History and Educational Policymaking

History and Educational Policymaking

Maris A. Vinovskis

Yale University Press

New Haven and London

For Diane Ravitch

Library of Congress Cataloging-in-Publication Data

Vinovskis, Maris.
    History and educational policymaking / Maris A. Vinovskis.
        p.   cm.
    Includes bibliographical references (p.   ) and index.
    ISBN 0-300-07571-5 (alk. paper)
        1. Education and state—United States.   2. Education—United States—
    History.   3. Federal aid to education—United States.   4. Education—
    Research—United States.   I. Title.
    LC89.V55   1999
    379.73—dc21   98–21496
                                                                            CIP

Printed in the United States of America

A catalogue record for this book is available from the British Library.

The paper in this book meets the guidelines for permanence and durability of the
Committee on Production Guidelines for Book Longevity of the Council on
Library Resources.

10 9 8 7 6 5 4 3 2 1

Contents

Acknowledgments

This volume owes its genesis and development to two different but sometimes overlapping groups—Washington policymakers and my colleagues in academia. Without the extraordinary and continued assistance from members of each, this book could not have been undertaken or completed.

My greatest debt is to Diane Ravitch, to whom this book is gratefully dedicated. As assistant secretary for the Office of Educational Research and Improvement (OERI), she persuaded me to come to Washington, D.C., as her research adviser and provided the guidance and encouragement that led to the work underlying many of these essays. Anyone who has worked closely with Diane recognizes and values her incisive intellect, her candor, and her genuine friendship and compassion. She was an outstanding OERI assistant secretary and is one of the few distinguished public intellectuals in America today.

Her successor, Sharon Robinson, has been equally generous and also indispensable to the completion of this project. Despite the concerns of a few political appointees about using my skills because of my service in the Bush administration, Sharon kept me on as her research adviser and allowed me to participate freely and openly in the agency's top-level meetings. When my earlier commitment to chair the Department of History at the University of Michigan required my return to Ann Arbor, she continued to bring me back occasionally as a consultant to OERI over the next two years. During my extended work with OERI in 1993–95, Sharon assigned me a series of challenging research and policy tasks. I will always appreciate her stimulating ideas, her nonpartisan leadership, and her personal friendship.

Many individuals in OERI and other units of the U.S. Department of Education as well as other policy analysts rendered valuable assistance. While I may not be able to thank each of them personally, I value their help. Among those who were particularly important to the work that has gone into this book are: Francis Alexander, Judith Anderson, Margo Anderson, Helen Barnes, Susan Berryman, Sue Betka, David Boesel, John Burkett, John Christensen, Joseph Conaty, Christopher Cross, Eve Bither, Blane Dessy, John Egermeier, Emerson Elliott, Chester Finn, Jr., Edward Fuentes, Sandra Garcia, Alan Ginsburg, Charles Hansen, Dick Hays, Eunice Henderson, Gregg Jackson, Naomi Karp, David Mack, Patricia McKee, Bruno Mano, Hunter Moorman, Laurence Peters, Val Plisko, Theodor Rebarber, Matilda Riley, Michael Ross, Lawrence Schweinhart, Marshall Smith, Steve Sniegoski, Charles Stalford, Deena Stoner, and Robert St. Pierre.

Among my academic colleagues, Jeffrey Mirel has provided extraordinary encouragement and assistance. He read the entire manuscript several times and made useful suggestions for organizing the book as well as for improving individual chapters. Our pancake breakfasts at the Northside Grill in Ann Arbor provided many opportunities for me to try out new ideas and new versions of the text.

Other scholars read individual chapters or commented on specific topics. Among them are David Angus, Norman Bradburn, P. Lindsay Chase-Lansdale, David Cohen, John D'Arms, Glen Elder, David Featherman, David Galenson, Sidney Fine, Raymond Grew, Joel Howell, Robert Kahn, Carl Kaestle, Valerie Lee, Earl Lewis, Jonathan Marwil, Robert McCaughey, Terrence McDonald, Samuel Meisels, Robert Michels, Gerald Moran, Jennifer O'Day, Bradford Perkins, Martin Pernick, Sonya Rose, William Rosenberg, John Rury, John Shy, David Scobey, J. Mills Thornton, Shep White, and Ernest Young. Naturally, the views expressed in this book are mine and do not necessarily reflect those of any of the individuals who kindly assisted me.

The publication of this book was greatly facilitated by the help of several dedicated individuals. Gladys Topkis, my editor at Yale University Press, was again helpful throughout the entire process, and Eliza Childs did a first-rate job of copyediting the manuscript. At the University of Michigan, Jeanette Diuble helped type several of the chapters, and Jennifer Mittelstadt did an excellent job of preparing the index and helping me to proofread the manuscript.

I also want to thank Sandra and Ginger Gardei for their hospitality on many of my trips to Washington, D.C. Sandra has always provided sympathetic understanding and encouragement for my work, while Ginger has made my trips there more memorable by taking me to her favorite movies.

Finally, but most important of all, I want to acknowledge the continued support of my family, who have managed to adjust to living with an as yet unreformed workaholic. Mary and Andris have listened patiently and thoughtfully to my lengthy and often repetitive attempts to explain what is happening in our nation's capital. They have also helped me to place my own efforts within a broader context and have sustained me when the political world periodically seems too frustrating and intractable.

An earlier version of chapter 2, "The Changing Role of the Federal Government in Educational Research and Statistics," appeared in the *History of Education Quarterly* 36, no. 2 (1996) : 111–28. An earlier version of chapter 3, "School Readiness and Early Childhood Education," appeared in Diane Ravitch and Maris A. Vinovskis, eds., *Learning from the Past: What History Teaches Us About School Reform* (Baltimore: Johns Hopkins University Press, 1995), 243–64, and is reprinted with permission of the publisher. An earlier version of chapter 6, "Education and the Economic Transformation of Nineteenth-Century America," appeared in Matilda White Riley, Robert L. Kahn, and Anne Foner, eds., *Age and Structural Lag: Society's Failure to Provide Meaningful Opportunities in Work, Family, and Leisure* (New York: John Wiley & Sons, 1994), 171–96, copyright © 1994 John Wiley & Sons, Inc. Reprinted by permission of John Wiley & Sons, Inc. An earlier version of chapter 7, "An Analysis of the Concept and Uses of Systemic Educational Reform," appeared in *American Educational Research Journal* 33, no. 1 (Spring 1996) : 53–85, copyright © 1996 American Educational Research Association. Adapted by permission of the publisher.

Introduction

History has long been regarded as a subject of great importance to both policymakers and well-educated citizens. In the seventeenth and eighteenth centuries, history was considered an indispensable guide for understanding how different structures of government might fare. During the late nineteenth and early twentieth centuries, social reformers saw a knowledge of history as central to improving the economy and society.

But as a new sense of professionalism and objectivity in history developed in the twentieth century, most academic historians moved away from producing the kind of historical research that was used by contemporary policymakers. Historians continued to stress the usefulness of history in theory though less often in practice. At the same time, the other social sciences, such as political science and sociology, increasingly emphasized the analysis of quantitative data and the creation of social science behavioral models rather than systematic investigation of historical developments.

The result has been that historians and history now are relatively unimportant to most policy analysts and decision makers. For example, whereas the federal Bureau of Education in the late nineteenth century stressed the need for historical case studies of school change to facilitate educational reforms, today the U.S. Department of Education downplays the value of historical analyses of pressing policy issues. Although many were undergraduate history majors, most federal and state policymakers continue to approach their work ahistorically.

Fortunately, there are some indications of change. The other social sciences are becoming more historically oriented, though a few crucial disciplines like political science still lag in this regard. Historians, especially those trained since the 1960s, show a greater awareness and receptivity to studies that have a more explicit policy orientation. And although most federal and state policymakers do not actively seek information about the past, they are more open to the use of relevant historical studies if they are readily available.

This book has grown out of my concern with and experiences in applying a historical perspective to policymaking, specifically in the area of education. As a scholar, for the past two decades I have investigated the history of colonial and nineteenth-century elementary and secondary education. As a concerned citizen, I have served as deputy staff director to the U.S. House Select Committee on Population (1978) and as a consultant to the Office of Adolescent Pregnancy Programs in the U.S. Department of Health and Human Services (1981–85). In 1992 I was appointed by Diane Ravitch as research adviser to the Office of Educational Research and Improvement (OERI) in the U.S. Department of Education. Following the change in administrations after the presidential election, I continued in that same post under the new OERI assistant secretary, Sharon Robinson. Having previously agreed to serve as chair of the Department of History, I had to return to the University of Michigan in August 1993. From October 1993 through November 1995 I also served as a consultant to OERI and have been appointed a member of the Independent Panel to review the federal Title 1 Program for the U.S. Department of Education.

Most of the chapters in this volume either were written while I was a staff member/consultant to OERI or draw heavily on that experience. These analyses, intended for a broad audience of concerned academics and policymakers, address significant current educational programs or problems. Earlier versions of four of the essays have been published elsewhere; each of these has been revised and expanded for this volume. Naturally, the views expressed in this book are strictly my own and do not necessarily reflect those of the U.S. Department of Education in either the Bush or Clinton administrations.

In the first chapter I shall look at how U.S. historians have dealt with policy issues in the past and trace the recent, gradual withdrawal of historians from the policy arena. Among other things, I shall look at changes in how historians viewed the policy role of their discipline, their personal participation in government activities, and the stated shifts in the utility of history in K–12 education. By analyzing the broad changes in how the history profession has dealt with policy, we will be in a better position to understand and appreciate the challenges of trying to provide a historical perspective on educational policies today.

The changing role of the federal government in educational research and statistics is explored in chapter 2. The 185-page study on which this essay is based was commissioned by OERI while I was a consultant to that agency. In this chapter I review the evolving role of the federal government in educational research and statistics at a time when some influential Republican members of Congress were rethinking the proper functions of the federal government in education and even considering abolishing the U.S. Department of Education. This chapter also provides a historical perspective on the strengths and weaknesses of OERI today and makes some suggestions for future improvements.

In chapters 3, 4, and 5, I shall focus specifically on early childhood education. School readiness and early childhood education are considered in chapter 3, in particular the creation and subsequent development by President George Bush and the nation's governors of the National Education Goal One—that "by the year 2000, all children in America will start school ready to learn." In this chapter I shall also explore the changes in early childhood education that occurred in the nineteenth and twentieth centuries and raise intriguing questions about why the United States periodically turns to such programs to correct what are perceived as major social problems.

Concerns about the fading effects of Head Start on at-risk children date to the mid-1960s. In chapter 4, I shall trace the origins of the Follow Through Program, which was set up in 1967 to help Head Start children make the transition into regular schools. Although it was initially intended to be temporary and experimental, the Follow Through Program survived for more than twenty-five years and cost more than a billion dollars. Yet its intellectual and conceptual impact on current policymakers has been minimal. The demise of Follow Through in 1994 went almost unnoticed and unmourned by both the public and policymakers. The interesting but rather troubling story of Follow Through is recounted in this chapter.

One of the frequently cited success stories in early childhood education is the newly created Even Start Program. The program works to improve the literacy of disadvantaged parents while at the same time providing early childhood education for their children. Its proponents argue that the program is much more effective than Head Start. Even Start has had a meteoric rise in funding, from $14 million in FY89 to $102 million in FY95. A recent independent evaluation, however, raised serious concerns about its usefulness and effectiveness. In chapter 5, I shall recount the development of the Even Start Program and critically review the recent evaluation by questioning some of its conceptual methodological assumptions and practices, concluding with the suggestion that we need another, more focused assessment of Even Start models if we are to discover what particular programs are most effective in helping illiterate adults and their young children learn to read.

One of the primary justifications for increased federal investment in schooling is that education enhances the economic productivity of its recipients as well as the overall competitiveness of the American economy. In chapter 6, which is based on a paper written for a conference on the relation between education and productivity sponsored by the National Center on Education and Employment at Columbia University, I shall analyze the changing views of the public and policymakers toward the economic productivity of education in colonial and nineteenth-century America and evaluate the limited evidence on the actual impact of schooling. This places the current discussions of human capital formation in historical perspective and challenges the argument of earlier historical studies that nineteenth-century schooling did not help most Americans.

The Clinton administration has emphasized the importance of systemic or standards-based reform in helping all American children improve their learning. The conceptual and empirical underpinnings of systemic reform have not been thoroughly investigated or discussed although this idea was the intellectual basis for much of the Improving America's Schools Act of 1994—the major federal compensatory education legislation. The analysis of the origins of the idea of systemic reform presented in chapter 7 details the variety of ways in which participants are now employing that term, often without awareness of its different uses and meanings. After reviewing the evolution of the concept, I shall critically assess its validity and usefulness and make some suggestions for subsequent improvements.

One problem in discussing educational research and reform is the lack of an overall analytic framework that can encompass both individual- and aggregate-level information while taking the changing historical context into account. In chapter 8, I shall develop a conceptual framework for describing and analyzing educational developments, based on a life-course approach. To test the usefulness of this framework, I use it to critique the recent OERI announcement of seven proposed new research and development centers. Overall, the life-course perspective appears to provide a detailed and useful framework and may encourage policymakers to be more historically conscious in their deliberations.

In the final chapter I shall return to the broader issue of the uses of history for educational policymaking. Drawing on the materials presented in this volume as well as on the work of other scholars, I shall explore in the conclusion how history has been or might be used by policymakers, including some general theoretical discussions and more specific practical suggestions for both policymakers and historians. I hope this chapter as well as the book as a whole will stimulate further explorations of this important but relatively neglected topic.

Part 1 History and Policymaking

Chapter 1 Historians and Policymaking: A Retrospective View

American views of the exact nature and utility of history have varied considerably over time. This is partly the result of changing perceptions of what constitutes the appropriate topics for and methodology of historical study, but it also reflects shifts in societal and personal expectations—including changing public attitudes toward what should be taught in elementary and secondary schools. Changes in the organization and functioning of government as well as in the role of academics in policymaking have created quite different settings for the uses of history. Thus, although there may be widespread agreement that history has played a vital role in our culture and society, we often have little appreciation of its complexity and changing functions.

In order to place the current efforts to use a historical perspective in educational policymaking in a broader context, I will examine the changing attitudes toward historical analyses in general in the United States. I will look at how historians here have produced their work and investigate what they have said about the usefulness of the study of history. The participation of historians in the policy arena will be analyzed with particular attention to such events as wars, when the federal government sought out their services. The role and value of history in the classroom will also be considered because training future citizens is often cited as a primary goal of the educational system.

In this chapter I will present a brief review of historical studies in colonial and antebellum America and then turn to the professionalization of the discipline after the Civil War. I will investigate the changing nature of the historical profession and the impacts of World War I and World War II on scholars and scholarship. Finally, I will conclude the chapter with an examination of the post–World War II era and how the study of history has fared in the past three decades. Unfortunately, since so little has been written about long-term changes in the relation between history and policymaking, this introductory chapter necessarily will be a somewhat lengthy and speculative endeavor.

COLONIAL AND ANTEBELLUM HISTORY

The earliest histories of the New World were travel accounts and promotional tracts. Although often written as historical narratives, they did not attempt to present a comprehensive and unbiased story. Rather, they were meant to encourage colonization and investment by emphasizing the virtues of life in the new territories. Moreover, many of them, like the accounts of early Virginia by Captain John Smith, were produced to justify the specific actions of the first settlers. Compared to the more professional historical studies emerging in Europe at this time (which focused on the major political and military events), these works provided information on a variety of mundane topics of interest to potential investors and settlers.[1]

The New England Puritans, more than their counterparts in the other colonies, continued writing histories in the seventeenth and eighteenth centuries. They portrayed New England as a unique link between the unfolding of God's will in the past and his plan for the future. God's presence was felt throughout these early histories, and his direct or indirect interventions were frequently chronicled. The Puritan histories initially focused on the struggles with the local Indians, but they later sought to document the historical precedents for the rights and liberties of the colonists. During the eighteenth century these studies became more sophisticated and often drew on European historical writings. These New England histories usually purported to be regional, but their focus was on developments in colonial Massachusetts. By the time of the Revolution, the practice of writing local histories had spread to all the colonies.[2]

For eighteenth-century Americans, the classics were a primary source of information about the past. Although only a small proportion of the population were trained in the classics, it was an important part of the education of the colonial elites.[3] Revolutionary political discourse, for example, drew heavily on historical events and symbolism from the ancients. Some historians have tried to downplay the importance of the classics for this generation,[4] but recent scholarship has reaffirmed the centrality of the classics for these decision makers.[5]

The classics provided models for both individual and national behavior. While the founding fathers thought that virtue resided within each individual, they also believed that experience and reason were essential for nurturing that virtue. Biographies of heroes from the past provided guidance for proper behavior. Similarly, lessons from the Greek and Roman city states helped late-eighteenth-century Americans to create and then to maintain republican governments.[6]

But the immersion of the founding fathers in the classics did more than just provide models for personal and national behavior; it affected how they perceived the world. For example, deep-seated fears of conspiracies against liberty grew in large measure out of their exposure to the classical writers who had been anxious about the continual threats to their freedoms in Greece and Rome.[7]

The founding fathers also drew heavily on British Whig historians for an understanding of how societies functioned historically. These works reinforced their classical views of the past and their sense of the fragility of republics.[8] Moreover, as the founding fathers tried to make sense of that recent conflict, they turned to their own historians who chronicled the American Revolution as a marked departure from events in Europe.[9]

The purposes of history for colonial Americans varied considerably. The earliest writers saw in historical narratives a means of promoting their enterprises and justifying their actions. The Puritans, in contrast, used history to reveal God's plans and to remind their children of the religious origins of the colonization of New England. For the generation of American revolutionaries, knowledge of history was for the prevention of tyranny—studying models from the past might enable one to create a republic capable of withstanding the seemingly inevitable corruption and decay of earlier political systems. The founders eagerly used the past as a broad guide for personal and state behavior, but they did not particularly try to employ historical knowledge to help them in the day-to-day operations of government.

History became even more popular in antebellum America and reached a much broader audience. Mass interest in the past, fostered in part by the immense popularity of such writers as Sir Walter Scott, grew rapidly in the early nineteenth century. As one recent scholar has put it: "Never before or since has history occupied such a vital place in the thinking of the American people as during the first half of the nineteenth century. Architecture, painting, theater, fiction, poetry, and oratory were filled with historical themes. About one-third of the best-selling books were historical, double the proportion it has ever been since. Popular magazines ran huge quantities of material on history and popular historical journals flourished. At least seventy-two historical societies were active on the eve of the Civil War, when there were only fifty-five towns in the country with a population over 15,000."[10]

History as a separate subject in schools also grew dramatically during the antebellum years. There were a few separate history textbooks and courses before the early nineteenth century, and they were mainly found in the private academies. In the decades after 1820, however, history as a separate subject became more commonplace in the public schools. Massachusetts, for example, passed legislation in 1827 that required the teaching of United States history, and by 1841 more than half of the towns in the Commonwealth offered such courses.[11]

Antebellum Americans offered a variety of reasons for the study of history in schools. A fairly typical rationale was stated in the preface of Charles Goodrich's popular American history textbook in 1823:

"1. History sets before us striking instances of virtue, enterprise, courage, generosity, patriotism; and, by a natural principle of emulation incites us to copy such noble examples. History also presents us with pictures of the vicious ultimately overtaken by misery and shame, and solemnly warns us against vice.

2. History . . . is the school of politics. That is, it opens the hidden springs of human affairs; the causes of the rise, grandeur, revolutions and fall of empires; it points out the influence which the manners of a people exert upon a government, and the influence which that government reciprocally exerts

upon the manners of a people; it illustrates the blessings of political union, and the miseries of faction; the dangers on the one hand of unbridled liberty, and, on the other, the mischief of despotic power. . . .

3. History displays the dealings of God with mankind. It call upon us often to regard with awe, his darker judgments, and against it awakens the liveliest emotions of gratitude for his kind and benignant dispensations. It cultivates a sense of dependence on Him; strengthens our confidence in his benevolence; and impresses us with a conviction of his justice.

4. Besides these advantages, the study of History if properly conducted, offers others of inferior importance indeed, but still they are not to be disregarded. It chastens the imagination, enlarges the range of thought, *strengthens and disciplines the mind.*" [12]

Perhaps one of the distinguishing characteristics of the antebellum period was the appearance, after the 1830s, of a series of very popular histories written by such literary scholars as George Bancroft, Washington Irving, John Motley, Francis Parkman, William Prescott, and Jared Sparks. While each of these authors had his own particular style and orientation, their overall goal was to produce thoroughly researched and well-written accounts of the past that would illuminate the workings of God throughout time and document the continual, though often temporarily interrupted, progress of mankind. Instead of focusing on the causes of temporal changes, these historians tried to capture the essence of a nation and its people. Moreover, they looked for the seeds of present-day society in the past and had a view of history that tended to emphasize continuity and stability. Later historians, however, would criticize them for their lack of attention and precision in using direct quotes or for sometimes making unwarranted assertions and statements based on their personal visions of the past. [13]

Few writers of antebellum history could make a living from that occupation, and most were either independently wealthy or had another profession (such as clergyman or lawyer). [14] Many, who were active participants in society, did not see the historian as separate or detached from the present. George Bancroft, for instance, was active in Democratic politics as well as being one of the foremost historians of his day. [15] Yet while they all saw the social value of history in illuminating and reinforcing existing values, they usually did not use history to provide them with immediate guidance for specific policymaking or for instructing other citizens how to cast their ballots in a particular election. [16]

Indeed, for much of the general public the primary value of history was as a more respectable and enlightened form of entertainment than romantic novels.[17]

THE PROFESSIONALIZATION OF HISTORY

Although the work of popular antebellum historians like George Bancroft continued to be praised and supported by the American public after the Civil War, younger historians increasingly rejected these studies as too moralistic and too florid.[18] At the same time, there was a slow but steady shift in the nature of the history discipline as professional historians gradually replaced the amateurs who had previously dominated the field. These new scholars, many of whom were trained in Germany and held academic positions in U.S. universities and colleges, denounced the work of the earlier amateur historians and strove to be more objective and scientific in their own investigations.[19]

The new scholars saw themselves as scientific historians. But there was no clear or simple definition of scientific history. Sometimes it referred to the effort to discover the general laws of history, but more often scientific history described a method for ascertaining the so-called objective facts of history—out of which later might emerge general laws. Henry Adams, president of the American Historical Association (AHA) in 1894, applauded the so-far unsuccessful efforts of historians to discover general laws:

> You may be sure that four out of five serious students of history who are living today have, in the course of their work, felt that they stood on the brink of a great generalization that would reduce all history under a law as clear as the laws which govern the material world. . . . Every professor who has tried to teach doubtful facts which we now call history must have felt that sooner or later he or another would put order in the chaos and bring light into darkness. Not so much genius or favor was needed as patience and good luck. . . . No teacher with a spark of imagination or with an idea of scientific method can have helped dreaming of the immortality that would be achieved by the man who should successfully apply Darwin's method to the facts of human history.[20]

While some historians awaited the discovery of a general law, most scholars were content simply to assemble the facts that would be used to build broader interpretations: "The scientific writer of history builds no Gothic cathedral, full of irregularities and suggestiveness, aspiring arches, niches filled with sacred or grotesque figures, and aisles dim with religious light,—that is the work of the literary historian. But he builds a classic temple: simple, severe, symmetrical in its lines, surrounded by the clear, bright light of truth, pervaded by the spirit of moderation. Every historical fact is a stone hewn from the quarry of past records; it must be solid and square and even-hued—an ascertained fact. . . . His design already exists, the events have actually occurred, the past has really been—his task is to approach as near to the design as he possibly can."[21]

The pursuit of scientific history took place in the context of the growing professionalization of the discipline of history. A small but increasing number of the post–Civil War cohort of historians were professionally trained and held appointments in a college or university.[22] In 1884 they organized themselves into the American Historical Association, bringing together professional historians and patrician amateurs. The AHA grew out of the American Social Science Association (ASSA) and modeled itself on the National Academy of Science. The new alliance among historians was dominated by the younger academic scholars who were less concerned with history as a means of political reform than of supporting scientific historical analyses. By 1900 it was clear that the AHA would be dominated by professional historians, and their amateur counterparts gradually lost interest in that organization and left.[23]

At the same time, other social scientists were creating their own associations. The anthropologists, economists, political scientists, and sociologists each developed separate organizations. Although there was some cross-fertilization among these groups, the separation of the disciplines increased over time. Moreover, whereas all the social sciences initially paid considerable attention to the role of history in their inquiries, by the 1920s most of them focused almost exclusively on the present. They also developed more generic analytic techniques, which did not necessitate contextualizing their findings historically. Scholars who were particularly interested in reforming society tended to be more attracted to the other social sciences. Those who went into history usually focused more narrowly on specialized research projects.[24]

Historians believed that the scientific study of history was useful for improving American society. But rather than trying to restructure or remake society as a whole, most professional historians felt that it was only necessary to introduce small and gradual reforms.[25] Even the so-called progressive historians, who emphasized the use of history to foster limited social reforms, rejected any broader societal changes.[26] In part this conservatism reflected the belief among most scholars that the current ills of society could be adequately alleviated through small-scale improvements. This orientation toward modest reforms also reflected the relatively homogeneous white, native-born, and middle-class background of the persons who became professional historians, persons who had fared relatively well in that rapidly changing society.[27] Authorities in colleges and universities also were quick to discipline or even dismiss scholars whose views were regarded as too radical.[28] As a result, while historians saw themselves contributing to the improvement of society, their reform efforts were moderate and usually noncontroversial.[29]

Compared to scholars in the other social sciences, such as political science or sociology, historians were less active and less visible in trying to reform late nineteenth- and early twentieth-century society. Historians also devoted less time to discussing the value of their discipline for improving society than their colleagues in the other social sciences. Yet reading through the addresses of the presidents of the American Historical Association provides ample testimony to the fact that most historians believed that their subject was not only scientific, but useful.[30]

Andrew White, the first president of the AHA, had been a historian at the University of Michigan and now was the president of Cornell University. He was also active as a diplomat and civil service reformer and had often written on the practical uses of history.[31] In his AHA presidential address he called for general as well as specialized histories as he felt that both could be used profitably to improve society. White listed a few of the lessons of history that his contemporaries were ignoring:

> Never was this want of broad historical views in the leaders of American opinion more keenly felt than now. Think of the blindness of one of the greatest things which gives renown to nations, involved in the duty levied by Congress on works of art. Think, too, of the blindness to one of the main agencies in the destruction of every great republic thus far, shown in the neglect to pass a constitutional amendment which shall free us from the dangers of coups d'etat at the counting of the electoral vote. Think of the cool disregard of the plainest teachings of general history involved in legislative carelessness or doctrinaire opposition to measures remedying illiteracy in our Southern States. Never was this want of broad historical views more evident than in our legislation now.[32]

Although most AHA presidents acknowledged the practical utility of history, each emphasized a somewhat different aspect of history as particularly important and relevant to the present. John Jay, for example, worried about the rapid influx of immigrants and saw in the teaching of American history a means of preserving our republic: "Our great authorities on history-teaching are agreed that rightly to understand, appreciate, and defend American institutions the true plan is to know their origin and their history, and so to learn the true policy required for our safety; and in this light history appears as the true basis of national character and of national wisdom, and there seems no reason to suppose that lessons in history may not be given in our common schools in a way to influence the ideas and character of our children."[33]

Most of these scholars did not hesitate to spell out clearly and directly the lessons learned from history—though some did acknowledge that more than one interpretation of the past was possible. Charles Francis Adams, who felt that history was extremely important to the present, deplored the fact that recent presidential campaigns ignored any guidance from the past. He called upon the American Historical Association to hold a special July session before each presidential election so that historians could comment on the major issues of the day.[34] Most AHA presidents did not hesitate to state their policy views explicitly, but Henry Lea cautioned his colleagues to be careful in drawing lessons from the past, especially in regards to passing moral judgments about the actions of historical actors: "I presume that you will agree with me that history is not to be written as a Sunday-school tale for children of larger growth. It is, or should be, a serious attempt to ascertain the severest truth as to the past and to set it forth without fear or favor. It may, and it generally will, convey a moral, but that moral should educe itself from the facts."[35]

Historians agreed that history provided valuable lessons, but a few pointed out that not all historical research and writing had to be done in service of the present. Writing in 1914, William Dunning, an expert on the still controversial issues of the Civil War and Reconstruction, agreed that historians could draw illustrations and lessons from the past, but he warned against inadvertently distorting the past when seeking answers for current problems. Dunning concluded by defending the importance of doing historical analyses even if the results did not directly address contemporary problems.[36]

Just as there were changes in the historical profession after the Civil War, so too were there important developments in the teaching of history in grades K–12. Following an initial slowdown in the teaching of history in the public schools after the Civil War, the subject received considerable attention from several national advisory groups and emerged stronger than ever in the early decades of the twentieth century. Moreover, the emphasis in high school history courses gradually shifted toward American history and toward present-day concerns.

Although there are no detailed studies of the period, interest in the teaching of history in the public schools in the two decades after the Civil War seems to have diminished. Amateur and professional historians devoted considerable attention to writing about such topics as the recent war, but school teachers and administrators seem to have paid less attention to the subject. Nevertheless, those who did teach history in newly emerging high schools often stressed its value as a vehicle for mental discipline as well as for the proper moral development of children.[37]

The National Education Association (NEA) in 1892 assembled the famous Committee of Ten to reexamine the entire high school curriculum. That committee appointed nine subcommittees to look in more depth at the curriculum, including a group on history, civil government, and political science chaired by Charles K. Adams, a prominent historian and president of the University of Wisconsin. The subgroup on the social sciences recommended that all students, regardless of their intended future occupations, should be taught the same curriculum and that the time devoted to the teaching of history should be considerably expanded. The subgroup rejected the existing emphasis on facts and called for more attention to the training of the mind: "To sum up, one object of historical study is the requirement of useful facts; but the chief object is the training of the judgment in selecting the grounds of an opinion, in accumulating materials for an opinion, in putting things together, in generalizing upon facts, in estimating character, in applying the lessons of history to current events, and in accustoming children to state their conclusions in their own words."[38]

The work of the Committee of Ten was followed several years later by a group created by the AHA—the Committee of Seven chaired by Andrew McLaughlin. This influential group reaffirmed many of the suggestions of the Committee of Ten and set out a strongly recommended four-year sequence of high school study which included "(1) Ancient History, with special reference to Greek and Roman History . . . , (2) Medieval and Modern European History . . . , (3) English History, [and] (4) American History and Civil Government."[39]

The AHA committee, noting that little had been said about the importance of history in the classroom, expounded at some length on the matter, stressing its value in fostering good citizenship:

> While we have no desire to underestimate the value of civil government as a secondary study, especially if it is written and taught from the historical point of view, we desire to emphasize the thought that appreciation and sympathy for the present is best secured by a study of the past. . . .
>
> While it is doubtless true that too much may be made of the idea that history furnishes us with rules, precepts, and maxims which may be used as immutable principles, as unerring guides for the conduct of the statesman and the practical

politician, or as means of foretelling the future, it is equally true that progress comes by making additions to the past or by its silent modification. All our institutions, our habits of thought and modes of action, are inheritances from preceding ages: no conscious advance, no worthy reform, can be secured without both a knowledge of the present and an appreciation of how forces have worked in the social and political organization of former times.[40]

Other committees and commissions also looked at elementary and second-ary education before World War I, but the reports of the Committee of Ten and the Committee of Seven were particularly influential in terms of the teaching of history.[41] The study of history was expanded in the public schools, drawing heavily on the recommendations of these experts.[42] There was also an increas-ing present-mindedness toward the teaching of history in an effort to be more useful. In 1914 one writer observed, perhaps with some exaggeration:

At the present time there are two groups or schools of history writers and history teachers, and these two schools are radically and sometimes unforgivingly opposed to each other. The older school, which may be termed the conservative, reactionary, stand-pat school, says that history should be studied for history's sake. Some of this school say that the primary, others say that the *only* object at which the teacher of history should aim is to impart as much knowledge of the history of the *past* as possible; that the function of history teaching is not to enable the pupil to under-stand or appreciate his social environment and the problems of his own time. These say that such a function is wrong because it is making the study of history bear almost wholly upon the present and the future—wrong because it is always drawing atten-tion to what we are to become. . . .

In very recent years another school of history writers and history teachers has arisen, which may be termed the insurgent, progressive, radical school. . . . Study the past and the present so that we may intelligently analyze the present and its problems. This school believes that historical facts or events are comparatively of little value unless they have a bearing upon the present world of thought and action.[43]

Thus, professional historians and history teachers viewed their subject mat-ter as useful, if not essential, for providing guidance for contemporary Ameri-cans. But many professional historians also were active in civic and political matters. Andrew White, whom I have already mentioned, was not only a distinguished historian, but a leader in Republican state and national politics as well as a prominent diplomat.[44] Moreover, the government frequently used history and historical analyses in its work. In the early twentieth century, the Supreme Court under Chief Justice Melville Fuller frequently used history in its deliberations and opinions.[45] And in the late nineteenth century, the U.S. Bureau of Education often turned to historians and historical analyses. For example, Herbert B. Adams, a prominent historian at Johns Hopkins, was commissioned to oversee in-depth scholarly studies of the development of higher education in the various states.[46]

THE IMPACT OF WORLD WAR I, THE INTERWAR YEARS, AND WORLD WAR II

The two world wars and the intervening years witnessed changes in how historians perceived their work as well as how it influenced their role in society. The heightened activism of historians during World War I was followed during the interwar years by a growing skepticism about the attainability of objectivity. Although the total number of historians increased after World War I, they were less active and influential in nonacademic matters than their predecessors. Teaching the traditional topics also became less important than preparing students for future citizenship through social studies courses that were heavily oriented toward the present. Despite these and other important changes, historians continued to believe that history was useful for both policymakers and society.

The outbreak of World War I in 1914 surprised most American historians and sharply challenged the idea that human history was gradually evolving toward a more progressive outcome. During the initial period of American neutrality, scholars as well as the general public expressed differing views on what the United States should do, but most American historians were sympathetic to the Allied cause despite their previous strong academic ties to Germany.[47] Arthur Lovejoy attacked German scholars for their willingness to serve the state at the expense of historical objectivity:

> We have learned much from German scholars about historical "objectivity" and the niceties of historical criticism; what we receive when we look for an application of these principles to contemporary events, is a clumsy compilation of fictions, irrelevancies, and vulgar appeals to what are apparently conceived to be American prejudices. . . . The incident has in it too much of instruction and warning for Americans of the same profession, to be allowed to pass without notice. . . . It seems . . . to show that the professional class, in a country where it has played the greatest part, has signally failed, at the most critical moment in German history, to perform its proper function—the function of detached criticism, of cool consideration, of insisting that facts, and all the relevant facts be known and faced.[48]

But not all scholars were as outspoken and single-mindedly against the German historians. H. Morse Stephens, president of the American Historical Association in 1915, candidly criticized his colleagues at home and abroad for overemphasizing their country's nationalism and fostering antagonism to other countries: "Woe unto us! Professional historians, professional students, professional teachers of history, if we cannot see, written in blood, in the dying civilization of Europe, the dreadful result of exaggerated nationalism as set forth in the patriotic histories of some of the most eloquent historians of the nineteenth century. May we not hope that this will be but a passing phase of historical writing, since its awful sequel is so plainly exhibited before us."[49]

Once the United States entered the war, there was strong pressure on everyone to support the Allied cause unequivocally. Most historians quickly and enthusiastically responded. Indeed, American historians were unique in their willingness to create their own wartime agency, the National Board for Historical Service (NBHS). Together with the Committee on Public Information, the NBHS recruited history professors to rally public opinion behind the war. Although most of the historians involved in these efforts earnestly sought to utilize only factual information, the manner in which they selected and presented those facts certainly was not intended as a dispassionate and objective analysis.[50] Moreover, the few outspoken scholars who were lukewarm to the Allied cause found themselves in deep trouble on their own campuses and were often scorned by their professional colleagues elsewhere.[51]

Historians also worked with faculty from other disciplines to provide special military training for students. In fall 1918 the nation's colleges and universities participated in the Students' Army Training Corps (SATC) under the direction and with the financial support of the War Department. Despite frequent tensions between the goals of an academic curriculum and the needs of the military, most professors cooperated with SATC, and historians helped to develop popular special war issues courses on many campuses.[52]

The propaganda excesses of historians on behalf of the war did not go unnoticed afterwards. Most of those who had participated in the propaganda efforts never expressed any private or public misgivings about their activities.[53] But other historians, such as Harry Elmer Barnes and Sidney B. Fay, challenged the one-sided portrayals of German war guilt and raised questions about the propriety of historians as propagandists.[54] And a scathing, vituperative article in the *American Mercury* denounced the propaganda contributions of American historians and brought the entire matter before the public.[55] In the early 1940s, William Hutchinson reassessed the actions of these historians and concluded "that except in a few instances their activities did not injure their reputations as scholars."[56]

The war also had an effect on the teaching of history. Special war courses were set up in many colleges and universities,[57] and historians, with the assistance of the Bureau of Education and other federal wartime agencies, encouraged high school teachers to develop similar courses. These courses purported to provide objective analyses of the historical background of the conflict, but most were biased interpretations heavily in favor of the Allied cause.[58] Although most of these special courses quickly faded after World War I, the emphasis on studying contemporary issues survived.[59]

The post–World War I period witnessed the expansion of the history profession as colleges and universities grew both in number and size. The estimated total number of history Ph.D.'s in the United States grew rapidly from 836 in 1921–22 to 3,168 in 1941–42; and about two-thirds of all history Ph.D.'s in 1939 were engaged in teaching in higher education.[60] Yet there was a perception that the quality of life in academia as well as the caliber of the graduate students in history was not as high as before. Some historians privately worried that the work produced by the profession failed to live up to the high prewar expectations.[61]

Throughout the interwar period, most historians continued to defend the usefulness of history.[62] James Robinson denounced the excesses of historians during World War I but praised the lessons learned from that experience. And he reiterated his belief that history was essential for every educated person: "I have been dealing with history in a very large—to some, it may seem, reckless way; thinking of it as an account of the mighty drama of our race; as absolutely essential in every scheme of education which aims at a general preparation for an intelligent life. Never before has the historical writer been in a position so favorable as now for bringing the past into such intimate relations with the present that they shall seem one, and shall flow and merge into our own personal history."[63] Even William Thayer, who pointed out the growing difficulty, if not impossibility, of predicting the future from the past, defended the utility of the discipline: "After making this confession which casts doubt on our ability to peer far into the future, shall I be charged with inconsistency when I declare that I believe history will become increasingly a vital concern. . . . 'History never repeats,' you may urge; and no doubt all the elements of any event may not be repeated in a later combination, but the gist may be repeated over and over again. A liar may never tell the same lie twice, or with the same results, but it will still be possible for the person who investigates the art of lying to generalize truth from the study of particular lies.[64]

A few historians resisted the calls for using history to address current issues and insisted that historians ought to investigate the past in its own terms and context. Charles McIlwain acknowledged that the public and policymakers employ the "lessons" of history, but he thought that the task of the professional historian was only to make sure that these lessons were really accurate reflections of the past:

> As historians, our real task is with history, not with its application; but when troubles come upon us, the question will always emerge . . . whether it belongs to the historian, even if not strictly *as* a historian, to find in all these facts and developments, assuming them to be accurate, any lessons of value that they may be practically useful. I sincerely believe that it does; but like that other "earnest desirer of his countrie's peace" already referred to, if I tried to urge any such lessons for our present troubles, I should be "telling my medicine" only as a bystander, and not as a physician. If there are any practical inferences to be drawn from this jumbled survey, therefore, I leave them for you to draw.[65]

If there was general agreement on the potential usefulness of history, there also was growing skepticism about the possibility of historians producing objective history.[66] Charles Beard, one of the most popular and outspoken historians of interwar years, argued that to some degree all historians are subjective in their selection and ordering of the past: "The historian who writes history . . . , consciously or unconsciously performs an act of faith, as to order and movement, for certainty as to order and movement is denied to him by knowledge of the actuality with which he is concerned. . . . His faith is at bottom a conviction that something true can be known about the movement of history and his conviction is a subjective decision, not a purely objective discovery."[67]

Other historians, while acknowledging some degree of subjectivity involved in the writing of history, rejected what they considered extreme statements on behalf of the relativity of all historical interpretations. McIlwain defended the efforts of historians to be as objective as possible:

> In this connection we are often told that each generation will rewrite its history of the past. Even if it does not wholly reconstruct this past, it will make its own choice of the parts to be noted, and these parts will be precisely those which are uppermost at the time when the history is written. One scarcely needs to be told that this is so, but some have told us more. They have said it ought to be done. At times they have

implied, if they have not actually said, that what is out-of-date now ought to be eliminated from history. . . .

But again these defeatists, for they are defeatists, would tell us more. Because it can never be done perfectly, it should not be attempted at all. At times they seem even to make a merit of our obvious, but unfortunate defeats. . . . The writing of history, they tell us, is only an "act of faith." . . .

How, in common sense, dare anyone say that we can know absolutely nothing positive about these past transactions, even if we cannot know all, even if we can know but little? And why should we be content merely to tint our picture with the colors that suit the changing taste of our own time? I am impressed by the sober words of the late Professor Tout in the opening part of his great work on English medieval administrative institutions. . . . "We investigate the past," he says, "not to deduce practical political lessons, but to find out what really happened."[68]

Most scholars continued to believe in the usefulness of history, even if their ability to produce objective history was acknowledged to be more limited than they had previously thought. But after World War I historians were less involved in public policy activities. To be sure, some prominent historians, like William Dodd, continued to serve in diplomatic positions,[69] and others wrote about specific policy issues,[70] but few historians were directly involved in political activity.[71] Professional historians devoted more attention and energy to scholarly research, teaching, and academic administration.[72]

There was also a general movement away from historical studies among American reformers and policymakers. Fascinated by the advances in the other social sciences, policymakers relied more on sociological surveys, psychological tests, and economic models than on historical analyses. In a few areas, such as the deliberations of the Supreme Court, history continued to be routinely employed,[73] but at the U.S. Bureau of Education, for example, much less attention was paid to historical studies.

History was gradually neglected or abandoned by the other social sciences. Whereas a historical perspective had been a vital component of most social sciences in the late nineteenth century, by the 1920s and 1930s it was often regarded as irrelevant. Scholars from such disciplines as political science, economics, and sociology became increasingly intellectually and physically separated from their colleagues in history; they also were less likely to use the past in their own investigations. Many scholars no longer saw history as central for an understanding of the contemporary world.[74]

The importance of history as a subject also receded somewhat in K–12 classrooms after World War I. The NEA's Committee of Ten in 1892 and the

AHA's Committee of Seven in 1899 had strongly endorsed the study of history in the secondary schools. The latter had recommended the study of (1) ancient history, (2) medieval and modern European history, (3) English history, and (4) American history and civil government. These recommendation were reiterated by the AHA's Committee of Five in 1910.[75]

In 1913 the NEA set up the Commission on the Reorganization of Secondary Education, which issued its report three years later. The report reaffirmed the value of history in the high school curriculum but proposed to abolish the traditional one-year course in ancient history and to replace it with a course in early modern European history. It also called for another course in modern European history (one-half or one year), as well as a course in American history (one-half or one year). Rather than separate courses in civics, economics, or sociology, the commission recommended a course on the problems of American democracy (one-half or one year).[76] Although the changes in history courses were rather limited, an assessment in the mid-1930s concluded that the NEA report had a major impact on the history curriculum:

> It would be difficult to overstate the influence of the report of this Committee. Three practices now very common may be traced directly to it. One of these is the practice in a multitude of present-day high schools of offering a course in problems of American democracy. Another relates to the common use of the expression "social studies." While the Committee did not originate this expression, it did give it respectability, thus assuring it a place in the vocabulary of a great many school people. The third is the one-year course in early European history. Probably one other present-day practice should be attributed to the Committee's influence, the one-year course in American history which has assumed such large proportions recently. It seems certain that this Committee was largely responsible for this course inasmuch as it was the first committee since the Committee of Ten to suggest a full year of American history in the upper grades of high school.[77]

The interwar years saw several additional changes in the history curriculum in elementary and secondary schools. The rise of junior high schools forced a reconsideration of the elementary school curriculum. History as an independent subject was largely eliminated in the primary grades. In the intermediate grades and the new junior high schools history was replaced in large part by new social studies courses. In the senior high schools, history continued to be taught, but more along the lines suggested by the NEA Commission Report of 1916.[78]

The AHA in the 1930s made yet another attempt to improve the teaching of history in the elementary and secondary grades. A Commission on Social

Studies was created, and under its auspices sixteen volumes were published—fourteen as individual contributions and two on behalf of the commission. The commission emphasized three major considerations in developing an appropriate curriculum—scholarship, the social environment, and student mental abilities. Unlike much of the ongoing drift away from rigorous scholarship and toward more attention to socially useful courses, the commission reaffirmed that scholarship was a fundamental, but not the sole determining factor in creating the social studies curriculum.[79] While not rigidly subdividing the existing social science disciplines, the commission listed them as "economics, politics, anthropology, psychology, sociology, geography, esthetics, ethics, imaginative literature, and history."[80] Not surprisingly, given its membership, the commission highlighted the role of history: "crowning them all is history, which began with the songs of bards and ends in philosophy. By taking for its data all that has been done and said on this earth since time began, history furnishes substance for philosophy and, in assuming an ordered form and progression, history becomes a philosophy, avowed or unavowed."[81]

Despite the efforts of the Commission on Social Studies, the general trend continued to be away from the more traditional divisions of academic history and toward a social studies focus, which emphasized the present at the expense of the more distant past. On the eve of World War II, the history curriculum had experienced considerable shifts. As one knowledgeable commentator put it:

> In the changing programs of the last twenty-five years, there has been, in the United States, a general decline in ancient history as a separate subject, and English history, as a separate subject, has almost disappeared. The two-year program in European history or world history has kept alive some interest in the Middle Ages. American history has in many cases been removed from the twelfth grade, which was once its almost undisputed place, and now often appears in the eleventh grade. Courses in problems of democracy have won wide recognition. Economics and sociology, along with government, have become conspicuous in programs for the twelfth grade, and sociology seems to be replacing history in primary grades. The topical treatment of history, anticipated by the McMurry type studies, has found in units of instruction something approaching general dogma in the treatment of a great variety of subject matter. . . . In the teaching of history, there has been increasing emphasis upon recent times.[82]

Historians were divided on the proper foreign policy course for the United States after Germany invaded Poland in September 1939. Some argued for providing immediate aid to the Allies, while others cautioned the United States to remain neutral and to focus primarily on its own defense needs. With the Japanese surprise attack on Pearl Harbor on December 7, 1941, however, everyone quickly rallied behind the U.S. war effort.

Historians drew on their earlier war experiences and avoided generating the extreme propaganda that some of them had produced during World War I. In the lead article in the *Mississippi Valley Historical Review* of September 1942, William Hutchinson cautioned his colleagues against such excesses. Conditions at home had changed, he noted, so there was less demand for that kind of propaganda.[83]

If historians participated less in writing propaganda for the war, they were more active in other areas, especially in gathering and interpreting intelligence for the war effort. The Office of Strategic Services (OSS), created in June 1942, was given a broad mandate to assemble and analyze war-related information as well as to carry out "special services" as needed.[84] One of the largest and most effective OSS branches was Research and Analysis (R&A), which specialized in collecting and researching vital information from abroad. Under the direction of William Langer, the distinguished Harvard University diplomatic historian, R&A, which grew to nearly one thousand employees by the end of the war, received critical acclaim for its work from Allied policymakers.[85] More than fifty major historians worked for OSS, including such prominent scholars as Crane Brinton, John Clive, Gordon Craig, John Fairbank, Franklin Ford, Felix Gilbert, Hajo Holborn, H. Stuart Hughes, Saul Padover, David Potter, Conyers Read, Carl Schorske, and Robert Wolff.[86]

The contributions of historians to the war effort through OSS and other state and federal agencies had a lasting effect on how they viewed their own role in society as scholars as well as how the public and policymakers perceived their usefulness.[87] Some of these activities continued into the postwar era as the OSS evolved into the Central Intelligence Agency (CIA) and the federal government recognized the importance of supporting foreign area studies in the universities.[88] Service in the armed forces provided many future historians with important early adult experiences.[89]

As in World War I, colleges and universities experienced considerable changes and hardships. There was a substantial decline in student enrollments, and many faculty members left the campus for war-related activities. The financial situation of many institutions suffered despite the efforts of the federal government to provide temporary assistance. Stress was placed on providing training useful to the war effort—especially in the sciences and mathematics. But some history courses were also revamped to focus more on present-day concerns and international developments. Compared to World War I, there were only a few incidents on campuses that challenged the academic freedom of the faculty.[90]

The education of elementary and especially secondary students was affected by World War II. High school enrollment declined from 7 million in 1940 to 5.5 million by the end of the war, reflecting both the increased number of adolescents going into the armed forces as well as those entering the lucrative war industries. As in higher education, the revisions of the curriculum focused more on changing the offerings in math and science than those in the humanities and social studies. In the latter areas, an emphasis on providing historical perspectives on current problems was commonplace.[91]

Following a *New York Times* survey which showed that Americans did not know much about American history, the American Historical Association, the Mississippi Valley Historical Association, and the National Council for the Social Studies created in 1943 a Committee on American History in Schools and Colleges to investigate the situation. After surveying high school students, military students, social studies teachers, members of *Who's Who,* and selected adults, the committee summarized its mixed findings:

> Do Americans know their own history? The answer to this question depends upon one's idea of history and the quality of the knowledge expected. If by knowing history one means the ability to recall dates, names, and specific events, the answer is fairly clear: Americans in general do not know this kind of history. If by knowing history one means the understanding of trends and movements, the appreciation of past events and persons, and the ability to see a connection between the experience of the country and the experience of the individual, the answer is that Americans in general do know a reasonable amount of American history.[92]

Of particular interest is the committee's discussion of why Americans should know their own history. The committee set forth four major objectives for the study of history:

> Laymen and educators are generally agreed that knowledge of our own history is essential in the making of Americans. The reasons for this belief may be summed up under four main heads. History makes loyal citizens because memories of common experiences and common aspirations are essential ingredients in patriotism. History makes intelligent voters because sound decisions about present problems must be based on knowledge of the past. History makes good neighbors because it teaches tolerance of individual differences and appreciation of varied abilities and interests. History makes stable, well-rounded individuals because it gives them a start toward understanding the pattern of society and toward enjoying the artistic and individual

productions of the past. It gives long views, a perspective, a measure of what is permanent in a nation's life. To a people it is what memory is to the individual; and memory, express or unconscious, guides the acts of every sentient being.[93]

The committee did not assume the centrality of history, but rather acknowledged that some of these objectives could be addressed by such disciplines as civics, geography, or sociology. But history made a unique contribution:

> The unique importance of history is based not only on its objectives, which are common to other school subjects, but on its methods and materials. History relates the social experience of our people in concrete and detailed form. It deals with specific and unique events instead of with averages and abstractions. It is interested in the experiences of groups of ordinary individuals as well as in the achievements of extraordinary persons. History arranges its materials in chronological order and thus is naturally led to stress the concepts of change and continuity, of development and decay. This time dimension cannot be given so much emphasis in any other school subject. In short, history attempts to present the facts of social experience in the same form and order in which the facts of individual experience occur.[94]

The experiences of World War II reaffirmed the usefulness of the past and contributions of historians, but it also saw another development that was to have an important bearing on the future—the increasing importance of science and medicine. The contributions of scientists and medical researchers were seen by policymakers and the public as significantly more important to the war effort than the efforts of historians and other social scientists. As a result, the postwar period witnessed a much greater expansion in federal support for scientific and medical research than for assistance to the social sciences in general or for history in particular.[95]

POST–WORLD WAR II DEVELOPMENTS

Celebrations of the Allied victories in World War II quickly gave way to growing concerns about threats from the Soviet Union.[96] Scholars acknowledged the dangerous role of irrationality and ideology in world affairs, at a time when the discovery and use of atomic bombs made human survival an open question.[97] As totalitarianism engulfed Eastern Europe and the Far East, American historians often called on their colleagues to meet the new challenges. In his 1949 AHA presidential address, Conyers Read argued that words are weapons and that historians have an obligation to abandon their dispassionate neutrality in order to defend democratic society:

The age we are leaving, the liberal age if you like, was characterized by a plurality of aims and values and a neutral attitude toward the main issues of life. In that age neutrality went so far that we ceased to believe, out of our fairness, in our own objectives. Confronted by such alternatives as Mussolini and Hitler and last of all Stalin have imposed, we must clearly assume a militant attitude if we are to survive. The antidote to bad doctrine is better doctrine, not neutralized intelligence. We must assert our own objectives, define our own ideals, establish our own standards and organize all the forces of society to support them. . . . Total war, whether it be hot or cold, enlists everyone and calls upon everyone to assume his part. The historian is no freer from this obligation than the physicist.[98]

Read wanted American historians to reassure the public of the positive future of our society, even if that meant distorting the understanding of the past and introducing social control:

Mankind still looks to the past to sustain his patterns of the present. If historians, in their examination of the past, represent the evolution of civilization as haphazard, without direction and without progress, offering no assurance that mankind's present position is on the highway and not on some dead end, then mankind will seek assurance in a more positive alternative whether it be offered from Rome or from Moscow.

This sounds like the advocacy of one form of social control as against another. In short, it is. But I see no alternative in a divided world. Probably in any planned world we can never be altogether free agents, even with our tongue and our pen. The important thing is that we shall accept and endorse such controls as are essential for the preservation of our way of life.[99]

Many historians, while not as outspoken or as fearful as Read, shared his general concerns and urged Americans not to return to their post–World War I isolationism. A few historians, notably Charles Beard, dissented and continued to espouse the cause of isolationism. Yet Beard and others who protested soon found themselves attacked by their colleagues.[100] Part of the problem was that historians after World War II increasingly began to feel that Beard and other progressive historians had become too involved in policy issues and had deliberately distorted their historical studies on behalf of their political causes. As Richard Hofstadter later sadly observed, Beard wrecked his earlier distinguished career as a historian by his continued obsession to attack Roosevelt's foreign policy:

Today Beard's reputation stands like an imposing ruin in the landscape of American historiography. What was once the grandest house in the province is now a ravaged survival. . . .

As one looks back upon it, Beard's professional life takes on more and more the aspect of a daring gamble . . . though, as a critic of speculative enterprise, he might have laughed at such a notion. But Beard did take moral and intellectual risks: he had never been content with the role of the historian or the academic alone; he had always hoped to be politically relevant, had always aspired to become a public force, and even more than the part of the sage he relished the part of the public moralist, the gadfly, the pamphleteer. With his ready pen and wide knowledge, his strong intellectual self-confidence and tireless energy, he had made himself foremost among the American historians of his or any other generation in search of a usable past. . . . Beyond this, the inevitable risk of the publicist, Beard took a further and more gratuitous risk: he finally geared his reputation as a historian so closely to his political interests and passions that the two were bound to share the same fate. This foe of the speculators put everything he had on the line, and though he had a long run at the tables, in the end he lost.[101]

Concerns about the communist threats abroad led to efforts by many academics, labor union leaders, and political leaders to eliminate communist influences at home. These fears were exploited by such unscrupulous politicians as Senator Joseph McCarthy (R-WI), who casually labeled many of his opponents as leftist sympathizers and denounced academics for being soft on communism. Although McCarthy was eventually censured by the U.S. Senate and died in disgrace, his activities had a chilling impact on many campuses and forced some left-oriented historians either to leave academia or to temper their ideas.[102] At the height of McCarthyism, 40 percent of social science faculty worried that their political views might be distorted and attacked in the classroom; about 27 percent occasionally went out of their way to point out that they did not have any extreme leftist or rightist leanings; and 9 percent toned down their writings because they were concerned about creating too much controversy.[103] Overall, Paul Lazarsfeld and Wagner Thielens, the researchers who conducted the faculty survey, concluded that there was "widespread apprehension among these social science teachers, but in general it [was] hardly of a paralyzing nature; the heads of these men and women [were] 'bloody but unbowed.'"[104]

If fears about the imminent threats from totalitarian governments abroad and internal enemies at home persuaded some historians to adjust their writings or teachings to contemporary political necessities, others continued to call for a more balanced and less presentist orientation in scholarship. Samuel Eliot Morison, who succeeded Read as the president of the AHA, acknowledged the value of history, but cautioned historians not to lose sight of their primary responsibility:

The historian's professional duty is primarily to illuminate the past for his hearers or readers; only secondarily and derivatively should he be concerned with influencing the future. He must frankly look backward, with frequent glances over his shoulder at the world in which he lives, and perhaps a prayer for the future world in which he hopes his descendants may live out their own lives. . . .

As one aspect of intellectual honesty, the historian should feel a sense of responsibility to his public. . . . But the historian who knows, or thinks he knows, an unmistakable lesson of the past, has the right and the duty to point it out, even though it counteract his own beliefs or social theories.[105]

In general, the immediate postwar period saw many historians quietly moving away from more presentist, reform concerns of the 1920s and 1930s. As the progressive historians like Beard and Becker became discredited, there was less interest in pursuing reform agendas.[106] At a special meeting of distinguished historians at the Historical Society of Pennsylvania in 1948, Pendleton Herring, a political scientist, called for a new history of American political democracy that was more relevant to current concerns: "The touchstone for historical writing is not accuracy nor objectivity, but relevance. The problem of the historian is always that of emphasis and selectivity, and the criterion that he applies, whether consciously or not, is that of relevance. . . . Great historians look both backward and forward; in their interpretation of the past and in their concern for discovering its relevance for the present they help to clear the contemporary minds for the tasks immediately ahead. Their function is fulfilled if they perform this duty for their own generation. As historians, their work is not ageless; it is rather as literary artists that the work of some takes on a timeless quality."[107]

But Herring's paper evoked considerable opposition from the historians. Most of the participants felt that focusing the study of the past in order to make it relevant for today's concerns was misguided and dangerous:

There were likewise fears in the way, fears that this doctrine of relevance might cause the historian to seek to justify current public policies and even tempt him to become propagandist. Examples were cited to show how past attempts to use the principle of relevance had produced history so distorted by contemporary emotionalism as to be practically worthless today. . . .

It was quite evident that most of the conferees would give but limited acceptance to relevance, and rather felt that the historian was responsible for re-creating the various epochs of the past and interpreting them as growing out of and contributing to those which precede and follow. Historians should try to be as independent of the present as possible.[108]

If many postwar historians were having some misgivings about trying to make their work more directly relevant, others continued to use their historical skills and perspectives outside of academia. Building on their government experiences during World War II, some historians continued to advise the State Department and the newly established Central Intelligence Agency about international affairs.[109] William Langer, who had headed up the Office of Research and Analysis in the Office of Strategic Services, rejoined government service to direct the CIA's Office of National Estimates (ONE).[110] Langer relied heavily upon his historical training and gathered about him other historians. In November 1950, for example, of the seven members of the board to oversee ONE, four were historians.[111] When Langer returned to the Department of History at Harvard in 1952, he was succeeded by Sherman Kent, his deputy and a former diplomatic historian from Yale University. Kent, who continued Langer's recruitment and use of historians, provided the CIA with useful long-term estimates. His failure to provide accurate analyses of the Cuban Missile Crisis, however, ended his otherwise long and productive career and led to his retirement in 1967.[112]

History continued to be an integral part of the high school curriculum, but there were concerns that its identity and importance were being lost as more attention was focused on social studies in general rather than on history in particular. A Harvard committee on "the Objectives of a General Education in a Free Society" reviewed the role of history in high school education and concluded that all students should receive training at least in both American and European history, though not necessarily during each of their four years.[113]

Overall, the percentage of public secondary school students (grades 9 through 12) enrolled in social studies rose from 78.8 percent in 1934 to 97.5 percent in 1949.[114] However, the growth of "life adjustment education" after the war, with its emphasis on preparing students for their own personal lives rather than teaching them rigorous academic subjects, meant that some of the social studies courses, including history, diluted their academic content and scholarly orientation.[115]

Richard Bauer, a professor at the University of Maryland, reviewed the status of history teaching in a series of articles in *Social Studies* in 1948. Although he admitted that history "has no utilitarian value for the average student," he argued "that history should be classified as a cultural rather than practical subject."[116] He went on to list six reasons for studying history:

"1. It will give one a better understanding of modern civilization by explaining how our institutions—whether economic, political, social, or religious—came into existence and what historical forces are at work in modifying them. . . .

2. It helps one to interpret current events. . . .

3. It provides an excellent background for other courses. . . .

4. It tends to sharpen one's critical faculties by providing many opportunities to make fruitful historical comparisons as well as to weigh and sift historical evidence. . . .

5. It often tends to develop a sense of sympathy and toleration for other classes, nations, and religions. . . .

6. It frequently stimulates a greater interest in the finer things of life by introducing us to the writings of the famous philosophers, scientists, and statesmen."[117]

Yet any lessons from the study of history, which other professional historians and teachers had stressed, seemed to Bauer to be much less attainable and useful:

> The historian of today is inclined to look with suspicion on all attempts to read lessons into history, largely because they tend to reveal, in so many cases, a glaring lack of historical knowledge and perspective. By tearing facts out of their historical pattern and conveniently rearranging them to support a given thesis, history can be interpreted to prove and teach almost anything. . . .
>
> In view of the widespread chaos and confusion in which the world finds itself today, a good case could be made for the thesis that history teaches no lessons at all. After experiencing hundreds of bloody and destructive wars in the past, mankind has not thus far learned to settle its disputes without periodically resorting to force and weapons.
>
> It is neither the business of the historian to read lessons into history nor to predict the future course of events, even though "he might anticipate them," to use the words of Carl Becker. His main function is to portray the past as sincerely, objectively, and truthfully as possible, without consciously injecting his own bias and prejudices.[118]

Given the lack of faith of some professional historians and educators in the usefulness of history in solving present problems, it is not surprising that those outside academia and the classroom also questioned the centrality that history had once occupied among the other disciplines. Howard Beale, who still believed in the value of history for addressing problems in the contemporary world, sadly acknowledged that:

History is fast losing the place of importance it once held. Government through the funds it appropriates to aid research and through its draft deferment policies shows clearly that it feels "practical" subjects are important but that the humanities and social sciences are at best luxuries that can be neglected in time of crisis. . . . Within colleges and universities history is rarely a "must" any longer as a basis for other work, and history except for recent American history is declining while other social studies grow.

Historians themselves are not always convincing on why history is important except that it always has been. Educated men recognize that history as a humanity must preserve and transmit the rich cultural heritage of the past, and to us historians this cultural heritage is one of the utmost importance. But the present world, preoccupied as it is with the struggle to survive, is chiefly interested in solving overwhelming current problems. History tells how men met the same problems in the past. Therefore, history both as humanity and as social study could become as important to the present world as any other field of human knowledge in finding intelligent answers to baffling contemporary problems. Some of us historians believe that, if more people knew more history and would heed it, past human experience could help create that better world so many have long wished for—or could at least prevent our repeating the same stupid and costly blunders each generation. In any case, if history is to preserve its place in the world, it will have to compete with the other social studies in discovering solutions for current problems.[119]

A fundamental problem, which Beale, but not many other historians, fully recognized, was that policymakers and the public were increasingly turning to the natural sciences for advice and guidance.[120] When they did need assistance from the social sciences in the late 1940s and 1950s, they relied more upon political scientists, economists, and sociologists than on historians.[121] At the same time, these other social scientists used the past even less in the 1950s, focusing more on contemporary quantitative and behavioral analyses.[122] As a result, the relative importance of history for addressing contemporary problems quietly but steadily diminished.

Rather than becoming disappointed and disheartened like Beale, most historians celebrated the gains in the history profession in the 1950s and early 1960s. The profession was expanding, and young historians had much less difficulty in finding employment. Academic hiring became more open and meritocratic, and prejudices against Jews and Blacks diminished somewhat.[123] Although the immediate aftermath of World War II did not see any fundamental shifts in scholarship, there was a continued reaction against the progressive interpretations of history. Sectional and class interpretations of America's past became more muted, and emphasis was placed on stability and continuity. Ideas and values reappeared as key factors in explaining political developments.[124] Although controversies among scholars continued, some analysts have labeled this period as one dominated by "consensus" historians.[125]

John Higham, in an influential overview of the history profession in 1965, looked back upon the post–World War II developments with considerable pride and satisfaction:

> It was suggested . . . that changes in American society and culture since World War II have somewhat revived the prestige and influence of the humanistic scholar and diminished the alienation between the professional historian and the American public. A new basis has been forming for a richer historical culture. We are now in a position to observe a parallel development on the level of theory: a revival of confidence in historical knowledge. The restoration of intellectual self-respect that has taken place since 1945 has not in any simple way resulted from improvements in social status. The intellectual transformation began before a new social adjustment became apparent, and contributed to it. But emancipation from skeptical and derivative theories of history might not have gone very far if the historian's morale and his position in American culture had not hearteningly improved.[126]

CHANGES IN THE PAST THIRTY YEARS

Major domestic and international developments in the mid-1960s had an important and unexpected impact on how historians related to policymakers. The election of Lyndon Johnson as president in 1964 and the "discovery" of poverty led to a rapid expansion of federal domestic programs under the rubric of the Great Society.[127] Although historical insights might have been helpful in designing these antipoverty programs, few historians were involved. Partly this was because potentially useful historical perspectives on such issues as early childhood training and Head Start had not yet been adequately researched.[128] But it also reflected the implicit belief among policymakers that, because the Great Society programs were unprecedented, the past had little guidance to offer.[129]

The lack of participation of professional historians went largely unnoticed, perhaps because two American historians—Arthur Schlesinger, Jr., and Eric Goldman—did have a visible role in Washington during these years. The first, Arthur Schlesinger, Jr., was a prominent, prize-winning historian who had written on Presidents Andrew Jackson and Franklin Roosevelt. His publications had been well received by both the public and professional historians, and his work often reflected his own liberal orientation. Schlesinger was active in Democratic politics and was one of the founders of the Americans for Democratic Action (ADA). He was an influential supporter of Adlai Stevenson's unsuccessful presidential bids in 1952 and 1956 and campaigned for John F. Kennedy in 1960. When President Kennedy assembled his team in Washington, Schlesinger came to the White House as a special assistant.[130]

Throughout much of his historical writings, Schlesinger employed the idea of regular cycles of political change in America. Periods of liberal reform were followed by periods of conservative reaction, which consolidated, but usually did not erase, the earlier advances. As additional problems accumulated and were left unresolved, a new phase of liberalism would emerge.[131] Schlesinger's cyclical theory of political change was incorporated into Kennedy's political outlook and used in campaign speeches. After Kennedy was assassinated in 1963, Schlesinger joined the Johnson administration for a short period before leaving for a distinguished chair at City University of New York to write a biography of Kennedy. The Kennedy book was widely acclaimed and received a Pulitzer Prize for biography, although some historians felt it was too contemporary and partisan.[132]

Schlesinger was one of the few major scholars of his generation to call for the historian to be a participant-observer. He argued that there had been a bias in the profession against participation and contemporary history, but that the situation today was quite different:

> As late as the days before the Second World War, a professional historian who carried his lectures up to his own time was deemed rash and unhistorical; a professional historian who wrote on contemporary events was considered to have lapsed into journalism; a professional historian who took part in events and wrote about them later was a rarity. Most scholars still felt that a generation or so was required before current events underwent the sea change into history. Today, however, few American universities would hesitate to offer courses which start with the Second World War and end with yesterday's newspaper. Only the most ascetic scholars now object to attempts to write serious accounts of the very recent past. And contemporary history has inevitably brought along with it eyewitness history as a vital component.[133]

Schlesinger went on to explain our recent acceptance of contemporary history:

> How to account for this unexpected emergence of contemporary history into academic respectability? The fundamental explanation lies, I think, in the acceleration of the rate of social change—an acceleration produced by the cumulative momentum of science and technology. Each decade generates both more innovations and more effective ways of introducing innovations into the social process. . . .

This steady increase in the velocity of history inevitably affects the psychology of the historian. What historians perceive as the "past" is today chronologically much closer than it was when historical change was the function not of days, but of decades. In the twelfth century, the historian's "past" was centuries back; in the nineteenth it was a generation or two back. Now it is yesterday.

At the same time, the emergence of a more extensive educated public than the world has ever known has increased the popular demand for knowledge about the problems that torment modern man—especially when, with the invention of nuclear weapons, these problems, if not brought under control, might rush civilization on to the final catastrophe. History becomes an indispensable means of organizing public experiences in categories conducive to understanding.[134]

Schlesinger acknowledged the dangers and difficulties of being a participant-observer and of doing contemporary history. But he also pointed to the advantages of having personal experiences—both in understanding the actual context better and in being more critical of the surviving documentation. "Practical experience may yield qualities of insight hard to achieve in the library; historians who know how laws are passed, decisions made, battles fought are perhaps in a better position to grasp the actuality of historical transactions."[135] Moreover, the participant-historian can better re-create the atmosphere of the situation because of his or her personal experiences in that or comparable situations, "Participation may not only sharpen the historian's judgment; it may also stimulate and amplify what might be called the historian's reconstructive imagination. To take part in public controversy, to smell the dust and sweat of conflict, to experience the precariousness of decision under pressure may help toward a better understanding of the historical process."[136] Indeed, the historian of contemporary affairs has to provide a more accurate and balanced portrayal of developments since others who disagree with his interpretation are in a position to challenge his analyses: "Far from historical truth being unattainable in contemporary history, it may almost be argued that in a sense truth is *only* attainable in contemporary history. For contemporary history means the writing of history under the eye of the only people who can offer contradiction, that is, witnesses. Every historian of the past knows at the bottom of his heart how much artifice and extrapolation go into his reconstructions; how much of his evidence is partial, ambiguous, or hypothetical; and how safe he is in his speculations because, barring recourse to spirit mediums, no one can easily say him nay, except other historians, and all they have to put up is other theories."[137]

Schlesinger's enthusiasm for the participant-historian was not widely shared by other scholars, but he played a unique role in the early 1960s as a bridge between historians and domestic policymakers. Although there is some debate over his actual role and importance in the Kennedy administration, he brought a historical perspective and consciousness to the White House. In addition, his Washington activities received considerable publicity and reinforced the image of the importance of intellectuals in the Kennedy administration.

President Johnson gradually replaced most of the original Kennedy staff with his own people. But Johnson, sensitive to the fact that his administration was not viewed as being sympathetic to intellectuals, appointed another prominent historian, Eric Goldman, as his "intellectual-in-residence." Goldman never developed a close personal relationship with President Johnson and often felt himself an outsider, partly because of his lack of prior experiences in government. Goldman did involve briefly several historians, such as Barbara Tuchman, David Donald, and Richard Hofstadter, in an advisory capacity, but these individuals did not play a major role in the Johnson administration. Nor was Goldman an influential adviser. Instead, he organized relatively minor events, for example, the ill-fated White House Festival of Arts in 1965, which floundered when several prominent participants dropped out because of their opposition to the Vietnam War. Discouraged with his role and experiences in the White House, Goldman resigned, returned to Princeton, and wrote about his personal observations of Lyndon Johnson as a tragic figure.[138]

The Vietnam War affected the opportunities for historians as policy advisers in the mid-1960s. Although President Kennedy escalated U.S. involvement in Vietnam in the early 1960s, his actions did not arouse much opposition on campuses. But after Johnson's election in November 1964, the American presence in Vietnam expanded more rapidly and deeply divided the nation and the academic community.

Whereas a historical perspective was not widely employed by domestic policymakers in the 1960s, State Department debates over Vietnam did involve detailed discussions of foreign policy in the 1930s as well as the lessons learned from the Korean War. Subsequent analyses of those discussions suggest that the historical analogies employed may not have been as appropriate or as simple as envisioned by the policymakers at the time, but there was little doubt that the past played a crucial role in those deliberations.[139] Perhaps one of the reasons why the historical analyses were not more accurate and helpful is that the policymakers seldom sought assistance from professional historians.[140]

Later, in the Nixon administration, Henry Kissinger, a distinguished and knowledgeable political scientist expert in international affairs, played a key role and provided a complex and overarching historical perspective on foreign affairs. Kissinger's unique view on the uses and value of history stemmed from his personal experience. As one analyst acknowledged: "Kissinger may well be the only political figure in Western civilization to have explored in a systematic and rigorous manner the basic question of whether history has any purpose. As a war veteran at Harvard, he undertook an ambitious, sophisticated examination of various European thinkers who had reflected on the past and had formulated a philosophy of history. . . . This study culminated in an almost 400-page undergraduate thesis entitled 'The Meaning of History,' which contains all the themes basic to his later political philosophy."[141]

Opposition to the Vietnam War mobilized students and faculty at the universities and colleges. A loose coalition of radical individuals and groups, often portrayed as the "New Left," often cited examples from history in their campaign against the establishment. More than most historians in the late 1960s, many of these self-proclaimed Marxists felt that scholarship and politics were inseparable. Some of their more hostile critics, such as Sidney Hook, argued that Marxism was so deterministic and conspiratorial that their historical work could not be considered objective, but the New Left scholars disagreed. Indeed, even before the debates on Vietnam, David Eakins had urged Marxists to be more objective than other scholars: "The Marxist, in all probability, will be one of the most controversial scholars in his academic area, and he should be. His analyses and conclusions, if consistent with his theory, will be fresh, challenging and critical. The Marxist should employ the highest standards of objectivity for the very reason that his work *is* challenging and critical. The scholar of any school who advances new theses and new interpretations must use stronger and more convincing evidence. He is not working in the safe realm of long and commonly accepted interpretations. He is breaking ground, perhaps even smashing ikons [*sic*], and his formulations will be examined the more sharply—and rightly so."[142]

While most left-oriented or Marxist scholars in the late 1960s accepted the importance of being involved politically and the potential usefulness of their work for changing society, there was considerable heated disagreement on just what types of historical work needed to be undertaken and if one should take liberties with the evidence to further the cause.[143] In retrospect, historians like Linda Gordon acknowledged that sometimes the demands of advocacy prevailed over objective scholarship: "I think I should start by saying that, advocacy or nonadvocacy, it *is* the responsibility of historians to tell the truth. Some may think that a needless moralism, but there were strands of our Left tradition, not only Stalinist, that said that it was not always necessary to tell the truth, and that, at times, it was justifiable to stretch the truth, to present the truth in this way or that way or some other way according to what was useful to the tasks at hand. (The Right also has this tradition of falsifying history.) Nor is truth telling simple: in reporting truths there is a necessity to interpret them correctly to the best of one's ability. The facts reported without the correct interpretation may be destructive."[144]

Eugene Genovese, one of the most active and outspoken socialist historians, defended the need for political activism, objectivity in scholarship, and the value of studying the more distant past:

> Socialists do not advocate pure scholarship and value-free social science because we do not advocate the impossible. But we do insist that the inevitability of ideological bias does not free us from the responsibility of struggle for maximum objectivity. . . . And we are terribly conceited: We are so convinced we are right that we believe we have nothing whatever to fear from the truth about anything. It is our contention, on the contrary, that only ruling classes have anything to gain from the ideological approach to history. Our pretensions, therefore, lead us to the fantastic idea that all good (true, valid, competent) history serves our interest and that all poor (false, invalid, incompetent) history serves the interest of our enemies—or at least of someone other than ourselves.[145]

The unrest on college campuses as well as the New Left challenge to traditional historians had several important consequences for historians and policymaking. On the one hand, the turmoil on campuses disrupted academic work and upset the public.[146] On the other hand, sharp academic disagreements stimulated new work that often led to a broader and more complex understanding of the past. For example, the so-called revisionists in educational history initially infuriated many scholars, but they generated rebuttals that led to significant advances in scholarship in the long term.[147]

The focus on history from the bottom up increased the popularity of social history at the expense of such more traditional concerns as political and diplomatic history.[148] While studies of ordinary Americans and the private sphere proliferated in the late 1960s and 1970s, the relative lack of attention to public institutions and international affairs moved historians away from the more immediate concerns of many domestic and foreign policymakers. Moreover, the lack of concern with traditional political topics made some social histories seem far removed from the immediate policy concern of the day. At the same time, however, the interest in social history encouraged some scholars to acquire social science training, which helped them to interact more effectively with quantitative information as well as with other social scientists.

Some conservative or liberal historians, who had previously shown considerable interest in or at least tolerance for contemporary policy-oriented history, now had second thoughts as they saw radical scholars demanding more immediate, partisan relevance for historical studies. Moreover, the apparent willingness of some of these new radical historians to manipulate the past on behalf of concerns in the present seemed to threaten the historical enterprise. Oscar Handlin, one of the interwar pioneers in the social history, denounced these practices:

> By contrast, historians in the 1970s and increasingly other scientists regarded the fact itself as malleable. As the distinction between fact and interpretation faded, all became faction—a combination of fact and fiction. The passive acceptance of that illegitimate genre—whatever mixes with fiction ceases to be fact—revealed the erosion of scholarly commitment. . . .
>
> The plea from utility was dangerous. In the 1930s it blinded well-intentioned social scientists and historians to the excesses of totalitarianism. It was inevitable in creating the omelette of a great social experiment that the shells of a few eggs of truth would be broken, so the argument ran. So, too, in the avid desire for peace, in the praiseworthy wish to avoid a second world war, Charles A. Beard abandoned all effort at factual accuracy. Yet the errors to which the plea for utility led in the past have not prevented others from proceeding along the same treacherous path in pursuit of no less worthy, but equally deceptive utilitarian goals.[149]

Whereas some historians did not abandon the the profession's potential contribution to policymaking, other scholars became more hesitant to do so. For example, C. Vann Woodward, whose book *The Strange Career of Jim Crow* had inspired many civil rights activists in the late 1950s and early 1960s, now wondered about the historian as participant. Reacting against some in the New Left who questioned the importance of academic freedom or civility, Woodward became cautious and more reluctant to engage in current policy debates.[150] Nevertheless, when he revisited these issues in the mid-1980s, Woodward still defended the role of historians in policymaking:

> I have been asked how, on looking back over three decades of controversy, criticism, and misunderstanding, I might feel about the whole Jim Crow venture in history-writing. Pressed for an answer, I would confess to feeling somewhat chastened and perhaps a bit wiser for the experience, but on the whole quite unrepentant. I readily admit the pitfalls and fallacies of presentists and instrumentalists, but

decline to be classified among them save as an interloper. Rejecting identification as a fulltime presentist, I nevertheless hold that since the historian lives in the present he has obligations to the present as well as to the past he studies. . . .

Anyone who accepts such a challenge must be prepared to make mistakes, to take criticism, and to be corrected. My advice is to stay out of the kitchen if you can't take the heat. I will admit reflecting that one such venture per career is probably enough. I was sobered but not deterred by the dangers of undertaking research on a controversial subject about which I had strong convictions.[151]

The radical intellectual attacks on the Johnson and Nixon administrations contributed to the growing public cynicism against the government and politicians in general.[152] Denunciations of the presence of the Reserve Officers Training Corps (ROTC), as well as other attacks on faculty who had government research contracts (especially those relating to defense or foreign affairs), discouraged some moderate faculty members from becoming more involved with policymaking. Given the generally liberal biases of social science faculty, the long string of more conservative Republican and Democratic administrations made service in Washington seem less desirable.[153] At the same time, the hostility toward the academic community of policymakers like Nixon contributed to the growing rift between academics and policymakers.[154] Thus, whereas World War I and World War II had provided considerable opportunities and incentives for professional historians to participate in government service either on campus or in Washington, the Vietnam War had the opposite effect, alienating the two sides from each other even further.

Changes in the academic job market in the 1970s and 1980s also had a profound impact on the history profession and its relation to public policy. The number of full-time college and university history faculty had risen rapidly: 5,000 in 1955, 7,000 in 1960, 10,700 in 1965, and 14,000 in 1970. The sense of well-being in the profession in the early 1960s, which we have mentioned earlier, reflected these substantial and steady increases in job opportunities. But there was a sharp decline in full-time history faculty to 12,900 in 1975 and 10,875 in 1980.[155] At the same time, the number of history Ph.D.'s continued to exceed the new positions available. The resultant crisis in the job market led to new questions about the future of the discipline and the role of historians outside academe.

The unexpectedly weak job market for academic historians discouraged some of the better undergraduate students from applying to history graduate programs and encouraged many of those who had entered to drop out. As the competition for academic positions became more intense, many history graduate students concentrated on more established areas of inquiry and avoided such risky endeavors as historical analyses of contemporary policies, a trend more marked because many faculty now questioned the wisdom of doing recent history.

Previously, most history Ph.D.'s had gone into teaching, and the necessity of finding employment elsewhere presented a serious challenge. Efforts were made to expand opportunities for history graduates in public or applied history. Although the terms "public" or "applied" history were not clearly specified, the emphasis was on using the past to inform the general public and policymakers. Leslie Fishel stated that "public history is the adaptation and application of the historian's skills and outlook for the benefit of public enterprises."[156]

Public historians worked in a wide variety of areas, such as archives and historical manuscripts; oral history; editing public and historic records; historic preservation and museums; the National Park Service; business corporations; and federal, state, or local governments. Although public and applied historians made important contributions to the public's appreciation of the past, most of these scholars were not directly involved in staffing or advising major government agencies. A few of the more distinguished historians participated in the newly created training programs for public historians, but these programs tended to be staffed by less-established scholars at the less-prestigious colleges and universities.[157] Moreover, many of the students in the public and applied history programs are more interested in receiving a master's than a doctorate. Public and applied history has made significant strides in the last fifteen to twenty years, but even its advocates admit that its impact on the history profession as a whole or on government policymaking in particular has been limited and uneven.[158] In 1994 Charles Cole, former president of the National Council on Public History (NCPH), reviewed twenty-one specially commissioned evaluations of the impact of public history. He concluded that although public history had made significant contributions in military history, the history of science, and the history of technology, overall it has not received adequate recognition and respect from academics.[159]

Related, but not often always identical, to public and applied historians are the recently self-identified policy historians. These scholars, from several different disciplines, are striving to create the study of policy history as a more systematic and recognizable field. Historians like Arthur Schlesinger, Jr., had done policy analyses in the past, but they had not created a visible and active subfield within the discipline. Policy historians established the *Journal of Policy History* in 1989 and today are in the process of organizing themselves.

Although most policy historians tend to be hopeful about the future of their endeavor, they candidly admit that much remains to be done. Hugh Graham, a distinguished senior scholar in the field, provides a rather pessimistic assessment of the current situation:

> Policy history has not found its identity. In light of the extensive development of policy studies in the social science disciplines in the United States since the 1960s, this is puzzling. The national reforms of the 1960s offered political historians an abundant feast, like the New Deal and the Reconstruction, to nourish a new generation of scholars. The growth of the policy sciences offered historians an overarching model of policy analysis for borrowing conceptual schemes. The development of the new field of public history during the 1970s provided institutional structures for exploring more systematically the relationship between historical analysis and public policy. Yet little of this promise has been realized. Indeed, our collective ability to understand and explain post–New Deal America has arguably deteriorated rather than grown since the 1960s.[160]

Graham identified several historians active in government service—David F. Trask (State Department) in foreign policy, Maeva Marcus (Supreme Court) in judicial analysis, and Stephen L. Reardon (Department of Defense) in military studies—and pointed out that the Society for History in the Federal Government had almost five hundred members in 1990. Yet he also acknowledged the limited impact historians have had on policy analysis:

> Nonetheless, in the expanding professional world of policy analysts who advise decision makers, historians have remained marginal. During the 1960s and 1970s, graduate schools of public policy were created at many of the nation's leading research universities—Harvard, Berkeley, Princeton, Minnesota, Michigan, Duke, Texas—and new public policy institutes crowded inside the Washington beltway. History courses, however, remained invisible in the curricula of the policy schools and historians were rarely found on their faculties or on the staffs of the policy institutes and think tanks. . . .
>
> In the modern marketplace for policy advice, historians compete at a disadvantage for the attention of decision makers, whose habit it is to turn to their experienced line staff, to lawyers and "hard" social scientists, or to policy analysts trained in systems analysis and operations research. Such policy advisers are trained in problem solving; they compare the costs and benefits of alternative solutions, predict outcomes, and recommend courses of action. Historians, on the other hand, are cautionary and seem more comfortable with negative advice. Historians are quickest to see what's wrong with politically tempting analogies. You can never step in the same river twice, we say. We refuse to predict. Given the generally weak instrumental case that policy historians have made for the importance of their advice to decision makers, and given

as well the severe economic pressures of recent years on public payrolls and private taxpayers, it is not surprising that political leaders, agency officials, and corporate decision makers have sought policy advice from lawyers and social scientists rather than historians.[161]

At the same time that there has been an effort to organize and mobilize the few policy historians, other scholars have been quietly, but steadily, producing useful monographs that address current concerns from a historical perspective. Partly this reflects younger scholars who have entered the profession and want to apply their historical skills to contemporary issues. It also reflects the passage of time: programs like the Great Society and events like the Vietnam War have become historical even for the more traditionally oriented historians. Although the authors of these studies do not necessarily see themselves as policy analysts or even applied historians, the topics they have investigated often provide useful historical policy perspectives—though often not as explicitly and specifically as decision makers in Washington or a state capital might like.[162]

Many of these historians see their role as helping policymakers by providing a broader context for contemporary issues, but they also stress their inability to offer specific solutions. Michael Katz, who often has provided historical perspectives on education and poverty policies, candidly acknowledges these limitations:

> I offer no concrete solutions. Historians and other social scientists who offer interpretative accounts of social issues always face a "last chapter" problem. Readers expect them to extract clear lessons from history, offer unambiguous recommendations, and foresee the future. My standard response—my role is to analyze and explain the problem; I have no special expertise in devising solutions—although honest, rarely satisfies. When historians tack on a set of conclusions, more often than not they appear utopian, banal, not very different from what others have suggested, marginally related to the analysis that precedes them and far less subtle. The reason, of course, is that no set of recommendations flows directly from any historical analysis. Understanding the origins and dimensions of a social issue can lead in very different policy directions.[163]

Unfortunately, given the nature of information dissemination among policymakers, few historical studies relating to public policy problems have found their way into the ongoing debates in Washington or Lansing. If historians and other social scientists are to have more impact on policymaking, special efforts will have to be made to share that information with a broader audience. Most policymakers and their staffs do not peruse scholarly monographs or history journals.[164]

Concurrent with the increase in policy-related work among historians, the federal government greatly expanded its use of academic advisers, both as outside experts and as staff. Starting with the Kennedy administration, the number of academics participating in Washington increased substantially, although the impact of these social scientists diminished somewhat after the mid-1970s as questions were raised about the efficacy of their advice as well as about their generally liberal outlooks during periods of relatively conservative and moderate administrations.[165] Yet, after the mid-1960s few prominent academic historians have gone to Washington as important political appointees or key staff members—except for those participating in such specialized and historically oriented federal agencies as the National Archives or the National Endowment for the Humanities (NEH).[166] Hundreds of social scientists have served each administration as policy advisers on preelection advisory groups, administration transition teams, and presidential task forces, but few historians have had that opportunity.[167] Whereas the number and percentage of professional historians in the first half of the twentieth century who had any government experience was sizable, it is difficult for most of us to name even one or two major academic historians who are active in government service today. This lack of experience with and access to the government makes it much more difficult for historians to write about policymaking as well as less likely for them to persuade decision makers to employ a historical perspective in their deliberations. This separation of historians and policymakers is all the more unfortunate because the latter usually see little need for knowledge of the past and therefore are unlikely to seek out such information or to consult historical advisers on their own.

Academic historians may not be as active in government as previously, but they are now much more involved in providing expert testimony in court cases that require information about the past. Although most in the profession have applauded the use of history and historians in these courts cases, some have questioned it.[168] For example, in the highly controversial Sears case, one in which the company was accused of discrimination against women in hiring and promotions, some feminists felt that it was inappropriate for historians to testify or let their work be used on behalf of the defendant.[169]

During the past thirty years, many of the AHA presidential addresses have continued to endorse the idea that history is useful and can make important societal contributions. Yet most AHA presidents spent little time addressing the issue of history and policymakers. Usually they made only brief references to the present in their introductory and concluding sections of their speeches.

William Leuchtenburg's lengthy and very thoughtful discussion of history and public policy in 1991 was the major exception. Leuchtenburg is a distinguished historian who is also a longtime activist in local, state, and national politics. After reviewing the views and experiences of historians with the policymaking process, Leuchtenburg concluded:

> In sum, in considering the long warfare between historians who favor engagement and those who oppose it, I would join issue on the one point on which they agree—that their positions are irreconcilable. Instead, I see a creative tension between the two attitudes. Scholars would do well to give a respectful hearing to both groups, for neither holds a monopoly of the truth. One can agree that history has value wholly apart from any utilitarian end it serves without accepting the conclusion that historians must refrain from public involvement, and one can acknowledge that historians have an obligation to their community without dismissing the sage admonitions that the skeptics raise.
>
> The historians who reject involvement might well ask themselves if they truly believe that, devoting their lives as they do to the study of history, they have nothing to contribute to the compelling public concerns of their only time on earth. . . .
>
> On the other hand, those of us who do take part in public affairs need constantly to remind ourselves that we are not omniscient, and that we must never, no matter how worthy the cause, compromise our commitment to, in John Higham's words, "the simple axiom that history is basically an effort to tell the truth about the past." We who are professors ought to remember that there are advantages, not only for ourselves but for society, to the detachment the campus affords us, and that unceasing involvement may diminish our capacity to see the world more clearly. When we do speak out, and we should choose those times wisely, we must take care to distinguish between doing so as historians and doing so simply as politically active citizens. Above all, we should take care not to create an atmosphere in the classroom in which the views that diverge from our own cannot freely be voiced, and we should respect the rights of others in the profession to express beliefs contrary to our own or to remain silent.[170]

One encouraging note is that the other social sciences are now more apt to make use of the past, and therefore in the long run policymakers may be provided with a more historically orientated analysis.[171] At the same time, however, graduate students in history are receiving less social science training so that the next generation of historians will have more difficulty in understanding and utilizing the vast array of quantitative information that policymakers and analysts have available to them today.[172] The net result may be that as policymakers develop more of an appreciation for information about the past, it will be delivered to them by social scientists other than historians.

There have also been important new efforts to reform the teaching of history in grades K–12. Reacting against history's subordination within social studies, professional historians have joined with elementary and secondary history teachers to emphasize the need for a more distinct and rigorous training in history.[173] The Bradley Commission on Schools, created in 1987, reaffirmed the importance and usefulness of the study of history for all students:

> History belongs in the school programs of all students, regardless of their academic standing and preparation, of their curricular track, or of their plans for the future. It is vital for all citizens in a democracy, because it provides the only avenue we have to reach an understanding of ourselves and of our society, in relation to the human condition over time, and of how some things change and others continue. . . .
>
> Without such understanding, the two foremost aims of American education will not be achieved—the preparation of all our people for private lives of personal integrity and fulfillment, and their preparation for public life as democratic citizens. . . .
>
> Beyond its centrality to educating the private person and the citizen, history is generally helpful to the third aim of education, preparation for work. It is needed for such professions as law, journalism, diplomacy, politics, and teaching. More broadly, historical study develops analytical skills, comparative perspectives, and modes of critical judgment that promote thoughtful work in any field or career.[174]

The effort to draft national history standards has caused the historical community to reconsider what students should know about the past. With funding from the National Endowment for the Humanities and the federal Department of Education, Charlotte Crabtree and Gary Nash of the National Center for History in the Schools at the University of California, Los Angeles worked with the National Council for History Standards to develop U.S. and world history standards. The national standards called for developing historical thinking skills and historical understanding. The original history standards were released in 1994 to considerable praise from professional historians and teachers. The draft of the national history standards also set forth the rationale for the usefulness of history for all citizens: "Without history, a society shares no common memory of where it has been, what its core values are, or what decisions of the past account for present circumstances. Without history, we cannot undertake any sensible inquiry into the political, social, or moral issues in society. And without historical knowledge and inquiry, we cannot achieve the informed, discriminating citizenship essential to effective participation in the democratic processes of governance and the fulfillment of all our citizens of the nation's democratic ideals."[175]

The national history standards included among the historical thinking skills a section on issues analysis and decision-making that reinforced those educators who wanted to emphasize the historical aspects of policymaking in the past: "*Historical issues-analysis and decision-making,* including the ability to identify problems that confronted people in the past; to analyze the various interests and points of view of people caught up in these situations; to evaluate alternative proposals for dealing with the problem(s); to analyze whether the decisions reached or the actions taken were good ones and why; and to bring historical perspectives to bear on informed decision-making in the present."[176]

Led by the former NEH director Lynn Cheney, opposition to the national history standards mounted quickly. Critics attacked the history standards and the accompanying teaching examples as being too negative about America's past. They also denounced the standards for paying too little attention to such important political leaders as George Washington and for ignoring key documents like the Constitution and the Bill of Rights. The U.S. Senate in a rare 99 to 1 vote denounced the draft history standards on January 18, 1995. Senator Slade Gorton (R-WA), who introduced the amendment, argued that: "This set of standards must be stopped, abolished, repudiated, repealed. . . . These standards are ideology masquerading as history. These standards would have us reinvent America's history. . . . America's story is both triumph and tragedy, but mostly triumph, of flawed yet unprecedented accomplishment. But in this teachers' and textbook manual it becomes a sordid tale 'drenched in dark skepticism,' as a *Wall Street Journal* editorial put it, emphasizing what is negative in America's past, while celebrating only politically correct culture and causes."[177]

Others defended the integrity and accuracy of the history standards, but with little success. Even U.S. Secretary of Education Richard Riley repudiated the history standards, stating that "the President [Clinton] does not believe and I do not believe that the UCLA standards should form the basis for a history curriculum in our schools."[178]

In an effort to salvage the standards, the Council for Basic Education assembled an independent panel of experts from both sides in the argument to propose revisions. The independent panel unanimously agreed on a set of revisions, including dropping all the teaching examples, which had been developed hastily and had attracted the most criticisms.[179] The suggestions of the independent panel were almost entirely accepted by the National Center for History in the Schools in their revision of the standards.[180] The revised national standards for history received a much better reception, but a few individuals and organizations continued to oppose any national standards—even if they are meant to be voluntary.

At the same time as this controversy, the National Assessment of Educational Progress (NAEP) released its study of the historical knowledge of students in grades 4, 8, and 12. The results were shocking—more than half (57 percent) of the high school seniors surveyed were performing below the basic level and only 11 percent were at or above the level of proficiency. Moreover, the NAEP assessment revealed sharp differences in achievements by race and ethnicity. While approximately half of white and Asian 12th graders were at or above basic level, only about 20 percent of black and Hispanic seniors were.[181] Thus, despite the recent outpouring of effort on behalf of K–12 history education, most American children did not know much about the past or how to think critically from a historical perspective.

The changes in the history profession during in the 1970s, 1980s, and 1990s have evoked different responses—in part due to when these assessments were made and what particular aspects of history were considered. For example, Michael Kammen, who edited an influential AHA-sponsored volume of scholarly reflections on the discipline in 1980, continued to be optimistic despite the numerous difficulties facing historians:

> History in our time confronts grave challenges as well as great opportunities. The challenges are to be found in the job crisis for history Ph.D.'s; in the decline of undergraduate enrollment in history courses at many colleges; in the way that history has been subsumed under social studies in so many of our secondary schools; in the way that church history has been pushed away from the core of theological studies in our divinity schools; in the misuses of history by politicians, policymakers, and jurists; and finally, in the dangers of vocational diversion and distraction. . . .
>
> There is a silver lining. . . . Insofar as historians do make themselves useful to society and find employment outside of academe, they not only help to counteract the job crisis for new Ph.D.'s but help to demonstrate the imperative of a historical perspective as well.[182]

Similarly, a 1994 evaluation of the historical profession by Joyce Appleby, Lynn Hunt, and Margaret Jacob acknowledged the philosophical and practical difficulties in trying to ascertain what actually happened in the past or in coping with the curriculum controversies over multiculturalism. Nevertheless, they remained hopeful that a middle way could be found to preserve a healthy skepticism about the present while not seeing everything as entirely relative:

A democratic practice of history, we will argue, encourages skepticism about dominant views, but at the same time trusts in the reality of the past and its knowability. To collapse this tension in favor of one side or the other is to give up the struggle for enlightenment. An openness to the interplay between certainty and doubt keeps faith with the expansive quality of democracy. This openness depends in turn on a version of the scientific model of knowledge, based on a belief in the reality of the past and the human ability to make contact with it, which helps discipline the understanding by requiring constant reference to something outside the human mind. In a democracy, history thrives on a passion for establishing and communicating the truth.

Even in a democracy, history always involves power and exclusion, for any history is always someone's history, told by that someone from a partial point of view. Yet external reality has the power to impose itself on the mind; past realities remain in records of various sorts that historians are trained to interpret. The effort to establish a historical truth itself fosters civility. Since no one can be certain that his or her explanations are definitively right, everyone must listen to other voices. All histories are provisional; none will have the last word.[183]

But not everyone was as calm and optimistic. Theodore Hamerow, for example, argued forcefully that the relative importance and status of history in our society has declined and that history faces a crises which many of his colleagues have not been willing to acknowledge or address:

The most serious aspect of the crisis, however, is not the employment situation, which will gradually become stabilized, but the decline in the importance which society assigns to historical scholarship. . . .

A gradual disenchantment set in . . . during the postwar years. It is still not entirely clear why it occurred, but the role of historical knowledge as a guide to the future came to be challenged by new disciplines which held out the promise of better answers than history could offer to the perplexities of our time. . . .

To our society, then, the methodology of historical scholarship appears inadequate for an understanding of the world in which we live. The brave phrases about history being our guide to the future, about knowing whence we have come so that we may know whither we are going, about those who cannot remember the past being condemned to repeat it, all sound a little hollow now. The promises historians made, to others as well as themselves, that they could steer a safe course for mankind amid the perils of an uncharted future seem naive and clearly unfulfillable. Here and there they may still be able to offer a piece of good advice, a sound analysis, a sharp insight, a constructive suggestion. But they can no longer pose as the guides and prophets of our age. No one would believe them, even if they tried.[184]

After surveying recent developments in the teaching of history at the college level, Hamerow reluctantly concluded that the future does not hold much encouragement in this area either:

> There is no need to make this sound too apocalyptic. It certainly does not imply that history is about to disappear from the college curriculum, the way theology or rhetoric disappeared. But it does seem that history as an academic discipline is approaching the position reached by the classics sixty years ago or by philosophy forty years ago, that is, branches of knowledge, once regarded as essential, which are still included among the course offerings of any respectable college as evidence of a commitment to higher learning, but no longer with a wide appeal to students and teachers. Such disciplines gradually come to perform a ceremonial rather than practical function in the academic community, a little like the cap and gowns worn in commencement processions. History is beginning to move in this direction, and while it still has a long way to go before it reaches the exoticism of Greek and Latin, the similarity of the process by which the classics arrived at their present situation is too close for complacency.[185]

Whether the optimism of scholars like Kammen or the pessimism of Hamerow is a better guide to the future of the history profession awaits the judgment of time. But most historians have believed that their profession can and should be useful in the present and that policymakers of all persuasions could benefit by employing a more historical perspective in their deliberations. Unfortunately, historians in recent years have not been able to provide much guidance for policymakers—partly because of their own limitations in producing appropriate studies and partly because of the indifference of decision makers to the input of policy historians. In the chapters that follow I shall explore the utility of using a historical perspective when addressing several contemporary educational problems and issues. This undertaking will, it is hoped, not only provide useful information for educators and other decision makers, but also allow us to assess some of the strengths and limitations of employing a historical approach in a specific policy area.

Part 2 The Federal Role in Educational Research and Statistics

Chapter 2 The Changing Role of the Federal Government in Educational Research and Statistics

With the election of a Republican-controlled Congress in 1994 and 1996, new questions have been raised about the federal role in education. Some members of Congress, for example, question the need for a federal Department of Education and have introduced legislation to abolish that agency. While there are few indications that the Department of Education will be terminated in the near future, disagreements over the role of federal government in education have intensified. During the current debates, the topics of the federal role in research and statistics have surfaced only occasionally. Attention more often is focused on either federal aid to education or federal regulation of schools.[1]

Since the Bureau of Education was created 130 years ago, most educators and policymakers have supported federal engagement in educational research and statistics, but a few individuals and groups have questioned that involvement. And proponents of a federal role in educational research and statistics differ over the nature and extent of that involvement. Moreover, there is considerable doubt about whether educational research or statistics actually helps K–12 students and teachers.

Different opinions about the nature and advisability of federal involvement in educational research and statistics are scattered throughout policy debates, federal agency mission statements, and academic discussions, but there has been little effort to systematically examine these diverse and changing views. Most current policy debates about the role of the federal government on these topics either ignore the historical context or create a somewhat mythical and misleading past.[2]

In this chapter, which is based on a longer and more fully documented analysis produced for the U.S. Office of Educational Research and Improvement (OERI), I shall consider some of the current issues in educational research and statistics from a broader historical perspective.[3] Among the diverse topics addressed are: (1) early federal involvement in educational research, (2) the establishment of a separate unit for federal educational research and statistics, (3) comparisons with other federal agencies and the other social sciences, (4) the fragmentation of educational research, (5) the inadequacy of research funding, (6) the disappearance of large-scale development and the change in dissemination, and (7) the political controversies surrounding educational research.

Naturally, given the limited time and space available, the issues raised here will not be discussed comprehensively. Instead, they will be explored briefly to suggest how a better understanding of the past may contribute to a more complex and a more useful analysis of some of the current problems facing federal educational research and statistics today. A longer historical perspective on educational research and statistics reveals not only what others have tried to do earlier, but also why many, if not most, of their efforts were not entirely satisfactory then or now.[4]

EARLY FEDERAL INVOLVEMENT IN EDUCATION
RESEARCH

Sometimes federal engagement in education is portrayed as a post–World War II or even a post-1960s phenomenon, but the government's involvement dates to the time of the American Revolution. The states, local communities, and parents had primary responsibility for schooling, and little public attention was paid to the role of the federal government in antebellum education.[5] Yet the federal government provided substantial funds for education in some of the territories and new states by distributing land grants for support of local schools. With the passage of the Morrill Act in 1862, the federal government provided more direct aid to education by financing land-grant colleges throughout the nation.[6]

Following the Civil War, the federal role in education expanded considerably with the creation of the Department of Education in 1867 (reorganized shortly afterwards as the Bureau of Education). Many proponents of a federal department had hoped for a very active and influential institution, but the Congress created an agency mainly to collect and disseminate educational statistics (as well as to work with states and local school districts to standardize educational data).[7]

Although collecting and disseminating educational data was less than the broader and more ambitious visions of some reformers, it was still regarded by educators as a major step forward. Nineteenth-century Americans believed that data collection and analysis was an essential component of educational improvement. Reformers hoped that once parents and school officials realized how much money some more enlightened communities were spending on education, they would become motivated to upgrade local public schools. State superintendents also used comparative school statistics to try to shame educationally backward districts to improve their public schools. Gradually, as many parents and local communities failed to respond to the repeated exhortations of reformers, however, the ability of educational data by themselves to stimulate school improvements was questioned.[8]

The collection, analysis, and dissemination of educational statistics remains the major mission of the National Center for Educational Statistics (NCES), but today there is more attention to the quality of the data collected as well as an increased reliance upon federally funded surveys and longitudinal investigations to complement information directly provided by state departments of education. Moreover, the few federal efforts to use comparative educational data to stimulate school reforms have often generated strong opposition from those states and local communities that perform at the weak end of the measurement spectrum. As a result, most policymakers today do not have as much confidence in the power of educational data by themselves to transform American public schooling.[9]

In the nineteenth-century, the Bureau of Education also tried to identify promising practices and to communicate that information to states and local schools. The bureau collected information on exemplary school practices and publicized it, but it did not undertake many new investigations itself. In addition, the early analyses by the bureau tended to be small case studies that employed traditional historical methods rather than the more sophisticated techniques of the other social sciences. Before World War II most of the bureau-sponsored research was done in-house and only rarely was work contracted to outside academics or institutions. The current Office of Educational Research and Improvement continues to identify and publicize promising programs and practices, but this is only a very small part of the agency's overall research and development mandate, and now an attempt is made to verify the effectiveness of the promising programs before information is disseminated to practitioners.[10]

In both the nineteenth and twentieth centuries, the federal government's involvement in collecting, analyzing, and disseminating educational data was seen as a legitimate and important function, and the need for centralized collection of educational statistics frequently was used as a rationale for expanding the role of the federal government in state and local education. As the federal government became more involved in funding and regulating state and local education, however, the Bureau of Education gradually moved away from its primary mission as a data-collection agency. As federal involvement in education expanded, education policymakers displayed much less interest in the actual collection and dissemination of educational data.[11]

Although federal collection of educational statistics has not generated much controversy, Washington's involvement in research and development has been challenged from time to time. Policymakers have questioned the relevance and usefulness of educational research and development; doubts have been expressed about the contribution of research and development to improving the schooling of children. Attacks on the liberal bias in educational research and curriculum development in the mid-1970s, early 1980s, and mid-1990s raised questions about the appropriateness of federal involvement. Combined with continuing doubts about the quality of the work produced, some critics contend that federal research and development monies have not been spent wisely or effectively.[12]

ESTABLISHMENT OF A SEPARATE UNIT FOR FEDERAL EDUCATION RESEARCH

A topic that has not received much attention recently is the question of whether the agency responsible for federal educational statistics and research should be a separate and independent entity. When the Bureau of Education was first created, its proponents wanted a separate education agency—but not necessarily an independent unit for analyzing data and research. As the bureau acquired responsibility for large projects (such as supervision of the educational system of the Alaska territory), the modest statistical and research activities of the office were dwarfed by the operations necessary to manage an entire territorial public school system. Faced with the growing neglect of its statistical and research duties, the bureau finally ended its supervision of Alaskan education in 1931 and returned to its historic mission.[13]

Similarly, the rapid growth of federal educational expenditures in the mid-1960s meant that research and development became more submerged within the Office of Education (the statistical and data-collecting functions had been set up separately as the National Center for Education Statistics in 1965). When the National Institute of Education (NIE) was created in 1972, Congress deliberately established it as a separate, independent agency apart from the Office of Education (OE). Although the detachment of NIE from the Office of Education posed some coordination problems, research and development greatly benefited by the additional attention they received in the new unit.[14]

When the federal Department of Education was created in 1979, NIE was placed within the new Office of Educational Research and Improvement. The National Institute of Education retained much of its former independence while housed under the new umbrella, but when OERI was reorganized in 1985, NIE lost most of its earlier independence and became just another operating unit within a larger agency that now included such diverse functions as statistical analysis and library programs. The reorganization of OERI was not the only, or perhaps even the most pressing problem facing the new entity, but over the next decade the number of serious researchers within OERI decreased (although NCES, one of the units within OERI, managed to attract and maintain many qualified statistical experts).

By the early 1990s there were few nationally recognized, practicing researchers within OERI; most of the top officials were not experienced researchers, and the agency in practice focused more on trying to identify and work closely with its customers than on providing intellectual leadership in substantive research and development areas. When OERI was allowed to hire new people in the late 1980s and early 1990s, few nationally distinguished researchers were recruited. In the past fifteen years, OERI has not been as successful as NIE in recruiting and attracting high-caliber academics and researchers.[15]

It is difficult to pinpoint precisely the reasons for the relative neglect of research and development in OERI, nor would it be fair to attribute the reorientation simply to the disappearance of NIE as an independent research unit. But submerging NIE within OERI and adding new responsibilities in the 1980s surely did not help to keep research and development at the forefront of the new agency's agenda. Whether the research and development functions of OERI again should be separated or whether the agency should be joined to another federal research entity, such as the National Science Foundation (NSF) or the National Institutes for Health (NIH), is not clear (as each of these proposals have serious shortcomings). But the decline of research and development capacity in OERI should be addressed immediately and candidly.

COMPARISONS TO OTHER FEDERAL RESEARCH AGENCIES AND THE OTHER SOCIAL SCIENCES

Comparisons are frequently made between NIE/OERI and other federal research agencies. Although such comparisons can be useful, the conclusions drawn can be misleading because of significant differences in subject matter and clientele. For example, throughout the hearings on the creation of NIE, there were frequent references to scientific and medical successes with the explicit suggestion that educational research now was poised to achieve similar breakthroughs.[16] Yet the sciences lend themselves more readily to large-scale, cumulative research efforts than do investigations of how human beings develop and learn. Moreover, the large amounts of money devoted to scientific and medical research have enabled these fields to advance rapidly while the more fragmented and underfinanced educational scholarship lags behind. Policymakers and the public also seem to have more respect for research in the sciences and medicine than for that in the social sciences or the humanities, so that they are more willing to support those endeavors as well as to be more patient in waiting for basic research results.

Nevertheless, we should also be careful not to deify medical and scientific research as scholars in these disciplines as well as policymakers have become more sophisticated and critical. Almost everyone is now more skeptical of the grandiose and exaggerated claims made on behalf of science and medicine in the 1940s and 1950s. Even the value of basic research, especially that of large-scale and expensive projects, is no longer immune to sharp questioning and federal budget cuts. We are now less likely to believe that the discovery of some simple technological-fix will radically transform our society.[17]

All too often discussions of educational research occur without adequate attention to comparable developments in the other social and behavioral sciences. Partly this is due to a natural tendency to focus only on one's own area of work, but the relative isolation of many educational researchers also plays a role—many researchers in education are not working closely with leading scholars in the other social and behavioral sciences. As a result, discussions of developments in educational research often seem divorced from the broader trends in academic discourse and analyses.[18]

Compared to some of the other social and behavioral disciplines (like sociology, political science, and economics), educational research appears to be relatively backward and underdeveloped. After the 1950s, other social and behavioral sciences made important conceptual and methodological strides, but educational research developed at a much slower pace and did not attract as many talented researchers. To many academics and policymakers today, education research appears to be second-rate theoretically and rather unsophisticated methodologically. The low regard for schools of education in the academic hierarchy is well documented and the quality of work coming from these institutions is often suspect. Thus recruiting capable researchers to work in schools of education or in OERI is more difficult than attracting someone to a sociology department or NSF.[19]

Although the social and behavioral sciences received much less financial support and public encouragement than the sciences and medicine, some major advances were made in these areas in the 1950s and 1960s. There was a concerted movement toward more rigorous, large-scale work, and these fields attracted some of the brightest and most able researchers. By the mid-1960s many academics and policymakers claimed that research findings from the social and behavioral sciences would make a decisive contribution to solving American domestic problems. Congress urged NSF to devote more of its resources to applied research in order to help overcome the crises in our cities and to save our deteriorating environment.[20]

Although the social and behavioral sciences made important gains, these advances did not live up to the exaggerated expectations. Disillusionment grew in the mid-1970s, and academics came to a better understanding of the inherent limitations of their disciplines in solving societal problems. Some policymakers characterized much of their work as irrelevant while others attacked it for subverting American values. Senator William Proxmire's (D-WI) "Golden Fleece" awards for trivial, wasteful research and the conservative attacks on NSF's Man: A Course of Study (MACOS) project undermined much of the early enthusiasm in the Congress for social and behavioral science research.[21]

This increasing disillusionment with the value and direction of academic social science research in general contributed to the questioning of the federal investment in educational research in particular.

FRAGMENTATION OF EDUCATIONAL RESEARCH

Much educational research and development during the past hundred years has been fragmented and episodic. Initially this was not viewed as a problem because the social and behavioral sciences in the late nineteenth and early twentieth centuries did not pursue large-scale cumulative research and development projects. Most of the research undertaken by the Bureau of Education were small case studies or occasional cross-sectional surveys intended to provide immediate and specific suggestions for school improvement. Nor did researchers and policymakers expect the federal government to support coherent, large-scale research initiatives in education. Indeed, even during World War II when the medical and scientific communities were launching ambitious and coordinated research and development programs, the Office of Education reduced expenditures on educational research in order to provide more immediate, practical assistance to the war effort.[22]

As the value of large-scale scientific and medical research projects was demonstrated during World War II, there was a belated, but growing awareness in some of the social and behavioral sciences of the need for comparable efforts.[23] Increasing dissatisfaction with the fragmentary and noncumulative educational research funded under the Cooperative Research Act of 1954 led to the creation of the R&D centers in 1964, as well as the recommendation by the Gardner Task Force for the establishment of large-scale educational laboratories.[24] But this suggestion was ignored almost immediately; the Office of Education proceeded to fund twenty small centers and laboratories.[25] The concept of R&D centers and regional educational laboratories has survived for three decades, but their portfolio of activities bears little resemblance to the initial vision. Under pressure from Congress and OERI, the current institutions moved away from large-scale development projects. Most of the existing centers and laboratories today support small, often fragmented research projects with relatively few of them funding sustained research or development projects.[26]

The fragmentation and impermanence of the educational research and development agenda of NIE/OERI has been reinforced by the rapid turnover of agency directors and the wholesale dismissal of OERI's professional staff in the early 1980s.[27] Frequent reorganizations of the office, while useful in some respects, have often diverted energy and attention away from the substantive research and development agenda of the agency.[28]

The extraordinary political turmoil faced by NIE/OERI during its brief history has made it much more difficult for the agency to concentrate on developing and implementing a more rational, long-range federal research and development policy. Despite numerous periodic efforts to create a long-term research plan, NIE/OERI has failed to develop a cohesive, meaningful strategy that would remain in effect for more than just a few years. Moreover, most of these long-term research plans consist of unconnected clusters of rather different activities than of a coherent and viable vision for improving education. We still need to create a broader framework for mapping and evaluating educational research and development that focuses on the evolving life course of individuals and takes into consideration the critical transitions which may be most amenable to appropriate interventions.[29]

INADEQUACY OF RESEARCH FUNDING

Complaints about the inadequacy of federal funding for educational research abound. Educators rightly point out that compared to the private industrial sector, health care system, or defense establishment, a much smaller percentage of total education expenditures are invested in research and development. Similarly, if one compares the funding of NIE/OERI to comparable federal agencies, such as NSF or NIH, the support for educational research is minuscule. In constant dollars, we are spending far less today on federal education research and development in OERI than when NIE was created twenty-five years ago.[30] Additional funds will be needed if we are to produce the type of serious, high-quality research and development necessary to have a major impact on educational improvements in the near future.

While the total amount appropriated for NIE/OERI was inadequate, the uncertainty of funding, especially in the 1970s and 1980s, was devastating to the agency. Given the large number of programs NIE inherited and the reductions in overall funding, almost no money was available for new initiatives in the first couple of years. Similarly, the unusually deep budget reductions for OERI in the early 1980s restricted the ability of the agency to implement any long-range plans.[31] Given the severity and abruptness of the recent reductions in federal educational research and development, perhaps it is not surprising that relatively few significant educational products and processes have been developed systematically.

The practice of earmarking funds for the centers and laboratories begun by Congress in the mid-1970s meant that an increasingly large proportion of the research and development budget was mandated for these institutions. In spite of periodic complaints about inappropriate congressional intervention, the set-asides for the centers and laboratories survive and limit the ability of the agency to maintain a balanced portfolio of activities. For example, field-initiated research, a vital and large component at such other federal agencies as NSF and NIH, was virtually eliminated due to the lack of flexibility in NIE/OERI funding. Combined with the increasingly regional orientation of the laboratories in the late 1970s and 1980s, OERI's national educational research and development program suffered greatly from both inadequate funding and lack of control over its scarce resources.[32]

Even given the difficult circumstances facing NIE/OERI, some critics of the agency argue that there is disappointingly little to show for those investments despite expenditures of several billions of dollars over the past two decades. They contend that while some modest improvements have been made, these gains do not justify the large sums of money that have been invested to date. These analysts often characterize NIE/OERI's work as fragmented and of low quality. Only in the area of educational statistics, which almost everyone agrees has improved considerably in the last decade, do they believe federal monies have been well spent.[33] Thus, while some of the critics of NIE/OERI are not necessarily against additional federal educational research or development funding in principle, they have little confidence in the ability of the agency to use those monies wisely to improve American education.

DISAPPEARANCE OF LARGE-SCALE
DEVELOPMENT AND CHANGES IN
DISSEMINATION

One of the major educational innovations in the 1950s and 1960s was investment in large-scale curriculum development. In response to the launch of Sputnik, NSF invested millions of dollars in developing its PSSC Physics curriculum for high school students in the late 1950s. Based upon its success, NSF expanded its curriculum development to other subjects.[34]

Following the lead of NSF, the Office of Education encouraged large-scale curriculum development by the centers and laboratories in the late 1960s. At first NIE continued support of curriculum development, but then retreated in the face of strong congressional opposition to the NSF-funded MACOS project in the mid-1970s. By the late 1970s and early 1980s, systematic development had been all but abandoned by NIE/OERI-supported R&D centers and regional educational laboratories.[35] The Office of Educational Research and Improvement downplayed the importance of development altogether, and what little development was done in the 1980s and early 1990s focused on small, short-term projects in some of the centers and laboratories. Despite occasional rhetoric about the importance of development, it received little emphasis in OERI. For instance, although still designed as "research and development centers," most centers minimized (or ignored entirely) the role of development; OERI staff had little appreciation or understanding of what development actually meant or entailed.[36]

With the reauthorization of OERI in 1994, however, Congress reiterated the importance of systematic development and provided a definition that harkened back to the vision of development from the late 1960s and early 1970s. Whether the intent of the legislation to spur more large-scale, systematic development will succeed remains to be seen. Certainly this would be a useful step toward translating more systematically research into practice. If it does, it would involve a major reversal and improvement of federal efforts to downplay systematic educational development for the past twenty years.

Dissemination has always been an important part of federal educational statistics and research activities. Indeed, the Bureau of Education from its inception worked hard to distribute data and other information to policymakers and educators. When one looks at the publication and distribution efforts of the Office of Education before the late 1950s, it appears that dissemination of information often may have received more attention than the generation or analysis of educational data.

With the creation of NIE, the Nixon administration tried to emphasize research and development and to minimize the role of dissemination (which they wanted to leave to the Office of Education). But members of Congress, many of whom implicitly assumed that there already was a "treasure chest" of good research and development findings, insisted that NIE greatly expand its planned dissemination activities.[37] Under congressional pressure, NIE spent an increasing proportion of its funds on dissemination so that by the end of the 1970s, more monies were spent on these activities than on basic research, applied research, or development. The emphasis on dissemination continued into the 1980s and early 1990s. A few R&D centers in the early 1990s, for example, spent more of their OERI funds on dissemination than on research and development.

Although NIE/OERI devoted more money and energy to dissemination than most other federal research units, legislators and practitioners continued to criticize the agency for emphasizing research and development at the expense of dissemination.[38] Moreover, although considerable OERI resources and attention have been devoted to dissemination, the agency has not developed as deep an understanding or an appreciation of the complexity of the process of reaching practitioners that it achieved in the late 1970s. Unlike NIE's more research-oriented initiatives on dissemination (such as the Research and Dissemination [RDU] program), much of the current efforts focus more on attempting to provide useful information directly to states and local practitioners without adequate attention to how information is most effectively transmitted.

POLITICAL CONTROVERSIES AND
EDUCATIONAL RESEARCH

Most federal research agencies have tried and, for the most part, succeeded in avoiding becoming embroiled in persistent, bitter political controversies over the legitimacy of their research agendas or funding practices. But recently, federal educational research has been the focus of numerous charges and countercharges about the political nature of its mission and about the unfair distribution of its resources. Yet few in OERI or the outside research community today seem to be willing to address these issues.[39]

Rather than acting as a dispassionate, objective statistical and research agency, the Bureau of Education and its successors have stressed their commitment to reforming and improving American education.[40] As long as everyone agreed with that goal, there was little controversy or suspicion that the agency could have had an implicit political orientation. The National Institute of Education was established to improve schooling and to reduce educational inequities. Few questioned NIE's mission because the agency was created by a Republican president and enacted by a Democratic Congress that shared those goals in the early 1970s.[41] The Carter administration pursued the promotion of ethnic and gender educational equity even more energetically. But conservative Republicans who came to power in the early 1980s did not accept the premises of NIE and characterized the inherited educational research and development agenda as blatantly biased and political.

The new leaders at NIE—such as Edward Curran and Robert Sweet—

sought to dramatically change the orientation of the agency in the early 1980s, but they insisted that they did not have a political agenda. Instead, Curran and Sweet viewed their mandate as the elimination of the political biases of NIE's earlier programs. But, in the process of creating a new federal research and development strategy, accompanied by the firing of many of the existing NIE professionals, Curran and Sweet created an equally one-sided agenda, which provoked even more contention.[42] Given the irreconcilable differences of opinion between these Reagan appointees and the more liberal members of the Democratic Congress (and even the new Republican secretary of education), it is not surprising that the office became highly politicized. Ironically, while each group accused the other of politicizing educational research and development, each maintained that they were only trying to re-create OERI as a more scientific and objective agency.

After Curran and Sweet departed, a series of moderate Republicans were appointed directors of OERI. They sought to reestablish a more objective and scientific federal research unit and emphasized the statistical role of the agency as well as its dissemination activities. Controversies over such topics as vouchers and school choice, however, persuaded some policymakers that the agency was still too political—despite the fact that the agency's involvement in these areas was relatively minor. Moreover, some leaders in Congress in the late 1980s and early 1990s, who wanted to restructure the agency significantly, argued that the political orientation and controversies of the early Reagan years were still in place, though these legislators had considerable difficulty in documenting any political wrongdoings in OERI at that time.[43] Again, each side viewed itself as the champion of establishing an objective, scientific OERI and chastised its opponents for trying to create a more politicized office.

Compounding the political controversies that have engulfed NIE/OERI are the ongoing and frequently bitter disputes over the control and funding of the R&D centers and regional educational laboratories (though in the 1980s and early 1990s debates over the centers have become much less contentious than those over the laboratories). The Council for Educational Development and Research (CEDaR), the organizational umbrella for the centers and laboratories, was created in the early 1970s and quickly became the most powerful and effective educational research and development lobbying organization in Washington. In order to protect the interests of the centers and laboratories, CEDaR often denigrated the leadership and operation of NIE/OERI, especially whenever the agency tried to dictate research and development agendas for the laboratories and centers or to control their funding. The often nasty episodic battles between NIE/OERI and CEDaR are legendary and created an atmosphere in which it became difficult for anyone to remain above the fray. In a rather unusual procedure for a federal research agency, NIE entered into formal, written agreements with CEDaR in the mid-1970s on how the centers and laboratories would be funded. An NIE director also felt it necessary to warn his professional research staff to restrain from openly criticizing these institutions.[44] Indeed, even today there is a strong undercurrent of belief among many OERI staff that any questions about the value or serious criticisms of the operation of the regional educational laboratories are strongly discouraged.

Adding to the political problems outlined above, the severe budget reductions in the 1970s and 1980s meant that competition for scarce federal research and development resources became even more intense. Combined with congressionally mandated expenditures for the centers and laboratories, the monies available for other projects and initiatives had to be diminished proportionately. Some directors of NIE/OERI blamed CEDaR for politicizing the agency's research and development agenda while other directors saw the wisdom of working more closely with a group that had such strong congressional ties. Thus, the continuing controversies over the centers and laboratories, which seem to flare up periodically, have contributed to the overall perception that NIE/OERI is a more politically contentious and vulnerable agency than such other federal research units as NSF or NIH.

Many educational researchers and policymakers would like to ignore the political controversies that have embroiled NIE/OERI, yet some political differences may be inherent in any institution that tries to reform and improve American education. Moreover, given the continued questioning of the wisdom of congressionally mandated funding for the R&D centers and regional educational laboratories, the external and internal political tensions surrounding these institutions are not likely to disappear altogether.

Rather than try to pretend that such political tensions and conflicts are not part of federal involvement in research and development today, perhaps we need a more open and candid analysis and discussion of this neglected topic. Does OERI really face political pressures different than those of such other federal research agencies as NSF or NIH? Do some of the professional research staff at NSF or NIH also feel that some of their agency's funding recipients cannot be criticized openly within their agencies? Would the current political pressures be any less or any different if OERI were a separate and a more independent research agency? What if OERI were merged with another federal research agency like NSF or NIH—would that have a beneficial or detrimental impact? Answers to such difficult and politically sensitive questions will not be easy or simple. But as the changing federal role in educational statistics and research is reconsidered, these issues will need to be addressed.

The views of the federal involvement in educational statistics and research have changed considerably during the past 130 years. While the federal responsibility for collecting, analyzing, and disseminating education statistics remains, there is a growing expectation that more should be done in the areas of research and development. Definitions of federal research and development, especially in terms of its scale and methodology, have become more ambitious and sophisticated over time. But the earlier visions of educational statistics and research significantly reforming American schooling still remain largely unfulfilled, in part because of the inherent practical limitations of any research endeavors and in part because of the inability of the federal enterprise to garner adequate funds and the intellectual leadership necessary to have a larger impact. As we reconsider and revise the federal role in educational statistics and research, perhaps this exploration of past efforts will facilitate a better understanding and appreciation of the historical context in which the earlier federal initiatives occurred as well as provide some useful guidance for future improvements. Although this historical analysis of the federal role in education research and statistics does not necessarily suggest any single course of action, it should encourage policymakers to reexamine their basic premises and to at least consider more diligently alternative ways of achieving current goals.

Part 3 **Early Childhood Education**

Chapter 3 School Readiness
and Early Childhood Education

President George Bush and the nation's governors established six national education goals after their meeting at the
Charlottesville Education Summit in 1989. The first of these
is perhaps the most widely known and highly esteemed: "By
the year 2000, all children in America will start school ready
to learn." The three objectives of this goal champion preschool programs, parent training and support, and child
nutrition and health care.[1]

Although the specific timetable for having all American
children ready for school was new, the stress on early childhood education, parental involvement, and improving the
health of children has a longer history. Most educators and
policymakers, however, are familiar only with the history as it
relates to the Head Start Program, and few analysts have
made any effort to place goal one within a historical framework. In this chapter I shall analyze the efforts to promote
early childhood education in nineteenth-century America;
discuss the creation and development of the Head Start Pro-

gram; and trace the concept, definition, and implementation of school readiness as a national education goal. Within this broader perspective I shall raise some questions that educators and policymakers need to consider as they attempt to implement the objectives of goal one.

EARLY CHILDHOOD EDUCATION IN THE
NINETEENTH CENTURY

Most educators and policymakers view early childhood education as a phenomenon of the past twenty-five years, but concern about educating very young children dates back to the early nineteenth century in the United States and the infant school movement. An examination of this phenomenon will reveal how quickly the enthusiasm for this form of early childhood education waxed and waned.

Some historians have argued that the concept of childhood did not exist in early America. Instead, children were perceived and treated as "miniature adults."[2] More recent scholarship suggests that colonial Americans did distinguish between children and adults, but they saw children as more intellectually and emotionally capable than many Americans do today.[3] Although some young children were taught to read, the Puritans were not especially concerned if they mastered their letters at an early age, as long as they eventually were able to read the Bible. The responsibility for education of young children was entrusted to the parents and not the schools.[4]

In the early nineteenth century there was a major change in when and how young children were educated in the United States.[5] The experiences of British reformers, who had set up infant schools for disadvantaged children in factory towns and large urban areas, provided useful models for Americans in the 1820s.[6] Although the reasons for creating infant schools in the United States were complex and varied, a key factor was the desire to help poor and disadvantaged urban children and their parents. Much of the rhetoric on behalf of investing in nineteenth-century infant schools sounds quite modern; claims were made about how much money would be saved by reducing the amount of welfare and crime: "For every dollar expended on Infant Schools, fifty will probably be saved to the community in the diminution of petty larcenies, and the support of paupers and convicts. This is a serious consideration: and it may be fairly doubted, whether in the boundless range of charity, for which this city is deservedly celebrated, there is any mode in which so large a harvest of safety, goodness, and virtue can be reaped from so slender a seed."[7] Middle-class women saw the efficacy of the infant schools for disadvantaged children, and many of them wanted to send their children to comparable institutions. The annual report of the Infant School Society of the City of Boston noted that "the infant school system was designed for the poor, and for them only was it introduced into this city; but the discovery has been made, that it is equally adapted to the rich. There is now hardly a neighborhood which has not its private infant school."[8]

The early infant schools were divided on what should be taught. Some focused on teaching three- and four-year-olds how to read. Because parents often wanted their young children to be taught reading, many infant school teachers introduced their pupils to the alphabet and the rudiments of reading. The widespread popularity of infant schools was such that by 1840 it is estimated that 40 percent of all three-year-olds in Massachusetts were enrolled either in an infant school or a regular private or public school.[9] Early childhood education became popular not just in the larger cities, but also in the countryside as educators and parents alike sang the praises of helping young children.

Some American educational reformers were attracted to the infant schools because they saw them as a way of introducing better pedagogical techniques into the regular classrooms (modeled after the work of Johann Pestalozzi), but this expectation was never fully realized. As infant schools were incorporated into existing primary schools, the nature of early childhood training offered shifted to resemble more closely what had already been practiced in the regular classrooms. The assimilation of infant schools into the public school system meant that much of their pedagogical distinctiveness was lost.[10]

The popularity of the infant schools was predicated on the belief that children could be taught at ages three and four and that such early education was beneficial. Many nineteenth-century reformers assumed that a child's early experiences determined their subsequent development.[11] This assumption was certainly compatible with the views of young children held by colonial and early nineteenth-century Americans, but there were some who felt otherwise. Amariah Brigham, a prominent young Connecticut physician, published a major treatise on early childhood learning in 1833 that warned educators and parents against infant schools. Brigham argued that overstimulating a child's mind deprived the developing brain of the energy necessary for growth and eventually resulted in an enfeebled mind: "Many physicians of great experience are of the opinion, that efforts to develope [sic] the minds of young children are very frequently injurious; and from instances of disease in children which I have witnessed, I am forced to believe that the danger is indeed great, and that very often in attempting to call forth and cultivate the intellectual faculties of children before they are six or seven years of age, serious and lasting injury has been done to both the body and the mind."[12] Far from helping young children, Brigham believed that infant schools doomed them to insanity in later life.

Although many working-class parents continued to send their three- or four-year-olds to an infant or elementary school, educators and the middle-class parents now repudiated infant schools. They accepted Brigham's arguments on the detrimental effects of early education and agreed with teachers who felt that the presence of such young children was disruptive to a well-ordered classroom. Moreover, there was a growing feeling, thanks in part to the influence of Heinrich Pestalozzi, that young children should be nurtured in the home rather than sent to school. As a result, by the eve of the Civil War hardly any three- or four-year-old children were enrolled in school.[13]

The demise of the infant schools was so complete that most historians and policymakers are not aware that such institutions for early childhood education predated the Head Start Program by nearly 150 years. When kindergartens spread in the United States after the Civil War, their proponents were careful not to identify them in any way with the failed infant schools. By restricting these new institutions to children over age five and deemphasizing the child's intellectual development, kindergartens were able to avoid the hostility that had developed against the infant schools. But the result was that by the end of the nineteenth century, few very young children were enrolled in any schools.[14]

DEVELOPMENT OF THE HEAD START PROGRAM

In the first half of the twentieth century efforts were made to provide some early education for children through nursery schools or day care centers, but these were largely related to other societal concerns. For example, as part of the Works Progress Administration (WPA) in the New Deal, the federal government sponsored nursery schools in order to provide jobs for unemployed teachers, and under the terms of the Lanham Act during World War II, the government funded day care facilities for mothers working in defense-related industries. But none of these efforts had a lasting impact on federal policy toward early childhood education, and most of them disappeared quickly once the larger crisis had subsided.[15]

President Lyndon Johnson's War on Poverty, however, had a major and long-lasting impact on early childhood education. Influenced by the changing scholarly views of the nature of early childhood and driven by the efforts to eradicate poverty, the Johnson administration created the Head Start Program, which has transformed how Americans perceive and educate preschool children.

The early twentieth-century idea that IQ was basically fixed at birth was challenged in the late 1950s and early 1960s by such scholars as Benjamin Bloom and J. McVicker Hunt.[16] Bloom argued that there was a "critical period" during the first five years of life and that early childhood programs could assist children from disadvantaged backgrounds. There was also a great increase in the 1960s in the proportion of child-rearing articles in the popular media that discussed the intellectual development of children.[17] The idea that children's IQs could be improved received reinforcement from several experimental early childhood programs in cities like Baltimore, Nashville, New York, and Syracuse.[18] Thus, the conceptual and intellectual foundations for Project Head Start were in place by the mid-1960s.

At the same time that ideas about the nature of childhood and IQ were changing, so, too, were views about poverty in the United States.[19] Poverty was rediscovered, and the Johnson administration made its elimination through education one of the major goals of the Great Society programs.[20] Led by the efforts of Sargent Shriver, director of the Office of Economic Opportunity (OEO), Project Head Start was created to help poor children overcome the disadvantages they faced when entering elementary schools.[21]

Head Start began as an eight-week summer program but was quickly converted to a full-year program. Although several key academic advisers suggested the gradual introduction of Head Start programs, Shriver insisted on a large-scale effort starting immediately in summer 1965. Particularly innovative and impressive was the involvement of parents in helping their children as well as in guiding the overall program. But while the Head Start Planning Committee envisioned the program delivering a variety of services to children (including health services), the tendency of many political leaders and the media was to focus on the cognitive benefits of the program.[22] Testifying before the House of Representatives, Shriver claimed that the Head Start Program could improve the IQ of children by eight to ten points.[23]

Some advisers and analysts were concerned that the long-term effects of the Head Start Program might be limited, but policymakers and the public remained enthusiastic about these projects. A seminal but controversial evaluation of Head Start by the Westinghouse Learning Corporation and Ohio University seemed to substantiate those fears by finding that the initial IQ score gains were only temporary and faded quickly once those children entered the regular schools: "Summer programs have been ineffective in producing any persisting gains in cognitive or affective development that can be detected by the tests used in grades 1, 2, and 3. . . . Full-year programs are marginally effective in terms of producing noticeable gains in cognitive development that can be detected by the measures used in grades 1, 2, and 3, but are ineffective in promoting detectable, durable gains in affective development."[24] The study did go on to mention sympathetically some noncognitive and nonaffective benefits of Head Start: "Furthermore, Head Start has been concerned with all aspects of the child: medical, dental, nutritional, intellectual, and sociopersonal. It is also a direct example of social action to help the poor; as such, it has been a facilitator of social change in the society at large. Many positive spin-off effects can be attributed to Head Start. It has pioneered in parent education and community development; it has mobilized resources for the group care of young children, stimulated research work in infant and child development, and fostered the further development of teacher competence."[25]

Favorable statements about the program by the Westinghouse Learning Corporation were quickly forgotten amidst the negative reports in the news media. A headline in the *New York Times* proclaimed that "Head Start Pupils Found No Better off Than Others."[26] The release of the Westinghouse Report on Head Start was met with widespread criticism from the academic community. Researchers pointed out that Head Start was not a single, homogeneous program and that certain projects may have been quite effective. Marshall Smith and Joan Bissell reanalyzed the Westinghouse data and claimed that it demonstrated that the full-year programs of Head Start had been effective, especially in the urban African-American Head Start centers.[27] But the authors of the original Westinghouse report responded by rejecting the conceptual and methodological critiques of their evaluation.[28]

In a retrospective glance two decades later, Edward Zigler candidly admits that despite the serious methodological shortcomings of that investigation, the adverse results should not have been unexpected because of the poor and uneven quality of many of the initial programs: "In short, there was no mystery behind the highly uneven quality of the Head Start programs in 1970. Despite the flaws in the Westinghouse report methodology, I doubt that any national impact evaluation at that time would have showed that Head Start had long-term educational benefits. Even if, as I suspected, a third of the programs were wonderful, their effects would most likely have been canceled out by an equal fraction of programs that were poorly operated."[29]

Thanks to the strong political constituency for Head Start among the parents, the program survived despite increasing doubts about its efficacy, yet the planned expansion of Head Start under the Nixon administration was postponed and the program was maintained at the same level of funding (in real dollars) for much of the 1970s and 1980s.[30] During the 1980s interest in Head Start revived as the proportion of mothers with young children in the labor force increased and as the percentage of poor children increased.[31] Early childhood education also gained an important boost when the longitudinal results from the highly visible, but controversial Perry Preschool Program in Ypsilanti, Michigan, seemed to demonstrate that such programs significantly increased high school graduation, reduced juvenile delinquency, and increased subsequent incomes among at-risk students. As with the nineteenth-century infant schools, the initial investment in the Perry School is cited as highly cost effective.[32]

The impressive results from the Perry Preschool Program have been challenged. The analysts of the program readily acknowledge that the high-quality care provided by that program does not resemble that of most Head Start programs and therefore the results from the former cannot be used to judge the latter. Moreover, critics have questioned the adequacy of the statistical design of that experiment because of the significant differences between the control and intervention groups, the lack of total random assignment, and the faulty methodology employed in the cost-benefit analysis.[33] Perhaps most intriguing and disturbing is the little noticed and belated finding that the Perry Preschool Program may not be equally effective with boys and girls. Helen Barnes, a researcher at the High/Scope Program who reanalyzed the longitudinal data, revealed that "most of the significant long-term outcome differences in the Perry study occur between the treatment and control girls. Although there are differences in long-term outcomes between the two male groups, in most cases they are not significant."[34] As her findings on the cohort at age nineteen were reported first in an unpublished master's thesis in 1989 and then in an unpublished Ph.D. dissertation in 1991, few scholars or policymakers noted this important caveat.[35]

In the most recent update of the Perry Preschool cohort, at age twenty-seven, however, the analysts acknowledge the existence of gender differences in the outcomes. Nevertheless, they still downplay the potential policy significance of those differences and emphasize the more positive results. For example, in the important executive summary of this lengthy and highly technical report, the positive results are repeatedly cited and emphasized. But the limitations and failures of the Perry Preschool Program are not even acknowledged in the executive summary.[36] Although it is understandable that the authors might want to highlight the achievements of their highly innovative and significant program, policymakers and the general public might have benefited from a more balanced presentation of their overall results.

The investigators also do not explore adequately the policy implications of the often sizable gender differences in outcomes in either the executive summary or the text. For example, while females in the program group did much better in schooling and graduating from high school than the females in the nonprogram sample, there were no real differences between program and nonprogram males.[37] Does this mean that quality early childhood programs like the Perry Preschool one help only the educational attainment of females? Do we need different types of preschool education for males and females? Are these striking gender differences in part the result of the particular characteristics of the sample and the setting in which the study was conducted?[38] Thus, although the investigators of the Perry Preschool experience have discussed and analyzed at great length the more positive and impressive findings, they seem to have ignored or minimized such equally important policy issues as gender differences.

The debate over the long-term effectiveness of early childhood education in general and the usefulness of the Head Start Program in particular continues.[39] Critics question the statistical rigor and methodological validity of the earlier evaluations of Head Start while its defenders point out that children who enroll in that program are more disadvantaged than the children who have not attended.[40] Ron Haskins has provided one of the more balanced summaries and assessments of the vast array of studies of the impact of early childhood education:

"1. Both model programs and Head Start produce significant and meaningful gains in intellectual performance and socioemotional development by the end of a year of intervention.
2. For both types of programs, gains on standardized IQ and achievement tests as well as on tests of socioemotional development decline within a few years (or even less in the case of Head Start studies).
3. On categorical variables of school performance such as special education placement and grade retention, there is very strong evidence of positive effects for the model programs and modest evidence of effects for Head Start programs.
4. On measures of life success such as teen pregnancy, delinquency, welfare

participation, and employment, there is modest evidence of positive impacts for model programs but virtually no evidence for Head Start."[41]

Another useful and somewhat more optimistic assessment of early childhood education programs by W. Stephen Barnett acknowledges the methodological weaknesses of most studies, but concludes that:

> The weight of the evidence establishes that ECCE [early childhood care and education] can produce large effects on IQ during the early childhood years and sizable persistent effects on achievement, grade retention, special education, high school graduation, and socialization. In particular, the evidence for effects on grade retention and special education is overwhelming. Evidence is weaker for persistent achievement effects, but this weakness is probably the result of flaws in study design and follow-up procedures. Evidence for effects on high school graduation and delinquency is strong but based on a smaller number of studies.
>
> These effects are large enough and persistent enough to make a meaningful difference in the lives of children from low-income families: for many children, preschool programs can mean the difference between failing and passing, regular or special education, staying out of trouble or becoming involved in crime and delinquency, dropping out or graduating from high school.[42]

Head Start was predicated upon the assumption that the early years of a child's life are the most crucial for their long-term growth and development. Proponents of the program used the perceived plasticity and determinative importance of early childhood to justify Head Start. But some child developmentalists extended this same logic to question Head Start by arguing that the program reaches children much too late. Burton White, for example, wrote that most of the important developments occur before the age of three:

> From all that I have learned about the education and development of young children, I have come to the conclusion that most American families get their children through the first six or eight months of life reasonably well in terms of education and development; but I believe that perhaps no more than ten percent at most manage to get their children through the eight- to thirty-six-month age periods as well educated and developed as they could and should be. Yet our studies show that the period that starts at eight months and ends at three years is a period of primary importance in the development of a human being. *To begin to look at a child's development when he is two years of age is already much too late,* particularly in the area of social skills and attitudes.[43]

If scholars like White think that early childhood care and interaction must begin sooner, others like David Elkind argue against rushing young children into early intellectual activity. Repeating the mid-nineteenth-century warnings against early intellectual activity, Elkind denounces the early intellectual stimulation of children in schools (but he does not oppose all out-of-home programs for children): "What harm is there in exposing young children to formal instruction involving the inculcation of rules? The harm comes from what I have called 'miseducation.' We miseducate children whenever we put them at risk for no purpose. The risks of miseducating young children are both short term and long term. The short-term risks derive from the stress formal instruction puts upon children with all its resultant stress symptoms. The long-term risks are of at least three kinds—motivational, intellectual, and social. In each case the potential psychological risk of early instruction is far greater than any potential educational gain."[44]

Other scholars implicitly raise questions about Head Start by challenging the notion that any early childhood experiences are so determinative of later developments. Work in lifespan psychology and life course analysis stresses the continuity of human development and minimizes the lasting and irreversible effects of any particular events—including early childhood experiences.[45] In spite of the growing popularity of lifespan psychology and life course analysis, however, few scholars or policymakers have seen how the implications of this approach might affect one's support for such early childhood education programs as Head Start.

A final and still rather new attack comes from those who question the efficiency of Head Start compared to alternative expenditures for helping at-risk children. On the basis of their extensive work with at-risk children in elementary schools, Robert Slavin at the Success for All Program at Johns Hopkins University argues that investing in individual tutoring in the early grades is more effective than funding Head Start. Indeed, after intensive testing of the effectiveness of the Success for All Program, Slavin and his colleagues conclude that "The evidence presented here dispels the idea that any one year of early intervention will have substantial lasting impacts on reading achievement. There is no 'magic bullet' that sets students on the road to success. . . . *Intensive* early intervention must be followed by *extensive* changes in basic classroom instructional practices if all students are to succeed throughout their elementary years."[46]

In spite of some academic challenges and uncertainty about Head Start in the 1980s, most educators, policymakers, and parents continued to endorse that program enthusiastically and unequivocally. Active lobbying by the National Head Start Association and others helped to persuade such key conservative Republican senators as Jeremiah Denton (R-AL) and Orrin Hatch (R-UT) to support the program. During the Reagan administration, Head Start was one of the very few domestic social programs that remained intact, and it was even endorsed by the president.[47]

EARLY EDUCATION AND SCHOOL READINESS

The election of George Bush as president in 1988 signaled a renewed interest by the federal government in education. Whereas Ronald Reagan tried to dismantle the newly created Department of Education and to reduce federal spending for education, Bush wanted to be seen as the "education president" and worked closely with the state governors to develop a national agenda for the improvement of education.

The National Governors' Association in the mid-1980s, reacting in part to the growing criticisms of the nation's schools, created seven task forces to examine the current state of affairs in education and to make recommendations. Governor Richard Riley of South Carolina headed the Task Force on Readiness, which held three hearings in late 1985 and early 1986 and commissioned several papers on school readiness.[48] This task force recommended:

> States must develop initiatives to help at-risk preschool children come ready for school. Possible state initiatives include: provide all in-home assistance for first-time, low-income parents of high-risk infants; develop outreach initiatives using community and religious organizations to assist and support young children with absentee parent(s) or guardian(s) as their sole source of nurturance; providing high quality early childhood development programs for all four-year-old at-risk children, and, where feasible, three-year-olds; provide all parents of preschool children with information on successful parenting practices; stress continued improvement of developmental and educational programs in existing day care centers for preschool children through center accreditation, teacher credentialing, and staff development; and, finally, develop state and local structures through which various public and private agencies can work together to provide appropriate programs for young children and new parents.[49]

Building on the initiative of the governors as well as on his own interest in education, the president of the United States, for only the third time in history, called for a meeting with the nation's governors to find ways of improving American education. The Bush administration objectives, which are listed below, were broad, and they included the unveiling of a set of national goals in early 1990.

"1. To demonstrate the President's interest in and commitment to education as a central national priority.

2. To engage the nation's governors in a substantive discussion of the nature of the challenge we face, of alternative ways of improving our educational performance, and of those ideas for reform that seem to have the greatest promise.

3. To set the stage for a series of education proposals and national goals to be unveiled in early 1990 possibly as part of the State of the Union Address."[50]

In the briefing book for the Charlottesville Education Summit, which was held in Charlottesville, Virginia, on September 27–28, 1989, the administration outlined six major areas for the discussion: (1) teaching: revitalizing a profession; (2) the learning environment; (3) governance: who is in charge? (4) choice and restructuring; (5) a competitive workforce and lifelong learning; and (6) postsecondary education: strengthening access and excellence. In the executive summary of the discussion of "the learning environment," one of the five specific items mentioned was "early childhood education: we must see to it that young children are provided with early childhood and pre-school experiences that prepare them for school success."[51] The specific mention of the importance of early childhood education was not surprising: almost all the preliminary administration documents for that education summit mentioned the importance of early education and the National Governors' Association had previously championed school readiness.[52]

Although the Bush administration did not want to commit itself to a particular set of objectives at the Charlottesville Education Summit, many governors wanted to issue a more specific joint statement at the conclusion of that meeting.[53] The resulting compromise stated that the president and the nation's governors would jointly establish national goals for education in early 1990 related to:

"• the readiness of children to start school;
• the performance of students on international achievement tests, especially math and science;
• the reduction of the dropout rate and the improvement of academic performance, especially among at-risk students;
• the functional literacy of adult Americans;
• the level of training necessary to guarantee a competitive workforce;
• the supply of qualified teachers and up-to-date technology; and
• the establishment of safe, disciplined, and drug-free schools."[54]

The drafting of the national education goals proceeded along two parallel tracks—one by the administration and the other by the National Governors'

Association. In the administration, Roger Porter, the White House domestic policy adviser, directed the activities and drew upon the staff of the Office of Educational Research and Improvement for assistance. Christopher Cross, the assistant secretary of OERI, in a set of briefing papers on the proposed education goals, provided four alternative ways of formulating the goal on early education:

> *Alternative Goal One:* By the year [2002], [all] children will be ready to begin first grade.
>
> *Alternative Goal Two:* By the year [2002], [halve] the differences among race/ethnic groups within the population with respect to their readiness to begin first grade.
>
> *Alternative Goal Three:* By [2002], disadvantaged students will participate in preschool educational programs with cognitive content [at least at the same rate] as more advantaged students.
>
> *Alternative Goal Four:* Increase the share of parents who provide positive educational experiences at home to their preschool children.[55]

The information in brackets in the above quote is for purposes of illustration only. The year 2002 was often suggested because that was the year when the children who were entering kindergarten in 1989 would graduate from high school. The other commonly used and eventually adopted year for the goals was 2000.

Throughout the discussions about the proposed national goals there was concern within the administration about how they could be measured and whether it was desirable to have more than one indicator for each goal. The question of school readiness posed a particular challenge since no adequate measurements had been developed to ascertain when a child was ready to enroll in a regular school. At the same time, specific recommendations could have immediate large-scale budgetary implications because they probably would entail an expansion of Head Start. Some suggested that a scale be developed for measuring the degree of "readiness" in children while others wanted to survey teachers on whether students were prepared to enter the first grade.[56]

Analysts for the Education Task Force of the Governors drafted their own set of recommendations for the national goals. They also favored having a few goals, but unlike the administration they wanted specific objectives under each of the goals and appropriate indicators for measuring progress. One of their four general goals was that "by the time they reach school age, every American should be healthy and ready to learn." Thus, the Education Task Force of the Governors highlighted the importance of early child development and explicitly linked health and cognitive concerns. Moreover, they proposed nine specific indicators for school readiness and set more immediate standards for the year 1995:

Objective: All children should be healthy.

Target and indicator: Reduce the incidence of low birth weight children by one-half by 1995 and by one-half again by 2000.

Target and indicator: Reduce the incidence of children who have not received recommended inoculations by 75% by 1995 and by 100% by 2000.

Target and indicator: Reduce incidence of malnourished aged 0–5 children by one-half by 1995 and by one-half again by 2000.

Target and indicator: Reduce to no more than 1 per 1,000 the prevalence of HIV infection among women to live born infants by the [sic] 2000.

Target and indicator: Reduce the number of crack- and cocaine-addicted babies by 50% by 1995 and by half again by 2000.

Objective: All children should be intellectually ready to learn.

Target and indicator: Give all four-year-old eligible children the opportunity to attend a yearlong Head Start program or its equivalent by 1995. By 2000, provide all eligible three-year-old children the same opportunity.

Target and indicator: Provide a high-quality preschool program to every disadvantaged three- and four-year-old.

Target and indicator: All three- and four-year-old children should be screened for potential disabilities and learning disorders by 1995. Increase the percentage of children who are identified as being at-risk who are served by one-half by 1995 and to 100% by 2000.

Target and indicator: Increase the percent of preschoolers who are ready to do school work upon entering school. Indicator: Need to develop a national assessment of school readiness and assessment tool to be administered to a sample of children for the express purpose of tracking progress on this goal.[57]

In the negotiations between the Bush administration and the nation's governors during December 1989, much of the specificity about the goals included in the earlier drafts by the National Governors' Association disappeared. President Bush announced the six national goals in his State of the Union speech on January 31, 1990. Goal one was simply stated as: "By the year 2000, all children in America will start school ready to learn." The text of the announcement acknowledged that no adequate assessments of school readiness existed and that it might be dangerous to develop such a scale: "Assessments indicating readiness for school generally are not administered by schools. Nor do the President and the Governors recommend that such an assessment, especially one that could wrongfully be used to determine when a child should start school, be developed for purposes of measuring progress toward this goal. Other current indicators of readiness may serve as proxies, and still others need to be developed."[58]

When the national governors met in February 1990, they reaffirmed the six national goals, but they also expanded the specific set of objectives under each of the goals. For goal one, the three objectives were:

All disadvantaged and disabled children will have access to high quality and developmentally appropriate preschool programs that help prepare children for school.

Every parent in America will be a child's first teacher and devote time each day helping his or her preschool child learn; parents will have access to the training and support they need.

Children will receive the nutrition and health care needed to arrive at school with healthy minds and bodies, and the number of low birth weight babies will be significantly reduced through enhanced prenatal health systems.[59]

Establishing indicators to measure the progress made on each of the six national goals was difficult, especially in regard to goal one and school readiness. In the first annual report of the National Education Goals Panel, under the heading of "what we now know," goal one was the only one for which it stated: "At present there are no direct ways to measure the nation's progress toward achieving this Goal." The report went on to note that the National Education Goals Panel would be considering an early childhood assessment system to monitor this goal.[60] The four variables specified as important for assessing a child's readiness for school were "direct indicators of the (1) knowledge, (2) social, emotional, and physical well-being, (3) language usage, and (4) approaches to learning of young children."[61] To obtain this information, they proposed "student profiles of a nationally representative sample of children conducted during their first year of formal schooling. The profiles would contain four sources of information: (1) parent reports, (2) teacher reports, (3) an individually administered examination, and (4) 'portfolios' of students' performance during their first year in school."[62] The specific empirical measures of school readiness reported, however, dealt with prenatal care, birth weight, routine health care, child nutrition, parent-child interactions, preschool participation, and preschool quality.[63]

The goals panel created a technical panel to work on this issue, but the following year it acknowledged that it still had no way of measuring progress toward goal one. It did endorse a national Early Childhood Assessment System that would obtain information on a nationally representative sample of kinder-gartners from their teachers, parents, and themselves. The National Education Goals Panel now specified that the gathering of this information would occur several times during the kindergarten year. The five critical areas of a child's growth and readiness for learning were specified as (1) physical well-being and motor development, (2) social and emotional development, (3) approaches toward learning, (4) language usage, and (5) cognition and general knowl-edge.[64] Again, the specific indicators presented about goal one were the same limited information presented the previous year, with the additions of data on continuity of health care, availability of health insurance or Medicaid, trends in nursery school enrollment, and preschool participation of children with dis-abilities.[65]

Given the broad and diverse definitions of a child's school readiness and the lack of any agreement on how to measure this concept, it is not surprising that different individuals and organizations use it in a wide variety of ways. Even within the Department of Education there is little coordination or discussion of how goal one should be defined and implemented. For example, OERI estab-lished an agencywide task force to look at what is known about each of the six national goals and what research remains to be done. That effort, however, was not closely coordinated with related activities in other parts of the federal government, including those of the National Education Goals Panel on school readiness.

Individuals and organizations outside of government also seized on the six national education goals to further their own reform agenda. Ernest Boyer, president of the Carnegie Foundation for the Advancement of Teaching and an active contributor to the National Education Goals Panel, wrote a highly influential book, *Ready to Learn: A Mandate for the Nation.*[66] Boyer interpreted goal one broadly and used it to justify the need for such diverse issues as a universal health insurance, a life cycle curriculum, neighborhood ready-to-learn centers, and full funding of an upgraded Head Start Program by 1995. In his discussions of these issues, however, Boyer tended to cite the more positive evaluations of programs like Head Start and ignore the more critical assess-ments of them. Moreover, he relied heavily upon the results of a 1991 Carnegie Foundation survey of kindergarten teachers even though the response rate was only about one-third.[67] Thus, although almost everyone agrees that we are yet to develop any effective and reliable assessments of school readiness, it has not prevented many analysts and policymakers from making ambitious and expensive recommendations on behalf of this goal. Although some have expressed reservations about the implementation and measurement of goal one, few have challenged its overall validity or usefulness. One of the sharpest critics of the Bush administration's America 2000 Program in general and of the school readiness goal in particular was columnist Phyllis Schlafly who fears further intrusion into education and the home:

> America 2000 has a concept of "school" that not only includes absorbing private schools into its system, but also includes expanding the public schools in order to "parent" children through their preschool years, in their after-school hours, and to provide non-school services. America 2000 wants to transform public schools into baby-sitters for pre-kindergarten kids, and into social service centers to provide meals, health care (probably including the controversial kinds), counseling and guidance. . . .
>
> Will government agents go into the homes and dictate how preschool children are raised—and then snitch on parents who reject the government's "suggestions"? This sort of thing is already being experimented with under the name "Parents as Teachers," but which many people call the "Teachers as Parents" program. Americans absolutely don't want that kind of Big Brother society.[68]

Whatever doubts some researchers have about the studies of the efficacy of Head Start or about measuring school readiness, or whatever misgivings some conservatives voiced about federal involvement in early education, most policy-makers have endorsed the program enthusiastically. Former President Bush sought a $600-million boost for Head Start for FY93 (27-percent increase), the largest funding increase proposed by a president up to then.[69] President Bill Clinton went even further and called for full funding of Head Start. As he stated in a major speech on education at the East Los Angeles Community College, "A country that found $500 billion to bail out the savings and loan industry can find $5 billion to full-fund Head Start."[70] During his first four years, President Clinton worked hard to increase funding for Head Start and succeeded in persuading a reluctant Congress to increase FY97 monies for Head Start to nearly $4 billion, a substantial 11.5-percent increase over the previous year.[71]

The six national education goals developed by the Bush administration and the governors focused public attention on the need to improve the educational system. They also centered federal, state, and local efforts on a particular set of educational priorities and have helped to forge a broad coalition of public and private support for these objectives. Although the political support for increased educational spending and innovations at the different levels has not been as strong or as consistent as that for other programs (such as assistance to the elderly), it appears to have risen in recent years.

Having all children ready to enter school is certainly one of the best known and most popular of the six national goals. It has attracted considerable attention and some additional resources for early education, especially federal funding of Head Start. This is an important achievement as federal funding of Head Start in real dollars was stagnant during the 1970s and early 1980s. In spite of the broad definition of school readiness, which includes concerns about children's health as well as educational reforms, however, there is little evidence to suggest that the national education goals have played a major role in garnering additional political support for the noneducational components of goal one.

The United States has turned to early childhood education on several occasions to correct what were perceived to be major problems in our society. The infant school movement addressed in large part the growing concern about urban crime and poverty in nineteenth-century America. Similarly, Head Start attempted to deal with the rediscovery of poverty in the mid-1960s. Continued concern about disadvantaged children today, as well as a growing fear about America's lack of competitiveness in the global economy, has spurred recent efforts on readiness to attend schools. In each of these instances there was genuine interest in helping young children, but all three movements were embedded within broader concerns about social and economic developments.

Infant schools, Head Start, and the school readiness movement all are based on the assumption that early childhood experiences are crucial to subsequent adult development. Proponents of these reforms believed that unless society reached the at-risk children at very young ages it would be difficult, if not impossible, to provide adequate remedial educational services later. Moreover, each of these movements was affected, in varying degrees, by the changing scientific and popular views of early child development. Each benefited by the emerging belief that young children were more capable cognitively and affectively than had previously been thought, but only the infant school movement was damaged irrevocably by a counterreaction, which asserted that early intellectual stimulation could permanently impair the child's brain.

The reformers involved in each of these movements shared the widespread belief that education by itself can alleviate many, if not most, of the disadvantages individuals have acquired as a result of their economic or ethnic background. Although the proponents of these changes did not ignore entirely other necessary societal reforms, they often underestimated the extent to which structural problems in the economy or society acted as barriers to social and economic mobility. Thus, early education often was portrayed as a panacea for solving problems that might have been equally or better addressed in other areas.

While almost all of the attention was devoted to preparing disadvantaged children for regular schools, very little effort was made to change the regular schools to accommodate those children. Nineteenth-century public school teachers and administrators frequently complained about the infant schools and often joined with others to eventually eliminate three- and four-year-olds from the public schools. In spite of early warnings that the initial cognitive gains of Head Start faded for students when they entered the elementary grades, surprisingly little effort was made to rethink and restructure the existing public schools. Although the Follow Through Program was created in 1967 for that purpose, it has never enjoyed the visibility or support that one might have expected. Similarly, although the early drafts of goal one by the staff of OERI in summer 1989 called for having all children ready for school and for having all schools ready for children, the latter part of this message was dropped in subsequent drafts in other parts of the Department of Education. Unfortunately, many public schools and teachers still have not succeeded in adapting their curriculum or teaching practices to the special needs of disadvantaged students.

After more than twenty-five years of experience with Head Start and a federal expenditure of more than $21 billion to serve 12 million children, we still are not certain of the actual impact of that program on the life course of disadvantaged children. Moreover, given the diversity of Head Start programs, we also do not know which Head Start models are best suited for children in different settings. Nevertheless, most policymakers and the public are convinced of the efficacy of Head Start—though some call for improving the overall quality of the program by reducing class sizes and attracting better trained teachers by substantially increasing their salaries. Finally, very little, if any, effort has been made to consider whether alternative expenditures on children, such as more individualized tutoring in the elementary grades, might be a more effective way of helping at-risk students.

Thus, ensuring that all children are ready for school is a laudable goal and one that has ample historical precedents in this country. But the uncertainty about the actual meanings of that goal and of the best ways of implementing it continue to present a serious challenge to policymakers and the public. Perhaps the pointed reminder about the importance of providing a world-class education for all our young children will help us in overcoming the often all-too-visible short-term difficulties and inefficiencies in having all children ready to learn when they enter school.

Chapter 4 Is It Time to
Reinvent Follow Through?
An Analysis of Past Efforts
to Sustain the Benefits
of Head Start

As noted in chapter 2, early childhood education in general and the Head Start Program in particular received renewed attention in the 1990s. Federal support for preschool programs waned in the 1970s and early 1980s, but Head Start is now enthusiastically embraced by most political leaders as well as by the American public. Both the Bush and Clinton administrations as well as the National Governors' Association have endorsed the eight national goals—the six that were adopted in 1989 and the two that were added in 1994—including goal one, which states that "by the year 2000, all children in America will start school ready to learn."[1]

At the same time that political leaders and the public were praising Head Start, some scholars questioned the long-term benefits of the program for the cognitive development of at-risk children.[2] The debates about the efficacy of Head Start found their way into the national media,[3] and some of the program's staunchest supporters admitted that the program had significant weaknesses as well as strengths.[4] Few contested the program's short-term beneficial impact, but there was growing concern that some of the more extravagant claims made on behalf of Head Start might lead to disappointment as Head Start became fully funded but many of the problems of at-risk children remained.

One response to these developments is to look for ways to improve the transition of Head Start students into the regular schools as well as to enhance the learning opportunities for at-risk children in the elementary grades. An earlier effort to maintain the short-term benefits of preschooling—the Follow Through Program—is usually totally forgotten in these discussions. Created in 1967 and envisioned initially as a large-scale public elementary school program modeled after Project Head Start, Follow Through reverted to an experimental program soon after its inception due to the lack of funding. This limited demonstration and evaluation program has survived for more than twenty-five years with a small, but very loyal and dedicated group of supporters. An analysis of the development and experiences of the Follow Through Program may be useful at this time, as we address problems similar to those that confronted policymakers in the late 1960s.

THE ORIGINS OF THE FOLLOW THROUGH PROGRAMS

Head Start was launched as part of the War on Poverty in summer 1965. Drawing upon the ideas that IQ was not fixed and that early childhood was the critical period for intellectual development, Project Head Start was designed to help poor children overcome their disadvantages by the time they entered elementary schools. The program was located in the Office of Economic Opportunity and had a strong parental and community focus.[5]

Although many academic advisers argued that Head Start should be introduced gradually and experimentally, Sargent Shriver, the director of OEO, insisted that it be implemented immediately as a large-scale, eight-week summer program. In part Shriver was anxious to use the popularity of Head Start to deflect the growing criticisms of other aspects of OEO.[6] The more knowledgeable proponents of Head Start downplayed the program's role in raising children's IQ and emphasized its broader objectives, but many of those testifying before Congress or addressing the mass media stressed the ability of that program to enhance the IQ of poor children.[7] As a result, Head Start became popularly identified with improving the cognitive development of poor children.

As Head Start flourished and there was widespread hope that this early intervention program by itself might eliminate most of the disadvantages faced by poor children, some policymakers called for comparable efforts in the elementary grades. Three months after the introduction of Head Start, President Johnson called for the creation of a full year Head Start Program and the "follow-through" of that program's achievements into the regular classes.[8] The idea of incorporating features of the Head Start Program into the regular schools was desirable to many policymakers at OEO. The immediate success and popularity of Head Start made it an attractive program to duplicate elsewhere. Thus, as the Johnson administration looked for new approaches and programs to eradicate poverty, the idea of continuing to work with children after they left Head Start seemed pedagogically sound and politically expedient.

Interest in continuing to help Head Start children as they entered the public schools received reinforcement as doubts began to surface about the lasting impact of that preschool experience. Edward Zigler, a prominent early childhood psychologist involved in the Head Start deliberations, privately voiced his doubts about the program's ability to improve dramatically the intellectual capabilities of children.[9] Ivor Kraft publicly speculated that "even the finest preschool experience for deprived and segregated children will wash out and disappear as the children pass through the grades."[10] Especially important to some policymakers were reports of the work of Max Wolf and Annie Stein. According to their study of a small sample of children who had attended Head Start in summer 1965, the children's IQ gains faded quickly during the first year of regular school.[11]

Sargent Shriver, in an address to the Great Cities Research Council on November 18, 1966, acknowledged that "the readiness and receptivity they [the children] had gained in Head Start has been crushed by the broken promises of the first grade."[12] President Johnson called for continuing to help Head Start children into the early grades and suggested the creation of a follow-through program in his State of the Union message: "We should strengthen the Head Start program, begin it for children three years old, and maintain its educational momentum by following through in the early years [of school]."[13] President Johnson in his message on children and youth a month later recommended to Congress the passage of a "follow-through" program.[14]

Not awaiting congressional approval, OEO funded a small $2.5-million pilot program for Follow Through. In June 1967 OEO transferred the Follow Through Program to the Division of Compensatory Education (DCE) within the Bureau of Elementary and Secondary Education (BESE) in the U.S. Office of Education. Congress formally legislated the Follow Through Program in 1967 amendments to the Economic Opportunity Act of 1964. The legislation stated:

"1. A program to be known as "Project Head Start" focused upon children who have not reached the age of compulsory school attendance which (A) will provide such comprehensive health, nutritional, educational, social, and other services as the director finds will aid the children to attain their full potential, and (B) will provide for direct participation of the parents of such children in development, conduct, and overall program direction at the local level.

2. A program to be known as "Follow Through" focused primarily upon children in kindergarten or elementary school who were previously enrolled in Head Start or similar programs and designed to provide comprehensive services and parent participation activities as described in paragraph (1), which the director finds will aid in the continuing development of children to their full potential. Funds for such programs shall be transferred directly from the director (of OEO) to the secretary of Health, Education and Welfare. Financial assistance for such projects shall be provided by the secretary on the basis of agreements reached with the director directly to local educational agencies except as otherwise provided by such agreements."[15]

It was anticipated that Follow Through would be a large-scale program with about 200,000 children enrolled in the 1968–69 school year and a budget of $120 million. Although the results of the pilot projects were expected to provide guidance for the expansion of Follow Through, research or evaluation was not intended to be a significant focus of the operating program, which was to provide additional compensatory education for children in grades K–3.

DESIGN AND EVALUATION OF THE FOLLOW THROUGH EXPERIMENT

The financial pressures brought on by the expenses of the Vietnam War as well as the growing disillusionment with the Office of Economic Opportunity resulted in a major reduction in funding for that agency for FY69. Only about $12 million in new funds were allocated to Follow Through for FY69.[16] Given the drastically reduced funding for FY69, Follow Through was scaled back and became an experimental program. This not only provided a rationale for continuing the program, but it also was consistent with the other broader evaluation efforts underway in the federal government. It was anticipated, however, that the experimentation phase would be short and that Follow Through would become a large-scale service program.[17] Congress was not asked to change the authorization of Follow Through to reflect its new experimental orientation. The legislative mandate continued to emphasize the service and community-oriented aspects of Follow Through rather than the new administrative goal of providing evaluations of alternative models. As a result, the initial ambiguity in Follow Through between a service and an experimental program was reinforced.[18]

The conceptual philosophy underlying the experimental orientation of the Follow Through Program was planned variation. The nature and contents of the local programs would be varied and their impact on students evaluated in order to determine which models were particularly effective. The White House Task Force on Child Development had recommended four sources of variation in Follow Through: (1) curriculum, (2) student-teacher ratios, (3) age and training of teachers, and (4) type of parental involvement. Eventually curriculum became the central factor in the planned variation, but in practice it was always hard to specify exactly what these differences meant.[19]

Given the limited number of Follow Through staff in Washington, D.C., as well as concern about excessive federal control over local education, Richard Snyder, the director of Follow Through's Research and Evaluation Section, decided to use different sponsors to provide models and guidance for the local projects. The programs of the sponsors ranged from highly structured academic approaches to ones that were more focused on the personal and emotional growth of the individual child.[20] Unfortunately, most of the sponsors did not have fully developed programs so that the development and implementation of these models had to proceed simultaneously.[21] Because local programs were free to choose their sponsors, systematic comparisons were more difficult.

Robert Egbert, the first director of Follow Through, and many others were anxious to expand the program as quickly as possible because they favored a large-scale public school service program for Head Start graduates. Thirty-nine communities and 2,900 students participated in the pilot program in FY67. By FY71 the number of projects had mushroomed to 178 sites and 78,100 students, which made the overall analysis of the Follow Through more difficult and much more expensive. Moreover, the number of sponsors grew from fourteen in FY69 to twenty-two in FY71. The funding for Follow Through rose from $3.75 million in FY67 to $69.0 million in FY71.[22]

The basic tension between running an experimental program and a service-oriented one was never clearly or satisfactorily resolved. Control of Follow Through projects was shared among several different groups, and no one had overall authority for crafting and executing a systematic planned variation experiment. Indeed, the idea of collegial and shared decision making was one of the cherished trademarks of Follow Through, though in practice this often broke down quite quickly. As a result, it was always difficult to develop and implement a systematic and comprehensive evaluation plan for the program as a whole.[23]

Follow Through was an anomaly in that it was funded through the Office of Economic Opportunity but administered in the U.S. Office of Education (USOE). This was an advantage in that it gave Follow Through relative autonomy within USOE, but it was a serious disadvantage when competition for scarce funding occurred: the program often lacked vigorous bureaucratic advocates as neither OEO nor the USOE saw it as one of their highest priorities.[24]

The Stanford Research Institute (SRI) was contacted belatedly to evaluate the program, but the initial design of the program had been compromised from the very beginning. The specific projects and their sponsors were selected and funded before an overall evaluation plan was developed. As a result, there was little agreement on the design or the administration of the local programs, especially since it was "clear from the outset that having a well-developed program model was not a precondition for participation in the experiment."[25] Although it was able to gather some of the appropriate data for children who entered the program in 1969 and 1970, SRI encountered serious difficulties from the more service- and community-oriented grantees who often did not accept the value of the planned variation approach. No serious thought was given at the time to the possibility of the random assignment of students to the Follow Through Program.[26]

Events continued to undermine the Follow Through experiment. The outcomes of the first-year evaluation (1968–69) were not positive, so it was quietly decided by everyone not to use them. Although this might have been a methodologically defensible position since it does take time to implement programs, the fact that the decision was made only after the results proved negative made it appear that Follow Through was trying to hide its failure. Moreover, questions about the procedures in granting the evaluation contract to Stanford Research Institute led to several internal and external reviews. None of the reviews challenged the methodological or conceptual aspects of the SRI contract, but they did criticize Follow Through for the lack of specificity in the contract and USOE for its inadequate direct control of the overall evaluation plans. In the midst of these difficulties, Egbert left Follow Through to become the dean of education at the University of Nebraska at Lincoln in 1971.[27]

As information about the inadequacy of the evaluation design and the problems in data collection became widespread and proved to be politically embarrassing, Garry McDaniels was recruited and assigned the task of correcting the shortcomings as well as possible.[28] Drawing on the help of the Huron Institute, McDaniels redesigned the program to make the planned variation idea more operational. He reasserted central control over all the major evaluation decisions and supervised the awarding of a new analysis contract to Abt Associates of Cambridge, Massachusetts (SRI continued to collect the data at the local projects). The data from the 1969 and 1970 cohorts were abandoned, and the new evaluation focused on students who entered kindergarten in fall 1971. Tension remained between the evaluation and service orientation of Follow Through, but the balance under McDaniels shifted more to the former. Rather than trying to collect data at all sites, McDaniels refocused the evaluation efforts on a smaller and more comparable subset of projects. Nevertheless, while there were considerable improvements in the new evaluation design, the overall Follow Through evaluation was basically flawed by the inherent complexity of the undertaking as well as by initial program decisions.[29]

In 1973 the Brookings Panel on Social Experimentation sponsored a conference on the planned variation experiences in education. They assembled a small group of experts in program experimentation and evaluation who focused on the conceptual and methodological (but not the substantive) issues involved in planned variation experiments. The conference examined the two federal education programs that were explicitly designed for planned variation—Follow Through and Head Start Planned Variation (HSPV).[30] Alice Rivlin and Michael Timpane, the organizers of the Brookings Conference, concluded:

"1. The evaluations of both Follow Through and HSPV suffered from the lack of clear-cut and measurable objectives. Participants in those programs simply did not know what was expected of them. Some saw their projects as social service providers while others viewed them as experimental programs. Nor was it clear whether their model projects were being compared to each other or to similar institutions like the regular Head Start programs or the normal public schools.

2. There was confusion about how much each local project should try to replicate exactly the educational model of their sponsor. Most of the confer-

ence participants agreed that it would have been most useful if each one of the sponsor's models had been as faithfully replicated as much as possible in order to test their effectiveness in different contexts.

3. There was widespread agreement that Follow Through and HSPV had been rushed too quickly into operation. More time should have been taken to develop and test each of the models more fully before trying to evaluate them on a large scale.

4. More attention should have been paid to the problems of measurement. Many of the existing, standardized tests were inadequate to address the specific concerns of the individual project. Moreover, more effort should have been made to obtain identical measures across all units in order to facilitate cross-site comparisons.

5. The use of voluntary rather than random communities for participation was not necessarily bad. Nor was there strong sentiment for having the sponsors assigned randomly to the sites. However, most participants did feel that greater efforts should have been made to assign random groups or students within those communities in order to provide for more rigorous treatment and control groups.

6. Several individuals at the conference felt that the planned variation experiments would have been more effective if fewer models had been tested. Moreover, the extremely large number of sites and students involved in Follow Through made that effort very expensive to evaluate and difficult to manage."[31]

Although the conferees continued to endorse a planned variation approach to assessment in education, they saw the need for a more systematic approach, involving five different stages and taking ten to twelve years to complete:

The strong consensus of the conferees that planned variation experiments of the future should have clearer objectives, more time, and cleaner statistical design was given concrete expression in a proposal for a five-stage process of development and testing of educational interventions. The experiment would begin as a highly controlled investigation at a single site involving random assignment to control and treatment groups and careful observations of inputs and outcomes. If the intervention appeared to have appreciable positive effects under these conditions, a couple of years would then be devoted to developing it further, creating a training program for teachers and instruments for measuring the program's implementation and outcomes. The intervention would next be tried out under natural conditions in a small number of sites, close enough to the sponsor's home base to be supervised without great travel and communication costs, and curriculum, training procedures, and measuring instruments would be revised in light of this experience. Not until after all of this development, small-scale testing, and revision had been successfully completed would a large-scale field test be undertaken to find out how the intervention works under a variety of conditions and with a variety of populations. In the final stage, full results of the field testing and training would be disseminated to those who wanted to adopt the intervention in their own school. The whole cycle, from initial experiment to dissemination of the field-test experience would take ten to twelve years.[32]

While some of the participants at the Brookings Conference expressed skepticism that sufficient improvements would be made to warrant continuation, "on balance, the conferees agreed that the preferred course was not to give up on planned variation in education, but to try harder, recognizing the pitfalls and building on the lessons of Follow Through and Head Start Planned Variation."[33]

The suggestion by the Brookings Conference participants that future experiments be developed through repeated stages of testing and improvement was not unexpected in the early 1970s. Systematic development was emphasized at the federally funded Regional Educational Laboratories and the Research and Development Centers. Thus, the proposed move away from the more static, longitudinal version of planned variation to a more dynamic, iterative testing orientation built upon and coincided with comparable developmental efforts in other areas of educational research and evaluation.[34]

SUBSTANTIVE FINDINGS FROM FOLLOW THROUGH

Abt Associates replaced the Stanford Research Institute as the analysts of the national evaluation of Follow Through in 1972. Abt Associates issued their findings about Follow Through five years later. The overall results of the evaluation were strongly negative: Follow Through was not an effective vehicle for helping at-risk children improve their school performance. In the *Harvard Educational Review*, the Abt evaluators emphasized three main findings:

"1. Each Follow Through model had very different effects on test scores in the various communities in which it was implemented. Differences in effectiveness between sites within each model were greater than overall differences between models. None of the seventeen models in the evaluation demonstrated that it could compensate consistently for the academic consequences of poverty. . . . Local circumstances and behavior clearly have more to do with children's test performance than do intentions, theories, and rhetoric of outside interveners. Taken as a whole, the evidence presented in our report suggests that if a local school system has the potential for effective compensatory education, then outside resources of the Follow Through kind can sometimes catalyze this potential. But if not, intervention seems likely to be somewhat disruptive and counterproductive. . . .

2. In most cases, the Follow Through groups scored about as one would expect similarly disadvantaged groups to score without Follow Through. Where differences were apparent, Follow Through groups scored lower more frequently than they scored higher. It appears clear, then, that the Follow Through strategy is not an effective tool for raising poor children's test scores. Not only are the effects unstable, but they are small, on the average, and a disquietingly large minority of them are in the wrong direction. . . .

3. With few exceptions, Follow Through groups were still scoring substantially below grade at the end of three or four years' intervention. Poor children still tend to perform poorly even after the best and brightest theorists—with the help of parents, local educators, and federal funds, and supported by the full range of supplementary services associated with community-action programs—have done their best to change the situation."[35]

Most of the critics of the Abt evaluation did not challenge this pessimistic assessment of the effects of Follow Through. As Ernest House and his colleagues put it: "Despite difficulties in design, scope of measurement, and analysis, the Abt Associates finding of the predominance of intersite variation remains valid. This finding is an important confirmation of contentions that the success of any educational innovation is dependent on contextual factors that can neither be implanted in the local scene nor controlled by outside parties."[36] The few who argued that Follow Through was effective with at-risk children criticized the narrow focus of the Abt national evaluation and cited more favorable individual, local reports and evaluations.[37]

The more controversial aspect of the Abt evaluation was the finding reported in their original study that "models that emphasize basic skills succeed better than other models in helping children gain these skills." Moreover, "where models have put their primary emphasis elsewhere than on basic skills, the children they served have tended to score lower on tests of these skills than they would have done without Follow Through." They went on to say that "no type of model was notably more successful than the others in raising scores on cognitive conceptual skills."[38]

The popular media were quick to announce that the Abt evaluation of Follow Through demonstrated that "basics are better."[39] But critics challenged Abt's categorization of the different types of local Follow Through projects as well as the specific measurements and analyses employed. The lack of adequate measures for noncognitive outcomes was particularly singled out. House and his associates argued that "the Follow Through evaluation does not demonstrate that models emphasizing basic skills are superior to other models."[40]

The Abt evaluators defended their finding that the models they labeled as "basic skills" did better, but they admitted that "even the model with the best overall showing had several sites with negative results. Such wide variability within each model implies that the 'model' is not a useful organizing concept for the Follow Through test data."[41] Some of the subsequent reanalyses of the data, however, suggested that students in the behavioral-oriented programs may have fared better on cognitive tests.[42]

Most of the attention about the Follow Through Program has been focused on the Abt national evaluation, but there were also a series of local evaluations that provided some information and guidance. For example, Ira Gordon and his colleagues developed and implemented the parent education model. Since little has been done to evaluate school-home partnerships, the researchers had to develop their own measures and procedures. Overall, they found that teaching low-income mothers to be more effective parents helped their children succeed in school. Unfortunately, the sample sizes in their various local evaluations were modest and the results often mixed, especially in regard to the cognitive gains of students participating at the parent education sites. Moreover, although the local evaluations provided some useful insights into the workings of the parent education model, these local studies did not negate the overall discouraging findings of the Abt Associates who had included this model in their broader, national assessment of the cognitive effects of Follow Through on students.[43]

The model sponsors tried to dispel the strongly negative view of Follow Through based upon the results of the national evaluations. Pointing to the benefits of Follow Through for parents, teachers, and classroom practices as well as drawing selectively upon some of the local, internal evaluations, they listed a series of major successes of the Follow Through Program:

> A significant number of major successes have been achieved by the Follow Through program participants even though not all expectations have been realized. These successes . . . include: (1) improvement in academic achievement and in school and home environments for children in communities associated with Follow Through

models; (2) advances in the development of comprehensive instructional models; (3) creation of several alternatives for training and support of school faculty and staffs; (4) progress in involving parents in the educational and political process of schooling; (5) knowledge about the potential of model-sponsorship as a way of improving schooling; and (6) new information concerning evaluation methodology for large-scale field studies.[44]

Yet even this more positive assessment of Follow Through from local evaluations did not counter effectively the disappointing cognitive test scores of those students in the national evaluations. Moreover, in many of their assessments, the local evaluators acknowledged the serious conceptual and methodological problems which were compounded by the fact that the results were not comparable across sites. As a result, even the most enthusiastic proponents of the effectiveness of Follow Through—its model sponsors—could only claim that the evidence provides "modest assurance that many Follow Through local-projects were achieving the models' goals with both children and adults."[45]

SURVIVAL OF FOLLOW THROUGH

Follow Through was an expensive program, both because it involved a large number of students and because it funded a large-scale evaluation. The program mandated a wide variety of services, and thus it cost more per student than most other elementary school programs. This added to the difficulties surrounding its acceptance in other educational institutions. From FY67 to FY74, the program cost $870 million (in constant dollars, 1982–84 = 100). Funding for Follow Through peaked in 1970 and then gradually declined (see figure 4.1).

Comparing the funding for Follow Through to the federal expenditures on the research and development centers and the regional educational laboratories, which were created in the mid-1960s to provide systematic and sustained research on educational problems, enables us to appreciate the relative size of the investment in Follow Through.[46] Although the funding for the centers and laboratories was never as generous as their proponents initially had hoped, these institutions received much of the available federal research dollars.[47] By FY69 the cost of Follow Through was greater than that of either the centers or the laboratories, and by FY70 more money was allocated to Follow Through than to the centers and labs combined.

Over the years, the Follow Through Program has been quite expensive. From FY67 to FY92, $1,541 million (all figures in constant dollars, 1982–84 = 100) was spent on Follow Through whereas $600 million was allocated to the

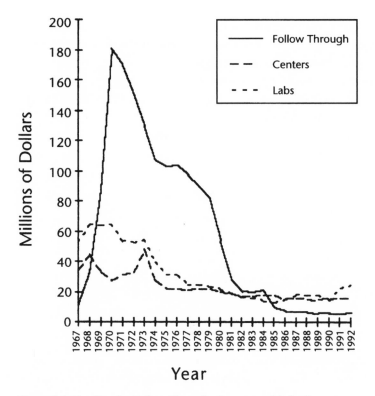

Figure 4.1. Funding for Follow Through, Centers, and Labs (in Constant 1982–84 Dollars)

research and development centers and $810 million to the regional educational laboratories. The growing criticisms of the Follow Through evaluation as well as the mounting costs of the program led some in the federal government to call for the end of this experiment, especially once the cohorts included in the study had completed the third grade. Beginning in 1973 efforts were made to phase out the funding for Follow Through.[48]

The initial plan had been to assemble data on cohorts of children who first entered school either in kindergarten or in the first grade and to follow their progress through the third grade. The first cohort consisted of children who enrolled in the 1969–70 school year. The original plans called for data collection to focus on all sponsors, sites, and children, but under the direction of Garry McDaniels in 1971 it was decided to eliminate sites that were unrepresentative or models that had too few local projects to be useful from a comparative perspective. Even the scaled down efforts required 2,200 data collectors in the field in 1972 and the assembling of vast amounts of information. Therefore, a decision was made to continue the study of the first three cohorts, focus only on the cities in the fourth cohort, and collect no data on the fifth cohort. Only limited data would be assembled on the first and second cohorts, though more detailed information would be gathered for the third cohort. With these changes, it was anticipated that the experimental phase of Follow Through would conclude by the school year 1976–77 or 1977–78.[49]

In spite of periodic efforts by different administrations during the 1970s to reduce or eliminate Follow Through, it had sufficient support among its constituents and legislators in Congress to protect it. The Office of the Assistant Secretary in the Department of Health, Education, and Welfare assessed the program in 1979 and concluded:

"• There was agreement that the *status quo* in Follow Through was unsatisfactory.
• Congress believed that Follow Through should be a *service program with a social action/anti-poverty emphasis and close links to Head Start;*
• *Office of Education policymakers believed that Follow Through should be a research, development and demonstration program.*"[50]

The assistant secretary of education decided that Follow Through should have two components. Most of the funds (80 percent) were to be utilized for providing services to at-risk children. The remainder (20 percent) were to be for research, development, and dissemination.[51] Thus, the historic division within Follow Through was reaffirmed, but now more specific weights were attached to the activities.

In June 1980 the National Institute of Education was asked by the Office of Elementary and Secondary Education to handle about one-third of the knowledge production activities of Follow Through. Approximately $2.7 million (in constant dollars, 1982–84 = 100) was to be transferred to NIE for the first phase of their five-year effort. Follow Through staff were expected to be closely involved throughout the research and evaluation portions of the NIE contract.[52]

The National Institute of Education proposed that Follow Through be assessed in two strands—the first emphasizing the immediate analysis of some existing projects, and the second investigating areas for future development. During the first strand, NIE would focus on improving the implementation of existing curricula or the use of better managerial methods, rather than on developing new curricula or instruction practices (the earlier evaluations of Follow Through had shown that none of the seventeen different curricula models were especially effective). In the first five years NIE proposed to fund such things as:

"• Means to increase instructional time in Follow Through classrooms through improved management of services;

• New patterns of in-service training and selection of teachers to gain better instructional management, including cooperative agreements between schools, teacher training institutions, and teacher associations or unions;

• New ways to systematically involve parent and community groups in planning and conduct of Follow Through programs, including the use of parents and families to provide instruction in the home;

• New uses of information systems, including testing and evaluation results, to bring better diagnostic and prescriptive information to bear on Follow Through student learning needs;

• New ways to facilitate support of school building and district administrators for the substantial changes typically required by innovative Follow Through procedures."[53]

The second strand of NIE activities would be to develop more speculative, broader areas for possible future analyses in the following five years (1985–90):

> Such thinking will be outside strictly educational areas as well as within them. Some preliminary areas of inquiry for this activity are the effects of media and new technology on early childhood learning, broad societal and environmental influences on early childhood education and extrapolation of research from other fields to Follow Through. This thinking will eventually be channeled into practical vehicles for improving schooling and learning. The intent is to cast a broad net to capture all the creative thinking possible that will benefit children eligible for Follow Through, and then continually assess the feasibility of converting these ideas into working models. The ideas closest to being ready for more rigorous testing will be identified, and a subset selected for funding in fiscal year 1985 or 1986.[54]

One line of inquiry that NIE pursued was based on the idea of active learning time (ALT). According to this approach, learning is dependent on the active participation of the student and varies according to the individual involved (slower students need more active learning time than quicker ones). In summer 1981 NIE funded four Follow Through pilot contracts to investigate more effective ways of helping disadvantaged children to learn actively in the classroom.[55]

As part of the planning process for its work on Follow Through, NIE planned three topical conferences and two public hearings for 1981–82. More than forty papers were commissioned on various aspects of past projects as well as on the future directions of the program. The commissioned papers and conference proceedings provide a useful, but contested assessment of Follow Through at the end of the 1970s. Although many participants called for improved rigorous, statistical evaluations of Follow Through models, a few rejected the social science approach altogether and argued for a more qualitative and humanistic orientation.[56]

Using some of the approximately two-thirds of the funds that remained funds for knowledge production, the Office of Elementary and Secondary Education continued to evaluate the success of the more service-oriented Follow Through projects. The rest of the funds in that subcategory were earmarked for disseminating information about the Follow Through models to interested service providers throughout the country.

The 1980 election signaled a major change in the attitude of the new administration toward Follow Through.[57] Rather than trying to improve the existing program, the Reagan administration proposed that the service portion of Follow Through, along with thirty-two other educational programs, be consolidated into Block Grants for Improving School Programs for FY82.[58] The proposed placement of Follow Through in a block grant was part of the broader movement within the Reagan administration to consolidate existing federal categorical programs and to forward federal funds directly to the states, which then would be given more discretion in spending the money. Some policymakers and analysts applauded the effort to give states and local authorities more leeway in determining how federal funds would be spent, but others suspected that important mandated categorical efforts might be underfunded locally or feared that the consolidation effort was a veiled excuse for diminishing or completely eliminating federal assistance.

The Reagan administration, like its predecessor, viewed Follow Through as a combination of a service and research program. Although the Reagan administration proposed putting the service portion of Follow Through into a block grant, they preserved the research portion as part of their federal Educational Improvement account. The administration requested $5 million (current dollars) for FY82 for Follow Through in the Educational Improvement account and designated those funds as part of a developmental activity.[59]

In the Omnibus Budget Reconciliation Act of 1981, however, Follow Through survived. The program was maintained temporarily as a categorical program, but it was to be phased in as part of an education block by October 1984.[60] The legislation provided assistance for Follow Through programs and allowed the secretary to fund research, demonstration, and pilot projects. The act also called for the evaluation of the programs by someone not directly involved in the administration of these projects. The diminishing support for Follow Through was evidenced by a dramatic decline in appropriations from $44.3 million in FY80 to $19.4 million in FY82 (in current dollars).[61]

The Reagan administration continued its opposition to Follow Through as a separate, categorical federal program. But the program survived due to congressional support. Follow Through was scheduled to be phased out in October 1984, but the Congress reauthorized the program for FY85 and FY86.[62] In 1986 Representative Tom Tauke (R-IA) introduced an amendment in the House to terminate Follow Through. The debate over Follow Through became quite animated. Since the same projects have been receiving funding since 1972, Tauke argued that it had in essence become a federal entitlement for a few school districts: "Now I understand why the Members who represent the 58 school districts out of the 14,000 in the country would be interested in trying to save the program; but this program on its own merits should end, because it has accomplished what it was supposed to accomplish; continuing to fund it is simply funding a pork barrel project for the 58 districts to get that money."[63]

Dale Kildee (D-MI), one of the representatives whose district contained a Follow Through project, defended the program and cited its "proven effectiveness." He then went on to denounce the effort to terminate Follow Through as a ploy to transfer more monies to the Defense Department:

> But let's look at the result of this amendment. Where is this money going? You know where it is going to go. We all know where it is going to go. Cap Weinberger is going to get the money. He has almost doubled his budget in the last 5 years. Where did he get those extra dollars? Not from extra taxes, we know that. We cut taxes in 1981.
>
> Cap Weinberger got his extra dollars by filching them from other programs. That is where he got his dollars. Let's not aid and abet him in his filching operation. That is what he is doing. Hey, Cap, leave the kids alone. Go get your money someplace else. Leave our kids alone.[64]

The amendment to terminate Follow Through failed on a roll-call vote of 161 to 245.[65]

The rationale for continued funding for Follow Through often shifted during the 1980s. For example, the House Committee on Education and Labor in 1983 argued that Follow Through should be reauthorized for at least one year in order to provide an opportunity for an in-depth evaluation of what had been learned during the past fifteen years.[66] The bill to temporarily reauthorize

Follow Through passed, but unfortunately the suggestion that the Department of Education commission an in-depth analysis and synthesis of findings from Follow Through was ignored.

When congressional hearings on the reauthorization of Follow Through were held in 1986 and 1990, the research and development aspects of the program usually were downplayed.[67] Moreover, none of the participants bemoaned the lack of the proposed detailed overview of Follow Through that had been advanced as part of the rationale for its continued funding three years earlier. Instead, most of the witnesses saw Follow Through as a means of supporting and disseminating information about a collection of proven programs to help at-risk children. As Eugene Ramp, chairman of the National Follow Through Association, put it:

> The programs that have come about through the Follow Through experience are, in some ways, not replicable, not easily replicable, in the sense that if Follow Through went away what we have learned in these models for other school districts and other Federal programs would no longer exist. . . .
>
> I look at the Follow Through programs and its 59 operating school districts as a national resource for other communities as well as other programs. And if you take [that] resource away, I'm not sure what you have, except perhaps you may have lost 20 years and over three-quarters of a billion dollar investment.[68]

One of the objections that the proponents of continued funding of Follow Through had to address was that the program had been assembling and analyzing data for over two decades. Indeed, some projects had remained in the program for nearly the entire period.[69] As supporters of Follow Through continued to search for a new rationale for continued funding of this long-term, experimental effort, some suggested shifting some of the focus to higher grades:

> *Extend Follow Through to higher grade levels.* There has been significant progress toward developing effective education for children from economically poor homes, but much remains to be accomplished. When Head Start began, it was hoped that a brief, enriched educational experience would enable the children enrolled to avoid future failure in schooling. When that hope was frustrated, Follow Through was initiated to provide effective education in kindergarten and the primary grades. Many successful programs have been developed in Follow Through, but more research and development activities are required now to extend the successes of Follow Through to the end of the elementary grades and beyond into the high school years. Clearly, there should be strong support of resource centers to communicate information about "exemplary" Follow Through programs. Based upon the successes of

Follow Through, similar levels of success at higher grade levels now appear to be practical possibilities.[70]

Others proposed to place more emphasis on the transition between Head Start and the regular schools. Although facilitating this transition for at-risk children was always considered an important goal of Follow Through, in fact often there had been little formal or informal contact between Head Start and the elementary schools. Therefore, Eugene Ramp, on behalf of the National Follow Through Association, proposed direct links between the Follow Through and Head Start programs:

> We would like to recommend that Follow Through be more closely aligned with Head Start. This does not necessarily mean major changes in the legislative or administrative requirements of the program. Nor does it mean that our appropriation be significantly increased. What we would like you to consider is requiring (legislating) some type of formal communication mechanism between the two programs. This could be as simple as a joint coordinating or planning committee. The purpose would be to increase Head Start's awareness of Follow Through models and to help them better prepare children for the transition into school. Though it is probably unrealistic to think our appropriation could ever reach that of Head Start, we would like you to consider eventually bringing Follow Through to within approximately one-tenth of Head Start's funding level, and then linking the two appropriations together on a percentage basis. For example, when Head Start gets a two percent increase, Follow Through appropriations automatically increase two percent.[71]

The supporters of Follow Through argued that if the program was to be placed into a block grant, it would not survive. In spite of the frequent testimonials of the popularity of Follow Through with parents and its effectiveness in helping at-risk children, the proponents claimed that state and local authorities would not be particularly sympathetic to funding Follow Through.[72] Even in such communities as Flint, Michigan, where Follow Through had operated successfully for nearly two decades, the local school district was unwilling to pick up any of the costs to replace the diminished federal dollars.[73] Yet, most of the participants at these hearings did not seem to appreciate the broader, logical implications of their position. Apparently, Follow Through programs could only be instituted and maintained with categorical federal dollars—a fact seemingly contradicted in some of their other testimony, which cited numerous examples of school adoptions of the program even though the local districts did not receive any specific federal funds for Follow Through.

The brief hearings on Follow Through before the House of Representatives in 1986 and 1990 were dominated by its supporters and beneficiaries. None of the more critical evaluators or commentators from the late 1970s were called to discuss the strengths and weaknesses of the program. Indeed, the strong negative findings from earlier national evaluations were ignored altogether; instead, supporters frequently cited the high rate of acceptance of Follow Through projects as exemplary by the Joint Dissemination Review Panel of the Department of Education as proof of their effectiveness, even though there are serious questions about how rigorously such a panel examines its exemplary programs.[74] In addition, the legislators were frequently impressed by anecdotal accounts of the effectiveness of Follow Through, such as when one mother testified that those of her children who participated in Follow Through fared better than those who had not.[75] Compared to the discussions of the evaluations of Follow Through in the 1970s, the testimony about the effectiveness of Follow Through in 1986 and 1990 was considerably less rigorous conceptually and statistically—even though elements of Follow Through were still designated as experimental and demonstration-oriented.

The Reagan and Bush administrations continued to oppose the funding of Follow Through but did not pay much legislative attention to this small program. For example, the Bush administration did not send anyone to testify against the program at the authorization hearing in 1990. Instead, the Department of Education submitted a letter to the House Subcommittee on Human Resources that stated:

> The Department, therefore, sees no need to reauthorize the Follow Through program when its authority expires in 1990. By the end of the current grant period the program will have had 24 years to test and disseminate its various models. The models have been proven effective. The only remaining task is for school districts to adopt or adapt the models to their particular circumstances. The Chapter 1 basic grants program, for which the FY 1991 budget request is $4.96 billion, is a logical source of support for the Follow Through models, particularly with its new emphasis on program improvement.
>
> Furthermore, the Department requests doubling the size of the Even Start Program to $48 million for FY 1991. The Even Start Program integrates early childhood education and adult education programs. Parents receive basic skills instruction and also receive help in becoming partners in their children's education. The Department believes that increased funding for Even Start could help make other programs such as Head Start and Chapter 1 become even more effective by helping disadvantaged children to sustain the progress made in preschool programs as they make the transition into elementary school. The Even Start Program, therefore, will address

the same goals as Follow Through, but will have a much more substantial impact on the education of at-risk youth. Finally, activities to improve educational programs for children in the early grades can also be carried out under the Chapter 2 block grant program.[76]

It is interesting to note how the Department of Education changed its opinion of the effectiveness of the Follow Through models. During the 1970s there was despair that none of the Follow Through models were effective in helping at-risk children, despite the hundreds of millions of dollars that had been expended on the program. Two decades later, and without the benefit of any new major national evaluation of the program, the Department of Education now claimed that "the models have been proven effective."[77]

The new and seemingly extravagant claims for the success of Follow Through models are not limited to the Department of Education. In a laudatory twenty-fifth anniversary publication about Follow Through, the success of the program in helping at-risk children is proclaimed without any reservations, although the earlier, more systematic evaluations of student outcomes had been so decidedly negative:

> As detailed in the individual descriptions of the various Follow Through models in the previous chapter, the success of Follow Through has been evidenced in a variety of ways. Professional growth and development of Follow Through staff, parent empowerment and school participation, community-school partnerships, and model adoption successes of all sorts accompany and reinforce what many feel to be the single most significant accomplishment any education program could hope to garner: consistently impressive gains in student achievement. Academic gains (as evidenced by standardized achievement tests) routinely skyrocket from below average to grade level and above in Follow Through programs nationwide.[78]

The stated goals of the program in the 1990s according to the Department of Education sounded familiar to anyone acquainted with Follow Through:

> The Follow Through program serves primarily low-income children in kindergarten and primary grades who were previously enrolled in Head Start or similar quality preschool programs. The goals of the program are—
>
> (a) To provide comprehensive services to help these children develop to their full potential.
>
> (b) To achieve active parent participation in the development, conduct, and overall direction of services to these children.
>
> (c) To produce knowledge about innovative educational approaches specifically designed to assist these children in their growth and development; and
>
> (d) To demonstrate and disseminate effective Follow Through practices.[79]

But Follow Through was now only a small $8.6-million (in current dollars) demonstration program administered in the Office of Elementary and Secondary Education in the U.S. Department of Education. In FY92 the program supported 12 sponsors and 34 local educational agencies, a far cry from its heyday in the early 1970s when it had a budget of $70 million (in current dollars), 22 sponsors, and 178 local schools. At a time when other early childhood programs were flourishing and the concerns about the transition from Head Start to the regular schools were increasing, few policymakers were aware of Follow Through and its twenty-five years of experience in this area.

The Clinton administration, like its immediate predecessors, tried to abolish the Follow Through Program, saying that the usefulness of the models created by the program had already been established and the continued implementation of the program could be carried out under the proposed Title 1 of the Improving America's School Act, the reauthorization of the Elementary and Secondary Education Act (ESEA) in 1994. The elimination of the Follow Through Program was also consistent with the attempts of the administration and others to simplify ESEA by reducing the number of small educational programs embedded within that legislation.

In 1994 Congress passed legislation that eliminated Follow Through, yet the program was quietly resurrected within the same legislation as the Innovative Elementary School Transitions Projects (section 1503).[80] During floor debates in the House, Representative John A. Boehner (R-OH) introduced an amendment to delete section 1503, arguing that the Innovative Elementary School Transitions Projects were merely a subterfuge to continue funding the same small number of recipients who had received Follow Through funding for the past twenty years: "The point we are trying to make here is that this is nothing more than a demonstration program that has gone on and on and on, and it is time to say 'no.' We can change the name. We can call it a pig or cow, but that will not make it oink. The fact is, this is Follow Through under disguise, and it ought to be eliminated from ESEA."[81]

Vocal congressional supporters of the program, most of whom already had one of the Follow Through projects in their district, maintained that the Innovative Elementary School Transitions Projects were not a continuation of the old program, but a new and innovative effort to help at-risk children.[82] These advocates focused most of their comments on the vital importance of helping at-risk children make the difficult transition from Head Start or Even Start Programs into the regular classrooms. As Representative Lynn C. Woolsey (D-CA) put it: "Study after study has shown that the early school years are crucial in setting the stage for future academic success. . . . However, Mr. Chairman, research indicates that the advantages of Head Start fade around the third grade. Mr. Chairman, we must support these students during their first years of elementary school if we want them to maintain the gains they made during their preschool years."[83]

Although the opponents of the proposed program did not object, in principle, to helping children during the transition from Head Start to the regular schools, they ridiculed the notion that a mere $10-million program would make much of a difference nationally. Moreover, they contended that districts that were interested in such efforts could readily fund them through the Title 1. But Representative Boehner resented that fact that this categorical program was designed to continue funding for the small number of Follow Through projects that had been receiving federal aid for several decades: "We are all familiar with pork in Congress. We all think it all happens in the appropriations bills, but it does not. This is nothing more than educational pork that ends up in 30 school districts in America. When we are trying to focus some attention on how to help disadvantaged children in Title 1, this is the last thing that we ought to be doing—taking out an authorization for $10 million in order to benefit just 30 school districts in America."[84]

A roll-call vote on the motion to delete the Innovative Elementary School Transitions Projects was defeated by a vote of 287 to 128.[85] The Clinton administration recommended funding for the program, but Congress, facing the growing budgetary pressures of the mid-1990s, refused to provide any actual funding for it in FY94, FY95, or FY96.[86] As a result, although the Follow Through Program in principle has survived under a new title, it has, in practice, ceased to exist more than twenty-five years after its inception as a temporary, demonstration program.

A rapid expansion of Head Start and a substantial improvement in the quality of those programs seems likely. At the same time, there are strong indications that the well-documented beneficial short-term effects of Head Start are not being sustained for many at-risk children as they enter the elementary grades. Comparable to the situation twenty-five years ago, there is a need to identify, develop, and implement programs to help maintain the gains of Head Start in the early elementary grades. In essence, it may be time to reinvent certain aspects of the original Follow Through Program, though the actual framework and details of any new initiative may differ considerably from the original program established in 1967.

For example, the original Follow Through Program focused mainly on the experiences of at-risk children in grades K–3, but it paid relatively little attention to the actual transition from Head Start to attendance in the regular public and private schools. Today, it is clear that we need to be concerned with both the transition and the nature of schooling in the K–3 grades.

The Follow Through Program in recent years had become a small, service-oriented effort to help children in grades K–3, though a very small portion of the funds were used for evaluations and research. As several analysts and policymakers have suggested, it was time to merge the service portions of Follow Through with the larger Title 1 program in order to address the needs of at-risk children better. Edward Zigler and Sally Styfco have argued persuasively that many of the federal education programs for young children should be consolidated.[87] The Congress took an important first step in that direction when it approved Representative Tom Tauke's (R-IA) amendment to the Follow Through legislation in 1990 to gave priority to Title 1 schools in receiving Follow Through funds.[88]

As the Follow Through programs and concepts are integrated into existing service programs like Title 1, there will still be a need to know what we have learned from the twenty-five years of experience with Follow Through. Surprisingly, the answer to this question will not be simple or straightforward. On the one hand, the major national evaluation of Follow Through by Abt Associates in the mid-1970s argued that none of the models was particularly effective in helping at-risk children, although those employing more behavioral-oriented approaches like DISTAR may have been somewhat more effective than others. The strong and unequivocally negative message from most of the analysts of the 1970s was that the Follow Through models were not effective. On the other hand, a decade later both the proponents and critics of Follow Through have declared that the program models have been proven effective in helping at-risk children. Even the Department of Education, which proposed to terminate Follow Through as a categorical program, proclaimed that the models worked.

Why the sudden and dramatic shift in the assessments of the effectiveness of the Follow Through models? Have the earlier negative views in the Abt Associates's national evaluation been challenged or revised? Have the local evaluations of Follow Through projects demonstrated convincingly their successes? Or are the supporters and opponents of Follow Through casually labeling the projects as successful, even though the type of conceptually and statistically rigorous evaluations necessary for making such statements may not have been undertaken?

Given that we have supported the Follow Through models for twenty-five years and have invested about $1.5 billion (in constant dollars, 1982–84 = 100), perhaps we should adopt the advice of the House Committee on Education, which in 1983 called for the creation of a bipartisan National Advisory Commission on Follow Through Education: "to review all Follow Through models and suggest those most conducive to replication. Furthermore, the Secretary of Education would be authorized to examine all past evaluations and 'sum-up' in one report what has been learned thus far. Particular attention would be paid to how effective these programs have been in narrowing the gap in successful educational performance between children from low-income families and children from non-low-income families."[89]

Although there are good reasons to be somewhat skeptical of the more recent pronouncements of the effectiveness of the Follow Through models, the entire question should be investigated further by a panel of outside experts.[90]

The service aspects of Follow Through may be effectively merged with the new Title 1 program, but the evaluation and demonstration aspects of the program should be preserved. We simply do not know enough about what programs and approaches are particularly effective in helping at-risk children make the transition from Head Start to the regular schools or how to best structure grades K–3.[91] Therefore, perhaps $5 to $10 million a year should be set aside specifically for evaluation and demonstration purposes.

Our twenty-five years with Follow Through as an experimental program has taught us many lessons on how to improve any further initiatives in this area. The new Follow Through Program should be explicitly and exclusively designated as a small demonstration and evaluation program. The earlier confusion and tension in trying to have Follow Through be both a service and a demonstration program severely handicapped the quality of the evaluation of the models. Moreover, the unnecessarily large number of local sites used and the excessively large sample sizes employed in the original Follow Through investigation should be avoided as it was logistically unwieldy and prohibitively expensive. Because much of the original data painstakingly collected were discarded without being carefully analyzed, we should acknowledge and apologize for the unnecessary and time-consuming testing burdens we placed on many of those students and teachers.

Instead of seeing the implementation and testing of demonstration models as the rather simple process envisioned in the original Follow Through Program, perhaps we should adopt a version of the proposed five-stage demonstration and evaluation model suggested by the participants at the Brookings Conference in 1973. This would involve steps ranging from the careful development and testing of single-site models using random assignment to the dissemination of the results from the large-scale field tests. Although such a process might require as long as ten to twelve years, the results would be more scientifically sound and more practical than what has been produced by most of the Follow Through projects in the past. Moreover, the length of the development and evaluation process might be considerably shortened if one started with individual programs that had already received some extensive testing, such as Johns Hopkins University's Success for All Program.

Finally, given the length of time that each cycle of demonstration and evaluation might take, one might adapt the National Institute of Education's strategy of the early 1980s to fund several strands of activity on a staggered basis. Thus, there would be an ongoing series of carefully designed and implemented demonstration models being developed and tested to address different issues in the transition from Head Start to the regular public and private schools. The overall cost of such an effort would be greater than some of the individual research or development projects currently financed by the Department of Education, but it probably would be possible to finance them entirely with the funds currently allocated to Follow Through.

Chapter 5 The Origins and Development of the Even Start Program

Since the mid-1960s fascination in Washington, D.C., with early childhood education has led to the proliferation of different preschool programs. Rather than focusing all of their attention and funds on a single popular program, such as Head Start, policymakers in both the Congress and the White House have supported different types of projects on early childhood education. Each of these early childhood education programs initially was hailed as a major innovation and its advocates were quick to cite preliminary data from ongoing evaluations to substantiate the importance and efficacy of these new initiatives.

One of the more recent and rapidly expanding early education programs is Even Start, a program that combines early childhood education with adult literacy training. The program has grown from $14 million in FY89 to $102 million in FY95.[1] Using preliminary results from the federally funded national evaluation by Abt Associates, policymakers claimed that Even Start is one of the most effective ways of helping disadvantaged children and their families to break the cycle of illiteracy and poverty.

In spite of the great enthusiasm for Even Start, almost no effort has been made to analyze simultaneously and critically its conceptual origins, program development, political support, and overall accomplishments. In this chapter, I shall discuss previous efforts in early childhood education and parent training in order to place Even Start within a broader historical perspective. Then I shall examine the legislative enactment of Even Start in 1988 and the subsequent growth of the program. The just completed national evaluation of the program will be described and assessed, and congressional reactions to its negative findings will be discussed. Finally, I shall conclude with some observations about the current value and future options for Even Start.

EARLY CHILDHOOD EDUCATION
AND PARENT TRAINING

Although many contemporary policymakers believe that early childhood education was initiated in the mid-1960s with the creation of Project Head Start, efforts to educate three- and four-year-olds in public and private schools date back to the early nineteenth century. As we saw in chapter 3, infant schools were established in many American communities in the 1820s and 1830s, and in 1840 approximately 40 percent of all three-year-olds in Massachusetts were enrolled in a school. A strong reaction against educating such young children occurred and by 1860 there were few, if any, young children attending schools.[2]

In the second half of the nineteenth century, the infant schools were replaced by kindergartens, which catered to slightly older children (ages five and older) and which did not emphasize intellectual training.[3] Nursery schools were added in the early twentieth century, though a few nursery schools had existed previously. By the 1920s the popularity of early childhood education had spread among child developmentalists and policymakers, but most of the nursery schools were intended for children of middle-class parents rather than those from less affluent backgrounds.[4]

Nursery schools received additional stimulus during the Depression as the WPA funded them as a means of supporting unemployed teachers. Federal assistance for local day care and nursery school facilities continued during World War II under the Lanham Act, which was intended to enable mothers to work in defense industries. After the war most of these day care and nursery school institutions closed as federal funding ended and many employed mothers, voluntarily and involuntarily, left the paid labor force.[5]

A few early childhood programs continued in the 1950s, but it was not until the mid-1960s, with the creation of Head Start for disadvantaged children, that they flourished. One of the most popular of the Great Society programs, Head Start changed from a summer program to a nine-month institution. Although Head Start was intended to be a comprehensive program offering health and social services as well as education, it became identified with rapid cognitive development for disadvantaged children.[6]

Head Start suffered a serious setback in 1969 when the Westinghouse evaluation of the program declared that the cognitive gains for disadvantaged children were only short term.[7] Strong parental support for Head Start saved the program, but funding levels in constant dollars remained relatively flat during the 1970s. Head Start managed, however, to escape the drastic cuts in federal spending that other domestic programs experienced in the early 1980s. Today Head Start thrives as policymakers in both parties vie with each other in endorsing the expansion and full funding of early childhood education.[8]

One of the fundamental assumptions of Even Start is the importance of involving parents in the education of their children. Recognizing the importance of parents in early childhood education is not new. Families had the primary responsibility for the education of their children in colonial America.[9] In the eighteenth and nineteenth centuries children were increasingly sent to private or public schools, but parents were expected to be involved in their education.[10] School administrators, however, complained that parents often showed little interest in the schools or in the education of their children.[11]

In the early decades of the twentieth century, the role of parents in raising their children and participating in school activities was reemphasized. The child study movement stressed the importance of parents in guiding the development of the children and the first nationwide program to educate parents was created. As early childhood education became increasingly identified with middle-class families in the 1920s, efforts were made to enhance parental education.[12]

Immigrant children and their parents did receive some early childhood training and adult education in the early twentieth century. While young children attended a nursery school or kindergarten at Hull House in Chicago, their mothers learned English in an adult education class. Similarly, some of the WPA nursery schools provided parent education for immigrant and poor parents. Yet few systematic efforts were made to link early childhood education for disadvantaged children with adult literacy training.[13]

Parents played a prominent role in Head Start. They played a key role in planning and running the programs as well as working with their own children. Many parents served as teachers in the program. Home Start was launched in 1972–75 as a small Head Start demonstration program to provide early childhood activities in the home.[14] Similarly, some of the Follow Through programs created in the late 1960s and early 1970s emphasized the importance of parental participation in the education of children in grades K–3.[15]

There was a movement in the mid-1980s to link generations in order to break the cycle of poverty that resulted from adult illiteracy. One of the pioneering efforts was the Parent and Child Education (PACE) program in Kentucky. The state legislature created PACE in 1985 to provide adult literacy training to parents and developmental assistance to their three- or four-year-old children. The experiences with PACE led to the creation of the National Center for Family Literacy in 1989. This nonprofit institution, funded largely by the Kenan Family Trust, established family literacy centers in Kentucky and North Carolina. They also have provided advice and guidance to approximately nine hundred other family literacy centers throughout the United States.[16]

According to the National Center for Family Literacy, there are four key components in any family literacy project:

> Family literacy programs provide developmental experiences for young children.
> Family literacy programs provide basic skills instruction to the children's parents or primary caregivers.
> Family literacy programs work with parents and children together, helping them to share in the learning experience.
> Family literacy programs bring parents together in peer support groups to share experiences and overcome obstacles to family learning.[17]

Although there can be considerable variation in how these four factors are implemented, they are seen as essential for any family literacy program and help to distinguish these efforts from other intergenerational literacy projects (which usually focus only on one or two of these components).[18]

PASSAGE OF THE EVEN START PROGRAM
IN 1988

Representative William Goodling (R-PA) led the efforts to create the Even Start Program. Goodling, a former school superintendent and ranking Republican on the House Subcommittee on Elementary, Secondary, and Vocational Education, introduced H.R. 2535 in 1985 "to establish a pilot program to develop methods for parents who are in adult literacy programs, and who have preschool-age children who may be educationally at risk, to acquire the skills necessary to work in the home with those children."[19] Drawing on his experiences with a similar program while he was superintendent of rural schools, Goodling wanted to link the current adult literacy programs with early childhood education to break the generational cycle of illiteracy. Rather than calling for a massive federal initiative, Goodling proposed funding three pilot sites (two urban and one rural). The funds earmarked for Even Start were to come from the Adult Education Program ($1 million) and from the Chapter 1 program ($2 million). The Even Start models were to be located in economically depressed areas and targeted families with a four- or five-year-old child.[20]

A comparable bill (S. 1723) was introduced in the other chamber by Senators John Chafee (R-RI), Lawton Chiles (D-FL) and Charles Mathias (R-MD). The proposed Senate program was similar to the House version, but there were a few differences. The Senate bill called for a $5-million pilot program with the funds coming from the Chapter 2 block grant program rather than from Chapter 1 and Adult Education. Chapter 2 funds were noncategorical assistance provided to the states for innovative efforts and the senators proposed earmarking some of these monies for Even Start. Disagreements over the source of funding for Even Start continued to divide many of its proponents.[21]

Whereas the House bill set the minimum for participation at age four, the Senate version allowed two-year-olds to enroll. Senator Chafee explained the difference by stating that "the rationale for this is a parent who begins the one-year program with a 2-year-old child will finish it when the child is at an ideal age, 3 years old, to take advantage of the home learning before the start of school."[22] It is worth noting that the implicit assumption in Chafee's discussion is that the illiterate parent or parents would first receive training and then use their new knowledge and skills to provide assistance to their own youngster. Similarly, Sharon Darling, then the director of adult and community education in Kentucky, testified that "adult educators need to work as partners with early childhood specialists to design model programs which appeal to the recognized needs of the parent first, and bring the child in to benefit from the parent's learning."[23] Most others, however, including Representative Goodling, stressed the importance of working simultaneously with parents and children rather than first providing the parent with basic literacy training.[24]

Although the hearings on the Even Start bill attracted some attention in 1985, it was not enacted (in part because the hearings on the bill were held at such a late date). Prospects for the program in the House improved in the second session of the 99th Congress when Representative Augustus Hawkins (D-CA), the powerful chair of the House Committee on Education and Labor, agreed to cosponsor Even Start as part of a bill that combined two rather different educational initiatives—Effective Schools and Even Start (H.R. 4463).[25]

The new House version of Even Start kept most of the features of the earlier bill. The amount of money remained at $3 million, but instead of getting $2 million of it from Chapter 1, the new legislation stipulated that it come from the Chapter 2 block grant (the other $1 million still was to come from Adult Education). The ages of the children eligible for the program now were set at three to seven. Thus, the new House version of Even Start moved closer toward the previous Senate bill.[26]

Interestingly, Goodling's Even Start bill of 1985 proposed funding three pilot projects with the $3 million requested. The new version by Hawkins and Goodling also requested $3 million, but did not specify how many pilot projects would be funded. Several of the witnesses testifying on behalf of the Effective Schools and Even Start Act of 1986 argued that approximately fifteen to twenty should be funded.[27] Thus, the new version of the legislation opened the way for much smaller projects, making any in-depth and rigorous evaluation of the proposed individual pilot models much more difficult.

The Hawkins-Goodling bill easily passed the House, but the Senate did not act upon it. The next year, the legislative strategy was revised. Rather than trying to enact Even Start as a separate piece of legislation, it was folded into the massive reauthorization of the Elementary and Secondary Education Act. Again, the House took the initiative by including Even Start as part of Chapter 1 of the Elementary and Secondary Education Act. Under the existing Chapter 1 legislation, local school districts could have used their funds to link preschool and adult education training. Yet only about 1 percent of Chapter 1 funds had been expended on preschool education and even less on the linkage of early childhood education and adult literacy training. Part of the broader strategy of the Chapter 1 reauthorization was to increase the use of those funds to finance early childhood education as well as secondary education. Therefore, the inclusion of Even Start as a specific and separate initiative within Chapter 1 reinforced the idea of using those monies to finance early childhood education.

The Bush administration did not support the creation of a separate Even Start Program within Chapter 1. It felt that the objectives of Even Start could be achieved within the existing Chapter 1 legislation and therefore did not see the value of creating yet another categorical program. As William Bennett, secretary of education put it:

Parts B and C of Chapter 1 of H.R. 5 would authorize two new programs: an Even Start program to integrate early childhood with adult education, and Secondary School Programs for Basic Skills Improvement and Dropout Prevention. These programs would be authorized at $50 million and $100 million, respectively, for fiscal year 1988, and at such sums as may be necessary for fiscal years 1989 through 1993.

Although I support the goals of these programs, I firmly believe that new categorical programs administered at the Federal level are not an appropriate means for achieving them, particularly in a time of severe budgetary restraints. The activities that could be carried out under these programs can already be carried out under Chapters 1 and 2 of the ECIA and under the Adult Education Act. Creation of new programs is thus unnecessary and would require bureaucratic proliferation, increased paperwork, and other administrative burdens. I instead urge that States be encouraged to exercise their discretion to achieve the important goals of Even Start and Secondary School programs through programs now in place.[28]

In spite of the lukewarm opposition of the administration, Even Start was easily included in the Chapter 1 reauthorization bill. There were a few differences between the House and Senate versions of the Even Start sections, but those were reconciled in the conference committee.[29] Rather than calling only for a pilot program, the new legislation authorized $50 million for FY89 and such sums as necessary for FY90–FY93. As long as the actual annual appropriations were less than $50 million, the Department of Education would make the grants directly to local groups; once the annual sum appropriated exceeded $50 million, the funds would be allocated to the states under a formula grant and the states would then distribute the monies to local groups. The $50-million annual appropriation was reached in FY92, so that the states now distribute the funds to their own localities.

Even Start was envisioned as a demonstration program in which local projects could receive federal funding for up to four years. The percentage of federal assistance would diminish from 90 percent for the first year to 60 percent in the final year.[30] Evaluation was to be built into the demonstration programs in order to facilitate the dissemination of the results—modeled in part on the evaluation section of the Head Start program.[31]

Both the House and Senate stressed that Even Start funds should be used mainly for coordinating and integrating current adult literacy and early childhood education services rather than duplicating existing programs. The important implicit assumption was that there were sufficient existing services of high quality and that they should be brought together to help clients. As the report of the House bill put it: "It is the purpose of the Even Start program to successfully combine adult basic education for parents and school readiness training for children into a single educational program. In many cases there may already be existing programs and other community resources for these purposes. Rather than supersede or compete, Even Start funds are intended to build upon these resources in order to create the specific programs described in this Part."[32]

Both chambers stressed the importance of having a family-centered approach. The report on the House bill stated:

> Programs assisted with funds under this Part must have two basic characteristics. First, they must be family centered. This means that they must focus on both the parents and the children as a unit. Services should take place in the home when possible and be designed so that parents and children can work on activities together. Second, the aim of the program must be to help the parents become active in their own children's development. Programs should not merely teach parents in one setting and children in another. The primary goal of Even Start is to help parents be their children's first teacher and become more literate in the process rather than teach the parents and children in separate and distinct programs.[33]

Unlike the earlier versions of Even Start in 1985 or 1986, which had set the minimum age of a child's participation at two, three, or four, the House-Senate version stated that children from ages one to seven were eligible. Given the very young ages at which children could enter Even Start, it was anticipated that some of them would be receiving basic child care while their parent or parents were enrolled in an adult literacy program.

Some minor modifications in the Even Start Program were made in the National Literacy Act of 1991 (P.L. 102–73). The program was renamed the "Even Start Family Literacy Program," and the eligibility for applying for funds was expanded to include other local groups (such as community organizations). The secretary of education was allowed to reserve up to 2 percent of the total appropriation for conducting evaluations and providing technical assistance. The eligibility requirement for children was lowered from ages one to seven to birth to seven, and families could continue to participate as long as any single member of that family was still eligible.[34]

The Even Start Program was again slightly modified in 1994 as part of its reauthorization as part of the Improving America's Schools Act (P.L. 103–382)—the new Title 1 program. Before 1994, the Even Start Program was restricted to parents beyond the normal school age. But now it was extended to include teenage parents as well as other family members, such as older siblings, spouses, and grandparents. Special set-asides were also designated for women in prison and their preschool children as well as for statewide initiatives. Despite these changes, the reauthorization legislation basically kept the goals and structure of the Even Start Program similar to what it had been before.[35]

DEVELOPMENT OF EVEN START

On October 27, 1989, Secretary of Education Lauro Cavazos announced the first seventy-six Even Start Program grants. The grants ranged in size from $62,330 to $504,717, with nearly half being less than $200,000. Only five of the awards were more than $250,000. Cavazos stated that "we see tremendous promise in this family-centered approach to education and feel it will have a major impact on both children and their parents."[36]

Appropriations for Even Start grew rapidly. The program received $14.8 million in FY89; $24.2 million in FY90; $49.8 million in FY91; $70.0 million in FY92; $89.1 million in FY93; and $91.4 million in FY94. During the first three years, 240 Even Start projects were funded and the average award was $180,000. In 1992–93, 340 projects served approximately 20,000 families and 60,000 participants.[37]

Most adults who participated in Even Start in 1992–93 were between the ages of twenty-two and twenty-nine (45.7 percent) or thirty and thirty-nine (30.6 percent). About 85 percent of the adults were females. One-fourth of them were African-Americans and another fifth were Hispanics. Approximately 79 percent had not completed high school and English was not the primary language for 34 percent of the adults. Many lived in single-parent (37.2 percent) or extended family (12.4 percent) households. Only about half the adults lived as couples.[38]

The adults in Even Start tended to come from poor families. In 1992–93 about 35 percent of the families had less than $5,000 annual income and another 31 percent received between $5,000 and $10,000. About three out of four of the adults were unemployed, and about half of the families listed government assistance as their primary source of income.[39] The children ranged from infants to seven-year-olds, with the focus somewhat on children in the middle ranges (19.5 percent were four-year-olds). Only a small proportion were identified as having special needs (7.0 percent) and most were able to speak English.[40]

In the first Even Start programs, the percentage of adults and children receiving some of the basic services was relatively low. For example, for 1989–90 only 54 percent of the adults participated in literacy training while 88 percent received parenting education and 90 percent of the children were in early education programs. Overall, only 46 percent of the participating families received all of the core services.[41]

The following year, the percentage of newly entering adults receiving literacy training rose to 81 percent, and 77 percent of the families received all of the core services. But for 1992–93, entering adult participation in literacy services dropped to 72 percent, and new families receiving all core services plummeted to 43 percent. Although there was a significant increase in the percentage of participants receiving the core services, there still was considerable variation among the programs in their participation rates.[42] The drop in the number of new adults or new families receiving services for the 1992–93 cohort reflects in part the expected start-up difficulties for many new Even Start projects that year.

Initially, most families did not remain long in the Even Start Program. In the first cohort, more than one-half dropped out by the end of the first year. But for the second cohort, beginning in 1990–91, two-thirds remained in the program for more than a year. Almost half of those who left for the 1992–93 program year did so because they either successfully completed the planned educational services (24 percent) or moved out of the Even Start project area (24 percent). Thus, as the program became more established it became more effective in working longer with the families. Nevertheless, the total amount of core services received by participants was never very high for most individuals.[43]

The Even Start Program was expected to draw upon and coordinate existing programs and services. Only where such services did not exist, was Even Start to provide them. Therefore, not surprisingly, approximately one-third of Even Start project funds went for program administration and coordination, local evaluation, case management and recruiting, and for other miscellaneous activities. The remaining two-thirds expenditures were for the provision of direct services (31 percent for early childhood education; 15 percent for adult education; 9 percent for parenting education; and 9 percent for support services to enable families to participate in the core services).[44]

The federal Even Start costs per family were substantial but they decreased as programs became more established and could serve large numbers of participants. Based on data from the in-depth study, the federal Even Start costs per family were $5,894 in 1989–90, $3,669 in 1990–91, and $2,503 in 1991–92. The total cost for all Even Start services for 1991–92 was $3,855 per family, $2,503 of which came from the federal Even Start Program (65 percent). The remaining $1,352 was provided by local matching, in-kind services or facilities, the value of other locally obtained core and support services, and other federal funding (e.g., the pro-rated cost of early childhood education provided by the Head Start program).[45]

PROPOSED EVALUATION OF EVEN START

The Even Start legislation called for an independent annual evaluation of the programs. The act specified that the evaluation was to determine the effectiveness of the programs in providing: "(1) services to special populations; (2) adult education services; (3) parent training; (4) home-based programs involving parents and children; (5) coordination with related programs; and (6) training of related personnel in appropriate skill areas."[46] The legislation also stated that "when possible, each evaluation shall include comparisons with appropriate control groups."[47] The results of these evaluations were to be summarized and sent to Congress by September 30, 1993, and the annual evaluations were to be "submitted to the National Diffusion Network for consideration for possible dissemination."[48]

The Office of Planning, Budget and Evaluation prepared a request for proposals that specified three evaluation objectives:

"1. Develop an Even Start evaluation model that includes data collection and evaluation standards for all Even Start projects.
2. Conduct an evaluation of Even Start and prepare an evaluation report to Congress in 1993.
3. Lay the foundation for a longitudinal study of the effects of Even Start on the cognitive development of disadvantaged children."[49]

The national evaluation contract was awarded to Abt Associates (with a subcontract to RMC Research Corporation) in January 1990. The contract ran from 1990 through 1995 and called for a two-part evaluation: (1) the National Evaluation Information System (NEIS) for all Even Start projects and (2) an In-Depth Study (IDS) of ten projects. Abt Associates would collect and analyze a common set of client and program characteristics using the NEIS. They would also do an in-depth study of ten sites, which would include a control group of children and adults who did not participate in Even Start. The IDS would include the design and implementation of a longitudinal study of Even Start children going into the public schools.[50]

In addition to the national evaluation of Even Start by Abt Associates, local projects were required to do their own evaluations. The results from these local evaluations were to be submitted to the Program Effectiveness Panel (PEP). Some local Even Start projects approved by PEP might be accepted as part of the National Diffusion Network (NDN) and given funds for disseminating information about their operations to other interested parties. Although the local projects were responsible for doing their own evaluations, Abt Associates would help them with their submissions to PEP. Indeed, Abt Associates observed that the "number of Even Start projects that are approved by the PEP is an outcome measure of the effectiveness of the entire program."[51]

Abt Associates designed a comprehensive conceptual model for evaluating Even Start, which included four elements: (1) program context, (2) program inputs, (3) program processes, and (4) program outcomes. The National Evaluation Information System would gather data on these four items for all Even Start projects. For program context, information would be gathered on the characteristics of the population served, the nature of the community, and the availability of existing early childhood education and adult basic education services in that area. For program inputs, information would be assembled on the program and staff resources as well as on the program regulations. The program processes include the design of the program, the available services at the site, the nature of the service delivery, and the services actually received by the clients. The program outcomes focus on both the parents and the children. The literacy behaviors, education skills, parenting behavior and skills, and personal skills of the parents would be documented and analyzed. The school readiness and subsequent school achievements of the children would be noted and analyzed.[52]

Data from NEIS provides a common core of information about the characteristics of the participants, the services they have received, and the nature of the Even Start project they attended. These data provide a rich source of descriptive information about the projects and allow for comparisons amongst the projects. They do not, however, provide data to assess the impact of the program because there were no experimental or quasi-experimental control groups selected for all of the Even Start projects. Therefore, Abt Associates proposed to develop a reference group based on an estimate of normal growth for such a population using cross-sectional information from those just entering the program. By comparing the outcomes of children in Even Start with the expected normal development of comparable children using the reference group, Abt Associates argued that they would be able to ascertain the impact of Even Start.[53]

The procedure for using an estimated reference group based on data derived from earlier Even Start participants was admittedly questionable. Therefore, Abt Associates also initiated an IDS at ten sites (selected from the first cohort of seventy-three Even Start projects). For these ten Even Start projects they attempted, whenever possible, to randomly assign families to the Even Start project or to a control.[54]

The Bush administration and the Congress did not wait for the results of the national evaluation of Even Start before expanding the program. Although the original idea was to fund a few pilot projects before proceeding to a large-scale service program, funding for Even Start almost doubled for the first three years ($14.5 million in FY89; $24.0 million in FY90; and $49.7 million in FY91). In addition, the Even Start proportion of the Department of Education expenditures on literacy programs rose from 7.5 percent in FY89 to 15.8 percent in FY91.[55] The rapid rise in federal spending on Even Start before the program was evaluated led Representative Steny Hoyer (D-MD) to ask in 1991: "The Department began a national evaluation of the Even Start program in 1990 and intends to continue collecting data through 1991. After doubling the program in 1991, isn't it unusual for the Department to make a request for such a significant increase in the Even Start program pending the collection of evaluation data?"[56]

John MacDonald, assistant secretary for elementary and secondary education, acknowledged that the national Even Start evaluation had not been completed, but defended the expansion by pointing to components of the Even Start Program that he claimed had been validated previously:

The Even Start model supports the National Education Goals of school readiness and adult literacy. In addition, the program has generated considerable interest at the State and local levels as a mechanism for bringing together local agencies that offer diverse services to young at-risk children and families. We believe that, after three years as a national demonstration program, it is time to make fuller use of the program's potential as well as the Even Start model, which integrates the educational needs of disadvantaged children and families in each project in order to coach young children in school readiness skills and provides adult literacy *and* parental activities for their mothers and fathers.

Ultimately, the national evaluation will reveal much about the success of the Even Start model and projects. In the meantime, however, the Even Start concept is neither unique nor untested. Twenty-five years of research strongly suggests the potential of family-oriented early interventions. Studies of compensatory programs for school-aged children cite the positive effects of parent reinforcement, especially in the area of reading. And evaluations of programs such as Head Start have produced a wealth of data that inform Even Start goals.[57]

Even before Abt Associates completed the national evaluation, the nature and direction of their work was clear from the first two annual reports, which provide information about methodology as well as some preliminary findings. The National Evaluation and Information System had been established and was providing useful descriptive information to the local programs as well as to policymakers concerned with Even Start as a whole. Compared to many other federal programs, this format provided more detailed and comparable data about the characteristics of the clients and service providers in Even Start. Moreover, federal officials were able to use information from these ongoing surveys to make appropriate adjustments in Even Start both at the national and local levels.[58]

The centerpiece of the Even Start evaluation was the In-Depth Study of ten purposely selected grantees with appropriate randomized control groups. As the Abt Associates put it:

> The best comparison group is one constructed by randomly assigning potential participants to Even Start or to a comparison group. Random assignment is the only way to ensure that the program and comparison groups are composed of similar families at the start of the study. When families are randomly assigned to groups, the characteristics of the participants, on the average, will not differ systematically from the characteristics of nonparticipants. Thus, differences in performance after program participation can be used to assess the effects of the program. Randomized experiments are difficult to implement and are expensive, but they provide the least ambiguous information for drawing conclusions about the effectiveness of a social program.[59]

The criteria for selecting the IDS sites, however, made them anything but typical of all of the Even Start projects. The seventy-three first-year grantees were given an opportunity to participate in the In-Depth Study, and thirty-two of them expressed interest. Ten sites were selected according to the following criteria:

> *Willingness to participate.* Projects are not required to take part in the IDS.
> *Willingness to implement a randomized study.* To the extent possible, the IDS will involve a series of project-level studies in which potential participants are randomly assigned to Even Start or to a control group. Grantees have raised legitimate questions about the feasibility of this approach (e.g., recruitment is ongoing rather than a one-time event), and research plans will be tailored to each project's circumstances.
> *Program model.* To be selected, a project should be implementing a set of activities that form a coherent program model, preferably one which focuses on the family as a unit rather than children and parents separately.

Level of implementation. The selected projects should be fully implemented. Staff should be in place, activities should be underway, families should be recruited, and initial start-up problems should have been solved.

Evidence of transferability. Projects selected for the IDS should have an approach that can be transferred to other sites rather than an approach that is primarily applicable to a particular local site.

Evidence of effectiveness. Projects selected for inclusion should be high-quality projects that can reasonably be expected to be successful at achieving their goals.

Focus on 3- and 4-year-olds. With a relatively small sample of projects and participants in each project, the IDS focuses on projects that serve a large proportion of 3- and 4-year-olds so that these children can be followed into the public schools within the time frame of this evaluation.

Geographic dispersion. Projects are selected to provide variation across regions of the country.

Variation in urbanicity. Some of the selected projects are urban, others are rural.[60]

Because all the projects were not fully implemented, the ten sites were chosen in two phases—six in summer 1990 and four in fall 1990. There was great variation in the nature of the projects: some were completely home-based while others were completely center-based. They also varied in the types of curriculum they offered as well as in the nature of the population they served.[61]

The IDS plan called for implementing randomized assignments in as many of the sites as possible. The initial design called for 20 families to participate at each site, with another 20 serving as the control group. Therefore, as many as 400 families would be included in the IDS.[62] But in practice, it was difficult to persuade all ten IDS sites to select randomized control groups. Five of the sites did not have any control groups and another one (at Birmingham, Alabama) had "a control group, but it was not statistically equivalent to the program group."[63] Because of the large number of families that dropped out of the projects, replacements had to be found which were not randomly assigned.[64] As a result, the IDS sample size of the projects with comparison families was considerably smaller than anticipated—101 families in the programs and 98 families in the control group.[65] Unfortunately, in the final evaluation report, readers are not provided with warnings about the problematic nature of some of the control groups used in the analysis.[66]

Given the unrepresentativeness of the participating IDS Even Start projects, the considerable heterogeneity among them, the nonrandomized nature of some of the controls, and the small sample sizes of the ones with controls, we should not have expected much definitive information about the impact of the overall Even Start Program on the participants. Even looking at the five remaining IDS projects together cannot provide much reliable data, and looking at differences among individual models is almost impossible.

In addition to analyzing data from the IDS, Abt Associates also used the data from the NEIS. As there were no randomized control groups developed for the NEIS data, Abt Associates sought external comparison groups using norms provided on the basis of standardized tests. For the Even Start children, there were no adequate reference standards. The PreSchool Inventory (PSI) administered to three- to five-year-olds had no national norms and the Peabody Picture Vocabulary Test-Revised (PPVT) given to three- to seven-year-olds had a national norm, but the population for that reference group did not match the characteristics of the Even Start participants. Adult literacy, as measured by the Comprehensive Adult Student Assessment System (CASAS), however, was deemed appropriate for comparison to the Even Start population.[67]

For estimating the Even Start Program effects on children, Abt Associates proposed "to develop no-treatment growth expectations from pretest scores; that is, to generate an expected growth rate from pretest scores; that is, to generate an expected growth rate (the mean number of additional items correct per each additional month of age) for Even Start children prior to their receiving Even Start services. Assessing the effectiveness of Even Start participation would be based on growth above the expected rate."[68] By subtracting the expected, nontreatment normal growth for this group from the actual changes revealed in the posttest, Abt Associates argued they would be able to quantify the effects of the Even Start treatment. Moreover, they planned to look at different subgroups of the participants to see if there were any differentials in the rates of their improvement.[69]

The idea of using cross-sectional pretest scores to generate an expected normal growth rate for a particular population is innovative and potentially useful. But it rests upon several assumptions that may render the results suspect. On the one hand, if the reference group is constructed from pretest scores of the initial cohort, it may not be accurate for subsequent ones as their characteristics may not be identical to the initial joiners. On the other hand, if pretest scores from later cohorts are employed to develop a reference group, they may not be accurate because children who are not enrolled in such a program by age five may no longer be similar to those who would have joined earlier.

Similarly, if the pretest and posttest of the children occurs within a short period of time, there is always the danger that the children will do better on the second test simply because they have had some recent experience with an identical test. In contrast, if there is a lengthy period of time between the pretest used to develop the reference norms and the posttest, there is the possibility that some historic event or change may have affected everyone in the cohort so that the pretest data based upon cross-sectional data are no longer a reasonable approximation of the actual longitudinal changes in a normal population.

Another complication with this procedure is the rate of attrition among program participants. Everyone who enters Even Start is included in the pretest scores, but only those who have remained for some time are used in the posttest scores. It may be that the less prepared and less interested participants are dropping out prematurely and that those who remain in the program are more capable and would have fared better than the average individual who was used to create the reference pattern of normal development. Finally, the children who entered the program were not immediately given the PSI or PPVT tests. This may bias the results because the cross-sectional group includes children who have some exposure to Even Start before being tested.

In any case, while the development of a special no-treatment reference group for Even Start participants based upon cross-sectional pretest PSI and PPVT scores is imaginative, the various possible biases in the data have not been thoroughly or carefully explored. As a result, whatever results are found by the use of this procedure probably should be regarded as very tentative and speculative. Even the In-Depth Study of the five sites, with the methodological problems mentioned above, is more reliable because of its use of control groups and usually randomized assignment of subjects.

FINDINGS FROM NATIONAL EVALUATION
OF EVEN START

Funding for the Even Start Program increased dramatically in the early 1990s in large part on the expectation that the ongoing national evaluation would demonstrate the efficacy of this initiative. But when the national evaluation was completed in January 1995, the results were quite disappointing. According to the IDS, although children and adults in the Even Start Program did improve over time, those in the control group did equally well.[70] Despite the efforts of Abt Associates, the RMC Research Corporation, and the U.S. Department of Education to emphasize the benefits of Even Start, the findings from the final report cast considerable doubts on the utility of this particular approach.[71] Naturally, because important components of the national evaluation of Even Start were methodology limited or flawed from the beginning, no definitive statements about the ultimate usefulness of this approach can or should be made at this time.

A series of tests were administered to the participants and to the control group at the five sites of the IDS in order to assess the impact of Even Start. The PreSchool Inventory was used to assess the readiness of children to enter school. While both the Even Start and control group children gained on the PSI from the pretest to the posttest eighteen months later, there was no statistically significant difference due to participation in the program. Similarly, no program difference was detected on the Peabody Picture Vocabulary Test-Revised measures of verbal or literacy-based skills or on the Child's Emergent Literacy Test (CELT)—though again both program participants and the control groups improved during the eighteen months. Perhaps one reason for the lack of an Even Start impact on the children is that nearly half of them were gone at the end of the eighteen months. Moreover, the majority of children in the control group (those not attending Even Start) were enrolled in some other type of early childhood education program by the time of the posttest, thus raising questions about the need for further coordination of existing services if these children already benefited sufficiently from available services.[72]

The effects of Even Start projects on parent literacy also were disappointing. Adults in the five In-Depth Study sites did no better than the control group on the Comprehensive Adult Student Assessment System, which measures adult literacy skills and their application. Nor were there any significant program effects on the extent to which parents use writing and reading as literacy tools in the home according to a questionnaire modeled on the California State Library's Adult Learner Program. Only in the likelihood of attaining a General Education Development (GED) certificate were the Even Start Program participants more successful.[73] Unfortunately, recent studies questioning the economic usefulness of a GED certificate cast some doubt about the importance of this accomplishment.[74]

Assessments of parents' personal skills, parental interactions with their children at home, and the extent to which the home environment fosters young children's growth and development yielded little evidence on any program effects of Even Start.[75] Similarly, there were no Even Start Program effects detected on social supports for families, family resources, or employment of the adults. Nor were parents in the program more likely than the control group to leave public assistance as their primary source of income. Parents' perceptions of the impact of Even Start, however, were positive and indicated satisfaction with participation in the program.[76]

If program effects from the more rigorous and scientifically designed In-Depth Study were almost uniformly disappointing, there were a few favorable findings based on data from a larger number of Even Start projects according to the National Evaluation Information System. Unfortunately, the methodological shortcomings of trying to assess program effects on the basis of constructing an expected hypothetical normal pattern of improvement in children over time from pretest cross-sectional data are so serious that we cannot place much confidence in those results. Moreover, comparisons of pretest and posttest results on the NEIS evaluation are hampered by the fact that the posttest results are based only on families that remained in the program long enough to be tested. Finally, even the findings from the NEIS investigations were not that positive overall, although they did suggest that those children and adults who received the most extensive services fared better.

The final evaluation report implicitly also raises some troubling issues for the current Even Start Program. Although most of the participants in Even Start are disadvantaged, some are less so than others. About one-third of the families have an annual income of more than $10,000, and 16.7 percent of them have an income over $15,000. Since there are no income cutoffs for participation in Even Start, the program includes a higher proportion of families with annual incomes greater than $15,000 than either the Head Start program or the Comprehensive Child Development Program (a family support program funded by the Department of Health and Human Services). In addition, 21 percent of Even Start adults have already graduated from high school or received a GED certificate.[77] Graduation from high school or making at least $15,000 annually does not necessarily mean that those families do not need further assistance; at a time of increasingly scarce federal resources, however, one does wonder whether those funds might be better redirected to others even less fortunate.

One explanation for the comparatively strong showing by the control group was that these children and adults were receiving similar services elsewhere.[78] But this raises questions about the need to set up a special Even Start Program. After all, the Even Start evaluation stressed the additional costs of starting new programs as well as the benefits that come from economies of scale in servicing more participants at each program.

As the total cost per participating family in Even Start seems quite high (including both federal and local contributions), one would like comparative cost information on delivering similar services through alternative individual programs, such as Head Start or existing adult literacy programs. Then the question for subsequent, more rigorous evaluations would be not only whether Even Start projects improve the child and adult development and learning, but at what cost relative to other alternatives. It may turn out, for example, that while one might identify and improve some Even Start models sufficiently to make a program difference, the additional costs may not be justified in terms of the marginal improvements for the children and the adults involved.

In spite of these serious methodological questions about the design and implementation of the national evaluation of Even Start, the program should be praised for its continued intellectual honesty in the face of such discouraging findings. Because most evaluations of the local projects lacked the scope and scientific rigor necessary to provide an overall assessment of the effectiveness of the Even Start concept, a national longitudinal evaluation of representative centers was essential. Without such an evaluation, the limitations of the current projects or the need to rethink the entire effort could not have been realized.

Given the methodological and conceptual limitations of the Abt and RMC Research Corporation evaluation, we should not abandon the Even Start Program prematurely. Instead, we need to devote more attention to identifying which components work best and what adjustments will be needed for implementing them in different settings. Then a more rigorous evaluation of some of the promising models should be undertaken not only to determine if Even Start works overall, but also to ascertain which particular models are the most helpful in different environments. At the same time, however, it would be useful to know if the coordination of existing services really does improve significantly the outcomes of illiterate adults and their young children. This will require not only a more careful conceptualization of the various models to be tested, but also a much larger sample size to allow for analyses of differences among the projects.

The NEIS cannot and should not be used as a substitute for a more rigorous longitudinal analysis, but it still can provide valuable information on the characteristics and general functioning of local Even Start projects. These standardized data will continue to be useful for local project administrators as well as for state and national policymakers, and they should be retained unless the system is unusually expensive (and then a sample of the projects could be followed).

Furthermore, rather than looking at the costs and benefits of the Even Start Program in isolation from alternative investments, more attention should be paid to other similar programs. St. Pierre and his colleagues at Abt Associates have nicely summarized the mixed findings from six of the better documented two-generation programs:

> Evidence about the short-term effects of two-generation programs is mixed. On balance, the evidence supports the following conclusions:
>
> Two-generation programs increase the rate of participation of children and their parents in relevant social and educational services.
>
> As currently designed, two-generation programs have small short-term effects on a wide set of measures of child development.
>
> Two-generation programs have scattered short-term effects on measures of parenting including time spent with child, parent teaching skills, expectations for child's success, attitudes about child rearing, and parent-child interactions.
>
> Two-generation programs have large short-term effects on attaining a GED, but these are not accompanied by effects on adult literacy. There are few effects on income or employment. There are no effects on the psychological status of participating mothers as measured by level of depression, self-esteem, or use of social supports.
>
> Many correlated analyses show that amount of participation is positively related to test gains and GED attainment.
>
> There is little evidence that two-generation programs are any more or less effective for important subgroups of participants.
>
> Where we find positive effects, those effects are generally small (except for effects on GED attainment).[79]

Future evaluations or discussions of the two-generation approach should be framed in a more comparative perspective. This will not only help us to understand alternative approaches, but also provide us with a more realistic set of expectations for what such programs may be able to accomplish in educating parents and their children.

CONGRESSIONAL RESPONSES TO THE ABT EVEN START EVALUATION

As noted earlier, the Even Start Program was created at the initiative of Representative William Goodling (R-PA), and it has enjoyed widespread bipartisan support in both chambers of Congress. Moreover, the program was quickly accepted by both the Bush and Clinton administrations, although Secretary of Education Bennett thought it could be handled better by being placed under one of the existing federal educational programs. When the unusually rapid increases in funding for Even Start were questioned, its congressional supporters assured their colleagues that the preliminary Abt evaluations provided ample empirical evidence of its effectiveness. So, when the unexpected negative results from the final Abt evaluation appeared in 1995, how did these supporters respond?

It was expected that the new leaders of Congress following the 1994 mid-term elections would be more skeptical of the federal role in education. Yet, the 104th Congress initially did not treat the Even Start Program much differently than its predecessors. The negative results of the Abt evaluation at first went either unnoticed or ignored in that Congress.

The House Committee on Economic and Educational Opportunities, now chaired by Representative Goodling, held hearings in January 1996 on what works in public education. Given the acrimonious partisan fights over the future of the federal role in education during the preceding year, many legislators welcomed the opportunity to emphasize the positive aspects of public education. As Chairman Goodling put it: "Several weeks ago I said to the staff, we hear so much bad-mouthing about public education that I'd like to have a hearing where we let the public know the good things that are happening in public education. Thus today we're trying to get this message out. . . . Since taking over the helm of the committee, I've consistently stressed two overarching themes when it comes to education: quality results and local control. In my view, these are the two most important elements needed to renew educational opportunity in this country."[80]

Representative William Clay (D-MO), the ranking minority member of the committee, agreed and commended the Republicans for focusing on the proven successes in the field of public education:

Throughout the first session of this Congress, many Members of the Majority acted as though it was open season on public education, promoting such radical proposals as a drastic reduction of the Federal role in education, or the eradication of public education all together. Such unwarranted attacks on our Nation's public schools have done a disservice to the legacy of bipartisan support for education in the Congress. . . .

Mr. Chairman, examples of success stories in public education deserve to be showcased and if successes can be replicated broadly, the Federal Government should work with State and local education agencies to do so. There is no reason for us to create incentives for families to abandon our public schools. The diverse needs of our students cannot be addressed by isolated alternatives such as taxpayer funded private school choice program. Our focus should be on working with States and localities to rejuvenate public schools instead of depriving them of vital resources. . . .

In conclusion, Mr. Chairman, we commend you for convening the hearing that applauds a few of the many successful things taking place in our Nation's public schools.[81]

One of the major educational successes cited by members from both sides of the aisle was the Even Start Program. And what evidence did the members of the House find so persuasive about the effectiveness of Even Start? They listened to the moving personal tribute paid by Christopher Atchinson, an Even Start parent; they also followed sympathetically the testimony of Mary Brown, an Even Start supervisor, who provided a testimonial on behalf of the program based on her own experiences.[82]

But what about the negative findings from large-scale, congressionally mandated evaluation of Even Start by the Abt Associates? The members of the House Committee on Economic and Educational Opportunities and the witnesses before them at this hearing simply ignored the dismal findings from that serious evaluation. The representatives did not mention the national evaluation, and no one from Abt Associates was asked to testify or provide information. Instead, they implicitly chose to leave their colleagues and the general public with the impression that Even Start was one of the programs in public education that worked. As with the Follow Through program (see chapter 4), some members of Congress conveniently ignored the negative findings and relied instead on the anecdotal testimony of one or two participants in the program. Moreover, none of the witnesses appearing before them drew their attention to the troublesome findings from the large-scale assessment, perhaps in some cases because they were not familiar with the results as they were not evaluation specialists.

When Representative Goodling appeared before the House Subcommittee on Appropriations on May 15, 1996, he assured his colleagues that the Committee on Economic and Educational Opportunities had "conducted a top-to-bottom review of the effectiveness of all programs under the Committee's jurisdiction."[83] Goodling, on behalf of his committee, praised the virtues of the Even Start Program:

> Mr. Chairman, for several years now, I have spoken out in favor of strong support for the Even Start family literacy program. It is one example of the Federal government's outreach to parents, which in turn helps their children. As you know, Even Start provides certain categories of parents with reading, writing and parenting skills to better enable them to assist with and support their child's education. After all, parents are their children's first teachers, and we need to do everything we can to support them in that capacity.

The quality of our workforce and our ability to compete is closely tied to the functional literacy of our people. Even Start helps insure quality and competitiveness through the family unit. When parents are equipped, they can in turn help ensure their children come to school ready to learn. Early intervention helps save dollars in the long run. As you face difficult funding decisions in the Fiscal Year 1997 Appropriations process, I would ask you to carefully consider the merits of this fine program.[84]

Once again, Goodling did not bring to the attention of the Appropriations Subcommittee any information about the Abt evaluation of the Even Start Program.

The disappointing results from the Abt evaluation eventually found their way into the congressional discussions because the Clinton administration brought this information before the House Appropriations Subcommittee on the Departments of Labor, Health and Human Services, Education, and Related Agencies during the FY97 appropriations process. The administration recommended level funding for Even Start for FY97. As part of its budget justification, it summarized the Abt evaluation:

Even Start is still evolving as a family-centered approach to school readiness and early intervention. The national evaluation of the program's first four years, completed in 1994, found that, while it did not have a significant overall effect on participating families, participants did experience some short-term gains. For example, participating children learned school readiness skills earlier than control group children (although control group children caught up once they entered preschool or kindergarten), and children developed better vocabulary skills when they had high exposure to early childhood education and when their parents had high exposure to parenting education classes.

The Department believes that, through the changes made by the 1994 reauthorization (promoting more intensive and sustained services), the technical assistance provided by the Department, and the growing maturation of the Even Start model, more significant and lasting gains will be found in the future.[85]

John Porter (R-IL), chair of that Appropriations Subcommittee, in the written questions to the Department of Education, challenged the wisdom of supporting Even Start: "Why does an administration that prides itself on supporting those programs that work propose to fund this program with such dismal evaluations?"[86] The new assistant secretary for elementary and secondary education, Gerald Tirozzi, agreed with Porter's reservations, but defended continued funding of Even Start:

Even Start is only six years old. It is still evolving as a family-centered approach to school readiness and early intervention. The 1993 evaluation showed that, in the program's first four years, Even Start projects demonstrated positive short-term effects on the learning of young children, but its overall effects on family literacy were not very strong. To address these findings, the Department's technical assistance to State Even Start coordinators and local projects has focused on service intensity and family retention issues that are key to program improvement. For example, a series of regional meetings, held in 1995, stressed approaches to providing intensive services; an issue of the Even Start newsletter was devoted to recruitment and retention issues; a recent guide to improving program quality includes self-assessment tools and sample benchmarks for recruiting and retaining families and for determining intensity levels in core service areas.

The Department is tracking the extent to which changes made in the 1994 reauthorization to promote more intensive and sustained services for families, the technical assistance provided by the Department, and the growing maturation of the Even Start approach will result in more significant and lasting gains.[87]

The House Appropriations Subcommittee acknowledged the findings from the Abt evaluation and recommended level funding for Even Start. Moreover, the subcommittee issued a stern warning to the Even Start Program: "The Committee believes that until more consistent results can be accomplished, funding for this program should be constrained."[88]

Reacting to the House Appropriations Subcommittee report on Even Start, Representative Goodling now addressed the findings from Abt evaluation by inserting his remarks in the *Congressional Record* three days later:

Mr. Speaker, as the Member of Congress who developed the Even Start Program, I was understandably disappointed by the language discussing Even Start in the committee report accompanying the Labor, HHS, and Education appropriations bill for fiscal year 1997.

The Even Start Program was first funded in 1989 and, therefore, the program has only been in existence for a short period of time compared to other major elementary and secondary education programs. Thus, I believe it is unfair to say there is little in the way of evaluations to support the request for funding this program.

I must admit that I, too, was disappointed with the last program evaluation. However, I never expected that the program would not have to undergo change in order to effectively carry out its goals. There is not a program in the Federal Government which cannot be improved. However, Even Start is new and we are just now learning what does and doesn't produce the positive results we are seeking.

For example, the interim evaluation reports called attention to the fact that adult participants were not benefiting as much as their children. As a result, the Department of Education started to stress with States and program providers the need for a stronger parent component. Additionally, early evaluations indicated that not all Even Start projects were operating all three program components. Again, this was corrected. . . .

  Mr. Speaker, the committee did not cut funding for this program, for which I am grateful. However, I would hope that any future discussion of the effectiveness of Even Start would take into consideration the information I have discussed today and not jump to the conclusion that this program has not proven its worth.[89]

Thus, although the evaluation findings from the Abt evaluation of Even Start finally did reach members of Congress, the process was rather slow and tortuous. The House Committee on Economic and Educational Opportunities did not mention the evaluation in its discussions of Even Start in January and May 1996. The House Appropriations Subcommittee, however, provided valuable, though limited, recognition of the Abt evaluation in its written exchange with the Department of Education following the committee's hearings. Representative Porter and his colleagues on the House Appropriations Subcommittee are to be commended for bringing the Abt evaluation to the attention of the Congress, even though they had little time or opportunity to explore the strengths and weaknesses of the Abt evaluation or its implications for policy. And while Representative Goodling's subsequent remarks in the *Congressional Record* were welcome and useful, they were not delivered on the floor of the House, but only inserted in the extension of remarks—hardly an appropriate forum for a balanced, in-depth discussion of the implications of the important Abt evaluation. Moreover, neither the administration nor the Congress addressed some of the most important policy issues. For example, it is not just a question of whether or not Even Start works, but how cost effective is it compared to alternative investments in such programs as Head Start, Success for All, or Title 1.[90]

Fortunately, Chairman Goodling in his extension of remarks in the *Congressional Record* called for a serious and careful reconsideration of the Even Start Program and one hopes that the House Committee on Economic and Educational Opportunities will pursue this matter at one of its first hearings in the 105th Congress.[91] Everyone in the administration and the Congress seems to agree on the need for further adjustments and evaluations of the Even Start models. The Department of Education is now exploring the possibility for undertaking another large-scale, rigorous evaluation of the program comparable to the earlier work of the Abt Associates.[92]

Enthusiasm for early childhood education remains high both among policy-makers and the public and seems to be immune to questions about its overall effectiveness. The Head Start program survived despite a very negative and damaging evaluation of its impact in the late 1960s (see chapter 3). Indeed, the fascination with early childhood training has spawned numerous other programs designed to provide those services in a more coordinated fashion.

Even Start, initially promoted as a pilot demonstration program in the mid-1980s, combines the focus on early childhood education and adult literacy into an integrated family-centered effort to improve education at both ends of the life course. But rather than waiting for empirical evidence of the utility of this approach, the U.S. Congress and the Bush and Clinton administrations have made it one of the fastest growing federal programs—from $14.8 million in FY89 to $102.0 million in FY95. Suggestions that the expansion of Even Start be delayed until the results of the mandated national evaluation were completed were rejected when proponents claimed that sufficient evidence of its effectiveness already existed.

A large-scale, sophisticated national evaluation of Even Start was mandated—part of the increasing trend in American domestic legislation to ascertain the effectiveness of new programs. The contractors of that evaluation, Abt Associates and the RMC Research Corporation, struggled conscientiously to produce a rigorous and useful analysis of Even Start, but the final research design and implementation was flawed in several crucial areas. Although the evaluators candidly admitted to many of these shortcomings, most administrators and policymakers seem not to have noticed these problems and continue to treat the national evaluation as scientifically impeccable and definitive.

Given the plausible and thoughtful assumptions behind Even Start, almost everyone expected the national evaluation to demonstrate convincingly that combining early childhood education with adult literacy and parenting programs would significantly improve the development of both young children and participating adults. Unfortunately, the results from the national evaluation provide little, if any, evidence of the program effectiveness of Even Start. Given the relatively high total cost of Even Start projects, questions about the survival or future direction of this program will need to be addressed.

Will Even Start, like its Head Start counterpart, survive politically because of continued enthusiastic support from program participants and administrators? Or will the relatively small-scale of the program, as well as the fact that it has been turned back to the states, weaken essential political support at a time when the national evaluation of the program raises questions about its utility altogether?

The idea of combining early childhood education with adult literacy and parenting training is still a potentially useful concept and deserves further scrutiny. Although the national evaluation of Even Start provides little comfort for its supporters, the analysis was sufficiently limited and flawed methodologically to rule out any definitive conclusions about the overall program at this time. Instead, we should try to identify any components of Even Start projects or some innovative models in their entirety that seem promising. These new models should be systematically developed and rigorously tested in a variety of settings. Then the effectiveness of these new Even Start projects should be compared to alternative early childhood and adult literacy programs. The final results from such a systematic development and evaluation project probably would not be available for five or six years, but it is important to initiate a long-term research investment now in order to ascertain how best to help children and adults in need. It would be a mistake to conclude prematurely that the Even Start concept does not work and to abandon attempts to improve the current models. Meanwhile, as the House Appropriations Subcommittee of the 104th Congress has suggested, nonexperimental expenditures on Even Start projects should be held constant or even reduced until we have additional, reliable assurances of the actual effectiveness of this approach.

Part 4 Other Research and Reform Efforts

Chapter 6 Education and the Economic Transformation of Nineteenth-Century America

One notable achievement of American educational history is the shift of focus away from narrow, laudatory analyses of schools toward more critical investigations of educational developments within broader social and historical contexts. Detailed studies of nineteenth-century communities as well as regional and national analyses of educational development have provided new information about education and enriched the overall study of social history.[1] The field of economic history has likewise expanded to deal with such broad social topics as the viability of slavery in the antebellum South and the decline of fertility in nineteenth-century America. And economists are exploring important new issues like human capital investment.[2]

Therefore one might expect that economic historians would also undertake analyses of the relation between education and economic development historically, but there has been little effort to consider the economic aspects of nineteenth-century educational development in the United

States. A few scholars have attempted to explore this topic, but most have ignored it, especially in regard to the economic rates of return to common schooling or to the impact of education on social mobility. As a result, we have only a limited understanding of the historical relation between economic and educational developments.

In the hope of stimulating research in this area, in this chapter I shall explore the period before the Civil War—a time of great change in both economic and educational spheres—with a special focus on the interrelation of economic and education developments. The industrialization in the United States during the first half of the nineteenth century coincided with common school expansion and reforms. Looking at educational changes in the decades before the Civil War from an economic perspective will provide us with a better sense of the relation between broad socioeconomic changes and schooling. It will also offer some preliminary discussion about how changes in schooling may have affected the nature of the education of individuals over their life course.

Rather than attempt to provide a comprehensive survey and explanation of educational developments in antebellum America, I shall concentrate on three issues: (1) the relation between early industrialization and the rise of mass public schooling; (2) nineteenth-century views of the economic productivity of education as seen from a late-twentieth-century perspective; and (3) nineteenth-century concepts about the relation between social mobility and education and whether they coincided with actual experience. Given the paucity of work on these topics, this chapter necessarily will be speculative at times. Nevertheless, it may provide us with a better understanding of the relation between schooling and economic changes in nineteenth-century America as well as suggesting new avenues for future research.

EARLY INDUSTRIALIZATION AND THE
DEVELOPMENT OF MASS EDUCATION

Only a few educational and economic historians have approached the study of educational development in America from an economic perspective. Most of these have concentrated on specific aspects rather than providing a detailed theoretical and empirical treatment of the subject. Samuel Bowles and Herbert Gintis, both economists, have produced a comprehensive neo-Marxist theory of the relation between educational and economic development in the United States. They applied their theoretical framework to explain the origins of mass public education in the two decades before the Civil War, the relation between corporate capital and progressive education in the early twentieth century, and the transformation of higher education in the 1960s and 1970s as a response to the emergence of a white-collar proletariat.[3] Although their theoretical and empirical work has been challenged, it remains as one of the few major attempts to link educational developments to the changes in the structure of the American economy historically.[4]

For Bowles and Gintis, there is a causal correspondence between the social relations of production and the characteristics of the educational system at that particular time. As they put it, "we have shown that changes in the structure of education are associated historically with changes in the social organization of production. The fact that changes in the structure of production have preceded parallel changes in schooling establishes a strong *prima facie* case for the casual importance of economic structure as a major determinant of educational structure."[5]

Like several other historians, Bowles and Gintis locate the origins and reform of American mass education before the Civil War and associate it with the industrialization of the economy:

> There can be little doubt that educational reform and expansion in the nineteenth century was associated with the growing ascendancy of the capitalist mode of production. Particularly striking is the recurring pattern of capital accumulation in the dynamic advanced sectors of the economy, the resulting integration of new workers into the wage-labor system, the expansion of the proletariat and the reserve army, social unrest and the emergence of political protest movements, and the development of movements for educational expansion and reform. We also find a recurring pattern of political and financial support for educational change. While the impetus for educational reform sometimes came from disgruntled farmers or workers, the leadership of the movements—which succeeded in stamping its unmistakable imprint on the form and direction of the educational innovation—was without exception in the hands of a coalition of professionals and capitalists from the leading sectors of the economy.[6]

A fundamental problem with many studies of antebellum education is that the terms educational "expansion" and "reform" are used interchangably without consideration of whether these two developments occurred simultaneously chronologically or in the same geographic areas. Nor is it clear what is meant by each of these terms. Should educational expansion be measured by looking at increasing rates of adult literacy, the shift from educating children in the home to educating them in schools, or the replacement of private schools by public schools? Similarly, given the wide variety of educational reforms proposed during the antebellum period, should we consider them equally important or were some innovations more central to the educational reform program than others? There are major differences where and when educational expansion occurred in nineteenth-century America, and the increases in education did not always coincide with attempts to improve the existing schools.

An often used benchmark for the origins of mass education and school reforms is the appointment of Horace Mann as secretary of the Massachusetts Board of Education. Bowles and Gintis adopt this strategy because it allows them to link the educational changes directly to the increasing industrialization of that state in the two decades before the Civil War. "Rapid growth in attendance paralleled these dramatic changes in the legal, financial and social structure of U.S. education. Twenty years before the Civil War, just under 38 percent of white children aged five-nineteen were attending schools. By 1860, the figure had risen to 59 percent. Thus Mann's ascendancy to the newly created Massachusetts State Board of Education in 1837, marked a major turning point in U.S. social history."[7]

Bowles and Gintis imply that their analysis is valid for the entire country, but most of their analysis is narrowly focused on educational and economic developments in Massachusetts, which led the nation in industrial and urban development. Therefore, its appropriate to ask whether Mann's appointment as secretary of the Massachusetts Board of Education really marked a major turning point in educational expansion as Bowles and Gintis claim. In terms of adult literacy, the period of change is the seventeenth and eighteenth centuries rather than the two decades preceding the Civil War. As Kenneth Lockridge has demonstrated, only about 60 percent of the men and 30 percent of the women among the first settlers of New England could sign their wills. By 1790 about 90 percent of New England males and 50 percent of New England females could sign their wills.[8] Indeed, by 1840 only 1.1 percent of the white population in Massachusetts ages twenty and above could not read and write.[9] Thus, if one measures educational attainment in terms of adult literacy, especially adult male literacy, most of it occurred well before the Commonwealth began to industrialize.[10]

Perhaps a more appropriate measure of educational expansion, from the perspective of Bowles and Gintis, would be to look at the replacement of parents by teachers as the primary educators of children. Bowles and Gintis argue that as households ceased to be sites for production in the early nineteenth century, it became necessary to shift the training of children to schools, which not only provided cognitive skills, but accustomed students to accept the same type of social hierarchy and discipline that they would encounter in the newly established factories.

> The expansion and continuing transformation of the system of capitalist production led to unprecedented shifts in the occupational distribution of the labor force and constant changes in the skill requirements for jobs. Training within the family became increasingly inadequate; the productive skills of parents were no longer adequate for the needs of children during their lifetime. The apprentice system of training, which, by custom, committed masters for a period of as much as seven years to supply apprentices with room and board as well as (sometimes) minimal levels of training in return for labor services, became a costly liability as the growing severity of depressions made the demand for the products of the apprentices' labor more uncertain. The further expansion of capital increasingly required a system of labor training which would allow the costs of training to be borne by the public. Equally important, the dynamism of the capitalist growth process required a training system which would facilitate a more rapid adjustment of employment to the business cycle and allow the constantly changing dictates of profitability to govern the allocation of labor.[11]

Was Mann's tenure as secretary of the Massachusetts Board of Education associated with a dramatic increase in school enrollments? Although it is difficult to obtain detailed records on school attendance before 1840, the available evidence suggests that Massachusetts school attendance was already high by 1800 and that it gradually increased during the next four decades. During the period 1840 to 1860, however, school attendance in Massachusetts declined dramatically as the percentage of children under age twenty enrolled in any school dropped from 67.4 percent in 1840 to 56.8 percent in 1860, in large part due to the elimination of the three- and four-year-olds who had been attending infant schools.[12]

With the lengthening of the school year and the increasing regularity of attendance, the average annual number of days of school per child under age twenty did increase slightly from 60.6 days in 1840 to 62.3 days in 1860.[13] Furthermore, there was a sizable shift from private to public schooling. In 1840, 18.7 percent of all those enrolled received at least some private schooling while in 1860 that proportion had dropped to 8.0 percent.[14] Nevertheless, it is still important to remember that even at the time when Mann first came to power, more than four out of five students were already going exclusively to a public school. Thus, whether one looks at the changes in the overall rate of school attendance, the average annual number of days of schooling received, or the proportion of students attending public schools in Massachusetts, the two decades before the Civil War did not witness a dramatic turning point.[15]

If the percentage of Massachusetts children attending school did not increase before the Civil War, what about trends in the rest of the United States? As Albert Fishlow pointed out more than twenty years ago, there was a substantial increase in the percentage of whites up through age nineteen attending schools between 1840 and 1860.[16] New England, which was one of the most industrialized areas, experienced declines in enrollment from 81.8 percent of whites under age twenty attending school in 1840 to 73.8 percent in 1860. The largest increases occurred in the largely agricultural North Central states where the percentage of attendance rose from 29.0 percent in 1840 to 70.3 percent in 1860.[17]

A similar picture emerges if we estimate the distribution of the total number of new students between 1840 and 1860 by region. Whereas the more industrialized regions of New England and the Middle Atlantic contributed only 2.7 percent and 21.7 percent, respectively, of new students, the North Central region accounted for 55.7 percent of the additional students during those two decades.[18]

Whether one looks at the state of Massachusetts specifically or at all regions of the country, there is little evidence to support the notion that industrialization preceded or caused the growth of mass public education in the United States. Mass public schooling preceded industrialization in Massachusetts, and the greatest increases in school attendance occurred in the largely agricultural North Central region. Thus, unlike the situation in much of Western Europe, "North American development, particularly Canadian industrialization, but also that in the United States, came comparatively much later. Importantly, it followed the attainment of near-universal levels of literacy (among the white population) and the establishment and expansion of public systems for mass elementary education (though not much secondary schooling)."[19]

Bowles and Gintis are correct, however, to point to the increased reform activity focused on schools during the 1830s, 1840s, and 1850s—much of it directed to the urban and industrializing communities of the Northeast. Educators like Henry Barnard and Horace Mann emphasized the need for such improvements as better trained teachers, more public funds for schools, more regular school attendance, and a consolidation and centralization of the existing public schools.[20] Whereas school promoters in the Midwest and the South were concerned about the quantity as well as the quality of schooling, in the Northeast the main emphasis was on the quality of education.[21]

Bowles and Gintis, like many of the other so-called revisionist historians of education, emphasize the importance of manufacturers, aided by professionals, in initiating common school reforms. Rejecting the more traditional interpretation of educational reformers as benign humanitarians, such scholars as Alexander Field, Michael Katz, Samuel Bowles, and Herbert Gintis stress that manufacturers were active in the school reform movement because of their fear of the social unrest caused by industrialization. Also contrary to earlier interpretations, which emphasized the contributions of workers, revisionists like Katz argue that schooling was imposed on the workers by the capitalists.[22]

Several observations can be made about the relation between early industrialization and antebellum school reforms. First, although educators devoted much of their energy to improving urban schools, they were also concerned with rural schools, which faced somewhat different problems. For example, while urban schools struggled to provide enough classroom seats and to get immigrant children to attend schools on a regular basis, rural schools were more concerned about extending the length of the school year. Therefore, the educational reform impetus in such states as Massachusetts was not confined to areas that were rapidly becoming urbanized and industrialized but was felt throughout society.

Second, reform efforts were not restricted to the Northeast as is often implied. Simultaneous with the activities of Mann were the educational reform efforts of John Pierce in Michigan, Calvin Stowe in Ohio, and Calvin Wiley in North Carolina. As a result, the suggestion that antebellum educational reforms arose mainly as a response to the social tensions generated by industrialization ignores the fact that parallel movements occurred in other, largely rural states.[23]

Third, the revisionists stress the leadership of manufacturers in promoting educational expansion and reform, but they frequently ignore the contributions of others, for example the clergymen. In his now classic study of the abolition of the public high school in Beverly, Massachusetts, in 1860, Katz stressed that support for that institution centered on the manufacturers and businessmen.[24] Yet he failed to acknowledge that the most influential and vocal proponents of the public high school on the Beverly School Committee were the Protestant ministers.[25]

Fourth, whereas the revisionists often portray public education as being imposed on an indifferent if not hostile working class, there are strong indications that many, if not most, workers welcomed the creation and maintenance of public schools. Although the workers were sometimes divided amongst themselves on certain aspects of educational strategy, such as the trade-off between the creation of public high schools and further funding for common schools, they recognized the importance of all children receiving at least some common school training.[26]

Finally, scholars like Bowles and Gintis portray schools as preparing students for the social relations of production by alienating them from each other through intense individualistic competition and by accustoming them to the bureaucratic hierarchical structures in schools, which parallel those of the workplace. For these analysts, schools correspond to the workplace and are dominated by the interests and needs of the capitalists.[27] But they ignore contradictory tendencies within schools, such as the emphasis on democracy and equality, and they deny any autonomy to the school system. As Martin Carnoy and Henry Levin have suggested:

> The dynamic of the American educational system . . . can best be understood as part of a much wider social conflict arising in the nature of capitalist production, with its inequalities of income and power. These inequalities lead to struggles by subordinate, relatively powerless groups for greater equality, economic security, and social control. In a politically democratic society, the State provides space for such struggles. In public education . . . the social conflict is expressed in the conflict between reforms aimed at reproducing the inequalities required for social efficiency under monopoly capitalism and reforms aimed at equalizing opportunities in pursuit of democratic and constitutional ideals.[28]

By now it should be apparent that the close, causal relation between early industrialization and the rise of mass public schooling proposed by Bowles and Gintis is not an accurate or adequate portrayal of educational development in America. It is, in fact, a much more complex phenomenon whose origins vary regionally. In New England, for which we have the most detailed studies, the impetus behind educating children came from the Puritan religion, which emphasized that everyone should be able to read the Bible, and was supplemented by the growing recognition that sons who planned to enter a profession or pursue a commercial career need additional schooling.[29]

The religious emphasis on the importance of education persisted throughout the entire period and was reinforced after the American Revolution by the need for an educated electorate. As barriers to white male suffrage were lowered and as political participation increased with the rise of political parties, schooling was seen as a means of educating the electorate and preserving the republic.[30] The role of mothers as educators of the next generation provided a convenient and important rationale for giving women more access to formal schooling as well.[31] Thus, the ideological justifications for providing schooling for almost everyone as well as the institutions designed to deliver these services were already in place in areas like New England before the urbanization and industrialization of 1820s and 1830s.

Although Bowles and Gintis, as well as other scholars, may have greatly exaggerated its impact on educational developments in New England, industrialization certainly contributed to an environment in which the already high levels of education could be sustained and improved. Nineteenth-century anxiety about unrest in urban settings, particularly where large numbers of immigrants were living, reinforced the belief that public education was necessary, not only to enhance the lives of individuals but also to preserve and protect society.[32] Furthermore, the increase in population concentration and growth of aggregate wealth caused in part by manufacturing made it easier to implement improvements in public common schools.[33] While the total direct costs of public and private schooling increased substantially during the antebellum period, education expenditures as part of the gross national product rose only slightly.[34] Early industrialization as well as other socioeconomic changes contributed to improvements in the quality of education in New England communities. Industrialization played a smaller role in the rapid expansion of public education in other regions, but there, too, the general social and economic transformation of society helped create a setting that fostered educational growth and improvement.

The beginnings of the rise of mass, formal schooling in late-eighteenth and early-nineteenth-century America had another implication. Whereas earlier families had been responsible for teaching their children how to read or write, they now relied on the private or public schools to handle those functions. Also, the institution of apprenticeship or informal and intermittent training throughout the life course that was common before the nineteenth century was replaced with formal and increasingly age-graded schooling.[35]

THE ECONOMIC PRODUCTIVITY
OF EDUCATION

Education, as a form of investment in human capital, was recognized as an important component of economic development in the 1960s. Numerous articles and books were published extolling the necessity of providing more schooling in the developing countries as a means of stimulating national economic growth and individual well-being.[36] Although the enthusiasm for a human capital approach diminished somewhat in the following decade as many of the exaggerated claims of the previous studies were corrected, there was renewed interest in the topic during the 1980s and 1990s.[37]

In the wake of these studies, efforts were made to investigate the economic productivity of education in the past. Scholars searched the writings of classical economists for any evidence of an awareness of human capital investment.[38] Others speculated on the role of education in the economic growth of the West.[39] A few individuals investigated the impact of schooling on nineteenth-century American economic development, but most economic and education historians have ignored this subject.[40]

In the seventeenth and eighteenth centuries, during the period of mercantilism with its emphasis on tangible wealth, some writers recognized the importance of learning and science in stimulating economic development. Although they seldom mentioned the word "education," pre-Smith economists referred to "art" as a word connotating knowledge or skill. One goal of public policy was to increase a nation's fund of knowledge and to make its citizens more skillful producers.[41]

Education received more explicit treatment in the writings of the English classical economists, such as Adam Smith and J. R. McCulloch, but their theoretical contribution to the current human capital debate was much more limited than some scholars have suggested. Although they sometimes mentioned education and a few even endorsed governmental support for schooling, they did not attach much importance to education in fostering economic growth.[42] Adam Smith, for example, briefly acknowledged that monetary rewards had to be provided to compensate workers for acquiring skills, but he did not develop the implications of his insights on the determinants of the relative wages paid to skilled and unskilled workers. Instead, he expressed concern that the increasing division of labor in a modern economy, which he strongly favored, might lead to social and political unrest, which education could help to contain. Social control rather than economic improvement of the individual became his major rationale for state aid to education:

> Though the state was to derive no advantage from the instruction of the inferior ranks of people, it would still deserve its attention that they should not be altogether uninstructed. The state, however, derives no inconsiderable advantage from their instruction. The more they are instructed, the less liable they are to delusions of

enthusiasm and superstition, which, among ignorant nations, frequently occasion the most dreadful disorders. An instructed and intelligent people besides, are always more decent and orderly than an ignorant and stupid one. . . . In free countries, where the safety of government depends very much upon the favourable judgment which the people may form of its conduct, it must surely be of the highest importance that they should not be disposed to judge rashly or capriciously concerning it.[43]

American economic writers, following the lead of their English colleagues, frequently alluded to the salutary effects of education, but they did not devote much attention to this subject in the first half of the nineteenth century. Compared to their English counterparts, however, they did mention more frequently the value of education in improving the productivity of workers.[44] But their emphasis was less on the benefits of schooling to the individual than on its impact on the nation as a whole by fostering useful inventions or preserving social and political tranquility. Willard Phillips, clearly drawing in part on the work of Adam Smith, saw in education both a means of increasing worker productivity and preserving the republic: "It is the leading policy of the country to extend instruction to all classes, it being well understood that not only the industrial productive faculties of the nation, but also its political existence, depend upon the intelligence and good sense of the great mass of the population. A people less free from paroxysms of passion, folly, and superstition, would at once demolish such a political fabric as ours."[45]

Similarly, Francis Wayland in his popular textbooks advocated government support for education in order to advance science and stimulate inventions as well as to disseminate that information by educating the public: "And, in general, it is evident that, with a given amount of labor and of capital, production will be exactly in proportion to the knowledge which the operator possesses of the laws which govern that department in which he labors, and to the degree in which his labor conforms to his knowledge. . . . Thus we see how it is, that an intelligent people is always industrious, and an ignorant people always indolent. Hence, one of the surest means of banishing indolence, is to banish ignorance from a country."[46]

Yet despite his recognition of the role of knowledge for the productivity of the worker, Wayland considered the moral character on an individual even more important: "For, where virtue, frugality, and respect for right exist, riches will, by natural consequence, accumulate; and intellectual cultivation will, of necessity, succeed. But, intellectual cultivation may easily exist, without the existence of virtue or love of right. In this case, its only effect is, to stimulate desire, and this, unrestrained by the love of right, must eventually overturn the social fabric which it at first erected. Hence, the surest means of promoting the welfare of a country is, to cultivate its intellectual, but especially its moral character."[47]

Thus, while American economists had a somewhat broader view of the role of education in economic development than the English classical economists, they both emphasized the importance of education for preserving the social and political harmony of the society. Education as an investment in human capital was mentioned by American economists, but it was not developed or stressed.

Some workers had another view of education: they saw in it an escape from the domination of their employers. During the 1820s and 1830s, workers banded together and called for free public education. Although the workers' attempts to organize themselves into a separate political movement failed, both the Democrats and Whigs sought to accommodate their demands for more public schooling (though the two parties disagreed on how that education should be provided and controlled).[48]

Yet the leaders of the workers who advocated free public schooling for everyone did not emphasize the economic benefits of education.[49] Instead, they saw in education a means for allowing workers to participate more equally and independently as employees and voters. Seth Luther, for example, in his pamphlet on education never discussed the role of education in raising the productivity of workers, but only its value for political participation. Furthermore, like many other leaders of the workers, Luther pointed out that the economic necessity for children to work in the factories and mills meant that they could not receive a common school education:

> The situation of the producing classes in New England is at present very unfavorable to the acquisition of mental improvement. That "the manufacturing establishments are extinguishing the flame of knowledge," we think has been abundantly proved. It is true there is a great cry about the schools and lyceums, and books of "*sentiment,* and *taste,* and *science,*" *especially* at Waltham. But of what use is it to be like Tantalus, up to the chin in water, if we cannot drink. . . . The whole system of labor in New England, more *especially in cotton mills,* is a cruel system of exaction on the bodies and minds of the producing classes, destroying the energies of both, and for no other object than to enable the "rich" to "take care of themselves," while "the poor must work or starve."[50]

In the two decades before the Civil War, working-class writers echoed educators and devoted more attention to the economic benefits of education to the individual. But their emphasis was not always identical to that of the educators or the capitalists. As Harvey Graff noted in his analysis of Ontario workers:

> Labor, in spite of its acceptance of hegemony and an apparent clamor for equal educational opportunity, deviated from the major premise of leading schoolmen who sought more education of the working class for greater productivity. Ambivalent about the proper role, form, and content of education, recognizing some contradictions, and often placing its benefits and application quite aside from their jobs, they sought to be free and independent, powerful in ways that would not have pleased the men who desired to have the masses educated. More fundamentally, they did not always equate education solely with the skills (in either an academic or a practical sense) required to gain and perform a good job.[51]

The individual in mid-nineteenth-century America who is most responsible for exploring and publicizing the idea of the economic productivity of education is Horace Mann. In his famous *Fifth Annual Report* he attempted to make a serious, though ultimately flawed, estimate of the actual rate of return to education based on information about the earnings of textile workers.[52] Merle Curti believed that Mann always emphasized the economic value of education during his tenure as the secretary of the Massachusetts Board of Education,[53] but a closer examination of Mann's writings suggests otherwise. Only when the Massachusetts House Committee on Education recommended abolishing the Board of Education did Mann undertake to demonstrate the importance of schooling to the economic development of the state.[54] Based upon a few replies to a questionnaire he sent to leading manufacturers or their agents at the textile mills in Lowell, Mann argued that education was the most productive investment any individual or community could make: "They [his evidence] seem to prove incontestably that education is not only a moral renovator, and a multiplier of intellectual power, but also that it is also the most prolific parent of material riches. It has a right, therefore, not only to be included in the grand inventory of a nation's resources, but to be placed at the very head of the inventory. It is not only the most honest and honorable, but the surest means of amassing property."[55]

He went on to compare industrialization in Massachusetts and England and concluded that the process was successful in the former because of the highly educated labor force in that state:

> It is a fact of universal notoriety, that the manufacturing population of England, as a class, work for half, or less than half the wages of our own. The cost of machinery there, also, is but about half as much as the cost of the same articles with us; while our capital when loaned, produces nearly double the rate of English interest. Yet, against

these grand adverse circumstances, our manufacturers, with a small percentage of tariff successfully compete with English capitalists, in many branches of manufacturing business. No explanation can be given of this extraordinary fact, which does not take into account, the difference of education between the operatives in the two countries.[56]

For Mann, education made workers more industrious, reliable, and punctual. Education also made it possible for the worker to tend to the increasingly complex machinery and encouraged the farmer to utilize chemical fertilizers and crop rotation to enhance the quality of their soil. Mann observed that educated workers were more apt to be content with their employment and less likely to join disruptive strikes. The major benefit of education for Mann, however, was the inventiveness of employees. Educated workers were more likely to discover and implement labor-saving ways of doing their jobs.

The businessmen who replied to Mann's questionnaires endorsed his views on the importance of education. Unlike Mann, however, these employers stressed better work discipline and loyalty to management rather than inventiveness as the most important advantages of educated workers. H. Bartlett, for example, briefly acknowledged that educated workers "more frequently devise new methods of operation" than uneducated ones, but then went on at much greater length about the positive effects of education on the social and work habits of the workers:

> I have never considered mere knowledge, valuable as it is in itself to the laborer, as the only advantage derived from a good Common School education. I have uniformly found the better educated as a class possessing a higher and better state of morals, more orderly and respectful in their deportment, and more ready to comply with the wholesome and necessary regulations of an establishment. And in times of agitation, on account of some change in regulations or wages, I have always looked to the most intelligent, best educated and the most moral for support, and have seldom been disappointed. . . . But the ignorant and uneducated I have generally found the most turbulent and troublesome, acting under the impulse of excited passion and jealousy.[57]

Only two of the four businessmen replying to Mann's questionnaire provided specific estimates of the differential in wages for educated and uneducated workers. J. K. Mills observed that literate workers on the average earned 27 percent more than illiterate ones, and J. Clark put that figure at 18.5 percent. The wage differential between the highest paid literate workers and the lowest paid illiterate workers was reported as 66 percent by Mills and 40 percent according to Clark.[58]

Based upon these replies, Mann claimed that educated workers earned about 50 percent more than uneducated ones. His estimate apparently is based upon a rough average of the reports from the two respondents, but there are several statistical and conceptual problems with his calculations. By using the extreme wage differentials of the literate and illiterate workers, Mann was looking at the unusual rather than the typical cases. If he had used their figures for the wage differentials for the average of literate and illiterate workers, his estimate of the value of education would have been reduced considerably. In addition, since almost everyone in Massachusetts was already literate at that time, a more appropriate question would have been what was the rate of return for an additional year of common school education rather than the advantage of literacy over illiteracy. Finally, because teenage children frequently were in the paid labor force in antebellum Massachusetts, the actual rate of return to education would be smaller due to the opportunity costs of attending school.[59]

If Mann's estimates of the rate of return for educated workers are limited and inadequate, his focus on this issue and attempt to measure it were innovative and important. Mann's contemporaries accepted his reasoning and calculations enthusiastically and without reservation. The *Fifth Annual Report* was widely cited and the New York legislature ordered 18,000 copies of it to be printed. A group of prominent Boston businessmen acknowledged his achievements in showing the economic benefits of public education: "You have demonstrated that the arm of industry is served, and the wealth of the country is augmented, in proportion to the diffusion of knowledge, so that each humble school-house is to be regarded, not only as a nursery of souls, but a mine of riches."[60] John D. Philbrick, another educational leader, said in 1863 that the *Fifth Annual Report* had "probably done more than all other publications written within the past twenty-five years to convince capitalists of the value of elementary instruction as a means of increasing the value of labor."[61]

Was Mann correct in claiming that education was an important factor in enhancing the economic productivity of antebellum American workers? Scholars continue to be sharply divided on this issue. Many analysts, such as Field, question the overall contribution of education to workers from a human capital perspective. They point out that early industrialization did not require additional skilled workers but, in fact, permitted less skilled ones to replace better trained artisans. The rise of mass education, according to these scholars, was not a response to a demand for better educated workers, but an effort to socialize a labor force becoming increasingly restive and unruly during the social transformation of the economy.[62]

Others, like Douglass North, argue that industrialization in America increased the demand not only for new labor-saving inventions, but for a more educated and skilled labor force capable of adapting and modifying English manufacturing techniques to the American setting: "While the operatives in the factory itself may not be required to possess substantial skills, the spread of manufacturing with expansion in the size of the market leads to vertical disintegration and the development of a host of highly trained and skilled ancillary and complementary functions. I am thinking not only of the development of specialized capital-goods industries and wholesale and retail marketing facilities, but equally of the wide variety of professional services which are required. Physicists, chemists, engineers, lawyers, etc., all are necessary to the spread of manufacturing."[63]

Analysts of nineteenth-century education as human capital often focus too narrowly on the manufacturing sector or concentrate mainly on the productivity of male workers. Yet schooling also provided opportunities for women to enter professions like teaching.[64] Indeed, after the coming of the Irish to the textile mills, the pay of female school teachers exceeded that of female mill hands.[65] Nevertheless, the actual rate of return to that education was limited by the fact that most female school teachers in antebellum America taught only for a few years before leaving the paid labor force when they married.[66]

At this time there is no way to decide definitively the impact of education on the nineteenth-century American economic development. Everyone seems to be agreed that education helped to foster an environment in which conflicts between labor and capital were minimized and the regularity and the discipline of the work force was enhanced. As Graff puts it: "The transition to both commercial and industrial capitalism in North America was a smoother one than in England, and perhaps elsewhere. Without ignoring or diminishing the significance of conflict and resistance, which certainly were present, their potential may well have been reduced as one direct consequence of the comparatively earlier and more extensive educational development and its intimate reciprocal relationship to economic change and industrialization. Schooling, in this formulation, paved the way for economic transformation."[67]

Similarly, most scholars, though not all, accept that education did improve the cognitive skills of workers and made them more adaptable to the technological changes taking place, but there is widespread disagreement on the importance of this contribution. Detailed micro-level studies necessary to resolve this debate are not available. A reasonable guess, however, would be that although the relatively high level of schooling among American workers in the Northeast was not caused by the skill demands of early industrialization, their education helped to speed the quick and efficient adoption of new labor-saving machinery and techniques in both the manufacturing and the agricultural sectors.[68] Mann's claim of a 50-percent rate of return to education is clearly exaggerated; perhaps a more realistic guess would be a rate of return in the range of 10 to 20 percent for a common school education.[69]

Interestingly, the identification of formal schooling with the economic productivity of education may have inadvertently contributed in part to a deemphasis of the importance of apprenticeship and lifelong learning in maintaining and enhancing the skills of older workers. Some policymakers and business leaders became increasingly persuaded that the key to economic growth and productivity rested more with early schooling than with adult training. This was reinforced by the growing negative views of elderly workers in the second half of the nineteenth century so that the education of the young in the schools seemed to be a more rational investment than retraining older workers.[70]

EDUCATION AND SOCIAL MOBILITY

America has frequently been characterized as a land of opportunity where anyone can succeed if they have good personal habits and are willing to work hard. According to this view, while inequalities of wealth and occupational status exist, those less fortunate have a real opportunity of improving their lives. Others dismiss this ideology as only a mask for the glaring and permanent subordination of the disadvantaged in our society. A few exceptional and token lower-class individuals may succeed, but most will be relegated to their inferior positions forever.

In antebellum America, the dominant ideology was that of social mobility. Inequities in wealth and power were often acknowledged, but it was said that everyone could improve their lives by being frugal, temperate, and hardworking.[71] Books and newspapers celebrated individuals who overcame their disadvantages to become business and political leaders.[72] A letter to the *Newburyport Herald* in Massachusetts, for example, advised that: "there is no avenue open to the rich man's son that is not equally accessible to the poor boy. If our boys would but look back, and learn the history of the men who are now the most successful around them, they would see that more than nine-tenths were once poor boys, with nothing to start with in the world but their own unaided energies, and who have advanced themselves by strict adherence to truth and correct principles. The same path is open to the boys of the present day, and the opportunities for improvement ten fold greater. Let no boy, therefore, feel that his chances for success are any less because he has not rich parents to help him along."[73]

But did social mobility really exist in that society? There is no easy answer, and it depends in part on how social mobility is defined and measured. Historians, drawing on the work of earlier sociologists, concentrate on occupational mobility. Most of these studies subdivide the nineteenth-century occupational structure into five broad categories: (1) high white-collar, (2) low white-collar, (3) skilled, (4) semiskilled, and (5) unskilled. Social mobility is also often measured by whether someone is able to move from a manual occupation (skilled, semiskilled, or unskilled) to a nonmanual one (high white-collar or low white-collar). Furthermore, while some studies focus on the career mobility of individuals, others look at the intergenerational mobility between fathers and sons.[74]

The findings from the social mobility studies of nineteenth-century America are somewhat mixed in terms of the opportunities available to the children of semiskilled or unskilled workers. The first case study, and perhaps still the most widely cited, is that of the lives of common laborers in the small urban community of Newburyport, Massachusetts, between 1850 and 1880. Stephan Thernstrom found that while many of the sons of the unskilled laborers who stayed in that community experienced a small increase in occupational status or were able to purchase their own homes, only about one out of every six was able to move into a skilled or white-collar occupation.[75] Similar results have been reported for Philadelphia in the four decades before the Civil War.[76]

Others have found higher rates of social mobility—particularly for the sons of the native-born population. Clyde Griffen's analysis of Poughkeepsie, New York, between 1850 and 1880 found that most immigrants and blacks did not fare well, but up to one-third of the sons of native-born fathers in manual trades moved up to nonmanual (white-collar) occupations, especially as owners of small craft and retail shops.[77]

A recent review of all the studies of nineteenth-century occupational mobility concluded that there was little difference between America and Europe in regard to overall career mobility, but that upward mobility among unskilled workers in the United States was slightly higher than in Europe. Compared to their European counterparts, American workers were less likely to experience downward mobility into the working classes. In addition, there was great diversity in the rates of occupational mobility among American cities with no simple explanations for the patterns. Furthermore, although upward mobility into skilled or nonmanual occupations was a distinct career possibility for some unskilled workers, the majority of them remained in the same occupational group or advanced only to a semiskilled position.[78]

Was education a key to social mobility in antebellum America? Certainly many educators drawing on the work of Horace Mann stressed the importance of education in enhancing the economic productivity of workers, but they did not focus on whether or not education promoted occupational mobility. In part their reluctance to discuss the impact of education on social mobility may be due to their efforts not to suggest that educated workers may become dissatisfied with more menial occupations. Nevertheless, implicit in their discussions of the value of education for the individual and the society is the belief that children through education could not only improve their education, but advance into better paying and higher status occupations.[79]

Most other nineteenth-century writers discussing social mobility, however, did not place much emphasis on the importance of education. Instead, they stressed the value of good habits and hard work as the essential ingredients for advancement. Although most of them assumed that a common school education was essential for everyone, few pointed to the specific advantages of additional years of schooling.[80]

Most studies of nineteenth-century careers have not discussed or tested for the role of education in promoting social mobility. The few historians who have commented on this issue are divided on the importance of literacy and education. Based upon a detailed study of three Canadian cities, Graff concluded that even literacy was not an important factor in helping individuals succeed, particularly among immigrants in unskilled or semiskilled occupations:

> Social thought and social ideals have, for the past two centuries, stressed the preemption of ascription by achievement as the basis of success and mobility, and the importance of education and literacy in overcoming disadvantages deriving from social origins. In the three cities, in 1861, however, ascription remained dominant. Only rarely was the achievement of literacy sufficient to counteract the depressing effects of inherited characteristics, of ethnicity, race, and sex. The process of stratification, with its basis in rigid social inequality, ordered the illiterates as it did those who were educated. Only at the level of skilled work and its rewards did literacy carry a meaningful influence. Literacy, overall, did not have an independent impact on the social structure.[81]

Several observations can be made about Graff's dismissal of the importance of education for helping individuals advance. First, he is taking only about those who are in the unskilled or semiskilled occupations. Therefore, individuals who are better educated may be able to avoid these occupations and use their educations to get ahead in skilled or white-collar occupations. Second, Graff's work is inadequate statistically. Relying only on a limited cross tabulation of his data, he cannot control for the effects of the other variables in ascertaining the impact of literacy. By subdividing his data into several groups, his sample size becomes too small to answer the questions he poses.[82]

In a study using multiple classification analysis, Michael Katz and his colleagues tested whether school attendance in Hamilton, Ontario, in 1861 led to more social mobility ten year later. They concluded that "School attendance itself, it is important to stress, did virtually nothing to promote occupational mobility. With other factors held constant, school attendance exerted no influence on the occupation of young men traced from one decade to another."[83]

Although this investigation of social mobility and education in Hamilton is more sophisticated than most comparable studies, it too suffers from some serious methodological weaknesses. The measure of education employed— whether or not someone attended school in 1861—is inadequate. Because children of all ages were in the multiple classification analysis, including those under age five, whether or not someone attended school in that year is not a reliable predictor of their eventual educational attainment.[84] A preferable index, the total number of years of schooling completed at the time social mobility was being measured, was not available. If one has to use a measure of school attendance ten years earlier, however, perhaps the analysis should be confined only to the population ages thirteen through nineteen so that any differentiation in school attendance is more likely to approximate the differences in the total amount of schooling ever received later.

Thernstrom, in contrast, argues for the importance of education for fostering social mobility, but he also fails to establish statistically that relationship. In his study of Newburyport, Thernstrom argued that a combination of misguided parental values toward education and the abject poverty of the family meant that lower-class children did not stay in school and therefore were severely handicapped in terms of their future social mobility. Irish parents, for example, were so determined to own their own homes that they withdrew their teenage children from school and sent them into the labor force in order to contribute to paying for the house mortgage. Furthermore, the depth of poverty among common laborers made it essential for their children to be earning money at an early age: "The relentless pressure of poverty—stemming from the depressed age level for common labor and from sharp seasonal fluctuations in employment opportunities—forced the children of Newburyport's laborers into the job market at an early age. Sometimes a laborer went several weeks without earning a cent; then the four dollars a week his twelve-year-old son earned as a bobbin boy was the family's sole source of support. Opportunities for formal education past the age of ten or eleven, as a result, were effectively nil for working class children."[85]

Thernstrom documents the low rate of social mobility among children of unskilled workers, but he does not demonstrate that this was due to their lack of education, in part because he studied only the children of the common laborers in Newburyport and not the rest of the population. He simply assumed that because children of working-class fathers received little education and those of more affluent parents must have had more education, education must be a key factor in explaining their subsequent differential occupational mobility.

Not only has Thernstrom failed to establish statistically the importance of education for explaining differentials in social mobility, but he has underestimated the extent of schooling received by children of common laborers. A more detailed analysis of the school attendance of all children in Newburyport in 1860 revealed that even among the children whose fathers were unskilled laborers, approximately 90 percent of them ages eleven or twelve attended school as well as a substantial portion of those ages thirteen to nineteen.[86] Thus, although children of unskilled fathers did receive less education in Newburyport than those from more fortunate homes, enough of them received sufficient education to question the notion that the only or perhaps the major reason for low social mobility among children from poorer backgrounds was their lack of education.

The few studies of schooling and social mobility in the nineteenth century focus on the impact of literacy or common school education on occupational advancement. They do not address the role of a high school education because it is usually assumed that few individuals attended such institutions, that those who did were almost always members of an already privileged middle or upper class, and that the few children of working-class families who did attend were unable to compete effectively with those from more advantaged homes.

The first public high school was established in Boston in 1821, but it was only in the late 1840s and 1850s that these institutions spread more rapidly in some states.[87] Looking mainly at the few urban high schools in nineteenth-century America, most scholars believe that even by the 1880s, "it was a rare thing to go to high school."[88]

A closer look, however, at certain states, such as Massachusetts, that led the way in establishing public high schools suggests that a much higher percentage of children attended high school than we had suspected—particularly in some of the smaller and medium-sized communities which had established them. In Newburyport almost one-third of the children in 1860 received some high school education at some point.[89] While high school attendance in New-buryport was higher than in many other medium-sized cities, nearly one out of five children in 1860 in Essex County towns with a public high school attended them. When we combine information on public high school attendance with private secondary school attendance for that county, 19 percent of all children in Essex County received the equivalent of at least some high school training. To be sure, most students attended one of these institutions for only a short period of time and did not complete the usual three-year course of high school instruction. Nevertheless, in some communities and regions of the United States, secondary education was more available and common than we had believed.[90]

Even if high schools were more accessible in some areas, were they reserved mainly for members of the middle or upper classes and unavailable to anyone whose father was in manual occupations? Based on his study of antebellum Massachusetts public high schools, Katz concluded that "high schools were minority institutions probably attended mainly by middle-class children."[91] Certainly children whose fathers were in white-collar occupations were over-represented in nineteenth-century public high schools. But in some communities a sizable minority of children from the working classes attended these institutions. In Newburyport, about one out of six children whose fathers were common laborers in 1860 received some high school education and almost four out of ten of those who fathers were in skilled occupations.[92] Again, although this proportion may be high compared to other mid-nineteenth-century communities, by the end of the nineteenth century a substantial minority of high school students were from blue-collar families.[93]

Some scholars argue that nineteenth-century public high schools simply reproduced the existing capitalist structure, not only by excluding children of working-class families, but by discriminating against them in terms of opportunities and rewards within those institutions. Again, the picture is much more complex and the few in-depth studies of high school education of that period suggest that once someone entered high school, their disadvantaged parental background was not an insurmountable barrier for success in those institutions. In fact, David Labaree's analysis of the Central High School of Philadelphia found that: "students obtained admission to the school through a mixture of class background and academic ability. However, once admitted, they found themselves in a model meritocracy where academic performance was the only characteristic that determined who would receive the school's valuable diploma. Therefore, although middle-class students were still the primary beneficiaries of the high school, since they constituted the majority of those admitted, this class effect was mediated through a form of meritocracy that held all students to the same rigorous academic standard."[94]

Did high school attendance promote social mobility or did it merely reinforce and legitimize the existing capitalist system? Again, scholars are divided on this question and the empirical support for either interpretation is limited. As mentioned previously, Bowles and Gintis or Katz challenge the notion that a high school education provided real opportunities for advancement for nineteenth-century Americans, but they do not provide much specific evidence on the impact of high school education on careers to bolster their arguments.[95] Similarly, Labaree, who has a more positive view of the value of a high school education, does not trace the students of the Philadelphia Central High School to their subsequent jobs to see what effect attendance actually had on their careers.[96] But Reed Ueda's analysis of the intergenerational occupational mobility for Somerville, Massachusetts, grammar and high school students in the last quarter of the nineteenth century found that: "The blue-collar son who was raised in the suburb and obtained the high school credential had powerful advantages over the average blue-collar son in Boston in obtaining white-collar employment. Blue-collar sons who went to high school in Somerville achieved a higher and faster rate of entry into the white-collar field than blue-collar sons in Boston of all levels of schooling."[97]

Similarly, Joel Perlmann's detailed, statistically sophisticated study of secondary schooling in Providence, Rhode Island, between 1880 and 1925 found that attending high school greatly improved one's chances for upward occupational mobility, even after controlling for the effects of family background. Furthermore, the advantages of a high school education were not reserved only for students from middle-class homes, but were also available for those from working-class families who were increasingly attending high schools in the early decades of the twentieth century: "The suspicion that secondary schooling did not help working-class boys, or immigrant working-class boys, who received it cannot be sustained. Education did not merely reflect the advantages of birth. Immigrant working-class boys who reached high school entered much more attractive occupations than others of similar social backgrounds, occupations."[98]

The exact relation between schooling and occupational mobility in nineteenth-century America remains to be documented. Several scholars have made important contributions to this effort, but none has established conclusively, one way or the other, whether or not schooling promoted occupational mobility and economic well-being for the individual worker.[99] Studies of the early twentieth century, however, suggest that schooling played a key role in fostering individual economic advancement.[100] Although comparable work for antebellum America remains to be done, enough fragmentary evidence exists to suggest that education may have helped individuals to improve their economic well-being and occupational status.

Nineteenth-century educational development was clearly related to and influenced by economic changes, but not as simply and directly as has been suggested by some. Mass public education was not caused or preceded by industrialization in antebellum America. Rather, it arose during the colonial period and early nineteenth century as a response to religious and political needs, particularly in New England. As a result, the United States was an unusually literate country when it first experienced industrialization.

If industrialization did not cause the rise of mass education, it did help to create an environment in which schooling could continue to flourish and improve. The potential and perceived turmoil associated with industrial development encouraged many Americans to support mass public education. Although industrial development was only one of many factors that caused nineteenth-century Americans to be anxious about their future, that fear was important in mobilizing support for public schooling. In addition, industrialization contributed to the general economic development of the United States and made the additional public expenditures for education more tolerable.

Although some industrialists and other capitalists certainly participated actively in antebellum school reforms, they by no means dominated them as some revisionists have implied. Nineteenth-century educational reform efforts were broad-based coalitions that brought together individuals and groups from very diverse backgrounds, including support from workers. In some ways, much of antebellum school reform was like an evangelical crusade by individuals who shared a deep though often naive faith in the power of education to redeem individuals and to preserve and protect the existing social and political order.

Schools did not simply correspond to the workplace and were not just an instrument of the capitalists. The schools provided cognitive skills and socialization that prepared children for their adult work roles, but they also taught democratic and egalitarian ideas that contradicted the unequal and hierarchical aspects of the antebellum society. Schools were a contested and semiautonomous domain where different individuals and groups sought to educate and to indoctrinate the next generation with what each considered were the proper views and values.

Most nineteenth-century classical economists did not devote much attention to the economic role of education. When they did discuss the subject, they stressed the importance of schools for disciplining the labor force and minimizing the tensions generated by industrialization. Although supporters of the workers in America wrote of the importance of free public schooling for everyone, they usually did not emphasize the value of education for enhancing the economic productivity of the individual or of the society as a whole. Horace Mann was the one most responsible for proclaiming and publicizing the importance of education for economic productivity. Although his methods of analysis were biased and inadequate statistically, he succeeded in convincing the public and many policymakers that education was a worthwhile economic investment for the individual and the society.

While most economists today continue to stress the importance of education as a form of human capital investment, some historians have expressed serious reservations about the economic productivity of education in antebellum America. Although the lack of adequate studies limits what we can say definitively about this issue, it does appear that public and private schooling contributed to the economic well-being of nineteenth-century Americans, though in a more modest fashion than proclaimed by such enthusiasts as Mann.

Nineteenth-century America also had a deep, abiding faith in the possibility and the reality of social mobility in their society. Current scholarship tends to support the notion that social mobility did exist for many Americans, but to a much more limited extent than we had previously assumed. Nevertheless, some scholars question the possibility of any real social mobility in antebellum America; they view the capitalist system as merely reproducing the existing social and economic structure.

There is also no agreement among researchers on whether or not education was an important factor in fostering social mobility. Many scholars question the importance of schooling, particularly at the primary levels, for helping children of blue-collar workers to get ahead. They also see the few secondary schools in that society as being reserved in practice almost exclusively for members of the more privileged classes. Other scholars detect the importance of education in contributing to the social mobility and economic well-being of at least some members of the working classes. They also tend to see the emerging public high schools as somewhat accessible to children from disadvantaged backgrounds and view these institutions as surprisingly egalitarian once someone was enrolled. Again, the controversy over the relation between education and social mobility in antebellum America cannot be resolved given the existing few studies. Yet the weight of evidence hints that schooling did contribute to the occupational advancement of individuals or their children, but that perhaps education was not as essential for everyone in the past as it may be today.

Finally, the rise of mass schooling and the emphasis on its role in fostering economic productivity and social mobility led to greater attention to early education. As schools replaced apprenticeship as the institutions for preparing future workers, children were sent at early ages to increasingly age-graded classrooms. Moreover, as economic productivity and social mobility became more closely and narrowly identified with schooling and as the biases against older workers grew in the second half of the nineteenth century, the perceived need for offering additional on-the-job training for older workers may have diminished. The relation between changes in schooling and the age-graded pattern of life course education remains to be investigated more thoroughly, but it is likely that the changes in the nineteenth-century schools and the economy may have played a key role in emphasizing the importance of formal schooling early in the life course

Chapter 7 An Analysis of the Concept and Uses of Systemic Educational Reform

Much of American educational development can be characterized as a series of ever-changing but often short-lived reforms, each of which responds to a perceived crisis and stimulates seemingly promising solutions. Unfortunately, many programs of educational reform fade rather quickly as the public and policymakers discover that the proposed changes have not provided significant and lasting improvements in student learning. The faddish nature of most educational reform is well documented and therefore many Americans are understandably skeptical and cautious whenever a reform initiative is launched. At the same time, we maintain faith in the potential efficacy of American schools and frequently turn to education to eradicate or alleviate social and economic problems.[1]

Several educational reforms were introduced in the 1980s and 1990s, including the recent bipartisan movement to implement by the year 2000 the eight National Education Goals.[2] One important component of these efforts has been the call for "systemic" educational reforms. While systemic reform is increasingly promoted, often there is little agreement on or understanding of what the term actually means or what it entails in practice. Frequently, systemic reform is used to describe attempts to create a more coherent, curriculum-driven reform effort, and at other times the phrase is employed to characterize efforts to provide more comprehensive educational and social services for school-aged children.[3]

In this chapter I shall trace the origin of the idea of systemic reform, place the concept within the context of educational developments in the 1980s and 1990s, and consider how systemic reform is being interpreted and applied by analysts and policymakers today. Although it may be too early to judge the long-term impact of the systemic reform movement on American education today, this is an opportune time to reexamine its conceptual meaning and relevance as well as to explore some possible mid-course adjustments.[4]

THE CONTEXT OF EDUCATIONAL REFORMS IN THE 1980S

Significant new ideas about educational reform do not arise in a vacuum. Usually they emerge in response to specific needs and reflect the thinking and educational practices already under way. For educational reform proposals to have a major impact, they must first become part of the public agenda for improving schools.[5]

The growing public dissatisfaction with the quality of education was reflected in and galvanized by the dire portrait of American schooling in the now-classic 1983 report of the National Commission on Excellence in Education, *A Nation at Risk: The Imperative for Educational Reform:*

> Our Nation is at risk. Our once unchallenged preeminence in commerce, industry, science, and technological innovation is being overtaken by competitors throughout the world. This report is concerned with only one of the many causes and dimensions of the problem, but it is the one that undergirds American prosperity, security, and civility. We report to the American people that while we can take justifiable pride in what our schools and colleges have historically accomplished and contributed to the United States and the well-being of its people, the educational foundations of our society are presently being eroded by a rising tide of mediocrity that threatens our very future as a Nation and a people. What was unimaginable a generation ago has begun to occur—others are matching and surpassing our educational attainments.[6]

Although some analysts questioned the accuracy of its portrayal of American schooling or the utility of its specific recommendations, most of the public and policymakers enthusiastically embraced *A Nation at Risk*. States and local areas instituted a variety of changes, such as more academically demanding high school graduation requirements, longer school days, new teacher preparation programs, and performance-based pay for teachers.[7] The initial phase of these reforms in the early 1980s, with its focus on more rigorous academic content and higher standards for students and teachers, is now often referred to as the "first wave" of the recent educational reforms.

While many state legislatures, governors, and local school boards were reexamining the nature of the curriculum and the role of classroom teachers, some researchers and educators were reconsidering the organization and governance of schools. One result of this reexamination was a shift toward decentralization and site-based management—local educators and administrators were to be given more control over managing their schools, but they also were to be held accountable for the results.[8] Some analysts labeled the restructuring of the organization and management of the schools as the "second wave" of school reform, but not surprisingly there has been considerable chronological and thematic overlap between the two phases.

One major hallmark of the education reforms undertaken in the 1980s has been the active involvement of the states in the implementation of reform measures in public elementary and secondary schools. Such states as California, Kentucky and South Carolina have taken the lead in developing new curriculum frameworks and student assessment tools, providing more comprehensive and integrated student services, and raising additional funding for elementary and secondary public education. While there has been considerable diversity in how the states have attempted to reform education, there have also been many commonalities as states have frequently borrowed ideas and practices from each other.[9]

Efforts were initiated in the 1980s to develop national education standards. Diane Ravitch, former assistant secretary of the Office of Educational Research and Improvement (OERI), identified three major factors that stimulated these activities:

First is the impetus that comes from disappointment with American students' performance in international assessments, particularly in mathematics and science.

A second source of this movement emerges from the participation of governors, business leaders, and visionary educators in school reform during the past decade. Those men and women who understood the idea of strategic planning, who knew that a change process must begin by identifying goals, found that education was not accustomed to goal-setting. . . .

A third reason for the movement for national standards is the example created by the National Council of Teachers of Mathematics, which has successfully developed voluntary national standards over the past several years.[10]

The National Governors' Association played a major role in the coordination of the education reform initiatives among the states. Working through seven task forces in the late 1980s, the National Governors' Association examined the current state of education in the United States and made recommendations for improvements. Their efforts culminated in the historic meeting with President Bush at the Charlottesville Education Summit in 1989 and led to the announcement of the six National Education Goals in early 1990.[11] The establishment of the six National Education Goals was especially significant because it provided a common set of objectives for the states and federal government in the Bush administration and continues to do so in the Clinton administration. While there is still considerable disagreement on how best to achieve these education goals, there is widespread agreement on their desirability and importance.[12]

As the end of the 1980s witnessed a federal and state convergence on the broad education goals, there was also a growing acknowledgement that all the proposed federal, state, and local educational reforms would have to be both comprehensive and integrated. Piecemeal or fragmentary reforms would not be adequate for achieving the six National Education Goals by the year 2000. The highly influential Business Roundtable, for example, issued in 1989 a ten-year agenda for its 200 corporate members that identified nine essential ingredients for implementing the National Education Goals:

"1. The new system is committed to four operating assumptions:
   • All students can learn at significantly higher levels
   • We know how to teach all students successfully
   • Curriculum content must reflect high expectations for all students, but instructional time and strategies may vary to assure success
   • Every child must have an advocate
2. The new system is performance or outcome based.
3. Assessment strategies must be as strong and rich as the outcomes.
4. Schools should receive rewards for success, assistance to improve and penalties for failure.
5. School-based staff have a major role in making instructional decisions.
6. Major emphasis is placed on staff development.

7. A high-quality pre-kindergarten program is established, at least for all disad-vantaged students.
8. Health and other social services are sufficient to reduce significant barriers to learning.
9. Technology is used to raise student and teacher productivity and to expand access to learning."[13]

Thus, by the end of the 1980s, numerous important and diverse educational reforms were underway throughout the United States. The states, guided in part by activities of the National Governors' Association, were playing an increasingly active role in directing and coordinating local educational efforts. The need for a more intellectually demanding curriculum generally had been accepted, and some education reform groups were beginning to call for a comprehensive and integrated effort to implement the six National Education Goals. The need for a coordinated federal, state, and local effort seemed partic-ularly essential as a growing number of studies suggested that educational achievement in the 1980s had made few real improvements in student out-comes despite the flurry of reform rhetoric and activity.

MARSHALL SMITH AND JENNIFER O'DAY'S
CONCEPT OF SYSTEMIC REFORM

The word "systemic" has been used frequently to talk about particular ap-proaches to family therapy or to indicate a review of an organization or institu-tion as a whole system, and it became, in the late 1980s and early 1990s, an influential description of and prescription for educational reform.[14] There are several different, but related, versions of the concept of systemic reform in education today. Jennifer O'Day and Marshall Smith are usually credited with having coined and popularized the phrase in regard to the current educational reforms, and I shall follow their definition here.[15] Smith and O'Day did not originate this particular approach to education—they drew heavily upon the recent initiatives in curriculum and assessment reforms in states such as Califor-nia—but their theoretical formulation of systemic reform has had considerable influence on other researchers and policymakers. Moreover, as the undersecre-tary in the Department of Education, Smith has played an important role in the Clinton administration's use of the idea of systemic educational reform in its policies.[16]

In the early 1980s, Smith, on several different occasions, commented on educational reforms already underway. In an essay coauthored with Brenda

Turnbull and Alan Ginsburg shortly after the election of President Reagan, Smith outlined his views on the federal role in education.[17] The authors strongly endorsed the goals of such earlier federal legislation as the Elementary and Secondary Education Act, but they argued that these programs had to be reformed because "economic and social conditions have changed since the programs were enacted. . . . state agencies have become more active since 1965. . . . the number and diversity of federal requirements can interfere with program effectiveness. . . . [and] we know more about how to deliver educational services."[18] They explored several options for improving the federal role, including fostering more coordination with the local schools because research had shown the importance of local commitment and capacity for the implementation of any educational reforms. They identified the lack of adequate research on program implementation as a major impediment to designing meaningful intervention programs:

> From the federal standpoint, though, all this new knowledge about effective schools leaves a crucial gap. We still know little about how the good schools got that way—and how average or poor schools can improve. Since the key ingredients in success seem to be local, outsiders are left wondering what constructive role they can play. Until more research identifies the potential contributions of specific outside stimuli (requirements, technical assistance, staff development, and other diverse approaches), the action implications for the federal government remain limited. We can say only that the federal government should stop preventing schools from applying their resources in a concerted and coordinated fashion to improve the instructional program as a whole. At present, fiscal controls are often used to isolate federal dollars and programs—and their recipients—from the regular school program.[19]

Smith later cowrote an essay on the impact of the federal government on elementary and secondary education from 1940 to 1980,[20] and he examined the federal Chapter 1 Program of the Elementary and Secondary School Act of 1965 by analyzing the characteristics of students who participated in that program in the early 1980s.[21] Smith's analyses of the effective school movement in the early 1980s reinforced his beliefs in the importance of coordinated and coherent education reforms at the level of the individual school. Admittedly, the research basis was less solid than its proponents claimed,[22] but there were strong indications that the effective schools movement, which emphasized the importance of changing the overall culture of the individual schools rather than attempting piecemeal reforms, was the best way to improve American schooling. In a 1985 article, Stewart Purkey and Smith listed thirteen characteristics of an effective school, but they argued that the existing research was unable to demonstrate which were the most essential or in what order they should be implemented.[23]

The key missing ingredient, according to Purkey and Smith, was knowledge of how to encourage the development of effective schools at the local level. Federal and state policy could provide assistance and even set general policy guidelines, but the impetus for the reforms had to come mainly from the local schools. After an extensive review of the limited research literature on the implementation of local reforms, Purkey and Smith concluded that a flexible combination of incentives and mandated requirements was the most effective way of proceeding. Interestingly, the possible role of federal or state curriculum frameworks, which was to receive so much attention later, was not explored in any detail.[24]

A significant influence on Smith's work on systemic reform was his participation in the Consortium for Policy Research in Education (CPRE), one of the five-year research and development centers funded in 1985 by the Office of Educational Research and Improvement. At the time CPRE consisted of a group of researchers from Rutgers University, the University of Southern California, Harvard University, Michigan State University, the University of Wisconsin, and the RAND Corporation (when the RAND Corporation dropped out, it was replaced by Stanford University).[25] The consortium was particularly interested in the role of the states in fostering local educational improvements and provided Smith and his colleagues with an important forum for analyzing and discussing school reforms. For example, CPRE cosponsored a "Policy Forum on New Roles and Responsibilities in the Public Schools" in spring 1987 to discuss the recent school restructuring reforms.[26]

The year 1988 was particularly crucial for the development of the concept of systemic reform. Although elements of the idea had been present, in various forms, in the writings of Smith and others, they had not been combined into a coherent vision. Three incidents were especially important in this development: (1) the request to Smith from Bassam Shakhashiri, assistant director of science and engineering education programs at the National Science Foundation, for ideas on how to conceptualize and organize statewide efforts to improve math and science teaching;[27] (2) a discussion at CPRE on the future direction of their work in preparation for OERI's competition for renewed center funding in 1990; and (3) an essay by Smith and O'Day about the state of research on teaching methods and effectiveness that suggested the need for state curriculum frameworks.[28] These efforts stimulated the thinking of Smith and led to his collaboration with O'Day to write the first, widely circulated essay on systemic reform.

Smith and O'Day surveyed the changing education scene and praised many of the local initiatives in the second wave of school reforms, but they also voiced concern that the scattered site-based reforms were not affecting most public schools, and they pointed to the need for statewide curriculum development and teacher training efforts to complement local school initiatives:

> Unfortunately, the very strength of this new approach [second wave of school reforms] may also be its shortcoming. While reliance on school-based initiative (even that stimulated by states) may be more likely to produce significant changes in classroom practice than have edicts from above, a strictly school-by-school approach makes it difficult to generalize such changes from the small number of initially active schools to the well over 100,000 educational institutions in cities, suburbs, and rural areas across the country. . . . Site-based management, professional collaboration, incentives, and choice may be important elements of the change process, but they alone will not produce the kinds of changes in content and pedagogy that appear critical to our national well-being. . . . However, we see in this process a more proactive role for the centralized elements of the system—particularly the states— one which can set the conditions of change to take place not just in a small handful of schools or for a few children, but in the great majority.[29]

Whereas much of Smith's earlier focus had been on the role of local schools or districts, in his essay with O'Day the emphasis shifted to the role the states could play in promoting educational changes. The key to change was systemic reform, which would combine state curriculum frameworks and assessments with site-based school reforms. O'Day and Smith identified three major changes as characteristic of an ideal model of systemic reform:

"1. Curriculum frameworks that establish what students should know and be able to do would provide direction and vision for significantly upgrading the quality of the content and instruction within all schools in the state. . . .

2. Alignment of state education policies would provide a coherent structure to support schools in designing effective strategies for teaching the content of the frameworks to all their students. . . .

3. Through a restructured governance system, schools would have the resources, flexibility, and responsibility to design and implement effective strategies for preparing their students to learn the content of the curriculum frameworks to a high level of performance."[30]

One major reason for urging the shift toward systemic reform, according to Smith and O'Day, is that the present system does not adequately provide for the needs of poor and minority students. Moreover, even the effective schools movement, which Smith had praised previously, apparently could not sustain itself without a systemic approach:

> The policy structure provides little support for generalizing or maintaining changes engendered by a more instruction-oriented school-by-school strategy. Without such support, schools with large numbers of already underserved students are particularly unlikely to be able to make the kinds of fundamental changes in instruction required by the new reforms. Where the changes do occur, it will be the result of the tremendous hard work, foresight, and knowledge of dedicated individuals in the affected schools. But personnel turnover, "burnout," and competing demands make the maintenance of such schools tenuous at best, and the history of school reform in the United States is replete with promising but eventually failed examples of school-by-school change.[31]

Partly as the result of such programs as Head Start and partly due to the basic skills movement of the 1970s and 1980s, African-American children had achieved some absolute and relative gains in their math and reading performances on the National Assessment of Educational Progress examinations. The more recent NAEP tests in 1990, however, ominously pointed to a reversal, and O'Day and Smith speculated that if systemic curriculum reforms were not instituted, poor and minority students might fall further behind their more affluent, white counterparts "because of the difficulty of implementing the reforms, particularly in schools with large numbers of disadvantaged students, it seems possible that a substantial new differentiation of curriculum will occur, albeit slowly, with a continued but diluted basic skills approach for the majority of low-income children and an increasing emphasis on problem solving and complex content for more advantaged students."[32]

Systemic school reform by itself, as Smith and O'Day point out, will not necessarily help all students equally because many of the poorer and more disadvantaged schools will not have adequate resources to offer the proposed new instruction. Simply expecting everyone, regardless of their access to the improved curricula, to measure up to the new standards is both unrealistic and unfair: "It is not legitimate to hold students accountable unless they have been given the opportunity to learn the material on the examination. Similarly, teachers or schools cannot legitimately be held accountable for how well their students do unless they have the preparation and resources to provide the students the opportunity to learn."[33]

Therefore, Smith and O'Day argue that "opportunity to learn" standards are needed to insure that all students have access to a quality education.[34] Since they recognize the dangers of the specification of inputs by bureaucracies, especially as most of the more traditional inputs do not seem to have much direct impact on student outcomes, O'Day and Smith define the opportunity to learn standards narrowly in scope and call for considerable flexibility in implementation; the opportunity to learn standards are to be based on the content and skills outlined in each of the state curriculum frameworks. They suggest four guidelines for establishing the opportunity to learn standards:

> First, standards should be parsimonious and well focused. . . . Too often they degrade into minimum standards and senseless bureaucratic exercises with long lists of easily measured but essentially meaningless elements. . . .
>
> Second, within the context of content-driven systemic reform, the purpose of school standards should be to provide operational specifications for assessing whether a school is giving its students the opportunity to learn the content and skills set out in the curriculum frameworks. . . .
>
> Third, the use of school standards in a systemic curriculum strategy is predicated on a different way of thinking about the relationship between school inputs and student achievement outcomes—a conceptualization that offers substantial promise of allowing a clear linkage between inputs and outcomes. . . .
>
> Finally, our understanding of what the essential resources are and of what constitutes quality in curriculum and instruction will change as systemic reform is implemented and as we understand more about teaching and learning. It will therefore be important to view school standards as dynamic and supportive of the entire school system's learning to improve over time.[35]

It is important to recognize that Smith and O'Day operationally define the resources for the opportunity to learn standards very narrowly in terms of the new curricula and instruction: "Obvious candidates include teachers and administrators knowledgeable of and able to teach the content of the frameworks and a planned school curriculum, professional development programs, assessments, and instructional materials and resources (such as laboratories), all in line with the frameworks. On the other hand, this highly targeted approach should help to guard against the kind of overregulatory 'wish list' that might otherwise be generated by the exercise of defining school standards. At the same time, however, it excludes from the standards some resources that many people (ourselves included) believe every school *should* have."[36] The only exception they make is that they "believe it critical to ensure through the standards that every school has a physically safe environment for all participants."[37]

Although O'Day and Smith argue for the value of each state having a single curriculum framework and each school having a coherent, overall curriculum, they do not believe that all schools within a state need an identical curriculum: "It is important also to note that ensuring access to the common content core does not necessarily mean all children receive exactly the same curriculum. Indeed, we would expect specific curricula to vary with the interests, backgrounds, and cultures of the students and possibly of their teachers and schools. Such diversity within a common core is an integral characteristic of systemic reform. . . . Individual schools, to maximize the opportunities for their particular students, must be free to choose the instructional strategies, language of instruction, use of curriculum materials, and topics to be emphasized."[38]

Smith and O'Day strongly believe in the need for an improved, coherent state curriculum framework coupled with site-based school reforms; they also endorse the necessity for related opportunity to learn standards. They are less certain, however, what should be done, even under ideal conditions, when students or schools fail to reach the desired performance (outcome) standards. Unlike some proponents of systemic reform, O'Day and Smith do not call for dramatically changing the existing school governance system, though according to their proposals local schools would be expected to adhere to the spirit of the state's curriculum framework. They consider several options for disciplining poorly performing students and schools but take a moderate position in regard to using rewards and sanctions. Throughout their discussion, the emphasis is more on trying to persuade students and schools to make the necessary adjustments themselves, but with the definite threat of stronger measures, if needed, at the state or district level to achieve compliance.[39]

OTHER VIEWS OF SYSTEMIC REFORM

There is some diversity in the definition of and use of the concept of systemic reform, and Smith and O'Day represent only one view. Whereas some of these variations are minor, representing only a slightly different emphasis, others are distinctly different and involve an entirely new definition. Rather than attempt a comprehensive review, in this section I shall explore only a few of the more significant and interesting versions of the concept of systemic reform.

The Smith and O'Day approach to systemic reform seems to require only a relatively loose coupling of national and local activities. For them, the crucial intermediary is the state, which provides the specific curriculum frameworks and assessments that local schools must address. Indeed, though the states may look to any of the emerging national curriculum frameworks or assessments for guidance, they are quite free to develop their own approaches as long as they include the cognitive rigor and coherence that O'Day and Smith see as essential to systemic reform.[40]

Some analysts call for a closer linkage between national objectives and local responses. For example, Chester Finn, cofounder of the Excellence Network and an assistant secretary of OERI in the Reagan administration, agrees with some of the basic tenets of systemic reform but recommends a single, national curriculum for everyone:

> *It is time to put in place a rich, solid core of common learning for all young Americans and an effective means of determining how well it is being learned.* Let's reject those old bugaboos that a "national curriculum" is a prescription for catastrophe and national exams are a plot to turn us into a land of dutiful robots. Let's instead open our eyes to the fact that we're living amid a catastrophe that might be ameliorated by embracing a national curriculum and an examination system to accompany it. . . . Note, however, that I do *not* mean a curriculum enacted by Congress and enforced by federal bureaucrats or judges. I visualize a *nationwide* core curriculum matched to the education goals set by the president and governors in 1990.[41]

Although all children would learn the same core curriculum, Finn's proposal would allow states and schools to supplement this instruction with some additional instruction to accommodate local interests.[42] Moreover, he is willing to leave the mechanics of how to organize and teach the curriculum at the local level to the schools and to vary the amount of time different students are given to master the materials. But he insists that both children and schools be held accountable for students understanding the content and acquiring the skills of the core curriculum through rigorous national examinations:

> We should institute a comprehensive new national examination program, similar to the "external exams" used in other countries—and to the Advanced Placement, International Baccalaureate, and New York Regents exams already in operation here. . . . Unlike its overseas counterparts, which typically click in at the end of secondary school, the new U.S. exams would be given at three stages in the typical student's school experience. Under the current grade structure, pupils would take suitable versions of them in grades four, eight, and twelve, as the governors suggested, in at least five subjects they identified. . . .
>
> The exams will appraise individual achievement but will be designed so that their results can be aggregated, analyzed, and compared at all the other levels we care about: the classroom, the school, the local system, the state, and the nation as a whole.[43]

Thus, Finn argues for flexibility in how children are taught, but he is firm in his expectation that schools will teach the national curriculum and all students will demonstrate competency in the skills and content of the core subjects before graduating.[44]

While some challenge Smith and O'Day's vision of systemic reform for not insisting on a national curriculum and a national assessment, others go in the opposite direction and question the wisdom and practicability of any mandatory linkage of national (or state) curriculum frameworks and local school instruction. William Clune, a professor at the University of Wisconsin and a member of CPRE, supports systemic reform but rejects any mandatory national or state system of instructional guidance for four reasons:

"1. *Standard curriculum, diverse needs.* State adoption of a standard curriculum is not required to make ambitious curricula widely available to schools and teachers. Acceptable models already exist, and more will regularly become available through multiple channels. . . .

2. *Absence of attention to delivery.* Whatever the curriculum, defining new goals for instruction is the easy part. The real challenges are at the delivery stage. . . . Yet the official enactment of high standards may distract attention from the problems of delivery and be confounded with real help for poor schools and real gains in student achievement.

3. *Problems with high-stakes exams.* In the absence of a realistic delivery structure, state-centered instructional guidance will probably rely on high-stakes examinations of students to force change in schools and classrooms. But the motivational power of high stakes automatically creates a vast, probably oppressive regime of teaching to the test, requires a highly prescriptive curriculum, creates misleading grade inflation, is inconsistent with the new constructivist and contextualized goal of teaching for understanding, and may well become transformed into an official system of student stratification. . . .

4. *Incompatibility with U.S. educational governance.* Adoption of a standard curriculum by the national government and 50 states is difficult enough (e.g., states tend to create multiple kinds of new standards and simply add them to the old ones), but the adoption problem is dwarfed by the implementation problem. Whatever is adopted at the top is filtered unpredictably through multiple intermediate layers of discretion shaped by preexisting cultures and agendas. The possibility of a prescriptive yet unpredictable system is difficult to imagine, but is the likely outcome of a standardized system."[45]

Clune accepts the value of systemic reform and the need for higher curriculum standards, but he feels that there may be several different, acceptable ways of achieving these goals at the level of the individual classroom or school:

> The system proposed here should be viewed as a completion rather than a rejection of the basic insights of systemic educational policy. Instructional change certainly does require higher standards and coherent, coordinated policy from outside the school. But on close inspection, the statist-centralized version of systemic policy built around authoritative curriculum frameworks is fatally flawed on the two grounds: A common curriculum is difficult, if not impossible, to apply considering the immense diversity of American schooling, and a tolerable link between policy at the top and change at the bottom is all but unattainable. The system recommended here solves both problems by creating a system of change agents (curriculum networks) using diverse curricula approved as ambitious and chosen by local schools and by emphasizing issues of capacity-building, such as teacher training and school finance.[46]

O'Day and Smith explicitly define the opportunity to learn standards rather narrowly—to provide measures of whether students have been given the opportunity to learn the proposed challenging curriculum. But among those who favor having opportunity to learn standards or school delivery standards, there is considerable debate about any federal or national involvement. The National Council on Education Standards and Testing (NCEST), for example, was deeply divided on the question of national versus state responsibility for school delivery standards. The final recommendation of NCEST was that state school delivery standards be established "to ensure that students do not bear the sole burden of attaining the standards and to encourage assurances that the tools for success will be available at all schools. . . . System performance standards would attest to the provision of opportunities to learn and of appropriate instructional conditions to enable all children to reach high standards."[47]

In discussing the recommendations of NCEST before Congress, Marshall Smith, a member of the council, explained that the school delivery standards would, in effect, become national ones—but by a different process than the national curriculum standards that were being developed by associations of educators: "The school delivery standards, on the other hand, would be developed collectively by the States. Now, what is something that's developed collectively by the States? That certainly seems to be national to me. It's a different form of national. It is developed collectively by the States and then used by the States themselves to oversee, to audit the kinds of schools, to ensure the kinds of opportunities to learn that's called for in the report."[48] Smith's preference, though, was for school delivery standards to be developed at the national level: "I recall the question you [Congressman Dale E. Kildee, D-MI] asked me during the Council meetings, and that was wouldn't you prefer to have the school delivery standards developed at the national level. My response was yes. But I needed very desperately—I wanted very desperately to get the concept of school delivery standards into this report, deeply embedded in the ways we begin to think about this process of changing American education."[49]

Other analysts have been even more outspoken about the need for national, rather than state, school delivery standards. Walter Haney, senior research associate of the Center for the Study of Testing, Evaluation and Educational Policy at Boston College, complained about the lack of national delivery standards:

> Let me mention that in my prepared remarks I indicate there are a number of aspects of the NCEST report that I personally do like. For example, at least the report raises the point that, when it comes to educational standards, we need to be concerned with standards not just for students but also standards for schools and school systems. What is odd, though, is why the standards for students should be national but the standards for schools should be up to the States. There's no rationale provided in the report for that distinction. Moreover, it seems pretty obvious to me, for both constitutional reasons and historical reasons of educational governance, quite the reverse set of priorities would be more appropriate than the priorities set out in the Council report.[50]

Rather than accept a restricted definition of opportunity to learn standards, some policymakers broadened the concept considerably to call for more federal funding of education and to specify a longer list of essential components of quality schooling. Keith Geiger, president of the National Education Association, praised the national education goals but called for an additional $100 billion in federal general aid funds for public elementary and secondary schools. Geiger went on to define more specifically the type of school environment that each student should have:

> *Teaching staff:* America's public schools must have a qualified teacher in every classroom. . . .
> *Education support employees:* Teachers should be relieved of duties that take them away from time spent teaching students. . . .
> *Class size:* America's public schools must have reasonable standards for adequate class size, including much smaller class size in the elementary grades. . . .
> *Course diversity:* Public school course offerings should reflect the broad array of

skills Americans need to maintain our Nation's economic and democratic institutions. . . .

Library: Every school should have a well-stocked library with age-appropriate materials and access to computer-based data systems. . . .

Staff and facilities for disabled students: Every school district must have the resources to provide adequate, appropriate facilities and staff with the preparation and skills to meet the individual needs of students with disabilities. . . .

Counselors and health care professionals: Every school should have properly licensed counselors able to assist with academic, emotional, and social issues and health care professionals to address medical emergencies and other health care needs. . . .

Instructional leadership: Every school should set aside time and resources to provide relevant inservice education for all staff and to work together to define the mission of the school and plan its implementation. . . .

Physical plant: Every public school student should be able to attend schools safe from drugs and violence and from environmental hazards.[51]

Some analysts and policymakers have embraced the idea of opportunity to learn standards; others express reservations about them or how they might be implemented. Linda Darling-Hammond, codirector of the National Center for Restructuring Education, Schools, and Teaching at Teachers College, favors opportunity to learn standards but acknowledges the tension between setting such expectations and allowing schools the flexibility to pursue instructional strategies at the local level. She calls for a few quantifiable resource measures as well as a more general set of standards for practice based on professional knowledge about children's learning in schools.

The first opportunity to learn standards, according to Darling-Hammond, would be standards for delivery systems measured at the state, school district, and school levels. Rather than try to specify such items as class sizes or teaching loads, she proposes to develop a set of indicators that would ensure equitable resources for all students. Darling-Hammond suggests three equity principles as guides in the construction of these resource indicators:

"1. *Equitable access to the school funding necessary to fulfill standards of excellence. . . .*

2. *Access to well-prepared, fully qualified teachers, whose knowledge of subject matter, pedagogy, curriculum, and assessment is grounded in deep understanding of how students grow, learn, and develop and how their various learning styles, talents, and backgrounds may best be addressed and nurtured. . . .*

3. *Equitable access to the materials and equipment necessary for learning: safe, clean*

physical facilities; textbooks and instructional materials; libraries, computers, laboratories, and other resources for inquiry."[52]

The school delivery standards proposed by Darling-Hammond are considerably broader than those suggested by O'Day and Smith yet somewhat less specific than those proposed by Geiger.

In addition to system delivery standards, Darling-Hammond calls for standards for practice that "embody what is known from research and systemic consideration of practice about approaches that support desired student learning."[53] She suggests a framework for standards of practice that might include:

School climate: students should encounter an environment that is respectful, purposeful, physically and psychologically safe, and personalized so as to ensure close, sustained relationships between students and teachers and attention to special needs.

Curriculum and assessment: all students should have access to a rich and challenging curriculum that fosters their critical thinking, creative and performance capabilities, develops their multiple intelligences and diverse talents, and encourages them to apply their learning in problem-solving situations. This should be supported by diverse assessment strategies that are appropriate and authentic measures of the goals being pursued as well as instructionally useful indicators of individual student growth and performance.

Teaching and learning experiences: all students should be taught in ways that are cognitively and developmentally appropriate, and that respect their individual experiences, learning styles, and learning needs. Teachers should use a wide array of multimodal teaching strategies, evaluate students' learning strengths and problems, and adapt their teaching to support student success. Student access to curricular and co-curricular opportunities should be inclusive and adaptive for maximum talent development rather than exclusive for purposes of limiting enrollment or participation.

Professional inquiry and development: schools should have mechanisms that help them to continually evaluate how well they are meeting students' needs and to provide ongoing supports for parent involvement, as well as teacher development, consultation, and school improvement.[54]

Andrew Porter, director of the Wisconsin Center for Education Research, has serious reservations about the use of opportunity to learn standards for school-by-school accountability purposes (though he sees their potential value for presenting a vision of schooling expectations or for gauging the extent and depth of the curriculum reforms): "Education has a long and not very productive history of having used inputs and processes for holding schools accountable. School accreditation programs and detailed lists of state requirements for school practices have not had the desired effects. Because school accountability on inputs and processes has not worked, there has been a shift toward school accountability in terms of outputs, what schools produce. Using school delivery standards/opportunity to learn standards would shift attention away from outcomes once again and back to processes."[55]

Instead of using opportunity to learn standards for school accountability, Porter suggests that value-added school assessments might be employed:

> While the technical details of value added school assessment are many and complicated, the concept is straightforward. Schools are held accountable for the value that they add to student achievement. A measure of baseline student achievement is required as well as subsequent measures of student achievement as students progress through school. To serve purposes of equity, school value added should be disaggregated by race (and/or socioeconomic status) and by sex to see if the school has similar value added for all students. South Carolina is one example where value added school assessment has been used for purposes of school accountability. South Carolina schools with high value added receive additional funds for instruction and staff in those schools receive salary bonuses.
>
> Value added assessment has several advantages over school delivery standards for purposes of school-by-school accountability. Value added school assessment keeps the focus on outcomes, where it belongs. The measurement problems for value added assessment are challenging, but they are nowhere near as complicated as the measurement problems for school performance standards, nor is value added school assessment as expensive. Value added school assessment avoids telling schools how to do what it is their business to do, staying away from the type of micromanagement that would be invited by school performance standards. Last and most important, value added school assessment reflects the fact that student achievement is a joint responsibility shared by student and school. Holding students and schools simultaneously accountable on the same output ensures that neither will be forced to take sole responsibility for that which is only partially under their control.[56]

The ideas cited thus far have been only somewhat dissimilar from the O'Day and Smith concept of systemic reform. But others are now employing the term "systemic reform" to mean something rather different. Frequently, states that have adopted the curriculum and assessment-driven approaches have also broadened their definition of systemic reform to include such features as early childhood education or the provision of health care facilities and services in the schools. For example, the Kentucky Education Reform Act (KERA) provides one of the most comprehensive packages of education reform. Under KERA, "for the first time, extra educational and social services are available at the school site for large numbers of children and their families, including preschool programs, family resource and youth centers, and extended school services."[57]

Systemic reform is also being used to refer to more general changes that affect the entire school system. That is how Robert Barkley, Jr., an analyst with the National Education Association, views systemic reform. He sees change "as being unalterably systemic in nature. That is, everything about schools and schooling is related. We cannot change one aspect of schools (i.e., personnel appraisal) without significant impact on other aspects (i.e., student assessment). The busing schedule does impact the curriculum, and just about every teacher knows this without question."[58]

Based on the writings of five experts on management or school reform, Barkley lists thirteen systemic change principles. As one can see, these principles draw heavily on the Total Quality Management (TQM) approach and explicitly emphasize process over specific outcomes:

"1. Purpose must be clearly articulated and widely 'known and owned.'
2. Purpose must be based upon a consciously developed philosophy rooted in shared theory.
3. Need for change must be broadly understood and accepted.
4. The 'top' must demonstrate the envisioned change.
5. Significant new investment and commitment must be made in educating/training prospective participants in the new theory and philosophy and relevant skills.
6. Participation in the new processes and approaches must be voluntary and active.
7. Power sources and relationships must be visibly altered.
8. Partner-customer-supplier relationships must be consciously developed.
9. Individual affirmation must be balanced with collaboration.
10. Process, at all levels, must be emphasized over end results.
11. Communication barriers must be eradicated and new channels developed.
12. Data-based decision-making must be required and enabled.
13. Efforts to learn and improve must be total, dynamic, and generative."[59]

For Barkley, "the degree to which the above are reflected in our Learning Labs determines the presence of and/or the prospect for systemic change. . . . The efforts of schools to change, like those of other organizations, will flounder to the extent they fail to attend to such principles."[60]

Some analysts use systemic reform to refer to a combination of a more general change in the overall system of education and an emphasis on state-level curriculum and assessment changes. Writing for the Midwest Regional Educational Laboratory, Charles Reigeluth of Indiana University, outlines systemic reforms for the Chicago public schools. While emphasizing the improvement of the learning experiences of students, he calls for major changes in the system of education at the building level, the district level, and the state level. Although he starts by focusing on reforms at the building and district levels, he concludes by seeing the need to integrate these efforts with state initiatives:

> Three considerations impact on the nature of the process for fundamental change. First, at this point in time, there is no new model (representing fundamental systemic change) that has been field tested, debugged, and proven effective. Therefore, a process to implement fundamental change must be a process to invent, debug, and continuously improve a new system, not just adopt one. Second, if a fundamentally different educational system is to be successful, all the key players must be content with their new roles: students, teachers, administrators, policymakers, and parents. Therefore, the change process must be one that results in *shared ownership* of the new system. Third, since fundamental change entails new roles for the key players, the process must be one that effects substantial professional development, particularly changing people's mindsets about education. . . .
>
> Finally, changes must occur on the *state level* for a truly systemic restructuring effort to be successful. State regulations that are barriers to experimentation and systemic change must be removed. . . . And incompatible parts of the state-level system must be changed for the new schools, such as curriculum frameworks, curricular materials, teacher development programs (pre-service and in-service), student assessment, and accountability mechanisms. A combination of the top-down and bottom-up approaches is recommended for this.[61]

Others use systemic change to describe pervasive alterations in a state's educational system. Rex Hagans and his colleagues at the Northwest Regional Educational Laboratory, explore two specific state efforts at systemic change in Oregon and Washington: "This analysis attempts to assist state efforts to achieve systemic change in the educational system. It assumes that true systemic change can be achieved only when the systems of the literally hundreds of communities, including local districts and local school buildings, change. These local 'subsystems' are the backbone of the state's educational structure and are the primary units for systemic change of the state's educational system."[62]

Applying general systems theory to educational change, Hagans and his associates emphasize the importance of improving the flow of information from the schools back to the upper levels of the administration:

General systems theory suggests that if we want to concern ourselves with systemic reform, we should be most concerned with (1) feedback of information to the regulatory system; and (2) ensuring that the regulatory systems are not in conflict with each other. To put it more simply, educational policy structures need to be systemically regulated by feedback from the other sub-systems of the educational community, rather than the other way around. The tenet of systemic reform is *not* "if we tinker with the system's elements, we can improve the output." Rather, it is "if we improve the nature, frequency, and quality of feedback, we can improve the output."[63]

They go on to provide a set of key parameters by which to judge the success of effecting systemic change:

Infusive: Does the initiative act so as to build upon existing knowledge, resources, and relationships and instill an increasingly shared commitment to a common vision and a set of commonly accepted outcomes at both the state and local levels?

Pervasive: Do the initiative's goals and actions promote and facilitate improvement in all the key components of both the state and local levels of the system (policy, human resource, community, and curriculum development)?

Potent: Are the initiative's goals and actions valued and embraced by all participants (parents, teachers, program staff, legislators) at all levels (state, community, school, program) of the system.

Coherent: Do the initiative's goals and actions increase and support congruence between the levels (state, community, school, program) and among the dimensions (including public understanding, aspirations, and assessment of outcomes)?

Sustainable: Do the initiative's goals and actions harness mechanisms within the infrastructure (fiscal resources, policies, professional incentives, and partnerships) to ensure long-term impact?[64]

Thus, the Northwest Regional Educational Laboratory's approach to systemic reform tries to provide a mechanism for evaluating and improving more specific educational reform initiatives based in part on the insights drawn from general systems thinking.

Finally, in this chapter I have dealt only with some of the leading proponents of systemic reform. Although they may differ amongst themselves in how systemic reform is defined or put into practice, they share a common belief in the validity and utility of this approach. As the concept of systemic reform becomes more popular, however, there will be more skeptics who question its basic assumptions.

Terry Astuto and his colleagues, funded by the Regional Laboratory for Educational Improvement of the Northeast and Islands, have challenged the underlying premises of systemic reform. Rather than praising recent efforts to develop national and state curriculum and assessment standards, they call for a fundamentally different view of education—one that focuses on the individual child and the local school:

> If you were involved in educational policy planning in Washington, D.C., or one of the state capitals, you would begin to develop the feeling that you were at the seat of life in educational reform. Even more exciting is the prospect that there is not only a solution to the vexation of reform in education but that the solution will be generalizable and lasting—currently described as "systemic reform." The marvelous attribute of systemic reform is that it will account for system variables in an ordered and comprehensive fashion that will maximize the impact of proposed system changes, monitor the changes in practice, and assess the output of the system in a fashion that will allow corrections to be made and accountability for breakdowns or failure to be established.
>
> Not everyone agrees with this scenario. The current authors disagree. We define the problem and solution in local terms—one student, one parent(s), one teacher, one principal, one classroom, one school. If reform in education occurs, the reformers will be the actors at the school level.[65]

They dismiss the idea that higher academic standards and more rigorous outcomes-based assessments will enhance student learning:

> Similarly, assessment of students through standardized performance testing generates many more problems than improvements. Test construction drives curriculum and instruction. Despite evidence of technical reliability and validity, teachers complain that tests do not measure what they teach. The dominant assumption about the merits of performance standards and assessments is so strong, that the focus of reform is to get better and better at designing valid and reliable systems. Alternative strategies for organizational improvement that build on the experiences of practitioners and focus on improved processes rather than product measurement are ignored.[66]

Rejecting what they see as top-down and external reforms, these researchers call for local initiatives that are more focused on teachers and students:

> The currently most popular reform initiatives place a high level of confidence in the efficacy of externally engineered interventions, e.g., setting standards, conducting assessments, formalizing power relationships, and establishing sanctions for failure. This fits a general lack of confidence in the self-motivation of individuals and the necessity to create and control work environments for teachers and students. . . .
>
> The last few years have provided evidence that our present policies governing educational reform are not working. They have not been discredited primarily because blame for their failure has been shifted by the national and state reformers to

inadequate implementation by inept local practitioners. This rationalization of the basic weaknesses of the policies will eventually fall of its own weight. The current knowledge base, not just in the field of education but in the broader fields of study reviewed in this monograph, provides convincing evidence that our path to reform is wrong. We're trying hard enough; we are just trying the wrong things. . . .

No one can reform our schools for us. If there is to be authentic reform in American education, it will be a grass roots movement. Systemic reformers will have to be resisted systematically. They are distracting us from the job at hand. The only system we have is the local community school, and external agencies should be worrying about how they can help and support these school units—not how they can dominate them. The current repressive and retrogressive policies will have to be rejected and replaced by hopeful teacher and student centered reforms. We are honestly sorry that those who would save our children and our schools by fiat cannot do it. But we will have to do it in individual communities through hard work, individual investment and effort, and local reformers who work on the line. Isn't that always the way?[67]

Thus, while systemic reform may be gaining in popularity and visibility in policymaking circles, it is by no means uncontested.[68] Whether the idea of systemic reform continues to thrive depends in large measure on how thoughtfully the concept can be defended and advanced intellectually as well as on how successfully it is implemented at the state and local levels.

SOME REFLECTIONS ABOUT SYSTEMIC REFORM

As the term "systemic reform" becomes more popular and more widely used, there is a danger that it will be employed to designate a variety of different reforms and in the process lose much of its current analytical focus and power. The increasingly broad and imprecise use of the term is already occurring. Because of this, it is important to know what exactly is meant by systemic reform.

From an analytic perspective, it may be more useful if the concept of systemic reform is employed in a limited sense to encompass reforms that particularly emphasize the role of states, are content-standards-driven, and seek to provide a coherent and close fit between curriculum and assessment at the local level. The O'Day and Smith model represents a reasonable framework for providing practical guidance and offers a useful point of departure for future policy debates. It might be possible to make some minor adjustments to their pro-posed vision of systemic change (such as opting for voluntary national rather than state content standards), while still maintaining the conceptual integrity of their overall approach. But if new components are added, such as an emphasis on early childhood education or the provision of comprehensive student health services, it may be better to designate these as supplements to systemic reform rather than trying to expand and redefine the concept itself.[69]

The concept of systemic reform has much to recommend it. Systemic reform recognizes the importance of voluntary national content standards and assessments, but it is also willing to let states develop their own curriculum frameworks and tests. It builds on the increasingly active and effective role of states in promoting some local school improvements while simultaneously tying national and state initiatives to other reforms. By stressing that the new standards frameworks should emphasize higher-order thinking skills as well as a deeper knowledge of subject-specific content, systemic reform properly attempts to unite broad curriculum improvements with site-based school restructuring efforts. Moreover, systemic reform is premised on the belief that all children can learn and that every student must be given equal and adequate access to both the new curriculum materials and effective teachers. Systemic reform recognizes the central role of teachers in any reform effort and calls for providing adequate resources and training for their professional development. Thus, systemic reform attempts to align the curriculum, student assessment, and teacher preparation into a coherent and comprehensive effort to help all students achieve high standards of excellence.

Whereas the potential benefits of systemic reform have received considerable attention, the possible shortcomings or limitations of this approach have generated less discussion. This is unfortunate. If the implementation of systemic reform is to have its intended positive effect on student learning within the American educational system, these weaknesses must be explored thoroughly and any necessary adjustments and improvements introduced quickly.

First of all, it is important to remember that while systemic reform provides a promising and plausible way of improving public schooling, it remains largely untested and unproven in the field. As Smith and O'Day have pointed out, most of the components of systemic reform have been so recently developed and implemented that there has been little opportunity to discover what impact they are having on students. Therefore, it is necessary to maintain considerable flexibility and open-mindedness in the implementation of systemic reform at the state and local levels and to be prepared to make adjustments on the basis of new information from related research or from direct experiences in the field.

Systemic reform relies heavily on the development of voluntary national and state curriculum standards. But when will such standards be available at the local level? And will the standards be coordinated sufficiently to form a coherent curriculum? Although considerable progress has been made in the creation of a set of national standards, much remains to be done. The National Council of Teachers of Mathematics has created standards for mathematics; standards for history have been completed; but standards for English may require several more years of preparation as the current contract for developing them has been terminated.[70] In addition, despite all of the rhetoric about coordination among different subject areas, most of the standards have been developed in relative isolation and without recognizing that other subjects must be taught as well.[71] A common complaint is that most disciplines involved in the creation of national standards have been too ambitious and are creating standards that will be difficult to implement fully given the limited time actually available for their subjects in most classrooms.[72]

Most of the discussions of systemic reform have focused on the benefits of having a common national or state curriculum. But what about the schools that have already successfully implemented local curriculum reforms? The Accelerated Schools Program (invented by Henry Levin), the School Development Program (created by James Comer), and the Coalition for Essential Schools (initiated by Theodore Sizer), for example, have reached well over 500 schools and are still expanding. Each of these reform efforts has its own guidelines. Will the imposition of a new set of standards hinder or threaten these reforms? Although the number of schools affected or the extent of their inconvenience may be small, they represent some of the most innovative and progressive schools in the nation. Therefore, proponents of systemic reform should explore ways of working with these reform-minded institutions to preserve and enhance their achievements.[73]

The O'Day-Smith model calls for state standards, but it allows considerable leeway at the school level for the sequencing of courses within the curriculum and how the courses are taught. This attempt at helpful flexibility could pose serious problems for students who move from one school to another. Approximately 17 percent of five- to nine-year-olds and 14 percent of ten- to fourteen-year-olds move each year, and a sizable proportion of these move to another county.[74] While systemic reform will reduce some of the educational dislocation felt by children who move, it will not eliminate it entirely (in some European countries that have more rigid national curricula, educational disruptions due to moving are less of a problem). Moreover, since systemic reform will allow states to produce curriculum frameworks that are considerably different from one another in such areas as social studies, there will be important implications for the proposed more coordinated and effective system of teacher preparation. Teachers trained to teach social studies in Michigan, for example, may not be prepared for the more discipline-oriented focus of the California curriculum.

And what about the development of an adequate assessment system for the new standards? As it is difficult to develop assessments before the curriculum framework is in place, it is clear that it will be some time before the assessment components of systemic reform can be completed. It is difficult to see how systemic reform can be fully in place within the next decade if we need to develop valid assessments.[75] Given the difficulty of developing and validating tests, much time and money will be needed for each state to develop its own assessment systems.[76] And it must be decided how often to test students. Would once, twice, or three times during their K–12 school years be best?[77] In view of these complexities, would it be more practical to work initially on a single national test rather than fifty state tests or even several regional ones?[78]

As states are free to create their own standards and assessments, will they stray into areas other than the core academic subjects identified in the eight national education goals? Some states have tried to establish standards that deal with student values and attitudes.[79] Critics attack these proposed outcomes-based standards as too vague, nonacademic, or threatening to more traditional family values. As George Kaplan, an analyst of the Christian Right and public education, explained:

> One does not have to be a zealot of the Religious Right to wonder who decided that public school bureaucrats—rather than parents and churches—should build children's self-worth and teach them what family and civic values are all about. These are red flags to the Christian Right. Adding insult to legitimate doubt, some state officeholders gave OBE's [outcomes-based-education] opponents too little time to air their objections, dealt high-handedly with them, and saturated OBE documents with educational jargon. This bureaucratic insensitivity only added fuel to the fire. Already disturbed by the sweep and depth of the new threat to schooling as they conceived it and to family solidarity as well, the Religious Right and its allies were also good and sore at the people who devised it.[80]

Thus, a small, but vocal group of citizens are challenging the entire outcomes-based reform approach and are increasingly forcing policymakers to reverse or slow down some portions of the systemic reform initiatives.[81]

One of the most important and difficult issues that will have to be resolved concerns the rewards and penalties for students, teachers, and local schools as they face these new tests and are judged to have succeeded or failed. Smith and O'Day have not spelled out exactly what should happen to individuals or institutions that do not perform adequately on the proposed state assessments; yet many of the high expectations for as well as the fears of systemic reform are based on what will be the nature and extent of the stakes involved. Testing systems in Europe and Japan are influential because they have a significant impact on the future educational and career opportunities of the students, yet many people in this country strongly oppose anything resembling the high-stakes examinations that are given abroad.[82] As a result, many proponents of systemic reform in the United States fear that evaluations of student, teacher, or school performances will be substantially weakened for fear of offending some-one. As a result, these assessments may become almost meaningless in prac-tice.[83]

Everyone agrees that all students should have the opportunity to learn. Yet if students are not given the opportunity to be exposed to the new curriculum or to have an effective teacher, it is unlikely they will be able to master the new standards. But there is considerable disagreement over the nature of the oppor-tunity to learn standards as well as the accountability of schools in meeting them. This disagreement stems, in part, from the fact that there is little compel-ling evidence that many of the older and more traditional indicators of school inputs have much of a direct impact on improving student outcomes.[84]

O'Day and Smith have a relatively narrow view of opportunity to learn standards that is based on all students having access to classes in the appropriate areas and to instructors competent to teach those materials. Other policy-makers provide longer, more specific lists of required classroom and school conditions. The danger exists, of course, that rigidly imposing an excessive number of opportunity to learn standards will stifle the initiative and freedom in local schools and classrooms that is often touted as an essential component of systemic reform.

Given the limited experience with and research on the proven effectiveness of any particular set of opportunity to learn standards, it is important to proceed very cautiously in this area. Focusing on providing equitable resources or on the notion of value added by the teacher and school might be a prudent beginning. Before any rigid and narrow opportunity to learn standards are imposed on schools, there should be convincing evidence that they are essential for systemic reform. Moreover, if the development and implementation of new assessments are sidelined until appropriate opportunity to learn standards are in place, then systemic reform efforts will be delayed considerably.[85]

Smith and O'Day have acknowledged that many local schools have developed effective reforms, but they argue that most of these reforms will not survive and that many other schools have shown little inclination toward comprehensive schoolwide reforms. Therefore, they believe that statewide systemic reforms are needed to stimulate and maintain such local reforms as school restructuring. Although their arguments are plausible to a certain extent, they are not entirely convincing. As Smith pointed out in his earlier writings, we do not have much conclusive evidence on what combination of local, state, or federal factors are necessary for stimulating and maintaining school reforms. Many of the earlier efforts at fostering comprehensive school-level changes, such as the Ford Foundation's Comprehensive School Improvement Program, the Experimental Schools Program, Individually Guided Education, and the Effective Schools approach failed to have the large and lasting impact their proponents had predicted.[86]

The idea of systemic reform as a stimulant for local school changes may sound promising and plausible, but almost no scientifically rigorous evidence has been brought forward to support this claim. Moreover, despite the fact that the issue of school reform diffusion and maintenance is a crucial component of the rationale for systemic reform, most discussions of this issue have been limited and somewhat cursory. Is systemic reform the best or only way to stimulate and sustain local school improvements? Will systemic reform impact schools and students the same way in all localities, or will hostile or indifferent administrators and teachers in the less reform-oriented schools subvert or circumvent the proposed initiatives?[87] Are there other ways of supporting local reform efforts, such as working through the ten federally funded regional educational laboratories or restructuring the federally sponsored National Diffusion Network, that are equally or more effective in facilitating site-based innovations?[88] In other words, we need to move from general and theoretical discussions of the potential impact of systemic reform on local schools to a more specific and focused analysis of the ties between statewide education mandates and local school and teacher responses.[89]

Moreover, some local reforms that were introduced in the late 1980s and early 1990s may not be as successful as their proponents had hoped. For example, the transfer of power to elected local school districts has not met initial expectations in terms of improved student outcomes. A recent review of the Chicago public schools concludes: "Despite the radical reform legislation and the transfer of considerable power to local school councils, there has scarcely been any demonstrable progress on outcome goals. Chicago schools continue to rank very low by national standards—even those of other big cities."[90]

The failure of any particular set of local reforms does not necessarily invalidate the plausibility of systemic reform, especially since some of these efforts have not incorporated all the key elements of systemic reform. There may be a danger, however, that policymakers and the public will become discouraged about any school reforms if they see highly touted local reforms, such as the one in the Chicago, fail to make any significant improvements in student outcomes. A growing skepticism about particular, well-publicized school reforms may indirectly diminish the support for other educational innovations such as systemic reform.[91]

If proponents of systemic reform have called attention to several potentially important and seemingly workable approaches for improving student learning, they have also often ignored other avenues for reform. Indeed, many policymakers who have endorsed the concept of systemic reform have acknowledged that it is not sufficient by itself to improve our educational system adequately. For example, Colorado Governor Roy Romer testified that: "High national standards and a system of assessments, while critically important, are not panaceas for the Nation's educational problems. Other elements of reform are necessary to enable us to reach high standards of achievement, including professional development, technology, incentives, early intervention strategies, and reducing health and social barriers to learning."[92]

One important factor that has been neglected by the proponents of systemic reform is the role parents play in the education of their children. There is considerable evidence that parents are essential elements in the education of children. Many analysts argue that parents play a more important role in the education of their children than the schools.[93] Yet most discussions of systemic reform do not give thorough attention to the role of parents and how they can be encouraged to become more active and effective partners with the schools in educating children. As a result, the public may receive the mistaken impression that school curriculum and assessment reforms by themselves will lead to improved student learning.[94]

A related issue is the question of motivating students to learn. Many analysts of international comparisons of schooling and student achievement, for example, argue that American children are less motivated to do well in school than their counterparts overseas. American culture simply does not place the same value on education that European or Japanese societies do.[95] Systemic reform will increase public awareness of education and reinforce the belief that schooling is vital to our nation, but we also need to find ways of motivating students in the classroom.[96] Moreover, there is growing concern that imposing high-stakes student testing may actually produce negative effects on student motivation.[97]

International comparisons have shown that differences in how students and teachers use their time in school plays an important role in their education. Students in other postindustrial democracies, for example, receive twice as much instruction on academic subjects than those in the United States.[98] Similarly, while teachers in countries like Japan have larger classes than their counterparts in the United States, the Japanese teachers are provided with more time to develop lesson plans and to learn from each other.[99] As the National Education Commission on Time and Learning has put it: "Time is the missing element in our great national debate about learning and the need for higher standards for all students. Our schools and the people involved with them—students, teachers, administrators, parents, and staff—are prisoners of time, captives of the school clock and calendar. We have been asking the impossible of our students—that they learn as much as their foreign peers while spending only half as much time in core academic subjects. The reform movement of the last decade is destined to flounder unless it is harnessed to more time for learning."[100]

There is growing research evidence that much of the learning gap between children from advantaged and disadvantaged homes occurs during the summer. The same research shows that this gap cannot be closed by sending these children to existing summer schools.[101] The proponents of systemic reform do not address this issue directly, but they implicitly assume that most learning improvements will occur within a classroom during the regular school year. The lack of attention to summer learning loss is particularly unfortunate, because this may be a major factor hindering the achievement of children from low-income families.

Many of the advocates of systemic reform have listed school environment as an essential factor in the learning outcomes of students. Safety, class size, libraries, laboratories, and computers have all been mentioned as important elements for the reform of schools. For example, O'Day and Smith place particular emphasis on the need for physical safety in the schools, but they do not use smaller class size or the presence of a school library as part of their opportunity to learn standards. It is not clear why some elements of the school and classroom environment are sometimes seen as an integral part of systemic reform while others are not mentioned.

Most discussions of systemic reform tend to treat each level of K–12 schooling as relatively equal in importance to overall learning. Reforms for the third grade, for example, appear to be given the same significance as those for the eighth grade. But are some periods of schooling particularly crucial for learning—such as the early years in school (perhaps K–4)? And are some aspects of childhood education, such as school readiness and the Head Start Program, especially critical?[102] By not considering in any detail the relative importance of different phases of schooling or child development, the advocates of systemic reform do not offer educators or policymakers much guidance in how to most efficiently allocate their scarce public school resources.

The opportunity to learn standards usually focus rather narrowly on having students be exposed to adequate curriculum materials and good teachers. But what about other problems that students from poor families may be experiencing, such as the lack of adequate medical or nutritional services? Can systemic reform really equalize the opportunities for these children without also addressing the social and health problems they bring into the classroom? For example, under what conditions can pregnant teenagers and young mothers hope to learn and compete effectively with their peers in the schools?[103] Considerations such as these have led some states to supplement their curriculum-oriented systemic reform efforts with the call for comprehensive social and health services for children from low-income families.

Perhaps one of the more disappointing aspects of the movement toward systemic reform today is the lack of much reliable research-based information on school effectiveness. Moreover, while everyone agrees that considerable research will be needed to provide guidance on the effectiveness of different approaches to systemic reform in various settings, there is little evidence that much of this work is being undertaken or even being contemplated. For example, the Office of Educational Research and Improvement, which in the late 1960s and mid-1970s spent considerable funds on the systematic development of educational products and processes, no longer emphasizes development.[104] Indeed, systematic, large-scale development has all but disappeared from the OERI-funded research and development centers or the regional educational laboratories.[105] As a result, when efforts will be made to implement, test, and adjust systemic reform throughout the nation, policymakers will receive little guidance or assistance from educational research.[106]

We are in the midst of an exciting and challenging period of educational reform. The American public and policymakers alike seem more committed than ever to improving the educational prospects of our children and are even willing to try new ways of restructuring curricula and schools. It is especially encouraging to see partnerships at the federal, state, and local levels working to produce more coherent and integrated reforms for American schools.

The concept of systemic reform has both described and stimulated recent educational reform efforts. Although there is still considerable disagreement and confusion over exactly what systemic reform means in theory and in practice, the general contours of this effort are becoming clearer—expanding the role of states in public education, emphasizing content standards-driven reforms, closely integrating intellectually challenging curriculum and assessments, believing that all students can learn, and providing the opportunity for all students to learn.

If systemic reform is to have any hope of long-term success in local schools and classrooms, it is imperative to conduct more thorough research and to initiate large-scale education development projects to help us learn which components of systemic reform, if any, are most effective in helping all children to learn. Meanwhile, in the absence of such important information, we must exercise considerable caution and humility in any attempt to implement systemic reform at the state and local levels today. We must also be prepared to acknowledge, if necessary, any overall limitations of systemic reform as a general strategy if the key assumptions upon which it is based become untenable in light of subsequent analyses or experiences.

Systemic reform by itself probably will not improve the education of our children sufficiently to reach all eight national education goals by the year 2000, but it may be a useful step toward a genuine but gradual improvement in the nation's schools. By thoughtfully and judiciously combining systemic reform with other essential aspects of learning, such as improved parental involvement, enhanced summer learning opportunities, expanded and improved early childhood education, or the provision of comprehensive social and health services for children from low-income families, perhaps we may be able to improve the learning of all children.

Chapter 8 A Life-Course Framework for Analyzing Educational Research Projects

One of the problems in investigating educational research and reforms from a broader, historical perspective is the lack of an appropriate overall framework for categorizing and analyzing the relevant information. Part of the difficulty is that we often need to look simultaneously at individual and aggregate levels but lack a conceptual framework that can encompass both. Another problem is that many analysts look only at selected aspects of education, frequently focusing exclusively on the roles of the classroom or the school on student outcomes, but do not try to place their subjects within a broader context. Finally, most investigators have not employed a conceptual map that can take into account a developing and aging individual who is influenced by a dynamic and often rapidly changing social structure.

To develop an appropriate framework for mapping and analyzing long-term research and reform priorities, perhaps we should focus our attention on the individual we are trying to educate while at the same time taking into consideration a myriad of factors that may influence that person's life (such as family, local school, and friends). Drawing on recent conceptual and empirical work on the life course, the proposed framework will follow the lives of the individuals while taking into account the various contextual and institutional factors that help shape their experiences. Although other conceptual schemes for organizing research and reform priorities may be plausible, the advantage of a life-course approach is that it places the child at the center without neglecting the roles of outside influences on his or her development and education. This life-course perspective may be useful to policymakers and analysts as they try to comprehend and visualize educational developments in a broader and more dynamic manner.

In this chapter I shall mention some of the schemes that education analysts have used, as well as trace the development of life-course analysis in disciplines like sociology, before presenting and discussing the proposed life-course framework. This framework was initially developed to facilitate planning for the Office of Educational Research and Improvement's five-year research priorities plan, but it should be useful and applicable in other circumstances as well.[1] Finally, I shall examine the recent OERI public announcement of the proposed seven new research and development centers using the life-course framework in order to explore the potential strengths and weaknesses of this approach.

DEVELOPMENT OF A LIFE-COURSE PERSPECTIVE

Most analysts have not needed an overall framework for studying educational changes because they focus primarily on particular grades in school or on specific issues. Many scholars analyze only specific phases of education, such as preschools, elementary schools, middle schools, high schools, or postsecondary institutions. Others investigate only certain topics, such as studying the history or mathematics curriculum or analyzing the nature of classroom discipline (and usually they consider these issues within the context of only a few grades in school). There are a few educators who do consider the bigger picture and try to analyze the entire educational system. For example, proponents of systemic reform look at the alignment between local and state curriculum and assessment practices. But even these investigators usually do not provide much detail on how these broader institutional or curricular changes actually will affect the lives of students in those schools.[2]

Many existing educational frameworks focus more on the interactions between educational institutions or among educators than on the impact these changes will have on individual pupils. Instead of being child-centered, these schemes analyze how curriculum is developed and implemented or how teachers are trained (with the explicit or implicit assumption that such improvements will eventually enhance the quality of schooling each child receives). Moreover, most of the existing educational frameworks concentrate on the role of teachers and schooling, but they ignore many other important influences on the child. Frequently the role of parents is acknowledged but not fully appreciated or analyzed. Such potential outside-of-school influences as after-school activities, summer learning, or social services are usually omitted or minimized.

Finally, even many child-centered approaches tend to look at a specific, short time period in a particular setting. Analysts recognize, for example, the diversity of children attending the fifth or sixth grade, but they sometimes fail to appreciate the varied paths and experiences that led those children into those classrooms. These conceptual schemes often fail to provide or encourage a dynamic and nuanced view of different children developing and progressing through our educational systems. Thus, the current educational frameworks may provide adequate models for handling the particular needs of the investigators, but they do not provide the broad and dynamic child-centered framework necessary for developing and mapping an agency's long-term research priorities.

Creating a broader and more flexible framework for understanding human development has not been confined to investigators of education. Indeed, much of the most innovative work in this area has come from sociologists like Evelyn Duvall and Reuben Hill, who developed models of the family life cycle in the 1940s and 1950s.[3] They created six- or nine-stage family life cycle models that reflected mainly changes in childbearing or child rearing based on some of the experiences of the youngest and oldest child. Such models often incorporated the entry of the oldest child into school as well as the departure of the youngest from the school. Among the advantages of the family life cycle approach was that it looked at the family as whole, acknowledged the importance of changes over time in the economic well-being of the family, and recognized the importance to the family of children entering and leaving school.

Although family life cycle models continue to be used, most scholars have abandoned them as too limited and inflexible. The focus on only one or two of the activities of the youngest or oldest child is seen as too confining. Yet to incorporate more activities and more children complicates considerably any family life cycle model. For example, Roy Rodgers expanded the Duvall and

Hill family life cycle models by including more changes in the experiences of the youngest as well as the oldest child; but this led to an unwieldy twenty-four-stage family cycle model. Family life cycle models also do not incorporate such other important developments as career changes or being in a single-parent household.[4]

Rather than trying to model changes in families over time, most scholars now concentrate on following individuals as they age. This approach, developed mainly in the 1970s and 1980s by sociologists and social psychologists is commonly referred to as life-course analysis (or life-span psychology). A useful summary of the life course is provided by Glen Elder, one of its most articulate and active proponents:

> The life course refers to pathways through the age-differentiated life span, to social patterns in the timing, duration, spacing, and order of events; the timing of an event may be as consequential for life experience as whether the event occurs and the degree or type of change. Age differentiation is manifested in expectations and options that impinge on decision processes and the course of events that give shape to life stages, transitions, and turning points. Such differentiation is based in part on the social meanings of age and the biological facts of birth, sexual maturity, and death. These meanings have varied through social history and across cultures at points in time, as documented by evidence on socially recognized age categories, grades, and classes. . . . Over the life course, age differentiation also occurs through the interplay of demographic and economic processes, as in the relation between economic swings and the timing of family events. Sociocultural, demographic and material factors are essential elements in a theory of life-course variation.[5]

The life-course perspective follows the aging and development of the individual while simultaneously taking into consideration the relevant contextual settings. It emphasizes the need to focus on important transitions (many of which are roughly age-graded) that the individual must make as she or he moves through different aspects of our society. Methodologically life-course analysis tends to follow age-cohorts of individuals longitudinally in order to understand the multiple pathways in which people led their lives. Most recently life-course analysis has stressed the importance of seeing the interactions between the developing individual and the organizations and social norms that facilitate and constrain the experiences of that person.[6]

Surprisingly, life-course analysis has not been as widely used by educators as by scholars in the other disciplines. But there are some important recent examples from the field of education that demonstrate the analytic power and utility of a life-course perspective. Indeed, there is every reason to believe that life-course analysis will become a permanent and prominent feature of educational research.

One of the more powerful and innovative examples of life-course analysis is the study of the effects of not promoting students in the first eight grades. Following a stratified cohort of 800 first-grade students in Baltimore public schools since 1982, Karl Alexander, Doris Entwisle, and Susan Dauber document the multiple pathways in which children advance through the first eight grades in school (and a sizable proportion left the Baltimore public schools altogether). Given the fact that approximately 40 percent of these students were held back at least once during that period, the multiple paths these students followed were quite diverse.[7] Using a life-course approach, Alexander and his colleagues try to ascertain whether those students who were retained fared better or worse than if they had been promoted. In spite of the seemingly insurmountable problems of developing appropriate control groups and measures of success, the authors carefully and thoughtfully analyze their data and arrive at a startling and at an undoubtedly controversial finding: "Instead of impeding their progress, repeating a grade helped retainees do better in their repeated year and for some years thereafter, although in diminishing amounts, until they made the transition into middle school. Rather than harming these children emotionally, retention led to improvement in their attitudes about self and school during the repeated year, and gave children a boost that often persisted until middle school."[8]

Similarly, in an in-depth, longitudinal analysis of all British children born during one week in March 1958, Alan Kerckhoff studies the cumulative effects of children being sent to particular schools or placed in certain ability groups. Tracing the lives of this birth-cohort through age twenty-three, Kerckhoff demonstrates the impact of parental background and of educational institutions on the life course of these children in school and in the labor force:

> There is abundant evidence in the earlier chapters of the significant effects of institutional arrangements on individual achievements. All of the analyses at each life course stage showed the same pattern of results. Even after controlling for an extensive list of individual characteristics and antecedent experiences at the beginning of each stage, those in some structural locations had higher achievements and those in other locations had lower achievements. The two most important features of the observed structural effects were their occurrence at every stage and their tendency to be cumulative. The analyses presented here have not clarified the reasons for those effects, but they have left no doubt about their size, pervasiveness, and cumulative impact on early adult outcomes.[9]

The work of Alexander, Entwisle, and Dauber demonstrates the importance and usefulness of using life-course analysis to study schooling. The complex pattern of school attendance as children age also reminds us of the diversity of educational careers and the need to contextualize the experiences of children. Moreover, their work is a model for seeing how the lives of children are influenced by the different types of curriculum and classroom settings to which they are exposed. Kerckhoff's analysis has also made a powerful conceptual and empirical case for the need to look at the interaction of individual and structural factors over time in order to understand the educational development of children and young adults, with particular attention to the cumulative effects of institutional education arrangements on the life course.

A LIFE-COURSE FRAMEWORK

Drawing on the life-course perspective, we can develop an overall framework for education that analyzes the lives of individuals as well as the impact of institutions that affect them directly and indirectly. The focus is on the individual, but some of the most immediate and direct influences on that individual—his or her local school, family, work, and other influences—are also considered (see figure 8.1). Although the life-course approach emphasizes the interactions between individuals and their immediate environment, it also acknowledges that the immediate organizations and norms that directly affect individuals are in turn influenced by broader and more distant factors, such as government activities, economic developments, social developments, and school-related activities (naturally the direction of influence in reality is two-way, but the diagram has been simplified to reflect influence only in a single, downward manner).

First, we should focus our attention on the developing individual and the factors that affect him or her most directly. The proposed framework for looking at an individual consists of a grid or matrix of the activities as that person ages (see table 8.1). In the fifth column from the left-hand side, the age of the individual is traced from birth to death (zero to 80 years as an illustration). One can then think of that column as representing the life course of an individual.

In the column next to age, the typical grade in school that an individual might be expected to attend is noted (ranging from preschool through graduate work). As United States schools are fairly closely age-graded today, the correspondence between the ages of the individual and her or his grade in school is

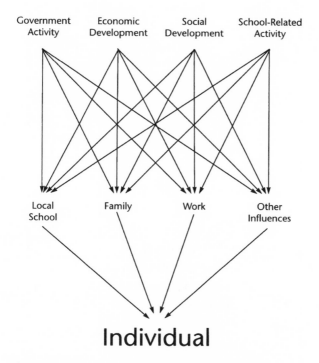

Figure 8.1. Life-Course Framework for Analyzing OERI Research Priorities

reasonably close.[10] But we do need to remind ourselves that for some populations, as in the case of the urban Baltimore sample described earlier, that correspondence is less than perfect. Moreover, not everyone is likely to attend college or graduate school; at the more advanced ages, the patterns of schooling are likely to be more erratic and unpredictable. Nevertheless, being able to designate approximate grades of pupils reminds us of the dynamics of the life course as children pass up the age-graded educational ladder and allows us to connect conceptually changes in the life course with patterns of school attendance.[11]

To the left of the age column, are four aspects of individual development that might be particularly important and interesting to us—physical development, cognitive development, emotional development, and moral development.[12] Naturally, one might think of other aspects of individual development that should be listed, or one could subdivide any one of these categories further for a particular analysis. If we were to focus on cognitive development, for example, it might be useful to subdivide that category according to six major, different

Table 8.1 Mapping an Individual's Life Course

Individual						Outside Influences																					
Age	Grade	Physical Development	Cognitive Development	Emotional Development	Moral Development	Local School									Family				Peers	Other Influences						Work	
						Teachers	Curriculum	Classrooms	Special Programs	School Environment	School Leadership	School Libraries	Social Services	Assessments	Parental Resources	Parental Involvement	Parental Characteristics	New Family Responsibilities		Media	Social Services	After-School Activities	Summer Learning	Public Libraries	Neighborhood	Nature of Job	On-the-job Training
0																											
1																											
2																											
3	preschool																										
4	preschool																										
5	kindergarten																										
6	1st grade																										

7	2d grade																							
8	3d grade																							
9	4th grade																							
10	5th grade																							
11	6th grade																							
12	7th grade																							
13	8th grade																							
14	9th grade																							
15	10th grade																							
16	11th grade																							
17	12th grade																							
18	college																							
19	college																							
20	college																							
21	college																							
22	graduate																							
23	graduate																							

(continued)

Table 8.1 Continued

	Individual						Outside Influences																								
							Local School									Family				Other Influences							Work	
	Physical Development	Cognitive Development	Emotional Development	Moral Development	Age	Grade	Teachers	Curriculum	Classrooms	Special Programs	School Environment	School Leadership	School Libraries	Social Services	Assessments	Parental Resources	Parental Involvement	Parental Characteristics	New Family Responsibilities	Peers	Media	Social Services	After-School Activities	Summer Learning	Public Libraries	Neighborhood	Nature of Job	On-the-job Training
					24	graduate																						
					25	graduate																						
					26																							
					.																							
					.																							
					79																							
					80																							

theories of intellectual development: (1) psychometric, (2) Piagetian, (3) neo-Piagetian, (4) information-processing, (5) learning, and (6) contextual.[13]

The first four columns on the left, representing facets of the individual, concentrate on changes within that individual and allow us to see how those developments might affect his or her learning over time. Much of this type of research is done by biologists, psychologists, and child development experts who are studying the life course or life span (the two words are sometimes used interchangeably) of the person. It is impossible conceptually or practically, of course, to isolate individual development from the social and historical context in which it occurs. Thus, one might study individual cognitive development within a classroom setting. But the emphasis in the left-hand portion of the matrix is more on the individual developing than on the impact of outside institutions on the life course of that person (which are categorized in the columns to the right of the age-column).

On the right of the age and grade columns are some local and most immediate institutions and settings which may have the most impact on the educational development of that person—the local school, family, other outside influences, and work experiences. The categories designated here represent some of the more important influences, but one could easily expand them to incorporate any necessary additional factors.

Each of these broad influences are then subdivided further for analytic purposes. Thus, the local school the individual attends might be subdivided into her teacher(s), the curriculum, the classroom(s), participation in a special education program, the overall school environment, the leadership of the school (usually the role of the principal), the nature of the school library, any social services received in school (such as school lunches or assistance from a school health program), and the assessment system (including both routine classroom grading practices and periodic outside assessments). Naturally, one could add or subtract from such a list or subdivide some of these categories further. For example, in some investigations one might want to divide the curriculum into smaller divisions, such as social studies or math and science. Similarly, one could differentiate among the social services provided for students in a particular school.

The logic of the resultant matrix consists of following the life course down the age column and then seeing what factors contribute to an individual's personal development as well as what impact institutions might have on the development of that person. It focuses only on those research activities that have as their focus looking at an individual developing or at the immediate institutions and norms that might affect her. Thus, the life-course matrix in table 8.1 allows one to plot any particular research activity on the basis of the age (or grade) of the intended pupil and the appropriate corresponding aspects of individual development or the influence of the immediate institutional activity or setting (such as classroom conditions or the curriculum offerings).

Using this matrix, one could map proposed research projects with a focus on the individual student or learning adult to see where one is investing its resources. One also can see what cells have been filled by existing projects and which ones remain empty. Rather than just placing a check mark in a cell where there is proposed activity, one could actually place the dollar amount allocated for that task to get a better sense of relative priorities. Thus, this matrix provides an opportunity to map the activities of a single project or of a combination of projects to provide a better sense of the overall research priorities of the agency focusing on the individual learner.

A particularly important benefit of this scheme is that it implicitly reveals where in the life course one thinks someone might intervene in order to improve the education and training of children. If one thought, for example, that the most strategic point for intervention was early childhood, then one would expect that many research activities would be focused on that time period. Similarly, if one hypothesized that parental involvement in school or the period of summer learning were especially crucial, then the resultant research priorities might be expected to occupy those cells in the matrix to a large degree (though, of course, considerations of what other agencies are doing, as well as the potential for research breakthroughs should also be taken into account).[14]

By itself the proposed life-course matrix does not necessarily provide much specific guidance on where educational interventions may be the most effective. Indeed, one could think of the matrix as a fairly neutral and simple framework which categorizes various school improvement activities by the age of the child or individual. Yet by drawing on the conceptual logic of life-course perspective, it does sensitize us to the changing needs of the developing child and the varied immediate influences on that person (including many that are outside the purview of the local school system). Moreover, the life-course perspective, with its emphasis on the importance of individuals making timely and appropriate transitions, also suggests that we may want to look closely at certain segments of the life course that are particularly important potential turning points in the normal educational experiences of children. Analyses of education suggest that such transitions as entering the formal school system, moving into the middle

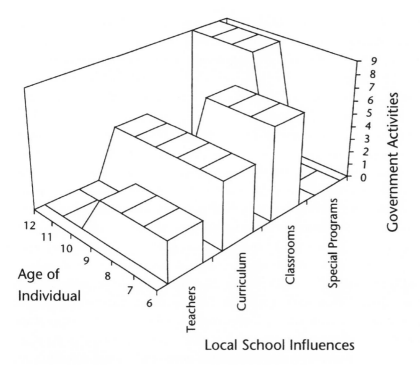

Figure 8.2. Government Activities to Improve Local School Influences
on the Life Course of an Individual

grades, going into high school, and leaving school for work are especially
important passages that may significantly affect the long-term educational and
career trajectories of individuals.[15]

The conceptual thrust of life-course analysis is to focus on the interactions
between the developing individual and the institutions immediately affecting
that person. Yet we all know that these institutions—the local school, family, or
work—are themselves affected by outside forces (and to a somewhat lesser
degree by the individual under scrutiny). Perhaps we can visualize this more
complex interaction by looking at figure 8.2, which depicts the aging individual
on the y-axis and the local school influences (teachers, curriculum, classrooms,
and special programs) on the x-axis. On the z-axis, for purposes of illustration,
are government activities designed to improve teachers, curriculum, classrooms, or special programs. (Instead of government initiatives, we might have
denoted such factors as school-related activities by foundations or professional
groups.) For example, the government programs represented in figure 8.2
might be designed to improve the skills of elementary school teachers or to

reform the curriculum of students aged six to twelve. Thus, one might visualize broader and more general programs to influence teachers or curriculum as represented by a plane that is perpendicular to the two-dimensional plane created by the intersection of the life course of the individual (e.g., aging of the individual) and the local institutions or activities that affect that person directly (e.g., teachers or curriculum).

Because it is cumbersome to diagram and difficult to follow a three-dimensional figure, it is probably more useful to create a two-dimensional table displaying some of the factors affecting the local institutions and activities that influence the life course of an individual (see table 8.2). For example, we might list on the x-axis a series of school-related activities, such as efforts to improve teachers, the curriculum, students assessments, or special school programs. These represent some major programs and activities that influence educational change at the macro-level. Teachers, curriculum, and student assessments are listed in both tables 8.1 and 8.2 because they can either affect the individual life course directly or be viewed as larger educational institutions or activities. Parental resources, however, play a prominent role in the life course of the individual (table 8.1) but are omitted in table 8.2 because educational policymakers have relatively little impact on the extent and nature of parental resources. Federal, state, and local school district regulations and funding, in contrast, were not depicted as direct influences on the life course, but they play an important role in the structuring and financing of local educational institutions (and therefore appear in table 8.2).

On the y-axis it might be useful to employ categories that would enable us to analyze larger institutions and groups. One might, for instance, provide a set of organizational and program subdivisions within an agency like OERI (for example, the five institutes, NCES, the regional educational laboratories, Fund for the Improvement of Education [FIE], Star Schools, National Diffusion Network [NDN], and the library programs). Mapping on this matrix would give us a good idea of the distribution of activities across the different programs.

Or, one might subdivide the tasks by the general levels of schooling they address—preschool, elementary school, middle school, high school, and postsecondary education. A division along these lines would encourage us to think more clearly and carefully about targeting our efforts to the different levels of education in our current school system. If one wanted further specification on grade level for certain programs, we could develop a matrix that employs the specific grades as outlined in table 8.3. On the one hand, one might want to think of an activity—teacher professionalization, for example—in broad terms

Table 8.2 Mapping Efforts to Influence Institutions and Activities That May Affect an Individual's Educational Development, by OERI Units, Level of Schooling, and Type of Activity

OERI Units	School-Related Activities											Other Activities							Government Activities												
	Teachers	Curriculum	Student Assessments	Special School Programs	School Physical Facilities	School Environment	School Libraries	Parental School Activities	School Management	School Finances	Alternative Schools	Social Services	Media (TV, film, newspapers)	Parental Involvement	Summer Learning Programs	Public Libraries	Adult Literacy Programs	Job Training Programs	Federal Regulations	Federal Funding	Federal Guidance	State Regulations	State Funding	State Coordination	State Curriculum	State Assessments	State Guidance	School District Regulations	School District Funding	School District Management	School District Guidance
Early childhood																															
At-risk																															
Student learning																															
Post secondary																															
Governance																															
NCES																															
Laboratories																															

(continued)

Table 8.2 Continued

	School-Related Activities												Other Activities						Government Activities												
	Teachers	Curriculum	Student Assessments	Special School Programs	School Physical Facilities	School Environment	School Libraries	Parental School Activities	School Management	School Finances	Alternative Schools	Social Services	Media (TV, film, newspapers)	Parental Involvement	Summer Learning Programs	Public Libraries	Adult Literacy Programs	Job Training Programs	Federal Regulations	Federal Funding	Federal Guidance	State Regulations	State Funding	State Coordination	State Curriculum	State Assessments	State Guidance	School District Regulations	School District Funding	School District Management	School District Guidance
FIE																															
Star schools																															
NDN																															
Other ORAD[a]																															
Library programs																															
Other OERI																															
Level of Schooling																															

Preschool															
Elementary															
Middle															
High school															
Postsecondary															
Type of Activity															
Policy analysis															
Basic research															
Applied research															
Development															
Statistics															
Technical assistance															
Dissemination															

[a]Office of Reform Assistance and Dissemination

Table 8.3 Mapping Efforts to Influence Institutions and Activities That May Affect an Individual's Educational Development, by Grade Level

Grade Level	School-Related Activities											Other Activities							Government Activities												
	Teachers	Curriculum	Student Assessments	Special School Programs	School Physical Facilities	School Environment	School Libraries	Parental School Activities	School Management	School Finances	Alternative Schools	Social Services	Media (TV, film, newspapers)	Parental Involvement	Summer Learning Programs	Public Libraries	Adult Literacy Programs	Job Training Programs	Federal Regulations	Federal Funding	Federal Guidance	State Regulations	State Funding	State Coordination	State Curriculum	State Assessments	State Guidance	School District Regulations	School District Funding	School District Management	School District Guidance
Preschool																															
Kindergarten																															
1st grade																															
2d grade																															
3d grade																															
4th grade																															
5th grade																															
6th grade																															

	7th grade	8th grade	9th grade	10th grade	11th grade	12th grade	College	College	College	College	Graduate education

across all K–12 grades when looking at a topic like state licensing of teachers. On the other hand, one might target K–4 teachers for special training in child development because of their crucial role in providing an adequate start for all students in school.

Another alternative would be to look at the different types of activities undertaken (see table 8.2). Similar to the questions asked on the current PMIS system in OERI, we could plot whether a particular activity might be considered as policy analysis, basic research, applied research, systematic development, data and statistical collection, technical assistance, or dissemination. As in the PMIS system, we could subdivide any individual project to reflect the approximate division of effort in each category. Assigning weights for any grantee or project is somewhat crude, but the overall pattern can be quite instructive and helpful (especially if the analytic categories are even more refined and accurate as in the current OERI-funded TORUS system).[16]

The use of OERI units, levels of schooling, and types of activity on the y-axis are only a few illustrations of the wide variety of analytic categories that may be useful in developing a matrix for mapping activities which represent institutions or larger collections of participants. Naturally, one could use more than one set of categories simultaneously to capture the different facets of OERI's research priority plan. One advantage of tying conceptually the study of programs and activities at the more aggregate level to our original life-course perspective is that it reminds us that often the otherwise highly desirable educational reforms we undertake may not make much of an immediate difference in improving the education and training of our present students. After making a compelling case for the need to revise our procedures for state licensing of public school teachers, for example, Linda Darling-Hammond and her coauthors candidly admit that this reform will have little immediate impact on the education of students today: "Licensing changes will not produce these benefits overnight. Indeed, the investment of both the time and the money required to implement programs such as the ones described here will probably not produce noticeable results for many years. However, steps in the direction of more meaningful and valid systems for licensing teachers will likely influence the preparation of teachers much sooner. These steps will also send a message that the state and the profession take seriously their obligations to safeguard the educational well-being of students by insisting on and supporting the competence of their teachers."[17] Thus, while the use of a life-course matrix by itself does not tell us necessarily whether to invest in such broader reforms as the licensing of teachers, it always reminds us of the importance of asking, among other questions, how each of the proposed changes will eventually affect the lives of the students we are trying to assist. Whereas we often will not have readily available the data or analyses to answer that question definitively, the life-course matrix encourages us to at least make those connections conceptually and reveals potentially important research gaps from a policy perspective.

In working with the proposed matrices (tables 8.1 and 8.2), it is important to keep in mind the different types of research each is designed to address. When a research project focuses on how to improve the curriculum, for example, but is not concerned with studying the interaction of that curriculum with the individual child, the matrix in table 8.2 could be used to plot that activity. In other words, whereas the first matrix in table 8.1 should be used when one is looking at an actual individual, the second matrix is really designed for categorizing activities to improve institutions, programs, or groups of individuals—such as professionalizing teachers, revising the curriculum, improving student assessments, or developing special school programs. In educational discussions, it is often difficult, if not impossible, to make the distinction because the analysts do not specify whether an activity occurs at an individual or aggregate level. One of the benefits of the proposed life-course framework is that it facilitates such an important analytic and policy distinction in our thinking.

Overall, the life-course framework proposed here encourages the analyst or the policymaker to see education in a much broader and more dynamic fashion. It continually forces us to ask how a particular educational reform or improvement will affect the individual child as she ages and traverses the educational system. Moreover, rather than focusing on the impact of teachers and curriculum on the development of the student, it calls for seeing the multiple, simultaneous influences of organizations and people outside the school system. By allowing us to map out proposed research projects, it also increases the likelihood that we will ask questions about alternative research strategies and try to explain why our particular research priorities may lead to significant improvements in learning at a crucial juncture in the life course.

APPLICATIONS OF THE LIFE-COURSE FRAMEWORK

The life-course framework has various applications. One of them is in program evaluation. To explore its possibilities in this context we used it to evaluate the priorities that were set for the educational research and development centers that were published in the *Federal Register*.[18] In this exercise we also drew on material from an earlier evaluation of the quality of research and development produced by the current OERI-funded R&D centers and the regional educational laboratories.[19]

The proposed expenditures on the centers and laboratories constitute a large proportion of OERI research and development investments for the near future. The general guidelines for the next lab competition have been set, and these, combined with the proposed priorities for the seven centers, represent a significant proportion of overall OERI research and development activities for five years. Therefore, at least implicitly if not explicitly, much of OERI's vision for reforming and improving American education has been set.

Overall, the proposed center research priorities were a thoughtful and useful improvement on earlier center solicitations. Reductions in the number of centers as well as improvements in specifying more clearly the nature of the centers were welcome additions. Using the life-course framework to assess the proposed OERI center research and development priorities, however, leads to at least nine general problems. These are:

1. Apparent lack of an overall OERI plan guiding center research and development priorities (or an OERI inventory of current research and development activities).
2. Too limited information for applicants either about OERI proposed research priorities or about existing research and development activities.
3. Too many centers for the limited amount of funding available.
4. Distinction between research and development priorities is unclear; no definition of development provided.
5. Little integration of proposed center research and development priorities with comparable existing OERI activities.
6. Too many mandated research and development tasks for some of the proposed individual centers given the limited funding available.
7. Inadequate integration of similar research and development tasks across the centers; lack of a convincing rationale for creating so many small, separate centers.
8. Failure to identify particularly crucial intervention points to improve significantly the education of individuals throughout the life course.
9. Some of the most important ways of helping disadvantaged children are not addressed.

Ideally a five-year research priorities plan would have been developed before undertaking a center and laboratory competition. But given the timing of the federal budget cycles, as well as the reorganization of OERI, the planning process has been reversed. Proposals for specific center and lab research and development tasks for the next five years have been developed and implemented before an overall OERI research priorities plan was formulated.

The absence of a formal five-year research priorities plan was regrettable, but it should not have precluded the agency from developing and employing an interim, preliminary research plan to guide the center and lab competitions. The notice of proposed center research and development priorities, however, made no mention of any such plan. Nor did the announcement suggest that OERI had inventoried its existing or contemplated activities to determine where in its overall scheme the proposed center research and development priorities fit.

If one mapped the proposed research and development priorities for the centers using the life-course framework developed here, it would be difficult to find any overall plan. The research and development activities of the individual centers sometimes appear to be somewhat disjointed and fragmentary. More important, there is little evidence of the integration of the seven centers amongst themselves or among the other activities within OERI and the Department of Education.

Thus, one of the major benefits of using a life-course framework would have been to encourage and to facilitate the mapping of diverse research and development efforts in order to help assess their overall coherence as well as their relation to each other. Application of this analytic tool to the proposed priorities of the seven centers might have alerted OERI to the apparent lack of an overall, underlying research rationale, and using the life-course framework might have assisted the agency in developing a more integrated approach to its center research and development priorities.

Lacking a long-term research and development plan but encouraged legislatively to base its activities on such an overall vision (or visions), OERI should have provided potential center applicants with additional information about other related research and development activities. Center applicants were expected to justify their proposals on the basis of what research and development had been completed as well as on what remained to be done. Some center applicants, for example, may have benefited by being aware of the work that is being funded by the Center for Research on the Education of Students Placed At-Risk or of the research and development requested of the regional educational laboratories or the Title 1 evaluations. If so, OERI should have provided some additional information about such projects in order to give all applicants an equal opportunity to compete. In the past this has not been an issue because the individual OERI centers were not designed or expected to be part of a larger, coherent research undertaking; therefore, relevance to a larger implicit or explicit research agenda was not a necessary or important part of a winning proposal.

When the original R&D centers were created in the mid-1960s, they were expected to conduct large-scale, coherent research on significant education problems. Over time, however, they have evolved into relatively small institutions supporting a wide array of often interesting, but usually fragmentary research projects.[20] Although the notice of proposed priorities does not specify the annual funding levels for the seven centers, one might speculate on the basis of the overall OERI budget that they could be in the range of $1.5 to $4 million. The recently funded OERI Center for Research on the Education of Students Placed At-Risk has an approximate annual budget of $5 million, probably a more realistic size for future centers.

An earlier analysis of five R&D centers funded in 1990 found that a sizable proportion of their FY92 awards went for administrative, overhead, and dissemination costs. The actual amount of money left for research ranged from 26.0 percent at the National Center for the Study of Writing and Literacy at the University of California at Berkeley to 62.5 percent at the National Resource Center on Student Learning at the University of Pittsburgh. Overall, only 52.4 percent of the OERI funds at the five centers studied were being used directly for research efforts.[21] Applying this rough estimate to the proposed centers, the amount of money annually available for research and development would range from $786,000 to $2.1 million. These sums may seem quite large, but large-scale research and development projects are very expensive and the total funds available for any individual center will not support many such efforts. Moreover, while the funding for some of these proposed centers compares favorably to current centers, it falls well short of what will be needed to implement the ambitious research and development agenda outlined in the *Federal Register* notice.

Throughout the notice on proposed center priorities, the terms "research" and "development" were linked whenever there were requests for addressing problems or topics. But there was little guidance on the desired mix of research or development activities or expenditures. Should a R&D center have focused 80 percent of its efforts on research and 20 percent on development? Or vice versa? Nor was there any indication of whether a particular issue should have been the focus of research or development activities. Given the high cost of doing good research (and probably higher cost of doing systematic development), someone made important choices on how much and what kinds of development, if any, should have been done. By default, that decision has been left to the applicants and their panel of reviewers rather than to directions from OERI. Although it may have been expedient and easier to let each applicant decide what mixture is best, it significantly reduced the ability of the OERI to direct research or development to specific areas that were deemed most promising for improving the education of children (and it also reduced the likelihood that the overall research and development portfolio of other OERI activities had been taken into consideration).

Although in principle the R&D centers always have stressed development (as evidenced by their designation as research and development centers), in practice, development has been ignored or minimized during the past ten to fifteen years. In the earlier study of five R&D centers, only 13.5 percent of the research dollars were spent on development (and much of that was for small-scale, short-term development of teaching materials and classroom practices).[22] The new OERI legislation in 1994, however, assigned to the R&D centers a major responsibility for development and provided a more precise and considerably more ambitious definition for that activity: "The term 'development'—(A) means the systematic use, adaptation, and transformation of knowledge and understanding gained from research to create alternatives, policies, products, methods, practices, or materials which can contribute to the improvement of educational practice; and (B) includes the design and development of prototypes and the testing of such prototypes for the purposes of establishing their feasibility, reliability, and cost-effectiveness."[23]

If the R&D centers were to undertake the type and amount of development activity envisioned in the legislation, then perhaps OERI should have provided applicants with a definition of this term as well as an indication of its relative importance. Because of the high costs associated with doing large-scale, long-term systematic development and the limited funds available for each center, OERI should have reconsidered the number of areas in which it envisioned supporting systematic development. Given the practices of the previous centers, the amount of systematic development that will be provided in the future is likely to be much less than Congress and OERI expect unless additional directives were to be issued.

Whereas each center's priorities by themselves may be plausible, it is not clear how they complement existing OERI or the U.S. Department of Education activities. Some of them overlap considerably with research and development activities provided or contemplated elsewhere. In some circumstances such overlaps may be warranted and welcomed; but in others it would be best not to duplicate work given the overall scarcity of funds. Moreover, it would have been more useful for centers to build on what was already being done rather than proposing a similar but separate line of inquiry.

The notice of proposed center priorities commendably set forth an ambitious but expensive research and development program. Among other considerations, it required that the centers "conduct scientifically rigorous studies capable of generating findings that contribute substantially to understanding in the field; [and] conduct work of sufficient size, scope, and duration to produce definitive guidance for improvement efforts and future research." Yet given the limited amount of funds available for research and development tasks, it is difficult to see how all the mandated tasks could have been completed with the required scientific rigor and definitive guidance. Moreover, while each of the proposed center studies may be useful and important, taken together they do not always appear to have provided "a coherent, sustained program of research and development to address problems and issues of national significance in its individual priority area" as the notice suggested. Rather than abandoning the laudatory principles enumerated in the *Federal Register*, it would have been advisable to reduce the number of mandated tasks for some centers, or at least to have made some of these tasks optional.

Given the limited center funding and the need for a more comprehensive, coherent agenda than in the past, perhaps these activities should have been reconfigured into four or five larger centers rather than the proposed seven smaller ones. Because there was no close coordination of the individual priorities among the proposed centers, it might have been useful to combine some of these centers (the new reconstituted centers could have been administered jointly by several of the institutes). The resulting economies-of-scale in administration and dissemination would have led to greater research and development productivity in the new package of larger centers.

From a life-course perspective, it was disappointing that OERI has provided so little guidance in identifying crucial intervention points for helping children. Rather than suggesting, for example, that certain transitions through the school system may be particularly important for the developing child, OERI has left these matters almost entirely to the discretion of the applicants and their reviewers. Similarly, the notice of proposed priorities did not provide much direction in terms of educational products or programs that might have been especially effective in helping individuals throughout their life course. One of the dangers in this approach was that while centers may do useful and thought-ful work in their respective areas, crucial transitions in the life course or impor-tant programs and services will have not been researched or developed.

Finally, the life-course perspective reminds us to view the developing indi-vidual from a broader perspective. Some priorities in the announcement did address these contextual concerns—such as calls for the study of the role of parents and community in fostering school readiness. But there may have been other important topics that were not researched or developed. For example, researchers have demonstrated a widening gap in learning and achievement between at-risk children and their more fortunate counterparts during the summer months (when most schools are out of session). Yet this summer learning gap was not addressed specifically anywhere in the proposed center competition (though it might have fit under the section on the structuring of out-of-school experiences). Thus, one needs to ascertain not only what topics and issues were examined by the proposed centers, but also which potentially important ones were ignored.

Each of the seven proposed absolute priorities were, according to the an-nouncement, addressed in a separate national education and development center. In the discussion that follows, I shall draw heavily on the life-course perspective to raise a few key issues about these proposed institutions.

The first R&D center was designed for "promoting the cognitive and social-emotional development of young children." The proposal called for conduct-ing research and development on children from birth and listed three topics to be addressed: (1) helping young children come to school prepared to learn; (2) researching and developing effective models and strategies for young children's learning; and (3) analyzing how various early childhood supports and services within the community can be designed and implemented to help young chil-dren's cognitive and social-emotional development.

By focusing on the early phase of child development, the proposed center fit nicely into a life-course perspective. Moreover, the priorities contained a bal-anced focus on the young child and the family, school, and community context in which that individual is developing. The discussion in the text also showed an appreciation for concentrating on the needs of children who were placed at a risk of failure.

This proposed absolute priority has much to recommend it, but it also raised some interesting questions. What were the approximate ages of the children who were to be investigated by this center? The notice suggested that one might look at children from birth through the elementary grades, but this is a large age range and it would be difficult to follow in practice given limited funds. Nor was it clear from the text of the proposal what studies, if any, were to be done on children ages one or two. Given the work of other agencies like the National Institutes for Health on early child development, should OERI really have focused its limited center funds on children in their first few years?

One of the strengths of the early childhood center was that it looked at getting children ready for the transition into formal schooling. While considerable work was being done on preschool education, much less effort was expended on children making the transition into the regular schools. Perhaps this section might have been expanded to include more attention to what happened to children once they arrived at that school (this might have been done by simply explicitly linking the effective models and strategies section to the issue of school transition).

One of OERI's major investments has been to help fund the development and assessment of the Success for All Program that works with children in grades K–4. Indeed, this is a focal point of much of the work of the Center for Research on the Education of Students Placed At-Risk. Will the proposed center on early childhood work closely with the "Success for All Program"? Should the new center develop or test alternative models or strategies for helping children in grades K–4? In other words, one could imagine a closer and more effective integration of this center's work with the existing bodies of research and development on this important transition point in the child's life course.

The focus on childhood supports and services was useful, but it was not clear whether scientifically rigorous and definitive work could be done on a topic as broad as from birth through the elementary grades. Since some work on the impact of integrated services does exist for preschool programs like Head Start, would it have made more sense to focus this effort on children once they have entered the regular school? How much of the work should have been concentrated on ascertaining the value of individual services in helping children learn and how much of it should have analyzed the impact of coordinating those services? And does OERI have a preference as to whether the work in this area is oriented more toward research or development?

Naturally, there were many other topics that might have been addressed by an early childhood center. One possibility was issues of individual cognitive development and its effects on learning, which could have been studied jointly with the National Institute on Student Achievement, Curriculum, and Assessment as it also called for research and development on "how students acquire knowledge and develop cognitive skills." The National Center for Educational Statistics was funding a major longitudinal study of kindergarten children; should the new center have helped in analyzing these data? What about the summer learning topic? Was this not a useful place to consider exploring that important topic (perhaps jointly with the National Institute on the Education of At-Risk Students)?

This brief review of the specific topics proposed for the early child development center illustrated how, even for a relatively narrow and focused area, important choices had to be made in order to arrive at a final research and development strategy. Given the limited funds available, one would not have expected all the topics discussed above to be analyzed by the new center. Perhaps OERI should have tried to specify more precisely and exactly, if possible, what types of research and development were needed so that the activities of the proposed center could have been targeted more directly and effectively on the most promising interventions to improve the education of developing young children.

These same types of questions about details and strategy should have been asked of each of the proposed research and development priorities of the other six institutions, but rather than going through each of the proposed centers at the same level of detail, I shall mention only a few additional considerations. The center on learning and achievement and the center on assessment will be discussed together because an argument can be made that they should have been merged into a larger and more coordinated center that encompassed both curriculum and assessment activities. Although both centers probably would have been supervised by the National Institute on Student Achievement, Curriculum, and Assessment, there was considerable danger that they would have gone in rather different directions unless they were brought together from the start (or unless OERI was more specific in its initial directives).

One potential problem for the two centers was that OERI did not specify the grade levels for the various activities. Nor did the notice of proposed priorities always indicate what subject matter should have been investigated. Thus, one can easily imagine a situation where the center on learning and achievement focused on improving the elementary reading and writing curriculum, but the center on assessment might have concentrated on high school English, language arts, and mathematics. As a result, important opportunities for aligning the development of the curriculum and its assessment were likely to be lost.

Moreover, the proposal for the center on student learning and achievement mandated that at least six quite different tasks must be done, ranging from analyzing the social context of learning to promoting effective professional development for educators. Given the high costs of research and development, it was unlikely that any center could do all six of these tasks without sacrificing the quality and generalizability of its work. OERI should have either reduced the number of tasks or made some of them optional. Some of these activities, as mentioned earlier, also might have been done in conjunction with other institutes (such as pursuing the topic on the development of cognitive skills).

The life-course framework helps remind us of the need to specify more precisely the grade level of various activities. Too often policymakers and researchers speak of improving curriculum or developing student assessments without acknowledging that only a very small part of a student's total life-course exposure to different school subjects or testing is being researched or developed. In the earlier study of the OERI-funded centers, for example, it was pointed out that although several different centers supported some work on teaching American history, most of it was quite fragmentary and episodic. None of the research appears to have been sufficiently rigorous scientifically or comprehensive enough to warrant the type of generalizability and definitive guidance for improvement envisioned in the present notice of priorities.[24] We need to be careful and clear about our expectations in the areas of curriculum development and assessment so that the activities we fund can actually meet the stated requirements.

OERI had created a five-year Center for Research on the Education of Students Placed At-Risk at an annual cost of approximately $5 million. It now proposed to add a second, related center to meet the needs of a diverse student population. The five topics of the proposed new center appeared to be useful and important, but one wonders if it would not have been better to distribute some of those issues among the other proposed centers rather than creating another new center altogether. Because a major at-risk center already existed, would it have made more sense to look at the specific needs of the diverse student population within the context of comparable work being done by the other proposed centers (especially since they were also likely to be interested in helping that same diverse student population)? For example, why couldn't we have combined the professional teacher development activities proposed by the center for learning and achievement with those for the center on diverse student populations? Could we not have designed activities to work with families and community-based organizations to help at-risk students that would have complemented the work of the other proposed centers? Maybe the structuring of out-of-school experiences could have been focused on summer learning and thereby address an issue of potential interest to several institutes. Certainly the requirement to recognize and build on the strengths of students from diverse backgrounds could have fit easily with the agendas of the other institutes. In other words, much of what was being proposed for the center on diverse student populations might have been combined with similar efforts at other centers, including some of the work being done by the at-risk center. Whether or not one creates a center on diverse students, more effort needs to be made to integrate that work with similar activities elsewhere.

The proposed center for state and local education reform efforts focused more on macro-level organizations and institutions than on the individual student or teacher. The topics it addressed were important and timely, but how much overlap was there with other research and development? The regional educational laboratories, for instance, were expected to spend approximately $100 to $150 million over the next five years to look at efforts to reform education systemically and to develop ways of "scaling-up" successful local reforms. What was the relation between the work proposed for the OERI-funded laboratories and this center? Similarly, how will the center agenda interact with the Title 1 activities that are being evaluated (especially since much of the Title 1 evaluation efforts seem to be focused on similar issues—challenging academic standards, alignment of curriculum and assessment, and school-level strategies)? How does the work of this center complement or duplicate that of the National Science Foundation state-level systemic reform investigations?

The center on state and local reform efforts had an extensive and ambitious seven-part agenda, but it was important that its priorities took into consideration the large amounts of related work underway elsewhere. Perhaps after carefully mapping the work of other agencies and institutions, it would have been possible for OERI to focus the work of this center even further. Many analysts and agencies, for example, seem interested in developing and implementing systemic reform, but less attention was being paid to financial and management issues. Or, many of the studies of systemic reform concentrated on school-level or state-level analysis of curriculum and assessment alignments without testing to see whether these changes would impact favorably on the learning of the child. Maybe the new center should have focused more on some of these important but relatively neglected topics and relied on other scholars and policy analysts for information and investigations of different aspects of systemic reform.

Finally, the proposed center for postsecondary education and adult work and the center for adult learning and literacy might have been combined into one larger center that addressed both agendas. The general topics covered by the two centers were compatible with each other and could have been effectively coordinated under one administrative umbrella. Combining the two centers and working jointly on the proposed priorities may have produced considerable savings and allowed for undertaking more rigorous and definitive work. By focusing on lifelong learning and the transition from school to work, the activities of these centers fit nicely into a life-course perspective. Assuming that the other centers had focused their attention on K–12 education, there should not have been much overlap with the work of the center on postsecondary student learning and assessment. Naturally, the crafting of these priorities should have taken into consideration any comparable work being done elsewhere in the Department of Education or Department of Labor.

Using a life-course perspective also suggests that some important topics may not have been covered by the funded centers. If one focused on the significant transitions in a student's life, the entry into the school system and the departure from it probably would have received adequate attention. But what about the important and difficult transition to the middle grades and schools? Some of the center projects would conceivably have addressed this matter, but it was just as likely that no successful applicant would make that particular transition a key part of her or his research and development agenda. If the transition to the middle grades was considered an important phase of the life course, and one that required further investigation, then the proposed priorities should have been rewritten.

Applying the life-course perspective to OERI's notice of proposed priorities for the centers has raised interesting and important questions about the coherence and effectiveness of the centers. It has also alerted us to the strengths and weaknesses of individual projects within the centers from the perspective of intervening at crucial points in the life course of individuals. Although the life-course framework does not necessarily tell us by itself where optimal research and development investments should be made, it does encourage us to ask appropriate questions and to integrate new work into existing initiatives. The life-course framework not only encourages such broader conversations, but it also provides us with an analytic framework for mapping current and proposed research priorities.[25]

One of the relatively few predictable events in education is the annual call for a long-term, stable research priorities plan. For nearly a quarter of a century, educators and policymakers have urged NIE and its successor, OERI, to develop such a plan. These requests have not gone unheeded. Perhaps a dozen or more quite different long-term plans have been drafted and implemented for a short time, but none have succeeded in guiding the agency as a whole for more than a few years.

This lack of real long-term research planning results mainly from the political weakness and organizational instability of a federal agency buffeted by changing congressional demands and frequent turnovers in directors. Moreover, much of the field of education research lacks the maturity and cohesiveness of some other science and social science disciplines. These factors, combined with the inadequate financial and staff resources and persistent outside earmarking of most of the agency's activities and expenditures, make it not surprising that an adequate long-term research plan has not been developed and successfully implemented.

A minor, though potentially important, factor in the failure to draft and complete a long-term research plan has been the lack of an overall framework for categorizing and guiding educational research in a more detailed and functional fashion. Although each long-term plan has had its own framework and rationale, most have been quite general and have not provided an opportunity to see how the different aspects of the overall research agenda fit together. By proposing such an overall analytic framework, perhaps we will be able to make a modest, but necessary, contribution toward developing a more workable and meaningful long-term research agenda for OERI.

The research framework proposed in this chapter—a life-course perspective—seems to provide some useful guidance for mapping existing or proposed research and development priorities while at the same time suggesting certain areas of investigation that might be particularly helpful. There might be other plausible schemes for accomplishing the same tasks, and these alternate frameworks should be developed and compared to the proposed life-course perspective. What we should not do, however, is to continue to accept uncritically the fragmentary nature of many of the individual education research and development investments funded by NIE and OERI in the past—even in the R&D centers and regional educational laboratories, which were designed specifically to provide more coherence and long-term direction to their activities.

The life-course perspective has much to recommend it. It focuses on the individual and reminds us that the fundamental goal of education is to improve the learning and well-being of each person. Programs to improve teachers or schools, for example, may be desirable and necessary, but they are only an indirect means of helping the learner. The ultimate success of our endeavors is not whether we have revised our curriculum or built new classrooms, but whether we have improved children's learning and enhanced their overall development.

The life-course perspective also emphasizes that learning is a lifelong process that begins at birth and continues through adulthood. Rather than seeing education mainly in terms of childhood and youth, the life-course approach points to the importance of learning and training throughout adulthood as well. Moreover, rather than believing that there is little we can do to remedy past difficulties and missed opportunities, this approach reinforces the belief that individuals can change and that society can provide additional opportunities throughout the entire life course.

The life-course framework allows us to appreciate how individual physical and cognitive developments are interrelated and how they affect the subsequent learning process. Important research advances in cognitive psychology and child development, for example, can be mapped and related to other learning opportunities within this framework. At the same time, the life-course perspective places the development of an individual within the broader familial and social context. In addition, rather than just focusing on the impact of schooling, this framework provides the means to analyze other important influences on the education of the individual, such as the role of family or the impact of activities outside the classroom.

The life-course perspective does not negate or minimize the importance of studying such vital topics as programs to improve teacher professionalization or efforts to develop statewide curriculum standards. Rather, it helps to remind us that when such reforms are advocated and implemented, we need to consider exactly how and when these changes will benefit the learning of the individual. The life-course perspective encourages us to make more explicit our assumptions about how macrolevel institutional changes can improve the education of our children and adults, and it suggests the need for sometimes documenting those linkages empirically.

Research growing out of the life-course perspective also points to the importance of focusing on key transitions in an individual's life. The transitions into formal schooling, the middle grades, high school, postsecondary education, and the labor force appear to be particularly important, and often difficult periods. Based on both research and practical experiences, we need to identify key potential turning points and then develop appropriate ways of helping individuals complete these transitions successfully.

The life-course perspective emphasizes that significant changes can be made throughout one's life, but it also demonstrates how the cumulative effect of a series of prior experiences and institutional placements can limit future opportunities. Rather than looking at particular aspects of the educational system in isolation, the life-course approach encourages us to acknowledge the key role that previous experiences and settings have on individuals. Understanding such dynamics might help us to revise our existing educational structures as well as to provide additional assistance to those who are disadvantaged.

Overall, the proposed life-course perspective provides a detailed framework for mapping existing research, plotting any additional useful research, and displaying future research proposals. As we map and analyze these different activities on the proposed grids, we will be able to identify research gaps and to assess the coherence and significance of OERI's long-range research and development strategy. It may be undesirable and unrealistic to expect that OERI or any other large research agency will arrive at a single, long-term research focus; but we should be able to identify and fund several clusters of coordinated research and development projects, each of which has the potential to make a real difference in children's lives and which together provide a balanced, coherent portfolio of research and development activities. The life-course perspective by itself cannot determine definitively what research and development should be done at OERI or elsewhere for the next five or ten years, but it will help us to plan these endeavors more thoughtfully and systematically.

Conclusion: The Uses of History in Educational Policymaking

The increasingly sharp separation between history and policymaking is in some ways a fairly recent development. During the colonial period and the early nineteenth century, people viewed history as an indispensable part of leadership training. History revealed valuable information about the past experiences of countries and city states and provided models of exemplary individual behavior. Moreover, a knowledge of American history was seen as essential for good citizenship because it fostered patriotism and civic virtue among the general population. In the late nineteenth and early twentieth century, when history became professionalized, scholars and policymakers alike believed that the past had important lessons for contemporary decision makers.

We should be careful, however, not to imagine a golden age when historians and policymakers worked closely and harmoniously together. Indeed, although both groups acknowledged the potential importance of learning from the past, in practice the early presidents of the American Historical Association often complained that members of the legislative and executive branches did not pay enough attention to history. Nevertheless, some of these earlier historians played active roles as participant-observers in government affairs, especially during such crises as World War I, World War II, and the beginnings of the cold war.

Yet over time the growth of professionalization and specialization among historians, as well as the decreasing interest in the past among scholars in the other social sciences, contributed to a growing estrangement between historians and policymakers. Today, despite occasional rhetoric about the uses and value of the past for decision makers, most professional historians have little impact or interaction with elected leaders at the state or federal level. Most historians are content to pursue their own investigations and debates, and most policymakers believe that a historical perspective has little to offer them.

In the last several decades few major professional historians have been involved in policymaking or have had much direct impact on decision makers outside of academia. Although the number of social science advisers to governments has grown substantially, historians have rarely been called on for advice. Few of the more recent writings on educational policymaking, for example, utilize a historical perspective.[1] And many educational historians, though producing first-rate scholarly work on colonial and nineteenth-century education, shy away from more contemporary policy-oriented analyses.[2] Nor is the next generation of social science policy advisers likely to be particularly historically oriented because public policy schools rarely, if ever, hire historians or offer history courses.[3]

At the same time history's popularity among the general public continues. The success of cable television programs like those found on the History Channel and the popularity of such historically oriented movies as "The Crucible," "Ghosts of Mississippi," "Glory," and "Nixon" testify to the enduring public interest in our past. But the information presented in these films is frequently altered for artistic or ideological reasons and does not reflect the more specialized and less accessible scholarship produced by professional historians today. Most professional historians do not write for a general audience, and the public's interest in the past is satisfied largely by those outside academia.[4]

One reason why policymakers and the public often are impatient or dissatisfied with advice from historians is that the past offers no easy lessons or prescriptions for future behavior. Americans have always liked straightforward, simple rules to guide their behavior. Benjamin Franklin's maxims for proper conduct were popular in the eighteenth century and have been modified and updated in numerous best-selling self-help books.[5] Similarly, the management consultant industry prospers by presenting a few concrete steps for increasing a company's efficiency and profits. Simple sayings and rules are easy to remember, but they are often difficult to interpret or put into practice.[6] Policymakers and the public frequently ask scholars what are the lessons of history and expect to receive a small set of useful insights, but when historians point out that there are no simple or easy lessons from the past, the audience's interest fades rapidly.[7]

Perhaps one of the best remembered and most quoted sayings is that of the philosopher George Santayana: "Those who cannot remember the past are condemned to repeat it." This has been an excellent advertisement for studying the past, but it does not tell us much about how to use historical information judiciously and effectively. One common response to Santayana's statement is the increased use of historical analogies. For example, in the foreign policy arena we are frequently reminded to "remember Munich"—the now infamous and futile effort of Neville Chamberlain to appease Adolf Hitler by agreeing to his takeover of strategic portions of Czechoslovakia in 1938. Although much can be learned from that event and appropriately used to inform us about the present, the episode can also mislead us into thinking that any compromises with hostile nondemocratic governments are bound to fail and therefore should always be resisted.[8] In certain situations, it may be more appropriate to say, as Arthur S. Schlesinger, Jr., put it: "Too often it is those who *can* remember the past who are condemned to repeat it."[9] The use of historical analogies is often helpful, but it depends on how well we understand the specific circumstances of the past and their similarity to the present situation. Perhaps one of the best things that we can learn from the past is to avoid simplistic and misleading historical analogies, which are frequently and casually evoked by decision makers and the public in favor of some particular policy alternative.[10]

Richard Neustadt and Ernest May suggest some useful steps that decision makers might take in order to develop an appropriate historical perspective on their problems:

> Faced with a situation prompting action, the first step in good staff work is to grasp its manifestations: What goes on here? The second step is to identify one's boss's concerns and one's own: If there is a problem to be solved (or lived with), what is it? And whose is it?
>
> Essential if these steps are to be sure-footed is an early effort to clear away impediments embedded in impressions of the past. . . .
>
> We urge that it become standard staff practice to start out by listing in three separate columns key elements of the immediate situation, namely those *Known*, *Unclear*, and *Presumed*. . . .
>
> An associated procedure is explicit identification of any past situations that appear

analogous or someone who matters seems likely to cite as such. Quickly jotting down the *Likenesses* and *Differences* can block use of potentially misleading analogies.[11]

Once these steps have been taken and an objective defined, they recommend three additional devices:

The first is the *Goldberg Rule.* With some definitions of concerns in hand ask, "What's the story?" How did *these* concerns develop. Take care not to pursue the wrong story. . . .

The second device is *time-lines:* Start the story as far back as it properly goes and plot key trends while also entering key events, especially big changes. . . .

The third device is asking journalists' questions: as the time-line answers "when" and "what," don't omit to ask also "where," "who," "how," and "why." . . . This is part of the point of invoking issue history: to get more thought on where to go and on how to get there before taking off.[12]

Surprisingly for many people, according to Neustadt and May, much of the role of history for decision-making has already been exercised—well before options for future action are even addressed: "Now, at last, we have reached the step where many people yearn to start and often leap for: arraying options. Except as it may be suggestive of the future, history has but a limited role here. For the most part options are defined by current conditions and capabilities."[13] They go on to discuss some additional steps in which history can play a role for policymakers, but conclude with a long and useful discussion of the importance of seeing time as a continuous stream. Indeed, for Neustadt and May knowledge of specific historical facts or events may be generally less important for decision makers than "the kind of mental quality that readily connects discrete phenomena over time and repeatedly checks connections."[14]

PROBLEMS OF ACQUIRING HISTORICAL POLICY INFORMATION

A major problem facing policymakers today is that government services and policy-related analyses are becoming increasingly segmented at a time when there is a need for more integration and synthesis. Federal service programs for children, for example, are often in practice narrowly categorical, fragmented, and uncoordinated. Not only are children's programs scattered across departments, they are separated from each other even within the same department. Congressional jurisdiction and oversight of these programs is also fragmented and uncoordinated. When the maze of federal programs for children interacts with an almost equally complex, but differently configured set of services at the state and local levels, the resultant service delivery pattern usually is chaotic, confusing, and unwieldy for the individual recipient.[15]

Similarly, the different academic disciplines dealing with children usually focus on only a few facets of that individual and often are not closely coordinated with comparable or related work in other areas of academic study. This specialization and fragmentation, widely recognized and often bemoaned, is difficult to overcome as synthesis across disciplines is intellectually challenging and very time-consuming. Yet dealing with this problem may be less difficult in academia than in the service sector, as it is easier to relate things intellectually and conceptually than it is to link and coordinate actual services. However, the reward structure in most academic disciplines generally encourages continued specialization and development of new research rather than an interdisciplinary syntheses of existing work.[16]

Much of historical scholarship is criticized as being too narrow and specialized. Yet the generally accepted paradigms for the history profession continue to call for addressing past human experiences in their broadest manifestations. Given the rapid growth of social history during the past three decades, one might argue that the overall purview of historians has expanded considerably, although in any particular area of analysis much of the work has become narrower and more focused. Because of this broad view, historians may be well positioned to bring together in a more coherent and dynamic fashion the diverse and often fragmented approaches of other scholars and policy analysts.[17]

Another area that needs further consideration is how policymakers acquire and use scholarly information. The few scholars who have written about the relation between history and policymaking have not devoted much attention, if any, to the varied and ever-changing nature and needs of the decision makers. As a result, there are often fundamental misperceptions about the types of policy settings in which a historical approach may be helpful.

We all carry at least implicit views of the past and are influenced by those perceptions in varying degrees. Most of us seldom contemplate how our understanding of the past affects our present thinking and behavior, yet a significant part of our general conceptual orientation and outlook probably is influenced by our usually unspoken and unstated interpretations of the past. Indeed, recent tests of high school students suggest that most of them do not have even a basic understanding of American history—let alone an ability and willingness to use it readily and thoughtfully later as adults.[18] Thus, while we all have a sense of the past, our knowledge and ideas about that past may not be very accurate.

Moreover, often there are important unstated assumptions that might be challenged or explored further using a historical perspective. In the field of environmental history, for example, William Cronon has written a thoughtful, but controversial historical essay on the changing meanings of the term "wilderness." Cronon tries to show that our current concepts about the "wilderness" are really social constructions rather than something "natural," and he argues that the rationale for protecting the environment should not be based simply upon an ahistorical, unconstructed definition of the concept.[19]

Presidential appointees in the executive branch usually do not have a good historical understanding of the problem area or agency to which they have been assigned. Although many appointees have had prior public service experience, the majority have not. And a substantial proportion of presidential appointees admit that they lack substantive knowledge of the relevant policies to which they have been assigned. Moreover, because most appointees serve less than two years in a particular post, they usually have little opportunity to develop a more in-depth understanding of their agency's past or even of its current needs.[20]

Career federal civil service employees provide some but often inadequate information about past practices. Members of the elite Senior Executive Service, for example, are encouraged to rotate from one assignment to another rather than to become experts in one area. Moreover, when new presidential employees arrive in an agency, they often want to select different career civil servants to advise them rather than to rely upon incumbents, especially when there is a political change in administrations. Given the nature of the federal pay scale, lower-grade employees have built-in incentives to shift jobs in order to advance professionally. Finally, as the more experienced career civil servants retire, they take with them an understanding of past practices and policies that might have been useful to future policymakers.[21]

Perhaps the most continuity in federal policymaking comes from the members of Congress, many of whom have served in the House or Senate for years. Especially important in this regard are the chairs of the committees and subcommittees who often have an interest in maintaining a smooth and stable legislative course. The chair's knowledge of his or her field and understanding of past policy developments has often been legendary, though it is limited by the fact that each chair has oversight over such a wide variety of different programs that it is very difficult, if not impossible, to be familiar with all the projects under their jurisdiction. In more recent years, this pattern of long-term oversight of federal programs by congressional members has been disrupted somewhat as a result of the increased turnover of representatives and senators.

Recent shifts in the partisan control of the House and Senate have also meant major changes in the key committees and their staffs. Rapid turnover in committee assignments is particularly evident in the area of education because many members of Congress do not regard educational oversight as a particularly important or desirable assignment.[22]

One of the most significant factors in the expansion of congressional oversight of federal programs is the great increase in congressional staff after World War II. The rapid growth of both personal and committee staff has meant that it is now easier to monitor the increasingly numerous and complex federal programs created since the mid-1960s. Some individuals have remained in their positions for a long time—subject periodically, however, to sudden shifts in partisan control of the House and Senate or changes in committee membership. Although congressional staff usually are more specialized and more focused substantively than their employers, significant staff turnover still limits the overall continuity in policymaking.[23]

Overall, my personal experiences as well as discussions with others suggest that domestic policymakers in Washington seldom look to the past for guidance on current work. Frequently there is a sense that everything is so new and unprecedented that an understanding of the past is irrelevant. Many policymakers in both the executive and legislative branches rarely look back further than a few years in their deliberations. This inattention to the past is compounded by the fact that few professional historians are either full-time federal employees or consultants.[24] And the few historians in the Department of Education are sometimes discouraged from pursuing their historical analyses or are located in positions far removed from the major policy decision makers.[25]

Even if federal policymakers were interested in having a historical perspective on their work, appropriate studies usually are not readily available. Few historical investigations are focused on the types of issues most helpful to a particular federal agency. And many of existing historical policy studies simply do not provide enough direct connections to the present to seem useful to policymakers.[26] The publications of historians do not receive the same respect and attention in government agencies as those of other social scientists.[27] Studies of how congressional members and their staffs search for new information suggest that it is unlikely that these policymakers consult historians—both because decision makers do not think that they particularly need historical information and because professional historical organizations are not especially active or effective in facilitating general policy-related communications between their members and Washington decision makers.[28]

There are some instances of improvements in the provision of historical information about current policy issues. The Congressional Research Service, for example, does a good job of providing background materials that take into account past legislative actions as well as provide information on some of the earlier relevant evaluations and studies for the members of Congress.[29] Similarly, recent White House efforts to provide briefings for new administration officials occasionally include a few historical case studies of agency developments.[30] The Office of Technology Assessment, which now has been eliminated, sometimes incorporated discussions of past policies in its position papers.[31] Yet, though all these efforts are useful and commendable, most have not provided the amount or type of in-depth historical discussion and analysis that policymakers might find most helpful.

The Department of Education appears to be especially negligent in its development and use of a historical perspective on its operations. The Office of Educational Research and Improvement, the lead research and intellectual agency of the department, has spent billions of dollars in the past three decades without much attention to historical studies of education.[32] Occasionally some historical work has been funded by OERI, but the findings from those studies usually have not been widely disseminated or utilized, even within the department.[33] In part this is because in recent years OERI has not been seen as a particularly relevant or important source of policy information and analysis. But is also reflects a long-standing, implicit bias or indifference within that agency and the department against historical analyses of current educational reforms and practices.[34]

Unlike the Congressional Research Service, the National Library of Education in the Department of Education has not defined as one of its missions the provision of detailed and timely analyses of current policy issues.[35] Moreover, although the National Center for Education Statistics provides useful statistical data and analyses, it has deliberately steered away from doing in-depth policy analyses—especially of topics that might be considered too politically sensitive or controversial.[36] And while the Office of Planning and Evaluation Service in the Department of Education frequently commissions useful evaluation studies, these are often done on an ad hoc basis and focus almost entirely on the present. For example, there are still no serious historical policy analyses of Title I of the Elementary and Secondary Education Act of 1965—the major federal educational compensatory program for the past thirty years—available in the U.S. Department of Education.[37]

Given the relatively rapid turnover of policymakers in Washington in both the executive and legislative branches, it is important that relevant documents and studies relating to substantive matters be collected, archived, and made readily available. Certainly the public legislative documents are well preserved and increasingly accessible through the Internet. Unfortunately, the same is not always true for documents generated by the executive branch. The domestic papers of the White House eventually are archived at the presidential libraries, but because these institutions are scattered throughout the country, it is difficult for policymakers to assemble relevant materials without considerable effort.[38] Moreover, most federal departments and agencies have an extremely poor record of archiving their own documents. Often some of the most important papers are available only in the personal files of the staff and these documents are periodically cleansed due to inadequate storage space or lost entirely when that employee changes jobs or retires. Even if the documents have been properly deposited with the National Archives, the materials are often poorly indexed and hard to retrieve.[39] Certainly the archiving practices and procedures of the U.S. Department of Education leave much to be desired.[40]

STUDYING CHANGES IN THE LIFE COURSE AND SOCIETY

Most studies of education have not employed an overall analytic framework and tend to focus only on some specific aspect of children or of their schools. The life-course framework, described in chapter 8, provides a broader and more comprehensive scheme of mapping and analyzing educational long-term change. It keeps the focus on the child while taking into account the myriad of potentially important influences on that individual. By concentrating on the developing child rather than on a static child placed in any particular grade or classroom, the life-course framework encourages a more dynamic and historical appreciation of individual change. It also emphasizes studying crucial life-course transitions, such as entering kindergarten or junior high school, that may be particularly stressful and yet very important for the education of the developing child. Thus, the complex interactions between the growing child and the various institutional forms of schooling she or he sequentially encounters can be documented and analyzed more readily from a policy perspective.

The life-course framework also reminds us that much of the education and training of children occurs in the home rather than in the classroom. Although educational reformers routinely acknowledge the importance of the home and parents, in practice they tend to focus their attention mainly on changing the school environment.[41] More traditional educational approaches also often fail to pay sufficient attention to such crucial nonschool experiences as summer learning. Several scholars have argued persuasively that at-risk children learn at about the same rate as middle-class children during the school year but fall behind during the summer months because of the limited educational opportunities in their culturally and economically impoverished neighborhoods and home environments.[42]

The life-course framework also helps us to cope conceptually with the increasingly fragmented, categorical educational and social service programs for children. Teenage mothers, for example, need educational as well as health and socioeconomic assistance. Yet federal programs for teen mothers are divided between the Department of Education and the Department of Health and Human Services. In theory these different federal initiatives are closely coordinated, but in practice during the past twenty years they have been kept far apart by both the executive and legislative branches. Part of that unfortunate separation can be traced to the legislative history of efforts to deal with teenage pregnancies and the care of young mothers. The life-course framework encourages policy analysts to acknowledge the service fragmentation and to take steps to address that problem.[43]

Another reason why historians may have something to contribute to policymaking today is that their work focuses heavily on long-term and large-scale changes and transitions. We have just discussed why historians may be well situated to integrate and analyze diverse and scattered information about the education of the developing child. The historian also may be helpful in analyzing school changes as well as investigating broader socioeconomic and educational transformations.

Public high schools, for example, have changed dramatically in the past 150 years. First created in Massachusetts in the early nineteenth century, they gradually spread throughout the nation. And rather than being designed mainly for middle- and upper-class students, they soon became more accessible to children of working-class parents as well.[44] In the twentieth-century, school attendance became a normal phase of adolescent life as the percentage of all fourteen- to seventeen-year-olds enrolled rose rapidly from 14.3 percent in 1909–10 to 50.7 percent in 1929–30; 72.6 percent in 1939–40; 83.4 percent in fall 1959; 92.0 percent in fall 1970; 90.3 percent in fall 1980; and 95.3 percent in fall 1993.[45] As teenage school attendance became almost universal in the 1960s, the concerns of the public and educators shifted from making high schools available to anyone wanting to attend to preventing any school dropouts.[46]

As high schools attracted more children from working-class families, many education leaders argued that the curriculum should be expanded to provide vocational and nonacademic opportunities for children not planning to attend college. Debates over the importance of providing more rigorous, academic training for those not expected to continue with their education continued throughout the twentieth century.[47] When we look at the actual courses taken by high school students, there has been a general overall decline in academic courses.[48] Moreover, starting in the late-nineteenth-century, public schools gradually came to provide many nonacademic services, such as school lunches, counseling, and health care, for children who needed them.[49]

As a result of these developments, the high school today has become more concerned about providing nonacademic opportunities and services for an increasingly diverse and impoverished population than one hundred years ago. Yet the average length of the school year and the school day has remained relatively stable since 1930, so that now there is less time for academic pursuits in the classroom.[50] Recent calls for higher academic curriculum standards and assessments are trying to reverse this trend, but are we prepared to sacrifice the nonacademic opportunities and services now provided in most public schools, especially in the inner cities where many at-risk children do not receive the care and attention they deserve? Will we be willing to expand the school year or school day to accommodate the proposed additional academic training? And if schools are to relinquish some of their nonacademic tasks, what other institutions in our society are available and willing to address those needs? By taking a longer, historical perspective, perhaps policymakers will better appreciate the diverse and ever-changing functions of schools in our society and take into consideration the overall educational, social, and health needs of adolescents as they redesign the functions of our high schools and other local institutions. This is not an argument against redirecting high schools toward a more academic curriculum, but a plea for trying to make those changes along with other necessary improvements in the family and neighborhood experiences of those adolescents. Moreover, by understanding the long, contentious history of the debates over the proper functions of high schools, it may be possible to anticipate and address some of the likely hostile reactions against the current efforts to enhance the academic quality of those institutions.

Another advantage of taking a longer, historical perspective on schooling is that the results of the few longitudinal studies of educational change may be more time-bound than educators and other policymakers realize. For example, the impressive, but contested impact of early childhood education at the Perry

Preschool in Ypsilanti, Michigan is frequently cited as proof of the effectiveness of early interventions (see chapter 3). But the quality of Ypsilanti schools in the mid-1960s may have been higher and the families and neighborhoods in that community more supportive and safer than they are today.[51] Similarly, the long-term benefits to pregnant teenagers attending Baltimore schools in the late 1960s may not be as easily replicated now, since conditions for disadvantaged children in those schools and the city as a whole may have deteriorated over the past three decades.[52] This may explain in part why many children of those adolescent mothers are faring worse today than their parents at comparable ages. Thus, policymakers assessing the potential long-term benefits of early model educational programs need to take into account subsequent changes in families and neighborhoods that may limit the ability of these institutions to improve upon or even duplicate the earlier successes.[53]

EDUCATIONAL REFORM AND PAST EXPERIENCES

One enduring characteristic of the American people and policymakers is faith in the ability of schooling in general or of specific education programs to produce fundamental improvements in society.[54] Education reformers like Henry Barnard and Horace Mann believed that the spread of common schools in antebellum America would not only help to preserve the Republic, but transform the very nature of American politics and the economy.[55] Infant school and Head Start were touted as institutions that would aid disadvantaged youth and help eventually to eradicate poverty altogether (see chapter 3). When kindergartens were first introduced in mid-nineteenth-century America, it was claimed that they, too, would lift immigrant and poor children into the ranks of the middle class.[56] And President Lyndon Johnson enthusiastically believed that the War on Poverty could be won with the passage of the Elementary and Secondary Education Act of 1965.[57]

Running through these educational initiatives is a naive belief that by simply educating the next generation one can eliminate many of the seemingly inscrutable problems facing society. These educational reforms are usually targeted at the poor, with the hope that through compensatory education programs, at-risk children can be redeemed and transformed into productive citizens. This vision exaggerates the actual impact of schools on children and minimizes the relative importance of parents in shaping the outcomes of their offspring. It also downplays the substantial structural barriers to social and economic mobility in our society and reflects the longstanding belief in America that individuals not only are responsible for their own well-being, but that they are capable of improving their lives if they study and work harder.[58] Although it may appear to be easier and less expensive to effect changes in public schools than in other powerful and intractable institutions, improving only the schools is unlikely to be enough to transform our society. Some analysts have argued that ending educational inequalities may reduce some disparities in our society, but that by itself this would not eliminate the increasingly sizable income and wealth inequalities.[59] Nor were improved educational opportunities by themselves enough to overcome the strong racial discrimination and barriers against blacks throughout much of our history.[60]

Related to the exaggerated faith in the general efficacy of education reforms is the more specific belief that early childhood education is the key to long-term individual and social improvements. There have been numerous examples throughout this volume of educators and the American public turning to early intervention programs—infant schools, kindergartens, Head Start, Follow Through, and Even Start—to solve problems of poverty and disadvantage. Yet in each instance, most of these early intervention programs had less impact than envisioned and the initial cognitive gains often could not be sustained over time. The life-course approach, which stresses the continuity of development and deemphasizes the absolute primacy of any particular phase, reminds us that while early childhood education programs may be quite helpful, their short-term benefits probably cannot be maintained without continued attention and assistance as children enter the regular schools.

One major reason for the unrealistic claims and subsequent disappointment of education as well as for other reform efforts is the nature of our political system, which in the short run often rewards those who make extravagant claims for their projects. As discussed earlier in this chapter, most education programs and services are categorical—focusing on some particular phase of the life course or problem area rather than trying to deal with the entire child. Fierce competition for public attention and funding by the increasingly numerous categorical programs leads to a bidding war among them. In order to succeed, each program finds it expedient to exaggerate its potential for success and to minimize its actual costs compared to its competitors. In this political and reform environment it is not enough just to say that one's program will provide some assistance for at-risk children; claims of dramatic, permanent improvements with high cost-benefit returns typically are expected before policymakers and the public are willing to provide more funds.

Yet experience has shown that, given the complexity of society and the difficulty of fostering long-term changes, most educational reforms at best produce only modest, though still important improvements. Patricia Graham, a historian and a former director of the National Institute of Education, explained that trying to change the direction of education is like trying to steer a battleship: you can make some small, but eventually important changes in the course, but whatever maneuvers you make will take considerable time to put into effect, especially if you are trying to introduce major changes.[61] And as David Tyack and Larry Cuban point out, most reforms are not only incremental, but are added onto the existing system so that the final product is often more jumbled and internally inconsistent than initially envisioned.[62]

When legislators and the public realize that a program's achievement has not matched the earlier exaggerated claims, they become disillusioned and angry—sometimes eliminating the program. Moreover, rather than focusing more resources on a few comprehensive and large-scale reforms that actually might make a difference, both the executive and legislative branches in the past twenty-five years have often resorted to establishing small, relatively inexpensive federal domestic programs of about $10 to $50 million, which claim to be able to solve some difficult and pressing social problem but in fact are doomed to failure because of their limited coverage and funding. Rather than learning from this all-too-frequent cyclical pattern of inflated claims and disappointing findings, we continue to look for the next "magic bullet" that will solve our difficult domestic problems. Thus, when President George Bush and the nation's governors issued the six national education goals in 1989, it was not enough to call for improvement in the math and science achievements of students; they insisted that by the year 2000 American students would be first in the world in math and science—a laudable but rather implausible goal.[63]

Our historical analyses of education programs like the infant schools, Head Start, Follow Through, and Even Start suggest that the public and policymakers often had unrealistically high expectations of education initiatives because these programs had not been developed properly. Much of the fault lies with policymakers who were unwilling to experiment and to develop more systematically the new educational models; instead, these leaders advocated the almost immediate creation and implementation of large-scale service programs. Sargent Shriver, for example, rejected advice to proceed slowly; instead he instituted on short notice a massive summer Head Start program in 1965. These summer programs subsequently proved to be ineffective, and they were quietly abandoned for year-round Head Start programs.[64] Similarly, suggestions that Even Start funding be limited while awaiting evaluations were summarily rejected as unnecessary by proponents claiming that the program had succeeded. Yet the large-scale Abt national evaluation found that, overall, the programs were not particularly effective, though this has not discouraged some of Even Start's more ardent supporters from claiming it has been successful and should be expanded.[65]

Perhaps one reason that some program advocates favor immediate implementation over experimentation is that once a larger constituency for the new services is created, it is politically more difficult to eliminate that new program even if the subsequent evaluations are disappointing. Indeed, Follow Through, which consisted of an uneasy mixture of a sizable number of service and experimental programs, survived for several decades despite the surprisingly strong negative results from its assessment in the mid-1970s.[66] As Diane Ravitch put it: "There is one sure way to achieve eternal life: Become a federal program. Many programs administered by the Department of Education long ago outlived their usefulness, but they continue to receive appropriations year after year, protected by friends in Congress. Most programs are seldom evaluated; on the odd occasion when a program gets a negative evaluation, its friends respond that it needs more money and more time."[67]

It is difficult to effect sustained educational change because there is not one American educational system, but many hundreds of local school districts that have different needs and orientations. Studies of schools have revealed the difficulty and complexity of trying to reform them. As Arthur Zilversmit's excellent but somewhat disheartening study of the interaction between progressive educational theory and practice in four Illinois schools over three decades demonstrated, "the ways in which the schools changed was a product of their own histories, developments within each community, and the personalities and goals of their superintendents."[68]

There are no simple or easy answers for improving schools. Good program development and evaluations are expensive, require considerable time, and are potentially dangerous politically if the results are disappointing. Yet they are essential if we are ever to figure out exactly which particular types of educational service delivery programs are most effective in helping at-risk children in different settings. Program development and evaluations are also needed for carefully scaling-up from a few local exemplary model programs to a large, national educational initiative. Indeed, the need for such long-term research and program development was part of the rationale in the mid-1960s for creating the regional educational laboratories and the research and development centers (see chapter 2). Unfortunately, during the past twenty-five years, neither the National Institute of Education nor its successor, the Office of Educational Research and Improvement, has made such systematic program development and testing part of its overall research agenda.

USES OF THE PAST AT THE AGENCY LEVEL

Much of the discussion in this chapter has centered on the possible uses of a historical perspective for addressing general educational policy issues. Naturally, the list of possible topics could be expanded to include school choice, the role of curriculum content standards, shifts in school finance and governance, or the controversy over multiculturalism. Each of these has important implications at the national, state, and local levels and has already attracted some useful historic studies.[69]

Historical analyses might also be profitably employed in the routine operations of a federal, state, or local agency because many key policy decisions are made and implemented there. Yet most discussions of the value of history do not explore such seemingly mundane but ultimately important sites for the uses of information about the past. Because most government institutions periodically develop strategic, long-range plans, a better understanding of an agency's past, including the history of earlier efforts to develop strategic plans, might be helpful in formulating and implementing new plans. For example, the Office of Educational Research and Improvement might have improved its five-year research plan by using a life-course framework (see chapter 8) and by paying more attention to the strengths and weaknesses of past planning exercises.

Knowledge of the past also might encourage and facilitate useful changes in an agency. Understanding that tasks were once done differently encourages policymakers to consider changes today. Knowledge of the past also reminds decision makers that the creation and evolution of current policies were not inevitable, so that proposed changes may seem less threatening. Placing the origins of present policies in their historical context also aids the policymaker in better understanding what his or her predecessors were trying to accomplish; this also makes it easier to assess an agency's success or failure in meeting those objectives. For example, rather than accepting the existing, long-standing OERI regional educational laboratory system as inevitable and immutable, policymakers should explore changing the system in light of its historical experiences and accomplishments as well as in response to present research and development needs (see chapter 2).

Agencies can also utilize information about the past to help accomplish their more immediate assignments. Continuing with the example of the regional educational laboratories, the congressionally mandated third-year review of these institutions would benefit by considering previous reviews of the laboratories. A review of earlier assessment procedures might suggest alternative strategies to the designers of the current laboratory evaluations, as well as providing clues to what impact the different approaches might have had on the functioning and achievements of the laboratories. Although past assessment practices cannot provide a simple blueprint for the present third-year evaluation, they might assist OERI officials in performing a more comprehensive and effective analysis.[70]

Historical knowledge can also help policymakers assess how well certain tasks are being done today compared to similar efforts in the past. The scope and usefulness of the Department of Education's proposed Title I evaluation should be compared to the Sustaining Effects Study in the late 1970s and to the Prospects Study in the early 1990s.[71] Similarly, the work and role of the new National Educational Research Policy and Priorities Board overseeing OERI might be compared to the activities of its NIE predecessor in the 1970s.[72] And the eventual design of OERI's third-year evaluation of the regional educational laboratories could be compared to previous assessments. By making such explicit comparisons, policymakers would be in a better position to appreciate the strengths and weaknesses of the current work and to encourage organizations to improve on their earlier efforts. At the same time, such comparisons might help agencies to stimulate a more historical and comprehensive understanding of their present activities.

Reviewing the earlier statements of administrators and experts provides yet another way of using the past to inform the present. Not only does it provide potentially valuable information about past practices, but it also allows us to ascertain which individuals have been particularly effective in analyzing and predicting the outcomes of educational reforms. Perhaps some individuals are more successful and reliable in presenting a balanced and realistic assessment of educational activities than others. Moreover, knowing that one's statements and claims may be scrutinized in the future might encourage educational administrators and policymakers to be more realistic in their expectations for new educational programs.

Social historians have discovered that many older workers enjoy and benefit considerably from studies and exhibitions dealing with their previous places of employment. It provides them with a richer understanding of their lives as well as a better appreciation of their achievements. Learning about the origins and development of agencies will help administrators to remember the tasks the agencies were initially created to address. And historical studies of government organizations also might help employees understand better their individual contributions to overall agency goals and accomplishments. To help reestablish the sense of dedication and pride in public service eloquently called for by President John F. Kennedy in 1961, we may need to develop a broader and more historical appreciation of the role and functioning of government agencies and to assist public employees in providing the high quality of services that all Americans deserve.

Knowing that future generations will judge what we accomplish today can stimulate more civic-minded and less narrowly partisan activities. Kennedy's realization that history would judge his actions reinforced his decision to proceed cautiously during the Cuban Missile Crisis. And President George Bush's desire to be remembered as the "education president" and President Bill Clinton's wish to enhance his place in history encouraged them to try to overcome more immediate, strictly political considerations. Similarly, career civil servants and congressional staff members might be more likely to focus on the long-term public interests once they realize that their work will be reviewed by policy analysts and historians.

Finally, the public's sense of fairness and justice can be satisfied in part by knowing that the few individuals in government positions of trust who commit illegal or morally questionable acts will be held accountable by historians. Moreover, those government officials and civil servants who maintain high ethical standards and pursue high-minded public policies despite intense pressure from lobbyists and politicians will be recognized and praised by future generations. Indeed, historians can play a useful role in explicating and publicizing the proper ethical and moral standards of behavior for public servants.

Lessons from the past provide no simple or straightforward guidance for policymakers. Yet a properly employed historical perspective can make important contributions to how we perceive and address the ever-changing yet always somewhat similar problems that confront us. Persuading policymakers to utilize more information about the past and historians to make such studies more readily available will be neither easy nor popular. But it is a worthwhile and necessary goal if government is to provide the type and quality of services that can truly help those most disadvantaged in our society today.

Notes

CHAPTER 1. HISTORIANS AND POLICYMAKING

1. On the early promotional literature about North America, see David Van Tassel, *Recording America's Past: An Interpretation of the Development of Historical Studies in America,* 1607–1884 (Chicago: University of Chicago Press, 1960), 1–9; Alden T. Vaughan, "The Evolution of Virginia's History: Historians of the First Colony," in *Perspectives on Early American History: Essays in Honor of Richard B. Morris,* ed. Alden T. Vaughan and George A. Billias (New York: Harper and Row, 1973), 9–39.

2. For discussions of Puritan and other early American histories, see Lester H. Cohen, *The Revolutionary Histories: Contemporary Narratives of the American Revolution* (Ithaca: Cornell University Press, 1980); Peter Gay, *A Loss of Mastery: Puritan Historians* (Berkeley: University of California Press, 1966); Van Tassel, *Recording America's Past,* 10–30; Harry M. Ward, "The Search for American Identity: Early Historians of New England," in *Perspectives on Early American History: Essays in Honor of Richard B. Morris,* ed. Alden T. Vaughan and George A. Billias (New York: Harper and Row, 1973), 40–62.

3. For a discussion of seventeenth- and eighteenth-century schooling, see James Axtell, *The School upon a Hill: Education and Society in Colonial New England* (New Haven: Yale University Press, 1974); Bernard Bailyn, *Education in the Forming of American Society: Needs and Opportunities for Study* (Chapel Hill:

University of North Carolina Press, 1960); Lawrence Cremin, *American Education: The Colonial Experience, 1607–1783* (New York: Harper and Row, 1970); Carl F. Kaestle, *Pillars of the Republic: Common Schools and American Society, 1780–1860* (New York: Hill and Wang, 1983).

4. Bernard Bailyn, *The Ideological Origins of the American Revolution* (Cambridge: Harvard University Press, 1967); Clinton Rossiter, *Seedtime of the Republic: The Origin of the American Tradition of Liberty* (New York: Harcourt, Brace, 1953).

5. Carl J. Richards, *The Founders and the Classics: Greece, Rome, and the American Enlightenment* (Cambridge: Harvard University Press, 1994).

6. Richard M. Gummere, *The American Colonial Mind and the Classical Tradition: Essays in Comparative Culture* (Cambridge: Harvard University Press, 1963); Richards, *Founders and the Classics.*

7. Richards, *Founders and the Classics,* 118–22. Bailyn, in contrast, minimizes the importance of the classics in developing the idea of a conspiracy against liberty but stresses the role of the writings of the British radical Whigs. Bailyn, *Ideological Origins,* 144–59.

8. Bailyn, *Ideological Origins.* On the educational views of the revolutionaries, see Lorraine S. Pangle and Thomas L. Pangle, *The Learning of Liberty: The Educational Ideas of the American Founders* (Lawrence: University of Kansas Press, 1993).

9. Cohen, *Revolutionary Histories.* For an attempt to link changing views of the American Revolution to the life stages of its participants, see Peter C. Hoffer, *Revolution and Regeneration: Life Cycle and the Historical Vision of the Generation of 1776* (Athens: University of Georgia Press, 1983). On the uses of history by ministers during these years, see Donald Weber, *Rhetoric and History in Revolutionary New England* (New York: Oxford University Press, 1988).

10. George H. Callcott, *History in the United States, 1800–1860: Its Practice and Purpose* (Baltimore: Johns Hopkins University Press, 1970), 25.

11. Agnew O. Roorbach, *The Development of the Social Studies in American Secondary Education before 1861* (Philadelphia: University of Pennsylvania Press, 1937), 119.

12. Quoted in Roorbach, *Development of the Social Studies,* 114–15. As Roorbach also points out, the uses of history varied somewhat according to whether one was studying ancient, universal, or U.S. history. Ibid., 123–28.

13. On the historians and histories of this period, see John S. Bassett, *The Middle Group of American Historians* (New York: Macmillan, 1917); Callcott, *History in the United States;* David Levin, *History As Romantic Art: Bancroft, Prescott, Motley, and Parkman* (New York: Harcourt, Brace, 1959); Van Tassel, *Recording America's Past.* There were other individuals and institutions that focused more on collecting historical facts than on interpreting them. For a discussion of this aspect of antebellum historical activity, see Callcott, *History in the United States,* 109–19.

14. Callcott, *History in the United States,* 67–82.

15. Lilian Handlin, *George Bancroft: The Intellectual As Democrat* (New York: Harper and Row, 1984); Levin, *History As Romantic Art;* Russell B. Nye, *George Bancroft* (New York: Washington Square Press, 1964).

16. Callcott, *History in the United States,* 175–214. Although historians who were active in contemporary politics tried to avoid introducing partisan biases in their scholarly works,

their enemies and even some of their friends felt that they did not always maintain that distinction in fact. Nye, *George Bancroft*, 136–94. Occasionally these activist scholars did use their historical knowledge to address contemporary issues. For example, in some of his political speeches Bancroft compared the situation in the United States to the decline of Rome. But most of Bancroft's comparisons were rather broad, as he often did not have specific insights or advice, historical or otherwise, on how to achieve the goals he was espousing. Handlin, *George Bancroft*, 115–73.

In addition to history, civics was introduced into the classrooms in the antebellum period. The focus of civic textbooks was more directly on the nature of the U.S. political system and the specific duties and responsibilities of citizens. There was, however, great overlap in subject matter among the emerging disciplines, and often textbooks and classes covered more than one subject. Roorbach, *Development of the Social Studies*, 165–201. As a result, although certain topics concerning citizenship may not have been addressed specifically in a history textbook or class, it does not necessarily mean that it was not covered elsewhere in the curriculum.

17. Callcott, *History in the United States*, 193–203.

18. Callcott, *History in the United States;* Handlin, *George Bancroft.*

19. For an excellent discussion of the changing nature of the history profession, see Peter Novick, *That Noble Dream: The "Objectivity Question" and the American Historical Profession* (Cambridge: Cambridge University Press, 1988).

20. Henry Adams, "The Tendency of History," *Annual Report of the American Historical Association for the Year* 1894 (Washington, D.C.: Government Printing Office, 1895), 18–19.

21. Edward P. Cheyney, address delivered to Graduate School of University of Pennsylvania, Oct. 3, 1907 quoted in Novick, *That Noble Dream,* 56.

22. On the slow but steady increase in professional historians in colleges and universities in the second half of the nineteenth century, see Charles Kendall Adams, "Recent Historical Work in the Colleges and Universities of Europe and America," *Annual Report of the American Historical Association for the Year* 1889 (Washington, D.C.: Government Printing Office, 1890), 19–42.

23. The best discussion of the creation and early development of the American Historical Association is David D. Van Tassel, "From Learned Society to Professional Organization: The American Historical Association, 1884–1900," *American Historical Review* 89, no. 4 (Oct. 1984): 929–56. On the development and demise of the American Social Science Association, see Mary O. Furner, *Advocacy and Objectivity: A Crisis in the Professionalization of American Social Science, 1865–1905* (Lexington: University Press of Kentucky, 1975); Thomas L. Haskell, *The Emergence of Professional Social Science: The American Social Science Association and the Nineteenth-Century Crisis of Authority* (Urbana: University of Illinois Press, 1977).

24. For a very useful, but often rather hard to read, overall analysis of the origins of the American social sciences, see Dorothy Ross, *The Origins of American Social Science* (Cambridge: Cambridge University Press, 1991). On the changing relation of the other social sciences to history, see Terrence J. McDonald, ed., *The Historic Turn in the Human Sciences* (Ann Arbor: University of Michigan Press, 1996); Eric H. Monkkonen, ed.,

Engaging the Past: The Uses of History across the Social Sciences (Durham: Duke University Press, 1994).

25. Novick, *That Noble Dream*, 47–85.

26. On the progressive historians during these years, see Ernest A. Breisach, *American Progressive History: An Experiment in Modernization* (Chicago: University of Chicago Press, 1993).

27. Alan Creutz, "Social Access to the Professions: Late Nineteenth-Century Academics at the University of Michigan as a Case Study," *Journal of Social History* 15 (1981): 61–64; Novick, *That Noble Dream*, 68–70.

28. On academic freedom during these years, see Richard Hofstadter, *Academic Freedom in the Age of the College* (New York: Columbia University Press, 1955); Novick, *That Noble Dream*, 63–68.

29. The noncontroversial aspects of the recommendations of historians resulted, in part, because scholars were discouraged from openly criticizing each other. As historians anticipated collecting and analyzing objective knowledge, they saw less need for controversies among themselves. Novick, *That Noble Dream*, 57–60.

30. The presidents of the American Historical Association were not typical members of that organization—they were more prominent and more accomplished—yet they provide a good indicator of the views of leading individuals in the field. Moreover, the AHA presidents often used the occasion to reflect on the broader and more philosophical purposes of their discipline, and so their speeches are a useful source of information on this topic. For a discussion and analysis of the content of AHA presidential addresses, see Henry Ausubel, *Historians and Their Craft: A Study of the Presidential Addresses of the American Historical Association, 1884–1945* (New York: Columbia University Press, 1950).

31. Glenn C. Altschuler, *Andrew D. White: Educator, Historian, Diplomat* (Ithaca: Cornell University Press, 1979).

32. Andrew D. White, "On Studies in General History and the History of Civilization," *Papers of the American Historical Association* 1, no. 2 (New York: G. P. Putnam's, 1895), 24.

33. John Jay, "The Demand for Education in American History," *Annual Report of the American Historical Association for the Year* 1890 (Washington, D.C.: Government Printing Office, 1891), 29. Jay was not alone in seeing the patriotic and civic values of American history. George Hoar, another AHA president who was not a prominent historian himself, rejected the negative views of American society and called for a greater appreciation of the virtues of our past as well as of our current political institutions: "The first duty of the historian, as I have said, as the first duty of every man in every relation of life, is to absolute truth. Yet if in anything the love of country or a lofty enthusiasm may have led him to paint her in too favorable colors, the sober judgment of time will correct the mistake. No serious harm will have been done. Certainly no youth was ever yet spoiled by reverencing too much the memory of his parents. If anything is to be pardoned to human infirmity, it is surely better to err on the side of ennobling the country's history than to err on the side of degrading it." George F. Hoar, "Popular Discontent with Representative Government," *Annual Report of the American Historical Association for the Year* 1895 (Washington, D.C.: Government Printing Office, 1896), 23.

34. Charles Francis Adams, "An Undeveloped Function," *Annual Report of the American*

Historical Association for the Year 1901 (Washington, D.C.: Government Printing Office, 1895), 49–93.

35. Henry Charles Lea, "Ethical Values in History," *American Historical Review* 9, no. 2 (Jan. 1904): 237.

36. William A. Dunning, "Truth in History," *American Historical Review* 19 (1914): 217–29.

37. William F. Russell, "The Early Teaching of History in Secondary Schools," *History Teachers' Magazine* 5, no. 7 (Sept. 1914): 203–8; Rolla M. Tryon, *The Social Sciences As School Subjects* (New York: Charles Scribner's, 1935), 79–84.

38. National Education Association, *Report of the Committee of Ten on Secondary School Studies with the Reports of the Conferences Arranged by the Committee* (New York: American Book Company, 1894), 170.

39. American Historical Association, *The Study of History in Schools: Report to the American Historical Association by the Committee of Seven* (New York: Macmillan, 1900), 34–35.

40. American Historical Association, *Study of History in Schools,* 19–20.

41. For example, the American Historical Associations's Committee of Five in 1910 basically endorsed the views of the AHA's Committee of Seven. American Historical Association, "The Study of History in Secondary Schools: Report of the Committee of Five," *Annual Report of the American Historical Association for the Year* 1910 (Washington, D.C.: Government Printing Office, 1912), 211–42.

42. Tryon, *Social Sciences As School Subjects,* 84–91, 131–208.

43. J. Madison Gathany, "The Reconstruction of History Teaching," *History Teachers' Magazine* 5 (1914): 223, as quoted in Tryon, *Social Sciences As School Subjects,* 88–89. Although Gathany may have exaggerated somewhat the presentist orientation of some historians, some prominent individuals fit his description quite accurately. See, e.g., the extended statements of David Snedden, the superintendent of Massachusetts schools on the role of history in the public schools. David Snedden, "Teaching of History in Secondary Schools," *History Teachers' Magazine* 5, no. 9 (November 1914): 277–82.

44. Altschuler, *Andrew D. White.*

45. John Daly studied the uses of history by the Supreme Court in the early twentieth century and summarized the uses of history by the Fuller Supreme Court: "It is impossible to say that the Court as a whole had any special attitude toward history. It can be asserted, though, that the majority of justices viewed history as a valuable aid in establishing a firm basis for resolving legal difficulties. Not all applied history with the same competency—which was to be expected—but aside from the criticism leveled at the historical interpretations in the opinions of Moody and Brown, and at Holmes' reluctance to use history at all, it can be said that the application of history by the judges was praiseworthy." John J. Daly, *The Use of History in the Decisions of the Supreme Court: 1900–1930* (Washington, D.C.: Catholic University of America Press, 1954), 100.

46. On the development of the Bureau of Education, see Donald R. Warren, *To Enforce Education: A History of the Founding Years of the United States Office of Education* (Detroit: Wayne State University Press, 1974). An examination of the annual reports of the Bureau of Education revealed that numerous historical studies were published in the 1870s, 1880s, and into the 1890s. Many of these studies were concerned with higher education, but most were publications of historical analyses without much attention to

their particular usefulness to policymakers. The assumption seemed to be that if you collected enough historical facts and analyses, something of value would emerge. But sometimes explicit efforts were made to point out the practical value of these historical studies. For example, in transmitting Herbert Adams's study of the College of William and Mary to the secretary of the interior, the commissioner of the Bureau of Education stated that the study demonstrated the value of an organic connection between political education and government. N. H. R. Dawson, "Letter to the Secretary of the Interior, Jan. 20, 1987," in Herbert B. Adams, *The College of William and Mary with Suggestions for the National Promotion of Higher Education,* Contributions to American Educational History, no. 1 (Washington, D.C.: Government Printing Office, 1987), 7–9.

47. On the reactions of American historians to World War I, see George T. Blakey, *Historians on the Homefront: American Propagandists for the Great War* (Lexington: University Press of Kentucky, 1970); Carol S. Gruber, *Mars and Minerva: World War I and the Uses of Higher Learning in America* (Baton Rouge: Louisiana State University Press, 1975).

48. Arthur O. Lovejoy, letter to the editor, *Nation* 99 (24 Sept. 1914): 376, quoted in Novick, *That Noble Dream,* 115.

49. H. Morse Stephens, "Nationality and History," *American Historical Review* 21 (1916): 236, quoted in Ausubel, *Historians and Their Craft,* 59.

50. Blakey, *Historians on the Homefront;* Gruber, *Mars and Minerva,* 118–61.

51. Gruber, *Mars and Minerva,* 163–212; Novick, *That Noble Dream,* 120–22.

52. Frank Aydelotte, *Final Report of the War Issues Course of the Students' Army Training Corps* (Washington, D.C.: War Department, 1919); Gruber, *Mars and Minerva,* 213–52.

53. Novick, *That Noble Dream,* 127–28.

54. Warren I. Cohen, *The American Revisionists* (Chicago: University of Chicago Press, 1966); Novick, *That Noble Dream,* 206–24.

55. C. Hartley Grattan, "The Historians Cut Loose," *American Mercury* 11, no. 44 (Aug. 1927): 414–30.

56. William T. Hutchinson, "The American Historian in Wartime," *Mississippi Valley Historical Review* 29, no. 2 (Sept. 1942): 182.

57. Gruber, *Mars and Minerva,* 213–52.

58. Lewis Paul Todd, *Wartime Relations of the Federal Government and the Public Schools, 1917–1918* (New York: Teachers College, 1945).

59. Tryon, *Social Sciences As School Subjects,* 216–24.

60. Dexter Perkins and John L. Snell, *The Education of Historians in the United States* (New York: McGraw-Hill, 1962), 16–22.

61. Novick, *That Noble Dream,* 168–205.

62. Ausubel, *Historians and Their Craft,* 50–119.

63. James Harvey Robinson, "The Newer Ways of Historians," *American Historical Review* 35, no. 2 (Jan. 1930): 255.

64. William Roscoe Thayer, "Fallacies in History," *American Historical Review* 25, no. 2 (Jan. 1920): 185. Thayer was one of the prominent historians who denounced the biases of German scholars while displaying his own in the process. For example, in the same speech he stated: "On the score of impartiality, therefore, the modern German historians did not greatly impress me; and since the war has disclosed that they, like the other

professional men, the teachers, and clergy, in Germany, were simply working to Germanize the world in order to make it an easier prey for German ambition, I have felt it a duty to repudiate them. If we are to raise history to the high place in the regard of men which it should occupy, we must purge it from the corruption which the Germans inflicted upon it. They used it simply as a higher form of the deception practiced by the imperial government." Ibid., 180.

65. Charles H. McIlwain, "The Historian's Part in a Changing World," *American Historical Review* 42, no. 2 (Jan. 1937): 223–24.

66. For an excellent discussion of the issue of historical objectivity during these years, see Novick, *That Noble Dream*, 133–278.

67. Charles A. Beard, "Written History As an Act of Faith," *American Historical Review* 39, no. 2 (Jan. 1934): 226.

68. McIlwain, "The Historian's Part in a Changing World," 208–9, 210.

69. William E. Dodd, Jr., and Martha Dodd, eds., *Ambassador Dodd's Diary, 1933–1938* (New York: Harcourt, Brace, 1941).

70. On the foreign policy debates in the 1930s, see William Langer and S. Everett Gleason, *The Challenge to Isolation, 1937–1940* (New York: Harper and Row, 1952), and William Langer and S. Everett Gleason, *The Undeclared War, 1940–1941* (New York: Harper and Row, 1953). During World War I and immediately thereafter, historians had been very active in the efforts to develop postwar peace plans. Lawrence E. Gelfand, *The Inquiry: American Preparations for Peace, 1917–1919* (New Haven: Yale University Press, 1963).

71. Novick, *That Noble Dream*, 245.

72. As one reads about historians during the interwar years, one gets the distinct impression that their activity and influence was reduced in both domestic and foreign affairs. This important topic, however, awaits more thorough and systematic work.

73. Daly, *Use of History*, 101–208.

74. McDonald, ed., *Historic Turn in the Human Sciences*; Ross, *Origins of American Social Science*.

75. For a further overview of these developments, see Henry Johnson, *Teaching of History in Elementary and Secondary School with Applications to Allied Studies*, rev. ed. (New York: Macmillan, 1940), 58–66.

76. Department of the Interior, Bureau of Education, "The Social Studies in Secondary Education," *Bulletin* no. 28 (Washington, D.C.: Government Printing Office, 1916), 35.

77. Tryon, *Social Sciences As School Subjects*, 20–21. Despite the importance of the commission's report, the earlier recommendations of the AHA committees continued to have a major impact in the 1920s. As Tryon put it: "It will be a surprise to those who have dared to suggest that the influence of the Committee of Seven ceased soon after the publication in 1916 of the report of the Committee of the Social Studies in Secondary Education to find that its influence was somewhat dominant during the 1920's. While ancient and English history both declined considerably during this decade, medieval and modern history held their own and American history increased in popularity." Ibid., 213.

78. Tryon, *Social Studies As School Subjects*, 213–37.

79. For a useful but brief discussion of the activities of the commission, see Johnson, *Teaching of History*, 74–83.

80. Charles A. Beard, *A Charter for the Social Sciences in the Schools, Report of the Commission on the Social Studies,* vol. 1 (New York: Charles Scribner's, 1932), 17.

81. Ibid., 18–19.

82. Johnson, *Teaching of History,* 83–84.

83. William, T. Hutchinson, "The American Historian in Wartime," *Mississippi Valley Historical Review* 29, no. 2 (Sept. 1942): 185. See also Merle Curti, "The American Scholar in Three Wars," *Journal of the History of Ideas* 3, no. 3 (June 1942): 241–64.

84. On the development of Office of Strategic Services (OSS), see Bradley F. Smith, *The Shadow Warriors: OSS and the Origins of CIA* (London: Andre Deutsch, 1983); R. Harris Smith, *OSS: The Secret History of America's First Central Intelligence Agency* (New York: Delta, 1973).

85. William L. Langer, *In and Out of the Ivory Tower: The Autobiography of William L. Langer* (New York: Neale Watson, 1977), 180–93.

86. For an excellent discussion of the participation of historians and other scholars in the intelligence community, see Robin W. Winks, *Cloak and Gown: Scholars in the Secret War, 1939–1961,* 2d ed. (New Haven: Yale University Press, 1996). Although the book focuses on the experiences of those from Yale University, it is much broader in many of its discussions. For a list of fifty members of the history profession who participated in the OSS, see Ibid., 495–98. On the impact of World War II on foreign area studies programs in the United States, see Robert McCaughey, *International Studies and Academic Enterprise: A Chapter in the Enclosure of American Learning* (New York: Columbia University Press, 1984).

87. There is no good list or study of the participation of historians in other federal activities during World War II. For example, Arthur Schlesinger, Sr., was on the Advisory Committee on Records of War Administration of the U.S. Bureau of the Budget. Arthur M. Schlesinger, *In Retrospect: The History of a Historian* (New York: Harcourt, Brace and World, 1963), 142–43. Many historians served in the armed forces, but little systematic information has been gathered about their participation. Scattered evidence suggests that among academics in general, a sizable proportion of them enlisted in the armed forces during the war. V. R. Cardozier, *Colleges and Universities in World War II* (Westport, Conn.: Praeger, 1993), 183–89. Some participated in editing and writing the official histories of World War II. James Cate, a University of Chicago historian, joined the Air Force and edited its official history. William H. McNeill, *Hutchins' University: A Memoir of the University of Chicago, 1929–1950* (Chicago: University of Chicago Press, 1991), 110.

    Yet not everyone was willing to drop regular teaching and research activities when called on to support the war effort. When the State Department invited Thomas Bailey, a prominent diplomatic historian, to go to Washington to summarize and analyze legation and embassy dispatches from abroad, Bailey refused by saying that he provided better service by educating public opinion on foreign affairs. Thomas A. Bailey, *The American Pageant Revised: Recollections of a Stanford Historian* (Stanford: Hoover Institution Press, 1982), 154–55.

88. There are numerous books on the development of the CIA. One useful starting point is Rhodri Jeffreys-Jones, *The CIA and American Democracy* (New Haven: Yale University Press, 1989).

89. For example, Bernard Bailyn served in the Army Signal Corps and in the Army Security Agency during World War II before entering graduate school in history in 1946. James A. Henretta, Michael Kammen, and Stanley N. Katz, eds., *The Transformation of Early American History: Society, Authority, and Ideology* (New York: Alfred A. Knopf, 1991), 6–7.

90. On the impact of World War II on higher education, see Cardozier, *Colleges and Universities in World War II;* I. L. Kandel, *The Impact of the War upon American Education* (Chapel Hill: University of North Carolina Press, 1948), 123–239. For a discussion of the impact of World War II on the University of Chicago, see McNeill, *Hutchins' University,* 102–32.

91. On elementary and secondary education during World War II, see Ronald D. Cohen, "Schooling Uncle Sam's Children: Education in the USA, 1941–1945," in *Education and the Second World War: Studies in Schooling and Social Change,* ed. Roy Lowe (London: Falmer Press, 1992), 47–58; Kandel, *Impact of the War,* 41–76. On the lives of children in schools during these years, see William M. Tuttle, Jr., *"Daddy's Gone to War": The Second World War in the Lives of America's Children* (New York: Oxford University Press, 1993); William M. Tuttle, Jr., "America's Home Front Children in World War II," in *Children in Time and Place: Developmental and Historical Insights,* ed. Glen H. Elder, Jr., John Modell, and Ross D. Parke (Cambridge: Cambridge University Press, 1993), 27–46.

92. Edgar B. Wesley, *American History in Schools and Colleges* (New York: Macmillan, 1944), 1.

93. Ibid., 14.

94. Ibid., 15.

95. For example, see Roger L. Geiger, *Research and Relevant Knowledge: American Research Universities since World War II* (New York: Oxford University Press, 1993); Daniel S. Greenberg, *The Politics of Pure Science* (New York: New American Library, 1967); Robert E. Kohler, *Partners in Science: Foundations and Natural Scientists, 1900–1945* (Chicago: University of Chicago Press, 1990); Bruce L. R. Smith, *American Science Policy since World War II* (Washington, D.C.: Brookings Institution, 1990).

96. There are a number of useful books on the post–World War II period. One recent and helpful analysis is James T. Patterson, *Grand Expectations: The United States, 1945–1974* (New York: Oxford University Press, 1996).

97. Timothy P. Donovan, *Historical Thought in America: Postwar Patterns* (Norman: University of Oklahoma Press, 1973), 3–31; Novick, *That Noble Dream,* 281–360.

98. Conyers Read, "The Social Responsibilities of the Historian," *American Historical Review* 50, no. 2 (Jan. 1950): 283.

99. Read, "Social Responsibilities of the Historian," 284. Read's presidential address may have received considerable attention, but it evoked sharp disagreement from some historians. For example, Howard Beale called Read's address "profoundly disturbing" and rejected his ideas about social control. Instead, Beale felt that "the best means of preserving democracy is to keep it by full criticism of it. To doubt that our values can be preserved if the people are told the truth is itself to question the very essence of democracy." Howard K. Beale, "The Professional Historian: His Theory and His Practice," *Pacific Historical Review* 22, no. 3 (Aug. 1953): 254–55.

100. Novick, *That Noble Dream,* 281–319

101. Richard Hofstadter, *The Progressive Historians: Turner, Beard, Parrington* (New York: Random House, 1968), 344–45.

102. There have been several books describing the impact of McCarthyism on colleges and universities in the 1950s. See, e.g., Ellen W. Schrecker, *No Ivory Tower: McCarthyism and the Universities* (New York: Oxford University Press, 1986), and Sigmund Diamond, *Compromised Campus: The Collaboration of Universities with the Intelligence Community, 1945–1955* (New York: Oxford University Press, 1992). Unfortunately, many of these have stressed the most negative aspects of domestic anticommunism without providing a broader and more balanced account. For a useful corrective, see Richard G. Powers, *Not without Honor: The History of American Anticommunism* (New York: Free Press, 1995). For a useful in-depth discussion of how these fears and sanctions affected the life of a young, prominent leftist historian, see Paul M. Buhle and Edward Rice-Maximin, *William Appleton Williams: The Tragedy of Empire* (New York: Routledge, 1995).

103. Paul F. Lazarsfeld and Wagner Thielens, Jr., *The Academic Mind: Social Scientists in a Time of Crisis* (New York: Free Press, 1958), 76, 78. Unfortunately, many of the more recent discussions of academia during these years have ignored the important work of Lazarsfeld and Thielens. Although Schrecker mentions this survey, she ignores most of its findings and relies more heavily on the writings and recollections of a few prominent activists during those years. Schrecker, *No Ivory Tower.* For a discussion of the uses of public opinion surveys to study issues related to academic freedom, see Maris A. Vinovskis, "Surveys of Academic Freedom among Faculty, Students, and the Public: A Review of the Literature and Suggestions for Future Research" (unpub. final report for OERI, Department of Education, Sept. 1991).

104. Lazarsfeld and Thielens, *Academic Mind,* 95.

105. Samuel Eliot Morison, "Faith of a Historian," *American Historical Review* 51, no. 2 (Jan. 1951): 264–65.

106. John Higham, Leonard Krieger, and Felix Gilbert, *History* (Englewood Cliffs, N.J.: Prentice-Hall, 1965), 212–32.

107. Pendleton Herring, "A Political Scientist Considers the Question," *Pennsylvania Magazine of History and Biography* 52, no. 2 (Apr. 1948): 121–22.

108. Ibid., 137–38.

109. On the role of diplomatic history and foreign policy, see Francis L. Loewenheim, ed., *The Historian and the Diplomat: The Role of History and Historians in American Foreign Policy* (New York: Harper and Row, 1967). On the origins and development of the CIA, see Jeffreys-Jones, *CIA and American Democracy.*

110. On Langer's brief description of his experiences as the director of ONE, see Langer, *In and Out of the Ivory Tower,* 218–22. Langer remained active in government affairs after he left the directorship of ONE. He served on the President's Foreign Intelligence Advisory Board in the Kennedy, Johnson, and Nixon administrations. Ibid., 222–23.

111. Jeffreys-Jones, *CIA and American Democracy,* 67.

112. On Kent's activities in OSS and the CIA, see Donald P. Steury, *Sherman Kent and the Board of National Estimates: Collected Essays* (Washington, D.C.: Central Intelligence Agency, 1994); Winks, *Cloak and Gown,* 81–96, 449–69.

113. Report of the Harvard Committee, *General Education in a Free Society* (Cambridge: Harvard University Press, 1945), 138–39.

114. David Angus and Jeffrey Mirel, "Rhetoric and Reality: The High School Curriculum," in *Learning from the Past: What History Teaches Us About School Reform,* ed. Diane Ravitch and Maris A. Vinovskis (Baltimore: Johns Hopkins University Press, 1995), 306.

115. Herbert M. Kliebard, *The Struggle for the American Curriculum,* 1893–1958 (New York: Routledge and Kegan Paul, 1986), 240–70.

116. Richard H. Bauer, "The Study of History," *Social Studies* 39, no. 4 (Apr. 1948): 154.

117. Ibid., 154–55.

118. Ibid., 155–56.

119. Beale, "Professional Historian," 227.

120. On the growing importance of science in the post–World War II period, see Geiger, *Research and Relevant Knowledge;* Greenberg, *Politics of Pure Science;* Bruce L. R. Smith, *American Science Policy since World War II.*

121. In the immediate aftermath of World War II, the federal government was relatively slow in enlisting the social sciences to help policymakers, and the National Science Foundation was instrumental in this area in the 1950s. For a discussion of the development of the use of social science research, see Otto N. Larsen, *Milestones and Millstones: Social Science at the National Science Foundation,* 1945–1991 (New Brunswick, N.J.: Transaction, 1992); Neil J. Smelser and Dean R. Gerstein, eds., *Behavioral and Social Science: Fifty Years of Discovery* (Washington, D.C.: National Academy Press, 1986).

122. McDonald, ed., *Historic Turn in the Human Sciences.*

123. Novick, *That Noble Dream,* 361–411.

124. Higham et al., *History,* 212–32; Maruan J. Morton, *The Terrors of Ideological Politics: Liberal Historians in a Conservative Mood* (Cleveland: Press of Case Western Reserve University, 1972); Novick, *That Noble Dream,* 320–60.

125. Higham is credited with coining and popularizing the expression "consensus" history to describe the 1950s. See. e.g., Higham, *Writing American History,* 138–56. But not everyone thought this was a useful or apt description. Oscar Handlin, for one, in discussing the lack of distinct schools of thought in American historical scholarship, argued: "In the first efforts to impart a political spin to scholarship the seekers after partisanship had to dream up a nonexistent category—the 'consensus' school—by jumbling together authors of the most disparate sorts. Tossed into the chaotic winds of scholarly discourse, that misleading term soon attained the status of a cliché that took the place of thought." Oscar Handlin, *Truth in History* (Cambridge: Harvard University Press, 1979), 81.

126. Higham et al., *History,* 132.

127. On the "War against Poverty" during the Johnson administration, see Irving Bernstein, *Guns or Butter: The Presidency of Lyndon Johnson* (New York: Oxford University Press, 1996); Gareth Davies, *From Opportunity to Entitlement: The Transformation and Decline of Great Society Liberalism* (Manhattan: University Press of Kansas, 1996); Marshall Kaplan and Peggy Cuciti, eds., *The Great Society and Its Legacy: Twenty Years of U.S. Social Policy* (Durham: Duke University Press, 1986); Sar A. Levitan and Robert Taggart, *The Promise of Greatness: The Social Programs of the Last Decade and Their Major Achievements* (Cambridge: Harvard University Press, 1976); David Zarefsky, *President*

Johnson's War on Poverty: Rhetoric and History (University: University of Alabama Press, 1986).

128. For a discussion of historical perspectives on early childhood education programs and Head Start, see chap. 2.

129. For example, policymakers might have consulted studies of federal programs created and developed during the New Deal.

130. For a discussion of Schlesinger's career and uses of history, see Stephen P. Depoe, *Arthur M. Schlesinger, Jr., and the Ideological History of American Liberalism* (Tuscaloosa: University of Alabama Press, 1994); Morton, *Terrors of Ideological Politics*, 27–49. There were a few other professional historians who participated in the Kennedy administration. One of the most notable was Edwin Reischauer who served as the ambassador to Japan. See Edwin O. Reischauer, *My Life between Japan and America* (New York: Harper and Row, 1986).

131. Schlesinger's ideas on the cycles of reform have evolved. For one version, see Arthur M. Schlesinger, Jr., *The Cycles of American History* (Boston: Houghton Mifflin, 1986), 23–48.

132. Depoe, *Arthur M. Schlesinger, Jr.*, 61–76.

133. Arthur Schlesinger, Jr., "The Historian As Participant," *Daedalus* 100, no. 2 (spring 1971): 342.

134. Ibid., 343.

135. Ibid., 348.

136. Ibid., 348.

137. Ibid., 351.

138. Eric F. Goldman, *The Tragedy of Lyndon Johnson* (New York: Alfred A. Knopf, 1969).

139. For useful discussions of the role of the past in the deliberations on Vietnam, see Ernest R. May, *"Lessons" of the Past: The Use and Misuse of History in American Foreign Policy* (New York: Oxford University Press, 1973), 87–142; Richard E. Neustadt and Ernest R. May, *Thinking in Time: The Uses of History for Decision Makers* (New York: Free Press, 1986), 75–90.

140. For an interesting discussion of the participation of historians in foreign policy deliberation before the mid-1960s, see Francis L. Loewenheim, ed., *The Historian and the Diplomat: The Role of History and Historians in American Foreign Policy* (New York: Harper and Row, 1967). One historian who did serve in the Reagan administration was Richard Pipes of Harvard University. Pipes was the director of East European and Soviet affairs on the National Security Council from 1981–82. For a short but insightful discussion of his experiences, see Richard Pipes, *How Washington Makes Soviet Policy: Observations of a Visitor* (Stanford: Hoover Institution Press, 1990).

141. For a discussion of the uses of history by Henry Kissinger, see Peter W. Dickson, *Kissinger and the Meaning of History* (Cambridge: Cambridge University Press, 1978), 4–5.

142. David Eakins, "Objectivity and Commitment," *Studies on the Left* 1, no. 1 (fall 1959): 49.

143. Novick, *That Noble Dream*, 415–38. On the experiences of the more radical history students and faculty during this period, see Howard Zinn, "The Politics of History in the Era of the Cold War: Repression and Resistance," in *The Cold War and the Univer-*

sity: Toward an Intellectual History of the Postwar Years, ed. Noam Chomsky et al. (New York: New Press, 1997), 35–72.

144. In this particular discussion, Gordon was pointing to examples from advocacy scholarship by feminists rather than the Vietnam War itself. Linda Gordon, "Interview," in *Visions of History,* ed. Henry Abelove et al., (New York: Pantheon, 1983), 85.

145. Eugene D. Genovese, *In Red and Black: Marxian Explorations in Southern and Afro-American History* (New York: Pantheon, 1971), 4–5.

146. There are numerous accounts of the disruptions on campuses during the Vietnam War. For discussions of developments at Berkeley and Harvard, see W. J. Rorabaugh, *Berkeley at War: The 1960s* (New York: Oxford University Press, 1989); Seymour Martin Lipset and David Riesman, *Education and Politics at Harvard* (New York: McGraw-Hill, 1975).

147. On some of the debates over revisionists among educational historians, see Walter Feinberg, Harvey Kantor, Michael Katz, and Paul Violas, *Revisionists Respond to Ravitch* (Washington, D.C.: National Academy of Education, 1980); Diane Ravitch, *The Revisionists Revised: A Critique of the Radical Attack on the Schools* (New York: Basic Books, 1977); Maris A. Vinovskis, *Education, Society, and Economic Opportunity: A Historical Perspective on Persistent Issues* (New Haven: Yale University Press, 1995), 125–41

148. Michael Kammen, ed., *The Past Before Us: Contemporary Historical Writing in the United States* (Ithaca: Cornell University Press, 1980).

149. Handlin, *Truth in History,* 409, 413.

150. For a discussion of Woodward's reactions to the turmoil of the 1960s and early 1970s, see John H. Roper, *C. Vann Woodward, Southerner* (Athens: University of Georgia Press, 1987), 232–67.

151. C. Vann Woodward, *Thinking Back: The Perils of Writing History* (Baton Rouge: Louisiana State University Press, 1986), 98–99.

152. The growing public alienation against the government and political leaders was a complex development and was influenced by a variety of factors besides the reactions to the Vietnam War. For a discussion of the changing attitudes of voters toward the government, see Warren E. Miller and J. Merrill Shanks, *The New American Voter* (Cambridge: Harvard University Press, 1996).

153. On the political orientation and attitudes of college faculty, see Everett C. Ladd, Jr., and Seymour M. Lipset, *The Divided Academy: Professors and Politics* (New York: McGraw-Hill 1975).

154. Stephen E. Ambrose, *Nixon: The Triumph of a Politician, 1962–1972* (New York: Simon and Schuster, 1989).

155. Ernest R. May and Dorothy G. Blaney, *Careers for Humanists* (New York: Academic Press, 1981), 2–3.

156. Leslie H. Fishel, Jr., "Public History and the Academy," in *Public History: An Introduction,* ed. Barbara J. Howe and Emory L. Kemp (Malabar, Fla.: Krieger, 1986), 12.

157. There were important exceptions. For example, such established scholars as Andrew Achenbaum at the University of Michigan, Ernest May at Harvard University, and Peter Stearns at Carnegie Mellon University have been active in training students for public history positions.

158. For useful discussions of the development and practice of public or applied history in the

United States, see Susan Porter Benson, Stephen Brier, and Roy Rosenzwig, eds., *Presenting the Past: Essays on History and the Public* (Philadelphia: Temple University Press, 1986); Barbara J. Howe and Emory L. Kemp, eds., *Public History: An Introduction* (Malabar, Fla.: Krieger, 1986); Phyllis K. Leffler and Joseph Brent, *Public and Academic History: A Philosophy and Paradigm* (Malabar, Fla.: Krieger, 1990); Phyllis K. Leffler and Joseph Brent, eds., *Public History Readings* (Malabar, Fla.: Krieger, 1992); David B. Mock, ed., *History and Public Policy* (Malabar, Fla.: Krieger, 1991). For a useful bibliographic introduction to this field, see David F. Trask and Robert W. Pomeroy III, eds., *The Craft of Public Policy: An Annotated Select Bibliography* (Westport, Conn.: Greenwood Press, 1983).

159. Charles C. Cole, Jr., "Public History: What Difference Has It Made?" *Public Historian* 16, no. 4 (fall 1994): 32. See also Page Putnam Miller, "Reflections on the Public History Movement," *Public Historian* 14, no. 2 (spring 1992): 67–70.

160. Hugh D. Graham, "The Stunted Career of Policy History: A Critique and an Agenda," *Public Historian* 15, no. 2 (spring 1993): 15. Graham has produced several thoughtful policy-oriented studies. See, e.g., Hugh Davis Graham, *The Uncertain Triumph: Federal Education Policy during the Kennedy and Johnson Years* (Chapel Hill: University of North Carolina Press, 1984); Hugh Davis Graham, *The Civil Rights Era: Origins and Development of National Policy, 1960–1972* (New York: Oxford University Press, 1990).

161. Graham, "Stunted Career of Policy History," 18, 20. Graham's critique of policy history was addressed by several scholars. Generally, they agree with his overall interpretation but question specific aspects of it, such as Graham's attributing the weakness of policy history, in part, to the strong position of social history in the discipline. Donald T. Critchlow, "A Prognosis of Policy History: Stunted—or Deceivingly Vital? A Brief Reply to Hugh Davis Graham," *Public Historian* 15, no. 4 (fall 1993): 51–61; Peter N. Stearns and Joel A. Tarr, "Straightening the Policy History Tree," Ibid., 63–67; Martin Reus, "Historians and Policymaking: A View from Inside the Beltway," Ibid., 69–75.

162. There are a large number of policy-related historical works available today. A very incomplete and eclectic selection follows: W. Andrew Achenbaum, *Shades of Gray: Old Age, American Values, and Federal Policies since 1920* (Boston: Little, Brown, 1983); Joan J. Brumberg, *Fasting Girls: The Emergence of Anorexia Nervosa As a Modern Disease* (Cambridge: Harvard University Press, 1988); Barbara Beatty, *Preschool Education in America: The Culture of Young Children from the Colonial Era to the Present* (New Haven: Yale University Press, 1995); Glen H. Elder, Jr., John Modell, and Ross D. Parke, eds., *Children in Time and Place: Developmental and Historical Insights* (Cambridge: Cambridge University Press, 1993); Roger L. Geiger, *Research and Relevant Knowledge: American Universities since World War II* (New York: Oxford University Press, 1993); Linda Gordon, *Heroes of Their Own Lives: The Politics and History of Family Violence* (New York: Viking, 1988); Carole Haber and Brian Gratton, *Old Age and the Search for Security: An American Social History* (Bloomington: Indiana University Press, 1994); Barbara M. Hobson, *Uneasy Virtue: The Politics of Prostitution and the American Reform Tradition* (New York: Basic Books, 1987); Michael B. Katz, ed., *The "Underclass" Debate: Views from History* (Princeton: Princeton University Press, 1993); Michael B. Katz, *Improving Poor People: The Welfare State, the "Underclass," and Urban Schools As History*

(Princeton: Princeton University Press, 1995); Marian J. Morton, *And Sin No More: Social Policy and Unwed Mothers in Cleveland, 1855–1990* (Columbus: Ohio State University Press, 1993); Richard E. Neustadt and Ernest R. May, *Thinking in Time: The Uses of History for Decision Makers* (Cambridge: Harvard University Press, 1986); James T. Patterson, *America's Struggle against Poverty, 1900–1980* (Cambridge: Harvard University Press, 1981); Elizabeth Pleck, *Domestic Tyranny: The Making of American Social Policy against Family Violence from Colonial Times to the Present* (New York: Oxford University Press, 1987); Diane Ravitch, *The Troubled Crusade: American Education, 1945–1980* (New York: Basic Books, 1983); Diane Ravitch and Maris A. Vinovskis, eds., *Learning from the Past: What History Teaches Us about School Reform* (Baltimore: Johns Hopkins University Press, 1995); Diane Ravitch, *National Standards in American Education: A Citizen's Guide* (Washington, D.C.: Brookings Institution, 1995); Glenda Riley, *Divorce: An American Tradition* (New York: Oxford University Press, 1991); David J. Rothman and Stanton Wheeler, eds., *Social History and Social Policy* (New York: Academic Press, 1981); David Tyack and Larry Cuban, *Tinkering toward Utopia: A Century of Public School Reform* (Cambridge: Harvard University Press, 1995).

163. Michael B. Katz, *Improving Poor People*, 7.

164. For useful discussions of how policymakers acquire and use social science information, see Laurence E. Lynn, Jr., ed., *Knowledge and Policy: The Uncertain Connection* (Washington, D.C.: National Academy of Sciences, 1978); Richard P. Nathan, *Social Science in Government: Uses and Misuses* (New York: Basic Books, 1988); William H. Robinson and Clay H. Wellborn, eds., *Knowledge, Power, and the Congress* (Washington, D.C.: Congressional Quarterly, 1991); David Whiteman, *Communication in Congress: Members, Staff, and the Search for Information* (Lawrence: University Press of Kansas, 1995).

165. For an excellent survey and analysis of the role of academic experts in the federal government, see Robert C. Wood, *Whatever Possessed the President? Academic Experts and Presidential Policy, 1960–1988* (Amherst: University of Massachusetts Press, 1993). For discussions of recent changes in the nature and practices of public policy analysts, see William N. Dunn and Rita Mae Kelly, eds., *Advances in Policy Studies since 1950*, Policy Studies Review Annual, no. 10 (New Brunswick, N.J.: Transaction, 1992); Marc K. Landy and Martin A. Levin, eds., *The New Politics of Public Policy* (Baltimore: Johns Hopkins University Press, 1995).

166. Among the few are Patricia Graham, who served as the director of the National Institute of Education in the late 1970s, and Diane Ravitch, who was the assistant secretary of the Office of Educational Research and Improvement in the early 1990s. In addition, I have had the opportunity to work in various agencies in the federal government.

   As part of the great expansion of the federal bureaucracy since the early 1960s, more individuals with history training have joined the permanent staff and made important contributions to federal agencies. Most of these staff members work closely within their area of expertise and do not necessarily have much contact with the top political appointees or upper-level policymakers. For analyses of the contributions and problems of historians working in federal agencies, see the works cited in note 159 above.

167. Among the few historians who served on such task forces was Edward Berkowitz, a senior staff member on President Carter's Commission of the Eighties. Edward D.

Berkowitz, "Commissioning the Future," in *History and Public Policy*, ed. David B. Mock (Malabar, Fla.: Krieger, 1991), 7–21. A few historians have also served on advisory groups created by private, nonprofit groups. For a discussion of the experiences of John Demos on the Carnegie Council on Children, see John Demos, *Past, Present, and Personal: The Family and the Life Course in American History* (New York: Oxford University Press, 1986), 186–212.

168. On the role of historians as expert witnesses in court cases, see Hal K. Rothman, "Historian v. Historian: Interpreting the Past in the Courtroom," *Public Historian* 5, no. 2 (spring 1993): 39–53.

169. On the Sears case, see Editors, "Women's History Goes to Trial: EEOC v. Sears, Roebuck and Company," *Signs* 11, no. 4 (summer 1986): 751–79; Katherine Jellison, "History in the Courtroom: The Sears Case in Perspective," *Public Historian* 9, no. 4 (fall 1987): 9–19; Ruth Milkman, "Women's History and the Sears Case," *Feminist Studies* 12, no. 2 (summer 1986): 375–400.

170. William E. Leuchtenburg, "The Historian and the Public Realm," *American Historical Review* 97, no. 1 (Feb. 1992): 17–18.

171. For useful discussions of the increased uses of history by the other social sciences, see McDonald, ed., *Historic Turn in the Human Sciences;* Monkkonen, ed., *Engaging the Past.*

172. On the problems of graduate students in history receiving social science training, see Jerome M. Clubb and Maris A. Vinovskis, "Training and Retraining in Quantitative Approaches to the Social Sciences," *Historical Methods* 17, no. 4 (fall 1984): 255–64.

173. Hertzberg, "Teaching of History."

174. Bradley Commission on History in Schools, "Building a History Curriculum: Guidelines for Teaching History in Schools," *History Teacher* 23, no. 1 (Nov. 1989): 11–12.

175. National Center for History in the Schools, *National Standards for United States History: Exploring the American Experience, Grades 5–12,* expanded ed. (Los Angeles: National Center for History in the Schools, 1994), 1.

176. Ibid., 7.

177. *Congressional Record* 141, no. 10, daily ed., (Jan. 18, 1995): S1026.

178. Richard W. Riley, "Statement by Richard W. Riley, U.S. Secretary of Education, Regarding U.S. History Standards," Department of Education, Sept. 4, 1995, 1.

179. Council for Basic Education, *History in the Making: An Independent Review of the Voluntary National History Standards* (Washington, D.C.: Council for Basic Education, 1996).

180. National Center for History in the Schools, *National Standards for History,* basic ed. (Los Angeles: National Center for History in the Schools, 1996).

181. Alexandra S. Beatty, Clyde M. Reese, Hilary R. Persky, and Peggy Carr, *NAEP 1994 U.S. History Report Card: Findings from the National Assessment of Educational Progress* (Washington, D.C.: Government Printing Office, 1996).

182. Kammen, *Past Before Us,* 44–45. Kammen also pointed to the proliferation of societies affiliated with the AHA, the growth of team research and collaborative analysis, and the shift in historical vision toward looking at human responses to structures of power as evidence of the strong and improving health of the history profession. Ibid., 45. More-

over, most of the twenty-one distinguished historians who reviewed their subfields of history voiced optimism about developments in their areas of specialty.

183. Joyce Appleby, Lynn Hunt, and Margaret Jacob, *Telling the Truth about History* (New York: W. W. Norton, 1994), 11.

184. Theodore S. Hamerow, *Reflections on History and Historians* (Madison: University of Wisconsin Press, 1987), 10–11, 13.

185. Hamerow, *Reflections on History,* 27–28.

CHAPTER 2. THE CHANGING ROLE OF THE FEDERAL GOVERNMENT IN EDUCATIONAL RESEARCH AND STATISTICS

1. For a discussion of the ongoing debates to abolish the U.S. Department of Education, see Wayne Riddle et al., "Education Department: Debate over Its Cabinet-Level Status," *CRS Report for Congress,* 95–693EPW, May 26, 1995.

2. There are surprisingly few studies of the changing federal role in education from a historical perspective. Some notable exceptions are: Hugh Davis Graham, *The Uncertain Triumph: Federal Education Policy in the Kennedy and Johnson Years* (Chapel Hill: University of North Carolina Press, 1984); Carl F. Kaestle and Marshall S. Smith, "The Federal Role in Elementary and Secondary Education, 1940–1980," *Harvard Educational Review* 52 (Nov. 1982): 384–408; Diane Ravitch, *The Troubled Crusade: American Education, 1945–1980* (New York: Basic Books, 1983); Harold Silver and Pamela Silver, *An Educational War on Poverty: American and British Policy-Making,* 1960–1980 (Cambridge: Cambridge University Press, 1991).

3. The longer study, upon which this essay is based, was commissioned by OERI when I served as a consultant to that agency. A preliminary 185-page draft of that report, "Changing Views of the Federal Role in Educational Statistics and Research," was completed in September 1995 and is available from the agency. Both that report as well as this essay have benefited from my continuing project, "Congressional Oversight of the Regional Educational Laboratories and the Research and Development Centers," which has been funded by a small grant from the Spencer Foundation. Naturally, the views expressed here are strictly my own and do not necessarily reflect those of either the U.S. Department of Education or the Spencer Foundation.

4. Given the limitations of time, in this chapter I shall focus mainly, but not exclusively, on the experiences of NIE and OERI in the post-1970s. I shall not attempt to provide a broader, in-depth analysis of program evaluations in other Department of Education agencies or a study of educational research done elsewhere (such as at the Department of Defense or at the National Science Foundation). For a useful essay on the history of educational research from the perspective of schools of education, see Ellen Condliffe Lagemann, *Contested Terrain: A History of Education Research in the United States,* 1890–1990 (Chicago: Spencer Foundation, Oct. 1996), 1–20.

5. For a discussion of education in early America, see James Axtell, *The School upon a Hill: Education and Society in Colonial New England* (New Haven: Yale University Press, 1974); Lawrence A. Cremin, *American Education: The Colonial Experience, 1607–1783* (New York: Harper and Row, 1970); Carl F. Kaestle, *Pillars of the Republic: Common Schools and*

American Society, 1780–1860 (New York: Hill and Wang, 1983); Gerald F. Moran and Maris A. Vinovskis, *Religion, Family, and the Life Course: Explorations in the Social History of Early America* (Ann Arbor: University of Michigan Press, 1992).

6. On the early involvement of the federal government in educational matters, see Maurice R. Berube, *American Presidents and Education* (Westport, Conn.: Greenwood Press, 1991); Paul H. Mattingly and Edward Stevens, eds., *"—Schools and the Means of Education Shall Forever be Encouraged: A History of Education in the Old Northwest, 1787–1880,"* (Athens: Ohio University Libraries, 1987); Howard C. Taylor, *The Educational Significance of the Early Federal Land Ordinances* (New York: Teachers College, 1922); David B. Tyack, Thomas James, and Aaron Benavot, *Law and the Shaping of Public Education, 1785–1954* (Madison: University of Wisconsin Press, 1987); George F. Zook, *The Role of the Federal Government in Education* (Cambridge: Harvard University Press, 1945).

7. The best work on the origins and development of the Department of Education in 1867 is Donald R. Warren, *To Enforce Education: A History of the Founding Years of the United States Office of Education* (Detroit: Wayne State University Press, 1974). Another study is Harry Kursh, *The United States Office of Education: A Century of Service* (Philadelphia: Chilton Books, 1965). Kursh has provided a useful introduction to the organization and functioning of the agency in the 1960s, but his book is written more for a popular audience than a scholarly one; the lack of footnotes makes it difficult to inspect the documentation that underlies his descriptions and analyses. A draft, unpublished history of the agency by Stephen Sniegoski, however, provides some useful insights, especially about the successive commissioners of education. Stephen J. Sniegoski, "History of the Department of Education and Its Forerunners" (unpub. manuscript, July 1995).

8. For a discussion of how nineteenth-century educational reformers used statistical information to further their educational efforts, see Charles L. Glenn, *The Myth of the Common School* (Amherst: University of Massachusetts Press, 1988); Edith N. Mac-Mullen, *In the Cause of True Education: Henry Barnard and Nineteenth-Century School Reform* (New Haven: Yale University Press, 1991); Maris A. Vinovskis, *Education, Society, and Economic Opportunity: A Historical Perspective on Persistent Issues* (New Haven: Yale University Press, 1995).

9. For a recent evaluation of the activities of NCES, see Richard C. Atkinson and Gregg B. Jackson, eds., *Research and Education Reform: Roles for the Office of Educational Research and Improvement* (Washington, D.C.: National Academy Press, 1992). A useful analysis of the evolution of the NAEP tests in NCES is provided by James A. Hazlett, "A History of the National Assessment of Progress, 1963–1973: A Look at Some Conflicting Ideas and Issues in Contemporary American Education" (Ed.D. diss., University of Kansas, 1974).

10. The most recent National Academy of Science evaluation of OERI concluded that major improvements were still needed to assess more rigorously which promising programs were the most effective. Atkinson and Jackson, eds., *Research and Education Reform,* 154–56.

11. For some discussions of earlier efforts to expand the role of the federal government in education, see Stephen K. Bailey and Edith K. Mosher, *ESEA: The Office of Education Administers a Law* (Syracuse: Syracuse University Press, 1965); Gordon C. Lee, *The*

Struggle for Federal Aid, First Phase: A History of the Attempts to Obtain Federal Aid for the Common Schools, 1870–1890 (New York: Teachers College, 1949); Michael P. Timpane and Stephen M. Barro, eds., *The Federal Interest in Financing Schooling* (Cambridge: Ballinger, 1978).

12. The best overall assessment of how educators and policymakers view OERI is by Carl Kaestle. Between May and August 1991 Kaestle interviewed thirty-three prominent and knowledgeable individuals who were or had been associated with the activities of NIE or OERI. The insightful analysis based on these interviews is available in Carl F. Kaestle, "Everybody's Been to Fourth Grade: An Oral History of R&D in Education," Report 92–1 (Wisconsin Center for Educational Research, Apr. 1992). A shorter version of this paper has been published as Carl F. Kaestle, "The Awful Reputation of Education Research," *Educational Researcher* 22 (Jan.-Feb. 1993): 23–31. For a thoughtful, but critical personal assessment of the role of OERI today, see Diane Ravitch, "Adventures in Wonderland: A Scholar in Washington," *American Scholar* 64 (autumn 1995): 497–516. See also the very useful analysis by the National Academy of Science: Atkinson and Jackson, eds., *Research and Education Reform.*

13. Victor W. Henningsen III, "Reading, Writing, and Reindeer: The Development of Federal Education in Alaska, 1877–1920" (Ed.D. diss., Harvard University, 1987); Kursh, *United States Office of Education;* Darrell H. Smith, *The Bureau of Education: Its History, Activities, and Organization* (Baltimore: Johns Hopkins University Press, 1923); Warren, *To Enforce Education.*

14. For an excellent discussion of the creation and functioning of NIE, see Lee Sproull, Stephen Weiner, and David Wolf, *Organizing an Anarchy: Belief, Bureaucracy, and Politics in the National Institute of Education* (Chicago: University of Chicago Press, 1978).

15. Kaestle, "Everybody's Been to Fourth Grade."

16. See, e.g., the comments of Daniel P. Moynihan, one of the chief architects of NIE, who anticipated major breakthroughs in educational research. U.S. Congress, House, Select Subcommittee on Education, *To Establish a National Institute of Education: Hearings . . . on H.R. 33, H.R. 3606, and Other Related Bills,* 92d Cong., 1st sess., Feb. 24, 1971, 86.

17. On American science policy in recent years, see Daniel L. Kleinman, *Politics on the Endless Frontier: Postwar Research Policy in the United States* (Durham: Duke University Press, 1995); Joseph P. Martino, *Science Funding: Politics and Porkbarrel* (New Brunswick, N.J.: Transaction, 1992); Alexander J. Morin, *Science Policy and Politics* (Englewood Cliffs, N.J.: Prentice-Hall, 1993); Bruce L. R. Smith, *American Science Policy since World War II* (Washington, D.C.: Brookings Institution, 1990).

18. On developments in the other social sciences, see Dean R. Gerstein et al., eds., *The Behavioral and Social Sciences: Achievements and Opportunities* (Washington, D.C.: National Academy Press, 1988); Otto N. Larsen, *Milestones and Millstones: Social Science at the National Science Foundation,* 1945–1991 (New Brunswick, N.J.: Transaction, 1992); Richard P. Nathan, *Social Science in Government: Uses and Misuses* (New York: Basic Books, 1988); Neil J. Smelser and Dean R. Gerstein, eds., *Behavioral and Social Science: Fifty Years of Discovery: In Commemoration of the Fiftieth Anniversary of the "Osburn Report,"* Recent Social Trends in the United States (Washington, D.C.: National Academy Press, 1986).

19. On the low regard for educational research, see Geraldine J. Clifford and James W. Guthrie, *Ed School: A Brief for Professional Education* (Chicago: University of Chicago Press, 1988); Kaestle, "Everybody's Been to Fourth Grade"; Arthur G. Powell, *The Uncertain Profession: Harvard and the Search for Educational Authority* (Cambridge: Harvard University Press, 1980); Lagemann, "Contested Terrain."

20. Larsen, *Milestones and Millstones;* Nathan, *Social Science in Government.*

21. Peter B. Dow, *Schoolhouse Politics: Lessons from the Sputnik Era* (Cambridge: Harvard University Press, 1991); Larsen, *Milestones and Millstones;* Nathan, *Social Science in Government.*

22. Office of Education, *Annual Report,* 1944 (Washington, D.C.: Government Printing Office, 1945), 2.

23. Roger L. Geiger, *Research and Relevant Knowledge: American Research Universities since World War II* (New York: Oxford University Press, 1993); Charles V. Kidd, *American Universities and Federal Research* (Cambridge: Harvard University Press, 1959); Larsen, *Milestones and Millstones;* Nathan, *Social Science in Government.*

24. For discussions of the state of educational research in this period, see Benjamin S. Bloom, "Twenty-five Years of Educational Research," *American Educational Research Journal 3* (May 1966): 211–21; Orville G. Brim, *Sociology and the Field of Education* (New York: Russell Sage Foundation, 1965); John B. Carroll, Arthur P. Coladarci, and B. Othenal Smith, "Neglected Areas in Educational Research," *Phi Delta Kappan* 42 (May 1961): 339–46; Arthur P. Coladarci, "Towards More Rigorous Educational Research," *Harvard Educational Review* 30 (winter 1960): 3–11; James S. Coleman, Lee J. Cronbach, and Patrick Suppes, eds., *Research for Tomorrow's Schools: Disciplined Inquiry for Education* (New York: Macmillan, 1969); Carter V. Good, "Educational Research after Fifty Years," *Phi Delta Kappan* 37 (Jan. 1956): 145–52. For a description of the Cooperative Research Program, see David L. Clark and William R. Carriker, "Educational Research and the Cooperative Research Program," *Phi Delta Kappan* 42 (March 1961): 226–30.

25. John Gardner, "Report of the President's Task Force on Education," Nov. 14, 1964. The report is available at the Lyndon Baines Johnson Presidential Library, Austin, Texas. The best analysis of the Gardner Task Force remains Charles P. Kearney, "The 1964 Presidential Task Force on Education and the Elementary and Secondary Act of 1965" (Ph.D. diss., University of Chicago, 1968).

26. On the development of the regional educational laboratories and the R&D centers, see Maris A. Vinovskis, "Analysis of the Quality of Research and Development at the OERI Research and Development Centers and at OERI Regional Educational Laboratories" (final report, OERI, Department of Education, June 1993).

27. Philip P. Zodhiates, "Bureaucrats and Politicians: The National Institute of Education and Educational Research under Reagan" (Ed.D. diss., Harvard University, 1988).

28. For a thorough and thoughtful analysis of the problems of the 1977–78 reorganization of NIE, see Grady McGonagill, "Reorganization—Faith and Skepticism: A Case Study of the 1977–78 Reorganization of the National Institute of Education" (master's thesis, Harvard University, Oct. 1981). See also Kaestle, "Everybody's Been to Fourth Grade."

29. For a life-course framework for mapping and evaluating educational research, see chap. 8.

30. Atkinson and Jackson, eds., *Research and Education Reform.*

31. Deborah A. Verstegen, "Educational Fiscal Policy in the Reagan Administration," *Educational Evaluation and Policy Analysis* 12 (winter 1990): 355–73; Deborah A. Verstegen and David L. Clark, "The Diminution in Federal Expenditures for Education during the Reagan Administration," *Phi Delta Kappan* 70 (Oct. 1988): 134–38; General Accounting Office, *Education Information: Changes in Funds and Priorities Have Affected Production and Quality,* GAO/PEMD-88-4 (Washington, D.C.: Government Printing Office, 1987).

32. Vinovskis, "Analysis of the Quality of Research." Fortunately, the amount of monies set aside for field-initiated research has been increased significantly for FY96 and FY97.

33. Kaestle, "Everybody's Been to Fourth Grade."

34. Dow, *Schoolhouse Politics;* Larsen, *Milestones and Millstones.*

35. Vinovskis, "Analysis of the Quality of Research."

36. Ibid.

37. Sproull et al., *Organizing an Anarchy.*

38. Kaestle, "Everybody's Been to Fourth Grade."

39. For a notable and thoughtful exception, see Kaestle, "Everybody's Been to Fourth Grade."

40. Warren, *To Enforce Education.*

41. Sproull et al., *Organizing an Anarchy.*

42. Zodhiates, "Bureaucrats and Politicians."

43. Kaestle, "Everybody's Been to Fourth Grade."

44. Vinovskis, "Analysis of the Quality of Research and Development."

CHAPTER 3. SCHOOL READINESS AND EARLY CHILDHOOD EDUCATION

1. National Goals Panel, *The National Education Goals Report: Building a Nation of Learners,* 1992 (Washington, D.C.: Government Printing Office, 1992), 58.

2. John Demos, *A Little Commonwealth: Family Life in Plymouth Colony* (New York: Oxford University Press, 1970); John Demos, "The American Family in Past Time," *American Scholar* 43 (1974): 422–46; John Demos, *Past, Present, and Personal: The Family and the Life Course in American History* (New York: Oxford University Press, 1986); John Modell and Madeline Goodman, "Historical Perspectives," in *At the Threshold: The Developing Adolescent,* ed. Shirley S. Feldman and Glen R. Elliott (Cambridge: Harvard University Press, 1990), 93–120; Walter I. Trattner, *From Poor Law to Welfare State: A History of Social Welfare in America,* 4th ed. (New York: Free Press, 1989); Michael Zuckerman, *Peaceable Kingdoms: New England Towns in the Eighteenth Century* (New York: Alfred A. Knopf, 1970).

3. James Axtell, *The School upon a Hill: Education and Society in Colonial New England* (New Haven: Yale University Press, 1974); Carl F. Kaestle and Maris A. Vinovskis, *Education and Social Change in Nineteenth-Century Massachusetts* (Cambridge: Cambridge University Press, 1980); David Stannard, "Death and the Puritan Child" in *Death in America,* ed. David Stannard (Philadelphia: University of Pennsylvania Press, 1975), 3–29; David Stannard, *The Puritan Way of Death* (New York: Oxford University Press, 1977).

4. Gerald F. Moran and Maris A. Vinovskis, *Religion, Family, and the Life Course: Explorations in the Social History of Early America* (Ann Arbor: University of Michigan Press, 1992).

5. Barbara Beatty, *Preschool Education in America: The Culture of Young Children from the Colonial Period to the Present* (New Haven: Yale University Press, 1995); John W. Jenkins, "Infant Schools and the Development of Public Primary Schools in Selected American Cities before the Civil War" (Ph.D. diss., University of Wisconsin, 1978); Dean May and Maris A. Vinovskis, "A Ray of Millennial Light: Early Education and Social Reform in the Infant School Movement in Massachusetts, 1826–1840" in *Family and Kin in American Urban Communities, 1800–1940,* ed. Tamara K. Hareven (New York: Watts, 1977), 62–99.

6. Phillip McCann and F. A. Young, *Samuel Wilderspin and the Infant School Movement* (London: Croom Helm, 1982).

7. Mathew Carey, *Miscellaneous Essays* (Philadelphia: Carey and Hart, 1830).

8. Infant School Society of the City of Boston, *Third Annual Report* (Boston, 1831).

9. Kaestle and Vinovskis, *Education and Social Change.*

10. For an excellent discussion of how the distinctiveness of kindergartens was often lost once they became incorporated into the public schools, see David Tyack and Larry Cuban, *Tinkering toward Utopia: A Century of Public School Reform* (Cambridge: Harvard University Press, 1995), 64–69.

11. J. R. Brown, *An Essay on Infant Cultivation* (Philadelphia: Clark and Raser, 1828).

12. Amariah Brigham, *Remarks on the Influence of Mental Cultivation and Mental Excitement upon Health,* 2d ed. (Boston: Marsh, Capen and Lyon, 1833).

13. May and Vinovskis, "Ray of Millennial Light"; Kaestle and Vinovskis, *Education and Social Change.*

14. Beatty, *Preschool Education in America;* Carolyn Winterer, "Avoiding a 'Hothouse System of Education': Kindergartens and the Problem of Insanity, 1860–1890," *History of Education Quarterly* 32 (1992): 289–314.

15. Judith D. Auerbach, *In the Business of Child Care: Employer Initiatives and Working Women* (New York: Praeger, 1988); Victoria L. Getis and Maris A. Vinovskis, "History of Child Care in the United States before 1850" in *Child Care in Context: Cross-Cultural Perspectives,* ed. Michael E. Lamb, Kathleen J. Sternberg, Carl-Phillip Hwang, and Anders G. Broberg (Hillsdale, N.J.: Lawrence Erlbaum, 1992), 185–206; Margaret O. Steinfels, *Who's Minding the Children? The History and Politics of Day Care in America* (New York: Simon and Schuster, 1973).

16. Benjamin S. Bloom, *Stability and Change in Human Characteristics* (New York: John Wiley, 1964); J. McVicker Hunt, *Intelligence and Experience* (New York: Ronald Press, 1961).

17. Julia Wrigley, "Do Young Children Need Intellectual Stimulation? Experts' Advice to Parents, 1900–1985," *History of Education Quarterly* 29 (1989): 41–75.

18. Edward Zigler and Karen Anderson, "An Idea Whose Time Had Come: The Intellectual and Political Climate for Head Start" in Edward Zigler and Jeanette Valentine, eds., *Project Head Start: A Legacy of the War on Poverty* (New York: Free Press, 1979), 3–19.

19. Edward D. Berkowitz, *America's Welfare State: From Roosevelt to Reagan* (Baltimore: Johns

Hopkins University Press, 1991); Marshall Kaplan and Peggy Cuciti, eds., *The Great Society and Its Legacy: Twenty Years of U.S. Social Policy* (Durham: Duke University Press, 1986).

20. Hugh D. Graham, *The Uncertain Triumph: Federal Education Policy in the Kennedy and Johnson Years* (Chapel Hill: University of North Carolina Press, 1984); Harold Silver and Pamela Silver, *An Educational War on Poverty: American and British Policy-Making, 1960–1980* (Cambridge: Cambridge University Press, 1991).

21. Edward Zigler and Jeanette Valentine, eds., *Project Head Start: A Legacy of the War on Poverty* (New York: Free Press, 1979).

22. Maris A. Vinovskis, "Early Childhood Education: Then and Now" *Daedalus* 122 (1993): 151–75; Edward Zigler and Susan Muenchow, *Head Start: The Inside Story of America's Most Successful Educational Experiment* (New York: Basic Books, 1992).

23. U.S. Congress, House, Committee on Education and Labor, *Hearings before the Subcommittee on the War on Poverty,* 89th Cong., 2d sess., 1966, 186.

24. Westinghouse Learning Corporation, "The Impact of Head Start: An Evaluation of the Effects of Head Start on Children's Cognitive and Affective Development," report presented to the Office of Economic Opportunity, contract no. B89–4536, vol. 1, 243.

25. Ibid., 255.

26. *New York Times,* Apr. 14, 1969, 1, 36.

27. Marshall S. Smith and Joan S. Bissell, "Report Analysis: The Impact of Head Start," *Harvard Educational Review* 40 (1970): 51–104.

28. Victor G. Cicirelli, John W. Evans, and Jeffrey S. Schiller, "The Impact of Head Start: A Reply to the Report Analysis," *Harvard Educational Review* 40 (1970): 105–29.

29. Zigler and Muenchow, *Head Start,* 154.

30. Daniel P. Moynihan, *The Politics of a Guaranteed Income: The Nixon Administration and the Family Assistance Plan* (New York: Vintage, 1973); Gilbert Y. Steiner, *The Children's Cause* (Washington, D.C.: Brookings Institution, 1976).

31. Kathleen A. Clarke-Stewart, "Infant Day Care: Maligned or Malignant?" *American Psychologist* 44 (1989): 266–73.

32. Lawrence J. Schweinhart and David P. Weikart, *Young Children Grow Up: The Effects of the Perry Preschool Program on Youths through Age 15* (Ypsilanti: High/Scope Press, 1980); John R. Berrueta-Clement et al., *Changed Lives: The Effects of the Perry Preschool Program on Youths through Age 19* (Ypsilanti: High/Scope Press, 1984); Lawrence J. Schweinhart, Helen V. Barnes, and David P. Weikart, *Significant Benefits: The High/Scope Perry Preschool Study through Age 27* (Ypsilanti: High/Scope Press, 1993). The positive results of the Perry Preschool Program are frequently cited without adequate acknowledgement of criticisms of that study. See, e.g., Beatty, *Preschool Education in America,* 199.

33. Edward F. Zigler, "Formal Schooling for Four-Year-Olds? No." in *Early Schooling: The National Debate,* ed. Sharon L. Kagan and Edward F. Zigler (New Haven: Yale University Press, 1987), 27–44.

34. Helen V. Barnes, "Predicting Long-Term Outcomes from Early Elementary Classroom Measures in a Sample of High-Risk Black Children" (Ph.D. diss., University of Michigan, 1991). More differences between the program and nonprogram males were discov-

ered at age twenty-seven in areas such as home ownership and earnings of employed males.

35. Ibid.; Helen V. Barnes, "Gender-Related Long-Term Outcomes from Early Elementary Classroom Measures in a Sample of High-Risk Black Children" (master's thesis, University of Michigan, 1989).

36. Schweinhart, Barnes, and Weikart, *Significant Benefits,* xv–xx.

37. Ibid., 54–80.

38. The discussion and analysis of gender differences is unfortunately limited in this otherwise thorough report. Ibid., 174–92.

39. Lawrence J. Schweinhart and Gary Gottfredson, "Good Preschool Programs for Young Children Living in Poverty Produce Important Long-Term Benefits: Pro and Con," *Debates on Education Issues* 1 (1990): 1–8.

40. Valerie E. Lee et al., "Are Head Start Effects Sustained? A Longitudinal Follow-Up Comparison of Disadvantaged Children Attending Head Start, No Preschool, and Other Preschool Programs," *Child Development* 61 (1990): 495–507.

41. Ron Haskins, "Beyond Metaphor: The Efficacy of Early Childhood Education," *American Psychologist* 44 (1989): 278.

42. W. Stephen Barnett, "Long-Term Effects of Early Childhood Programs on Cognitive and School Outcomes," *Future of Children* 5, no. 3 (winter 1995): 43.

43. Burton L. White, *The First Three Years of Life* (New York: Prentice-Hall, 1975), 4.

44. David Elkind, "Early Childhood Education on Its Own Terms" in *Early Schooling: The National Debate,* ed. Sharon L. Kagan and Edward F. Zigler, (New Haven: Yale University Press, 1987), 98–115.

45. Orville G. Brim and Jerome Kagan, eds., *Constancy and Change in Human Development* (Cambridge: Harvard University Press, 1980); W. Andrew Collins, ed., *Development during Middle Childhood: The Years from Six to Twelve* (Washington, D.C.: National Academy Press, 1984); S. Shirley Feldman and Glen R. Elliott, eds., *At The Threshold: The Developing Adolescent* (Cambridge: Harvard University Press, 1990).

46. Robert E. Slavin, Nancy L. Karweik, and Barbara A. Wasik, "Preventing Early School Failure: What Works?" Center for Research on Effective Schooling for Disadvantaged Students, Report no. 26 (Nov. 1991).

47. Zigler and Muenchow, *Head Start.*

48. National Governors' Association, *Task Force on Readiness: Supporting Works* (Washington, D.C.: National Governors' Association, 1986).

49. National Governors' Association, *Time for Results: The Governors' 1991 Report on Education* (Washington, D.C.: National Governors' Association, 1986), 14–15.

50. Roger B. Porter and Stephen M. Studdert, memo to John H. Sununu on President's Education Summit Conference for Governors (White House, Aug. 14, 1989), in the author's possession.

51. White House, briefing paper for the Education Summit Meeting (White House, Sept. 27, 1989), in the author's possession.

52. National Governors' Association, *Time for Results.*

53. Julie A. Miller, "Small Group's Insider Role in Goals-Setting Provides Clues to Education Policymaking," *Education Week* 9, no. 25 (Mar. 14, 1990).

54. *New York Times,* Oct. 1, 1989, 22.

55. Christopher Cross, memo to John Porter (OERI, Nov. 30, 1989), in the author's possession.

56. Ibid.

57. Ray Scheppach and Michael Cohen, memo to Governors on Education Task Force and Administration Representatives on Background for Dec. 7 Meeting (Dec. 5, 1989), in the author's possession.

58. Office of the Press Secretary, National Education Goals (White House, Jan. 31, 1990), in the author's possession.

59. National Governors' Association, *National Education Goals* (Washington, D.C.: National Governors' Association, Feb. 25, 1990).

60. National Goals Panel, *The National Education Goals Report: Building a Nation of Learners,* 1991 (Washington, D.C.: Government Printing Office, 1991).

61. National Goals Panel, *National Education Goals Report,* 1992, 191.

62. Ibid., 191.

63. National Goals Panel, *National Education Goals Report,* 1991, 33–38.

64. National Goals Panel, *National Education Goals Report,* 1992, 19.

65. Ibid., 59–72. It is very difficult to develop appropriate measures to assess the development of young children. For an excellent introduction to the most recent work in this important area, see Samuel J. Meisels and Emily Fenichel, eds., *New Visions for the Developmental Assessment of Infants and Young Children* (Washington, D.C.: Zero to Three, National Center for Infants, Toddlers, and Families, 1996).

66. Ernest L. Boyer, *Ready to Learn: A Mandate for the Nation* (Princeton: Princeton University Press, 1991).

67. Ibid., 161.

68. Phyllis Schlafly, "Course Outline for a Blackboard Empire," *Washington Times,* Feb. 21, 1992, F4.

69. *Education Daily,* Jan. 22, 1992, 1.

70. *Education Daily,* May 15, 1992, 1.

71. Jeffrey L. Katz, "Education Programs Get Big Boost in Spending," *Congressional Quarterly* 54, no. 40 (Oct. 5, 1996): 2867–70.

CHAPTER 4. IS IT TIME TO REINVENT FOLLOW THROUGH?

1. National Governors' Association, *The National Education Goals Report: Building a Nation of Learners,* 1992 (Washington, D.C.: Government Printing Office, 1992), 58. There were originally six national goals, with two added in 1994. For an analysis of the origins of goal one, see chap. 2.

2. For a balanced and thoughtful assessment of the studies on the impact of Head Start, see Ron Haskins, "Beyond Metaphor: The Efficacy of Early Childhood Education," *American Psychologist* 44, no. 2 (1989): 274–82.

3. See, e.g., John Hood, "What's Wrong with Head Start," *Wall Street Journal,* Feb. 19, 1993, A14; "Head Start Must Catch Up," *Daily Report Card: The National Update on America's Education Goals* 2, no. 170 (Feb. 17, 1993): 2–3; Mary Jordan, "As Politicians Expand Head Start, Experts Question Worth, Efficiency," *Washington Post,* Feb. 19, 1993, A4.

4. For example, Albert Shanker, president of the American Federation of Teachers, wrote: "Many of us saw its [Head Start's] shortcomings, but we were reluctant to open up the issue, to raise doubts. We were afraid that if we offered suggestions for improving Head Start, the end result would be no improvements and the program might suffer cuts instead of being expanded.

   "But now, we're in a different period. Because we have a Democratic president and a Democratic Congress, we can, for the first time in years, talk openly about shortcomings and needed improvements without fearing that such a discussion will be used to sabotage the very programs we want to improve." Albert Shanker, "A New Head Start," *New Republic* 208, no. 10 (Mar. 8, 1993): 43.

5. For discussions of the origins of Head Start, see Harold Silver and Pamela Silver, *An Educational War on Poverty: American and British Policy-Making, 1960–1980* (Cambridge: Cambridge University Press, 1991); Maris A. Vinovskis, "Early Education: Then and Now," *Daedalus* 122, no. 1 (winter 1993): 151–76; Edward Zigler and Jeanette Valentine, eds., *Project Head Start: A Legacy of the War on Poverty* (New York: Free Press, 1979); Edward Zigler and Susan Muenchow, *Head Start: The Inside Story of America's Most Successful Educational Experiment* (New York: Basic Books, 1992).

6. For a discussion of the problems of the War on Poverty, see Edward D. Berkowitz, *America's Welfare State: From Roosevelt to Reagan* (Baltimore: Johns Hopkins University Press, 1991); John C. Donovan, *The Politics of Poverty* (New York: Pegasus, 1967); Marshall Kaplan and Peggy Cucit, eds., *The Great Society and Its Legacy: Twenty Years of U.S. Policy* (Durham: Duke University Press, 1986).

7. For example, when Shriver testified on behalf of Head Start, he emphasized the value of the program for increasing the IQ of children. Testimony of Sargent Shriver, U.S. Congress, House, Committee on Education and Labor, *Hearings before the Subcommittee on the War on Poverty Programs,* 89th Cong., 2d sess., Mar. 8, 1966, 186. Sheldon White, who has reviewed much of the materials on the origins of Head Start, suggests that the major players in the creation of that program did not subscribe to the IQ-modification theory that many policymakers and the public seemed so eager to accept. Sheldon H. White, letter to Maris Vinovskis, OERI, Department of Education, Mar. 23, 1993.

8. U.S. President, "Remarks of President Lyndon B. Johnson on Announcing Plans to Extend Head Start," *Published Papers of the President,* no. 467, bk. 2 (June 1, 1965 to Dec. 1, 1965), 953–54.

9. Zigler and Muenchow, *Head Start,* 10.

10. Ivor Kraft, "Are We Overselling the Preschool Idea?" *Saturday Review* 48, no. 51 (Dec. 18, 1965): 63.

11. Max Wolff and Annie Stein, "Six Months Later: A Comparison of Children Who Had Head Start, Summer 1965, with Their Classmates" (New York: Ferkauf Graduate School of Education, Yeshiva University, Aug. 1966) [ERIC no. ED 015025]. Robert Egbert, one of the early participants and first director of Follow Through, emphasizes the importance of the Wolff and Stein study. "The decision to request a Follow Through program resulted largely from a single report that was based on kindergarten data from four New York City schools." Robert L. Egbert, Marijane E. England, and Rosalind Alexander-Kasparik, "A Glance Back at Follow Through's Beginnings," in *Follow*

Through: A Bridge to the Future, ed. Betty J. Mace-Matluck (Austin, Tex.: Southwest Educational Development Laboratory, 1992), 11. While not denying the importance of reports of the Wolff and Stein work, Richard Elmore convincingly presents a much broader view of the origins of Follow Through. Richard Elmore, "Follow Through: Decision-Making in a Large-Scale Social Experiment" (Ph.D. diss., Graduate School of Education of Harvard University, 1976).

12. Quoted in Robert L. Egbert, "Some Thoughts about Follow Through Thirteen Years Later" (paper commissioned by the National Institute of Education, 1981), 7 [ERIC no. ED 244–733]. John Henry Martin and Jule Sugarman prepared that speech for Shriver. Carol Doernberger and Edward Zigler, "Project Follow Through: Intent and Reality," in *Head Start and Beyond: A National Plan for Extended Childhood Intervention,* ed. Edward Zigler and Sally J. Styfco (New Haven: Yale University Press, 1993), 44.

13. U.S. Congress, House, "State of the Union Message by President Lyndon B. Johnson," *Congressional Record,* 90th Cong., 1st sess., Jan. 10, 1967, 113, pt. 1:37.

14. U.S. Congress, House, "Message on Children and Youth by President Lyndon B. Johnson," *Congressional Record,* 90th Cong., 1st sess., Feb. 8, 1967, 113, pt. 2:2882.

15. Quoted in Egbert, England, and Alexander-Kasparik, "Glance Back at Follow Through's Beginnings," 11–12.

16. Although $15 million was allocated to Follow Through, $3.5 million was used to replace the money that had been advanced for the pilot project.

17. For an analysis of the shift of Follow Through from a large-scale program to a smaller, experimental one, see Egbert, England, and Alexander-Kasparik, "Glance Back at Follow Through's Beginnings"; Elmore, "Follow Through"; Doernberger and Zigler, "Project Follow Through," 43–72.

18. Because the legislation continued to depict Follow Through as an extension of Head Start, each local project had to provide the full array of social, medical, psychological, and nutritional services in addition to its educational offerings. As a result, Follow Through was allowed to vary only the educational services offered while maintaining the full complement of the other services, thus seriously limiting the experimental opportunities.

19. For a detailed and critical discussion of the initial design of the planned variation of Follow Through, see Elmore, "Follow Through," chap. 5.

20. For a description and analysis of the Follow Through models, see W. Ray Rhine, ed., *Making Schools More Effective: New Directions from Follow Through* (New York: Academic Press, 1981).

21. Problems of implementing the available models continued to plague the local projects. For an analysis of the difficulties from the perspective of the sponsors, see Walter Hodges et al., *Follow Through: Forces for Change in the Primary Schools* (Ypsilanti: High/Scope Press, 1980).

22. For figures on the number of sites, sponsors, students, and funding, see Robert L. Egbert and Marijane E. England, "A Brief History," *Follow Through: Program and Policy Issues,* ed. Eugene A. Ramp and Colleen S. Pederson (Lawrence: University of Kansas, 1992). The more recent data on Follow Through has been furnished by the Office of Compensatory Education, Department of Education.

23. For a discussion of the problems of designing and implementing the evaluation of Follow

Through, see Richard F. Elmore, "Design of the Follow Through Experiment," in *Planned Variation in Education: Should We Give Up or Try Harder?* ed. Alice M. Rivlin and P. Michael Timpane (Washington, D.C.: Brookings Institution, 1975), 23–45; Garry L. McDaniels, "Evaluation Problems in Follow Through," in Ibid., 47–60.

24. Alice M. Rivlin, *Systematic Thinking for Social Action* (Washington, D.C.: Brookings Institution, 1971), 102–3.

25. Elmore, "Follow Through," 199.

26. Elmore, "Follow Through."

27. Few of the published accounts of the Follow Through Program discuss these serious difficulties experienced by the agency. For a critical but balanced account of these events, see Elmore, "Follow Through," chap. 6.

28. Rosemary Wilson replaced Egbert as the program director, but McDaniels played the leading role in the agency in redesigning the evaluation of Follow Through.

29. Elmore, "Follow Through," chap. 6; Garry L. McDaniels, "Evaluation Problems in Follow Through," in *Planned Variation in Education: Should We Give Up or Try Harder?* ed. Alice M. Rivlin and P. Michael Timpane (Washington, D.C.: Brookings Institution, 1975), 47–60. When McDaniels left Follow Through in 1973 to work at the newly created National Institute of Education, he was replaced by Eugene Tucker. The evaluation of Follow Through was transferred to the Office of Planning, Budgeting, and Evaluation (OPBE) in spring 1974 and Tucker reported to John Evans, director of OPBE, rather than to Rosemary Wilson, director of Follow Through.

30. The HSPV program was created in 1969 and modeled after the Follow Through Program. Both programs emphasized differences in curriculum rather than other program inputs, such as social or psychological services. (The legislation for both Head Start and Follow Through required the provision of a comprehensive set of services.) For a discussion of HSPV, see Lois-Ellin Datta, "Design of the Head Start Planned Variation Experiment," in *Planned Variation in Education: Should We Give Up or Try Harder?* ed. Alice M. Rivlin and P. Michael Timpane (Washington, D.C.: Brookings Institution, 1975), 79–99; Marshall S. Smith, "Evaluation Findings in Head Start Planned Variation," in ibid., 101–11; Carol Vanduesen Lukas, "Problems in Implementing Head Start Planned Variation Models," in ibid., 113–25.

31. Alice M. Rivlin and P. Michael Timpane, "Planned Variation in Education: An Assessment," in *Planned Variation in Education: Should We Give Up or Try Harder?* ed. Alice M. Rivlin and P. Michael Timpane (Washington, D.C.: Brookings Institution, 1975), 1–21.

32. Ibid., 18.

33. Ibid., 21.

34. For a discussion of the changing role of development in the regional educational laboratories and the research and development centers, see Maris A. Vinovskis, "Analysis of the Quality of Research and Development at the OERI Research and Development Centers and at the OERI Regional Educational Laboratories" (final report, OERI, Department of Education, June 1993).

35. Richard B. Anderson et al., "Pardon Us, but What Was the Question Again? A Response to the Critique of the Follow Through Evaluation," *Harvard Educational Review* 48, no. 2 (May 1978): 161–70. For another valuable perspective that reinforces the importance of

local school contexts affecting educational reform efforts, see David Tyack and Larry Cuban, *Tinkering toward Utopia: A Century of Public School Reform* (Cambridge: Harvard University Press, 1995), 60–84.

36. Ernest R. House et al., "No Simple Answer: Critique of the Follow Through Evaluation," *Harvard Educational Review* 48, no. 2 (May 1978): 154.

37. Walter L. Hodges, "The Worth of the Follow Through Experience," *Harvard Educational Review* 48, no. 2 (May 1978): 186–92.

38. Linda B. Stebbins et al., *Education as Experimentation: A Planned Variation Model, Volume IV–A, An Evaluation of Follow Through* (Cambridge, Mass.: Abt Associates, 1977), xxv–xxvi.

39. L. Feinberg, "'Basic' Teaching Methods More Effective Study Says," *Washington Post*, June 20, 1977, 1, 8; James J. Kilpatrick, "Basics Better in Education, Cambridge Group Finds," *Boston Evening Globe*, July 1, 1977, 19.

40. House et al. "No Simple Answer," 156.

41. Anderson et al. "Pardon Us, but What Was the Question Again?" 168.

42. Egbert and England, "Brief History," 25. Others argued that while the more behavioral-oriented programs may have been useful for improving students' basic skills, they failed to instill proper social skills and values, and this limited the students' long-term progress.

43. Gordon E. Greenwood et al., "Parent Education Model" in *Making Schools More Effective: New Directions from Follow Through,* ed. W. Ray Rhine (New York: Academic Press, 1981), 49–93. Greenwood and his colleagues were not entirely discouraged by the lack of more positive cognitive gains for the Follow Through students since they assumed that because helping parents become better educators was a lengthy process, the beneficial effects for the child may not appear until much later. I am indebted to Professor Gordon Greenwood of the University of Florida for sharing his reflections on the parent education model in a telephone conversation on May 10, 1993.

For analyses of other local evaluations of some of the different Follow Through models, see Wesley C. Becker et al., "Direct Instruction Model," in ibid., 95–154; Eugene A. Ramp and W. Ray Rhine, "Behavior Model Analysis," in ibid., 155–200; David P. Weikart, Charles F. Hohmann, and W. Ray Rhine, "High/Scope Cognitively Oriented Curriculum Model," in ibid., 201–47; Elizabeth C. Gilkeson et al., "Bank Street Model: A Developmental-Interaction Approach," in ibid., 249–88.

44. Hodges et al., *Follow Through,* 73.

45. Ibid., 53.

46. One could also compare the expenditures on Follow Through to such programs as Head Start, but the comparison to the centers and labs is particularly appropriate because these two sets of federally funded education institutions had large research and development components.

47. On the early development of the centers and laboratories, see Richard A. Dershimer, *The Federal Government and Educational R&D* (Lexington, Mass.: Lexington Books, 1976).

48. Robert L. Egbert, "Some Thoughts about Follow Through Thirteen Years Later" (unpub. paper, National Institute of Education, 1981) [ERIC no. 244–733].

49. For details of the planned design of Follow Through, see McDaniels, "Evaluation Problems in Follow Through."

50. As quoted in Jeffrey Schiller et al., "Plans for Follow Through Research and Development" (unpub. paper, National Institute of Education, Oct. 1, 1980) [ERIC no. ED244–727].

51. Ibid.

52. Information about the Follow Through activities of NIE are described in Schiller et al., "Plans for Follow Through Research and Development." Given the budgetary reductions for Follow Through, only $769,000 (in constant dollars, 1982–84 = 100) were given to NIE for 1981.

53. Schiller et al., "Plans for Follow Through Research and Development," 11.

54. Ibid., 12.

55. Beatrice Gross and Ronald Gross, "Towards Improved Compensatory Education: Findings of Five Conferences to Plan Fresh Follow Through Research" (unpub. paper, National Institute of Education, 1982) [ERIC no. 254–335]. An alternative way of describing this approach was to label it "academic learning time." For a more detailed discussion of academic learning time, see Carolyn Denham and Ann Lieberman, eds., *Time to Learn* (Washington, D.C.: National Institute of Education, 1980).

56. For summaries of the conferences, see Gross and Gross, "Towards Improved Compensatory Education"; Beatrice Gross and Ronald Gross, "Frontiers of Research and Evaluation in Compensatory Education" (unpub. paper, National Institute of Education, 1982) [ERIC no. 254–337].

57. It is difficult to reconstruct some of the policy discussions and positions of the Carter and Reagan administrations because the records of the Follow Through Office were destroyed. Apparently, when the Reagan appointees arrived at the Department of Education, a GS-15 employee discarded the records of the Follow Through Office. Therefore, much of the following discussion is based on congressional hearings and interviews with some of the participants. A search was made of the computerized list of the Department of Education materials deposited in the National Archives, but no relevant Follow Through records were located.

58. U.S. Congress, House, *Hearings before a Subcommittee of the Committee on Appropriations, Part 6: Department of Education,* 97th Cong., 1st sess., May 15, 1981, 275–314.

59. Ibid., 850–52.

60. Congressional Quarterly, *Almanac, 97th Congress, 1st Session . . . 1981* (Washington, D.C.: Congressional Quarterly, 1982), 500.

61. The authorizations for the program had dropped as well during those years. *Omnibus Budget Reconciliation Act of* 1981, Public Law 97–35, 97th Cong., 1st sess. (Aug. 13, 1981), 42 UCS 9801–42 USC 9867.

62. Congressional Quarterly, *Almanac, 98th Congress, 2d Session . . . 1984* (Washington, D.C.: Congressional Quarterly, 1983), 485–87.

63. *Congressional Record,* 132, no. 55, daily ed. (Apr. 29, 1986): H2227.

64. Ibid., H2224. Representative James Jeffords (R-VT) disagreed with Kildee's assertion that the Follow Through money would be diverted to the Defense Department: "I think that we ought to recognize that in the appropriations process, there is going to be so much money set aside for education. Cap is probably not even interested in $7.5 million; he would not know where to put it. He does not have a drawer that small. What we

would be doing is making more money available for education in other areas." Ibid., H2225.

65. Congressional Quarterly, *Weekly Report* 44, no. 18 (May 3, 1986): 971.

66. U.S. Congress, House, *Follow Through Amendments of 1983*, 98th Cong., 1st sess., May 16, 1983, Report no. 98–160, 2 [ERIC no. ED241–132].

67. While there were hearings on the reauthorization of Follow Through and other programs in 1984, the focus was on Head Start. Little mention was made of Follow Through in those hearings, perhaps in large part because the officials who testified were from the Department of Health and Human Services rather than the Department of Education, which administered Follow Through. U.S. Congress, House, Subcommittee on Human Resources, Committee on Education and Labor, *Authorizations for Head Start, Follow Through, Community Services, and Establishing Child Care Information and Referral Services,* 98th Cong., 2d sess., Mar. 21, 1984.

68. Testimony of Eugene A. Ramp, U.S. Congress, House, Subcommittee on Human Resources, Committee on Education and Labor, *Reauthorization of the Follow Through Program,* 99th Cong., 2d sess., Feb. 20, 1986, serial no. 99–103, 4.

69. For example, the Follow Through programs in Flint, Michigan, and Washington, D.C., were started in 1969 and continued in the early 1990s.

70. Testimony of W. Ray Rhine, U.S. Congress, House, Subcommittee on Human Resources of the Committee on Education and Labor, *Reauthorization of the Follow Through Program,* 99th Cong., 2d sess., Feb. 20, 1986, serial no. 99–103, 37.

71. Testimony of Eugen A. Ramp, U.S. Congress, House, Subcommittee on Human Resources of the Committee on Education and Labor, *Hearings on the Reauthorization of the Follow Through Act,* 101st Cong., 2d sess., Feb. 21, 1990, serial no. 101–93, 48.

72. Rhine stated: "I'm not really optimistic about the ability of Follow Through to compete in most States. In my own State of Missouri, for example, I think that to come in as a new influence, requesting State support, is just, on the face of it, not going to be a very inspiring thing to happen as far as State legislators are concerned." House Subcommittee, *Reauthorization of the Follow Through Program,* 1986, 110.

73. Ibid., 111.

74. In an analysis of the Program Effectiveness Panel (PEP) and National Diffusion Network (NDN) at the Office of Educational Research and Improvement, the National Academy of Sciences reviewed the previous studies of the Joint Dissemination Review Panel and the National Diffusion Network. The National Academy study concluded that "there have been a few studies of PEP's predecessor, the Joint Dissemination Review Panel (JDRP), and of NDN. They have generally found that JDRP and NDN do help to put innovations into the schools, but that enduring improvements in student outcomes are seldom achieved." Richard C. Atkinson and Gregg B. Jackson, eds., *Research and Education Reform: Roles for the Office of Educational Research and Improvement* (Washington, D.C.: National Academy Press, 1992), 81.

Moreover, apparently the majority of local Follow Through programs were never submitted to the JDRP. By 1980, nineteen of the thirty-three local projects submitted for review were approved. Hodges et al., *Follow Through,* 53.

75. Helen Suber, a Follow Through parent, testified: "I, for one, would not have done

without the Follow Through program. I have two sets of children, and they've seen a 12-year difference in them. So, that makes me a dynamite Follow Through parent. And the reason for that is that the older children did not have access to Head Start and Follow Through. The last set of kids, after that 12 years, the last set did. And there's a tremendous difference in there." House Subcommittee, *Reauthorization of the Follow Through Program,* 1986, 112. Ms. Super was quizzed in much greater detail by Representative Kildee (D-MI) about the progress of the Follow Through students compared to those who had not attended.

76. U.S. Congress, House, *Hearings on the Reauthorization of the Follow Through Act,* 1990, 4–5.

77. Ibid., 4. At the same time, the Department of Education felt that the Even Start Program was more effective than the Follow Through models they had praised in the previous paragraph. Ibid., 5.

78. Mace-Matluck, ed., *Follow Through,* 86.

79. Department of Education, "Follow Through Program: Fact Sheet" (1992).

80. U.S. Congress, House, *Improving America's Schools Act: Conference Report to Accompany H.R. 6,* 103d Cong., 2d sess., 1994, Report 103–761, 92–97.

81. *Congressional Record,* 140, no. 22, daily ed. (Mar. 3, 1994): H1010.

82. For example, Representative Jolene Unsoeld (D-WA) argued: "This is not a Follow Through Program. This a new authority that provides grants to LEA's for innovative transition projects. In order to be funded under this authority, projects must enter into formal transition agreements with Head Start, Even Start, and other local preschool programs, and they must involve parents in the planning, operation, and evaluation of transition projects." Ibid., H1010.

83. Ibid., H1011.

84. Ibid., H1012.

85. Ibid., H1014–H1015.

86. James J. Marshall, Charles J. Edwards, and Alvin C. Lin, *Title I Handbook* (East Providence, R.I.: Newsletter Press of New England, 1995), B/37, C/123.

87. Edward Zigler and Sally J. Styfco, "Strength in Unity: Consolidating Federal Education Programs for Young Children," in *Head Start and Beyond: A National Plan for Extended Childhood Intervention,* ed. Edward Zigler and Sally J. Styfco (New Haven: Yale University Press, 1993), 111–45.

88. The clear intent of Tauke's amendment was to move toward the consolidation of the Follow Through program and the Chapter 1 program. As he put it, "Chapter 1, if expanded, could have something to offer these children. We should not attempt to expand a $7 million program [Follow Through] to the size and scope of Head Start and Chapter 1 when we would do better to develop ways to co-ordinate these two very large programs. The theory behind my amendment is that in years to come Chapter 1 should provide a continuum of services to Head Start children but this will take time. What my amendment proposes to do is to allow the Follow Through Program, which has been built upon the strengths of Head Start to serve as a bridge between Head Start and chapter 1 as we move toward our goal." *Congressional Record,* 136, no. 62, daily ed. (May 16, 1990): H2367.

89. U.S. Congress, House, *Follow Through Amendments of* 1983, May 16, 1983, 2.

90. Some Follow Through proponents have recommended that the Department of Education commission a large-scale study of the student participants in Follow Through to see whether, in the long run, they have fared much better than their nonparticipating peers. Others have argued that this would be an expensive undertaking and not likely to yield much useful information given the strongly negative findings about the program in the short term. For a discussion of this option, see Ramp and Pederson, eds., *Follow Through: Program and Policy Issues.* Although it probably does not make too much sense to spend millions of dollars tracking the original Follow Through sample, it may be possible to work with a much smaller subsample, and this could be useful. In any case, one might also be interested in reanalyzing the existing national data sample, if it is readily available, using some of the more sophisticated statistical techniques that have been developed recently to investigate program and individual-level data simultaneously. Certainly the more prominent and promising local evaluations should be assessed more carefully by a panel of experts.

91. Efforts are being made to address some of these issues. For example, the Administration on Children, Youth, and Families in the Department of Health and Human Services has funded some transition projects. Craig Ramey has been commissioned to evaluate these efforts. As much as possible, information from such other projects should be incorporated into any new Follow Through initiatives so that there is ample coordination among the various projects. Although some overlap and duplication is inevitable, and not necessarily undesirable, given the scarce funds available for educational research and development care must be exercised when building upon these earlier efforts.

CHAPTER 5. THE ORIGINS AND DEVELOPMENT OF THE EVEN START PROGRAM

1. While Even Start focuses on family literacy as a whole and not just on early childhood education, concerns about the educational development of young children were perhaps the major consideration throughout the legislative process for many members of Congress. The focus of this chapter will be the early childhood aspects of Even Start, but the adult literacy and parenting aspects of Even Start will also be considered when appropriate. For an introduction to and analyses of the broader, family literacy approach, see David K. Dickinson, ed., *Bridges to Literacy: Children, Families, and Schools* (Oxford: Blackwell, 1994); Lesley Mandel Morrow, ed., *Family Literacy: Connections in Schools and Communities* (Newark, Del.: International Reading Association, 1995). By far the best, single scholarly summary and analysis of two-generation programs is Robert G. St. Pierre, Jean I. Layzer, and Helen V. Barnes, "Two-Generation Programs: Design, Cost, and Short-Term Effectiveness," *Future of Children* 5, no. 3 (winter 1995): 76–93. A slightly different version of this essay is available in Robert G. St. Pierre, Jean I. Layzer, and Helen V. Barnes, *Regenerating Two-Generation Programs* (Cambridge, Mass.: Abt Associates, 1996).

   For useful introductions to the Even Start Program, see Patricia A. McKee and Nancy Rhett, "The Even Start Family Literacy Program," in *Family Literacy: Connections in Schools and Communities,* ed. Leslie Mandel Morrow (Newark, Del.: International Reading Association, 1995), 155–66; Robert G. St. Pierre and Janet P. Swartz, *The Even Start Family Literacy Program: Early Implementation* (Cambridge, Mass.: Abt Associates, 1996).

As part of the growing efforts in Congress to reduce the budget deficit, the Even Start Program was level-funded for FY96. The president's recommendation for FY97 also proposed a continued level funding for the program. James J. Marshall, *Title I Update: Understanding and Implementing the Title I Program,* vol. 16, no. 4 (Arlington, Va.: Education Funding Research Council, May 1996), C/123.

2. On the origins and demise of infant schools, see Dean May and Maris A. Vinovskis, "A Ray of Millennial Light: Early Education and Social Reform in the Infant School Movement in Massachusetts, 1826–1840," in *Family and Kin in American Urban Communities,* 1800–1940, ed. Tamara K. Hareven (New York: Watts, 1977), 62–99; Carl F. Kaestle and Maris A. Vinovskis, *Education and Social Change in Massachusetts* (Cambridge: Cambridge University Press, 1980); Alan R. Pence, "Infant Schools in North America, 1825–1840," in *Advances in Early Education and Day Care* (Greenwich, Conn.: JAI Press, 1986), 1–25.

3. On the role of kindergartens, see Barbara Beatty, *Preschool Education in America: The Culture of Young Children from the Colonial Period to the Present* (New Haven: Yale University Press, 1995); Caroline Winterer, "Avoiding a 'Hothouse System of Education': Kindergartens and the Problem of Insanity, 1860–1890," *History of Education Quarterly* 32, 3 (1992): 289–314.

4. Hamilton Cravens, "Child-Saving in the Age of Professionalism, 1915–1930," in *American Childhood: A Research Guide and Historical Handbook,* ed. J. M. Hawes and N. Ray Hiner (Westport, Conn.: Greenwood Press, 1985), 415–88; Victoria L. Getis and Maris A. Vinovskis, "History of Child Care in the United States before 1950," in *Child Care in Context: Cross-Cultural Perspectives,* ed. Michael E. Lamb et al. (Hillsdale, N.J.: Lawrence Erlbaum, 1992), 185–206.

5. Sonya Michel, "The Politics of Childhood: Federal Programs for Children from the WPA through Head Start" (paper presented at the annual meeting of the Organization of American Historians, Washington, D.C., March 1990).

6. On the origins of Head Start, see Edward Zigler and Jeanette Valentine, eds., *Project Head Start: A Legacy of the War on Poverty* (New York: Free Press, 1979); Gilbert Y. Steiner, *The Children's Cause* (Washington, D.C.: Brookings Institution, 1976).

7. Westinghouse Learning Corporation, *The Impact of Head Start: An Evaluation of the Effects of Head Start on Children's Cognitive and Affective Development. Executive Summary,* Ohio University Report to the Office of Economic Opportunity, ED036321 (Washington, D.C.: Clearinghouse for Federal Scientific and Technical Information, June 1969).

8. Maris A. Vinovskis, "Early Childhood Education: Then and Now," *Daedalus* 122, no. 1 (winter 1993): 151–76; Edward Zigler and Sally J. Styfco, eds., *Head Start and Beyond: A National Plan for Extended Childhood Intervention* (New Haven: Yale University Press, 1993).

9. Gerald F. Moran and Maris A. Vinovskis, *Religion, Family, and the Life Course: Explorations in the Social History of Early America* (Ann Arbor: University of Michigan Press, 1992).

10. Carl F. Kaestle, *Pillars of the Republic: Common Schools and American Society,* 1780–1860 (New York: Hill and Wang, 1983).

11. See, e.g., Jacob Abbott, "The Duties of Parents, in Regard to the Schools Where Their Children Are Instructed," in *The Introductory Discourse and Lectures Delivered before the American Institute of Instruction, in Boston, August* 1834 (Boston: Carter, Hendee, 1835), 81–98.

12. Steven L. Schlossman, "The Formative Era in American Parent Education: Overview and Interpretation," in *Parent Education and Public Policy,* ed. Ron Haskins (New York: Ablex, 1983), 7–39; Steven L. Schlossman, "Before Home Start: Notes Toward a History of Parent Education in America, 1897–1929," *Harvard Educational Review* 46 (1976): 436–67.

13. Little research has been done on the relation between early childhood education programs and adult literacy training, and most of these efforts in the first half of the twentieth century were done separately rather than being linked together as a strategy for working with the entire family. For a discussion on immigrants and education, see Maris A. Vinovskis, "Immigrants and Schooling in the United States," in *Immigrants in Two Democracies: French and American Experience,* ed. Donald L. Horowitz and Gerard Noiriel (New York: New York University Press, 1992), 127–47.

14. Kathryn D. Hewett, *Partners with Parents: The Home Start Experience with Preschoolers and Their Families* (Washington, D.C.: Government Printing Office, 1977).

15. Gordon E. Greenwood et al., "Parent Education Model," in *Making Schools More Effective: New Directions from Follow Through,* ed. W. Ray Rhine (New York: Academic Press, 1981), 49–93.

16. For discussions of programs trying to deal with both parents and young children, see Jack A. Brizius and Susan A. Foster, *Generation to Generation: Realizing the Promise of Family Literacy* (Ypsilanti: High/Scope Press, 1993); Barbara Dillion Goodson et al., *Working with Families: Promising Programs to Help Parents Support Young Children's Learning* (Cambridge, Mass.: Abt Associates, February 1991); Jean I. Layzer and Robert G. St. Pierre, *Early Childhood Programs: Adding a Two-Generation Perspective* (Cambridge, Mass.: Abt Associates, 1996); Douglas R. Powell, *Families and Early Childhood Programs* (Washington, D.C.: National Association for the Education of Young Children, 1989); Robert G. St. Pierre and Jean I. Layzer, *Improving Family Literacy Programs: Lessons from Other Intervention Programs* (Cambridge, Mass.: Abt Associates, 1996); Kevin J. Swick, *Teacher-Parent Partnerships to Enhance School Success in Early Childhood Education* (Washington, D.C.: National Education Association, 1991).

17. Brizius and Foster, *Generation to Generation,* 15.

18. For a helpful discussion of the different assumptions of family literacy programs and how well those assumptions are supported by research, see Elsa Roberts Auerbach, "Which Way for Family Literacy: Intervention or Empowerment?" in *Family Literacy: Connections in Schools and Communities,* ed. Lesley Mandel Morrow (Newark, Del.: International Reading Association, 1995), 11–27.

19. U.S. Congress, House, Committee on Education and Labor, *The Even Start Act—H.R. 2535: Hearing before the Subcommittee on Elementary, Secondary, and Vocational Education of the Committee on Education and Labor, November* 20, 1985, 99th Cong., 1st sess., 1986, serial no. 99–82, 1.

20. House Committee, *Even Start Act—H.R.* 2535.

21. There was continued controversy over several different attempts to earmark any of the Chapter 2 funds. Many state and local officials were anxious to protect the flexibility in that block grant program to fund activities which they could not support through the regular categorical programs like Chapter 1.

22. Testimony of Senator John Chafee, House Committee, *Even Start Act—H.R.* 2535, 7.

23. House Committee, *Even Start Act—H.R.* 2535, 20..

24. The sequencing of educational services was never entirely clear. Even Sharon Darling, who in her written testimony seemed to expect that the illiterate parent would be trained first, blurred that distinction in her oral presentation: "This program will bring the parent into a school setting with a preschool youngster, and if that program is successful, it could expect to raise the educational level of the parents of the preschool children through basic skill instruction so that we could turn that around in the home. It would enhance their parenting skills. It would increase the developmental skills of the preschool youngster because they would be working with a developmental child specialist while their parents were working with an adult educator." House Committee, *Even Start Act—H.R.* 2535, 17.

   The question of whether to provide services directly to children or indirectly to them through their parents has important policy and cost implications. Robert St. Pierre, vice president of Abt Associates, points out that while direct services to children may be more expensive, they also may be more effective. This entire matter awaits further research. Robert St. Pierre, letter to Maris Vinovskis, Aug. 18, 1996.

25. The Effective Schools portion of the legislation was the larger of the two programs. Whereas Even Start was to be authorized at $3 million, the Effective Schools program was to receive 10 percent of the Chapter 2 funds, which would have been almost $50 million in FY86. Congressional Quarterly, *Weekly Report* 44, no. 24 (June 14, 1986): 1328.

26. *Congressional Record*, 132, no. 82, daily ed. (June 17, 1986): H3807–H3809.

27. See, e.g., the testimony of Gerald Tirozzi on behalf of the Council of State School Officers. U.S. Congress, House, Subcommittee on Elementary, Secondary, and Vocational Education, *The Effective Schools and Even Start Act: Hearing before the Subcommittee on Elementary, Secondary, and Vocational Education, April 17, 1986*, 99th Cong., 2d sess., 1987, serial no. 99–144, 8. On behalf of the National Council of State Directors of Adult Education, Art Ellison wanted to increase the maximum number of grants from twenty to twenty-five. Ibid., 107.

28. William J. Bennett, letter to Augustus F. Hawkins, chairman of the House Committee on Education and Labor, Apr. 20, 1987, in the author's possession.

29. For the House version of the bill, see U.S. Congress, House, Committee on Education and Labor, *School Improvement Act of 1987: Report Together with Additional Views,* 100th Cong., 1st sess., 1987, Report no. 100–95; for the Senate version of the bill, see U.S. Congress, Senate, Committee on Labor and Human Resources, *The Robert T. Stafford Elementary and Secondary Education Improvement Act of 1987,* 100th Cong., 1st sess., 1987, Report no. 100–222. Details of the final set of reconciliations between the two versions can be found in U.S. Congress, House, *Elementary and Secondary Education: Conference Report to Accompany H.R. 5,* 100th Cong., 2d sess., 1988, Report no. 100–567.

30. However, after the four years of federal funding, the projects were eligible to reapply as a new grant for additional support.

31. U.S. House, *School Improvement Act of 1987,* 15.

32. Ibid., 13.

33. Ibid., 14.

34. Paul M. Irwin, *National Literacy Act of 1991: Major Provisions of P.L.* 102–73 (Washington, D.C.: Congressional Research Service, Nov. 8, 1991).

35. For a very useful discussion on the new Title 1 program and its Even Start component, see James J. Marshall, Charles J. Edwards, and Alvin C. Lin, *Title I Handbook* (Arlington, Va.: Newsletter Press of New England, 1995), B/36–B/37, B/209–B/214.

36. Department of Education, "News," Oct. 27, 1989.

37. Robert G. St. Pierre et al., *National Evaluation of the Even Start Family Literacy Program: Final Report* (Washington, D.C.: Department of Education, 1995), 2, 4, 125. A useful, shorter summary of that evaluation is available in Robert G. St. Pierre et al., *Improving Family Literacy: Findings from the National Even Start Evaluation* (Cambridge, Mass.: Abt Associates, 1996).

38. St. Pierre et al., *National Evaluation . . . Final Report,* 41, 45–47, 50, 55.

39. Ibid., 44, 58.

40. Ibid., 59, 63.

41. Ibid., 128.

42. Ibid., 129, 131.

43. Ibid., 134, 136.

44. Ibid., 233.

45. Ibid., 232–33.

46. House Committee, *Elementary and Secondary Education,* 44.

47. Ibid., 45.

48. Ibid., 45.

49. Robert G. St. Pierre et al., *National Even Start Evaluation: Overview* (Cambridge, Mass.: Abt Associates, 1990), 3.

50. Ibid., 4.

51. Ibid., 6.

52. For a description of the Abt conceptual model of Even Start, see Robert St. Pierre et al., *National Evaluation of the Even Start Family Literacy Program: Status of Even Start Projects during the 1990–91 Program Year and Preliminary Estimates of Program Effects* (Cambridge, Mass.: Abt Associates, Nov. 2, 1992), 3–8.

53. For a detailed description and discussion of this approach, see Stephen Murray et al., "Evaluating Program Effectiveness for the National Even Start Evaluation: Deriving Estimates of Effect from Reference Groups" (Abt Associates, Apr. 2, 1991).

54. St. Pierre et al., *National Evaluation of the Even Start Family Literacy Program . . . during the 1990–91 Program Year,* 29–36.

55. U.S. Congress, House, Subcommittee of the Committee on Appropriations, *Hearings, Departments of Labor, Health and Human Services, Education, and Related Agencies: Appropriations for 1993,* Part 6, 102d Cong., 2d sess., 1993, 225.

56. U.S. Congress, House, Subcommittee of the Committee on Appropriations, *Hearings, Departments of Labor, Health and Human Services, and Related Agencies: Appropriations for* 1992, Part 6, 102d Cong., 1st sess., 1992, 443.

57. Ibid., 443–44.

58. Although Abt Associates looked at the data from the local projects for consistency and trained the local record keepers, it did not examine the accuracy of the data.

59. Murray et al., "Evaluating Program Effectiveness," 4.

60. St. Pierre et al., *National Even Start Evaluation: Overview,* 36–37.

61. Ibid., 38.

62. Ibid., 40.

63. St. Pierre et al., *National Evaluation of the Even Start Family Literacy Program . . . during the* 1990–91 *Program Year,* 30.

64. For example, eight of the twenty-two families at the Reading, Pennsylvania, program were nonrandom replacements. Ibid., 31.

65. Ibid., 34.

66. St. Pierre et al., *National Evaluation . . . Final Report.*

67. Ibid., 5.

68. Ibid., 7. The methodology used in this procedure was based on earlier work by Abt Associates for the Giant Step study in New York.

69. Ibid.

70. St. Pierre et al., *National Evaluation . . . Final Report.*

71. Although the executive summary of the national evaluation as well as the longer study itself report disappointing findings about the impact of the Even Start Program, both documents attempt to minimize the bad news and to maximize the limited good news.

72. Ibid., 157–82.

73. Ibid., 183–201.

74. Stephen Cameron and James Heckman, "Determinants of Young Male Schooling and Training Choices" (National Bureau of Economic Research Working Paper no. 4327, Apr. 1993). Policymakers in other fields may have overemphasized the importance of receiving a GED as well. For a useful analysis of changing attitudes toward education and job training for parenting teens, see Jennifer Mittelstadt, "An Educated Education Policy? Discussions of Education and Job Training for Parenting Teens in Federal Hearings, 1975–1995" (seminar paper, Department of History, University of Michigan, Apr. 19, 1995).

75. St. Pierre et al., *National Evaluation . . . Final Report,* 201–18. There was a program difference only on the number of reading materials, but because this was just one of ten positive items on the home environment measures, the authors of the evaluation urged a cautious interpretation of this particular finding.

76. Ibid., 219–30.

77. Ibid., 44, 50, 63.

78. For example, the evaluation reports that "by the second posttest the percentage of Even Start and control children reported to be in early childhood education were nearly identical (77 percent versus 80 percent), meaning that most children in the control group were receiving an early childhood program." Ibid., 163.

79. St. Pierre, Layzer, and Barnes, "Two-Generation Programs," 89.

80. U.S., Congress, House, Committee on Economic and Educational Opportunities, *Hearing on What Works in Public Education,* 104th Cong., 2d sess., Jan. 31, 1996, 1.

81. Ibid., 2–3.

82. Ibid., 3–19.

83. U.S., Congress, House, Appropriations Subcommittee on the Departments of Labor, Health and Human Services, Education, and Related Agencies, *Hearings on Departments of Labor, Health and Human Services, Education, and Related Agencies Appropriations for 1997,* Part 5, 104th Cong., 2d sess., 1996, 1432.

84. Ibid., 1433.

85. House Subcommittee, *Hearings . . . Appropriations for 1997,* Part 5, 1996, 808.

86. Ibid., 64.

87. Ibid.

88. U.S. Congress, House, *Report on Departments of Labor, Health and Human Services, and Education, and Related Agencies Appropriations Bill,* 1997, 104th Cong., 2d sess., 1996, Report no. 104–659, 215. Interestingly, while the Senate went along with the funding recommendations of the House for the Even Start Program, it did not mention any of the difficulties facing that program in the short paragraph it devoted to Even Start. U.S. Congress, Senate, *Report on Departments of Labor, Health and Human Services, and Education and Related Agencies Appropriation Bill,* 1997, 104th Cong., 2d sess., Report no. 104–368, 1996, 171.

89. *Congressional Record,* 142, no. 102, daily ed. (July 11, 1996): E1256.

90. Members of Congress are not the only ones who have been ignoring the topic of the relative costs of the Even Start Program. Most scholarly discussions of the Even Start also do not acknowledge or address the cost issue. See, e.g., McKee and Rhett, "Even Start Family Literacy Program." For one notable exception, see St. Pierre, Layzer, and Barnes, "Two-Generation Programs."

91. *Congressional Record,* 142, no. 102, daily ed. (July 11, 1996): E1256.

92. A meeting to discuss future plans for a possible reevaluation of Even Start was held in February 1997 by the Department of Education. A third national evaluation of Even Start is now underway.

CHAPTER 6. EDUCATION AND THE ECONOMIC TRANSFORMATION OF NINETEENTH-CENTURY AMERICA

1. For some overviews of studies of American educational history, see Sol Cohen, "The History of Education in the United States: Historians of Education and Their Discontents," in *Urban Education in the Nineteenth Century: Proceedings of the 1976 Annual Conference of the History of Education Society of Great Britain,* ed. D. A. Reeder (London: Taylor and Francis, 1977), 115–32; Lawrence A. Cremin, *Traditions of American Education* (New York: Basic Books, 1977); Michael B. Katz, "The Origins of Public Education: A Reassessment," *History of Education Quarterly* 16, no. 4 (winter 1976): 381–407; Carl F. Kaestle, *Pillars of the Republic: Common Schools and American Society, 1780–1860* (New York: Hill and Wang, 1983).

2. For discussions of trends in economic history, see Peter D. McClelland, *Casual Explanation and Model Building in History, Economics, and the New Economic History* (Ithaca: Cornell University Press, 1975); Robert W. Fogel and Stanley L. Engerman, eds., *The Reinterpretation of American Economic History* (New York: Harper and Row, 1971); Alexander J. Field, ed., *The Future of Economic History* (Boston: Kluwer-Nijhoff, 1987).

3. Samuel Bowles and Herbert Gintis, *Schooling in Capitalist America: Educational Reform and the Contradictions of Economic Life* (New York: Basic Books, 1976).

4. The most detailed critique of Bowles and Gintis from a Marxist perspective is Mike Cole, ed., *Bowles and Gintis Revisited: Correspondence and Contradiction in Educational Theory* (London: Falmer Press, 1988).

5. Bowles and Gintis, *Schooling in Capitalist America*, 24.

6. Ibid., 178–79.

7. Ibid., 154.

8. Kenneth A. Lockridge, *Literacy in Colonial New England: An Enquiry into the Social Context of Literacy in the Early Modern West* (New York: W. W. Norton, 1974). For other discussions of colonial literacy, see Linda Auwers, "Reading the Marks of the Past: Exploring Female Literacy in Colonial Windsor, Connecticut," *Historical Methods* 4 (1980): 204–14; Lee Soltow and Edward Stevens, *The Rise of Literacy and the Common School in the United States: A Socioeconomic Analysis to 1870* (Chicago: University of Chicago Press, 1981). As all of these readings point out, the use of mark-signatures to estimate literacy rates provides only a crude approximation of the actual ability of individuals in the past to read and write. Several more recent studies of colonial literacy, often using different sources, found a higher rate of female literacy than suggested by Lockridge. See William J. Gilmore, *Reading Becomes a Necessity of Life* (Knoxville: University of Tennessee Press, 1989); Gloria L. Main, "An Inquiry into When and Why Women Learned to Write in Colonial New England," *Journal of Social History* 24 (1991): 579–89; Joel Perlmann and Dennis Shirley, "When Did New England Women Acquire Literacy?" *William and Mary Quarterly*, 3d ser., 48 (1991): 50–67; Gerald F. Moran and Maris A. Vinovskis, *Religion, Family, and the Life Course: Explorations in the Social History of Early America* (Ann Arbor: University of Michigan Press, 1992); Gerald F. Moran and Maris A. Vinovskis, "Education and Literacy in Eighteenth-Century America," in *Essays on Eighteenth-Century America*, ed. William G. Shade (forthcoming).

Interestingly, recent work has shown that literacy rates were much lower in the French colonies in North America in the seventeenth and eighteenth centuries. Roger Magnuson, *Education in New France* (Montreal: McGill-Queen's University Press, 1992); Andris A. Vinovskis, "Literacy in 18th Century Michigan: An Analysis of the Marriage Register at Fort Michilimackinac," (unpub. senior honors thesis, Department of History, Albion College, 1996).

9. Calculated from Secretary of State, *Sixth Census or Enumeration of the Inhabitants of the United States as Corrected at the Department of State in 1840* (Washington, D.C.: Blair and Rives, 1841).

On the increase in literacy in nineteenth-century Scotland and England, see Robert D. Anderson, *Education and the Scottish People, 1750–1918* (London: Clarendon Press, 1995);

David F. Miller, *The Rise of Popular Literacy in Victorian England: The Influence of Private Choice and Public Policy* (Philadelphia: University of Pennsylvania Press, 1992).

10. One should not make too much of the differences between males and females in colonial Massachusetts in their ability to sign wills because this probably exaggerates the differences in their abilities to read. Many colonial women were able to read the Bible but had never been taught to write. Gerald F. Moran and Maris A. Vinovskis, "The Great Care of Godly Parents: Early Childhood in Puritan New England," in *History and Research in Child Development,* ed. Alice B. Smuts and John W. Hagen, Monographs of the Society for Research in Child Development 50, nos. 4–5 (Chicago: University of Chicago, 1985), 24–37.

11. Bowles and Gintis, *Schooling in Capitalist America,* 157–58.

12. Carl F. Kaestle and Maris A. Vinovskis, *Education and Social Change in Nineteenth-Century Massachusetts* (Cambridge: Cambridge University Press, 1980), 246–47. Several earlier estimates of Massachusetts schooling show roughly the same general trends, but they have not made the appropriate adjustments for the deficiencies in the statistical data. Albert Fishlow, "The American Common School Revival: Fact or Fancy?" in *Industrialization in Two Systems: Essays in Honor of Alexander Gerschenkron* (New York: Wiley, 1966), 40–67; Alexander James Field, "Educational Expansion in Mid-Nineteenth Century Massachusetts: Human-Capital Formation or Structural Reinforcement?" *Harvard Educational Review* 46, no. 4 (Nov. 1976): 521–52.

As late as 1840, approximately 40 percent of all three-year-olds in Massachusetts were attending infant schools or the regular public schools. For a discussion of early childhood education in the first half of the nineteenth century, see Dean May and Maris A. Vinovskis, "A Ray of Millennial Light: Early Education and Social Reform in the Infant School Movement in Massachusetts, 1826–1840," in *Family and Kin in American Urban Communities,* 1700–1930, ed. Tamara K. Hareven (New York: Watts, 1977), 62–99; Carl F. Kaestle and Maris A. Vinovskis, "From Apron Strings to ABCs: Parents, Children, and Schooling in Nineteenth-Century Massachusetts," in *Turning Points: Historical and Sociological Essays on the Family,* ed. John Demos and Sarane S. Boocock (Chicago: University of Chicago Press, 1978), S39–S80.

13. Kaestle and Vinovskis, *Education and Social Change,* 246–47. Some scholars argue that the increases in the length of the public school year in Massachusetts occurred in the more urban and industrial communities. Alexander James Field, "Economic and Demographic Determinants of Educational Commitment: Massachusetts, 1855," *Journal of Economic History* 39, no. 2 (June 1979): 439–59; Martin Carnoy and Henry M. Levin, *Schooling and Work in the Democratic State* (Stanford: Stanford University Press, 1985), 85. But the large increase in the average length of Massachusetts public schools from 1826 to 1875 actually occurred in the smaller communities rather than the larger and more industrial cities. Maris A. Vinovskis, *The Origins of Public High Schools: A Re-Examination of the Beverly High School Controversy* (Madison: University of Wisconsin Press, 1985), 12–14.

14. Calculated from Kaestle and Vinovskis, *Education and Social Change,* 238–47. The estimate of private school attendance in 1840 includes students who went to both a public

and a private school in the same year. This occurred because public schools at that time—but not in 1860—were often closed for lack of funds, later reopening with the same teacher who was now paid by the parents of the students who continued to attend. If we eliminate those students who attended both private and public schools in 1860, the percentage of students in private schools only would be 12.9 percent—thus greatly reducing the shift from private to public schooling from 1840 to 1860.

15. Bowles and Gintis admitted that school attendance did not increase in Massachusetts during the two decades before the Civil War, but they do not seem to realize how this seriously undermines their theory. Instead, they simply observed that in this respect Massachusetts was atypical of the rest of the nation. Bowles and Gintis, *Schooling in Capitalist America,* 173.

16. Fishlow, "American School Revival."

17. Vinovskis, *Origins of Public High Schools,* 123.

18. Ibid., 15.

19. Harvey J. Graff, *The Literacy Myth: Literacy and Social Structure in the Nineteenth-Century City* (New York: Academic Press, 1979), 231. Graff, however, does not seem to be aware that his description of the timing of educational development and industrialization undermines the assertions of Bowles and Gintis.

20. Edith N. MacMullen, *In the Cause of True Education: Henry Barnard and Nineteenth-Century School Reform* (New Haven: Yale University Press, 1991); Jonathan Messerli, *Horace Mann: A Biography* (New York: Alfred A. Knopf, 1972); Maris A. Vinovskis, *Education, Society, and Economic Opportunity* (New Haven: Yale University Press, 1995).

21. There are many useful surveys of antebellum reforms, such as Robert L. Church, *Education in the United States: An Interpretative History* (New York: Free Press, 1976); Lawrence A. Cremin, *American Education: The National Experience, 1783–1876* (New York: Harper and Row, 1980). The best balanced treatment of antebellum educational reformers and their critics is Kaestle, *Pillars of the Republic.*

22. For some of the recent work on antebellum education by revisionist historians, see Bowles and Gintis, *Schooling in Capitalist America;* Alexander Field, "Educational Reform and Manufacturing Development in Mid-Nineteenth-Century Massachusetts" (Ph.D. diss, University of California, Berkeley, 1974); Michael B. Katz, *Reconstructing American Education* (Cambridge: Harvard University Press, 1987). For a critique of the revisionist approach, see Diane Ravitch, *The Revisionists Revised: A Critique of the Radical Attack on the Schools* (New York: Basic Books, 1978).

23. Carl F. Kaestle, "The Development of Common School Systems in the States of the Old Northwest," in *". . . Schools and the Means of Education Shall Forever Be Encouraged": A History of Education in the Old Northwest, 1787–1880,* ed. Paul H. Mattingly and Edward W. Stevens, Jr. (Athens: Ohio University Libraries, 1987), 31–43.

24. Michael B. Katz, *The Irony of Early School Reform: Educational Innovation in Mid-Nineteenth Century Massachusetts* (Cambridge: Harvard University Press, 1968).

25. Vinovskis, *Origins of Public High Schools;* Vinovskis, *Education, Society, and Economic Opportunity,* 125–41.

26. Kaestle, *Pillars of the Republic;* Ira Katznelson and Margaret Weir, *Schooling for All: Class, Race, and the Decline of the Democratic Ideal* (New York: Basic Books, 1985); Vinovskis,

Origins of Public High Schools. Sometimes the revisionists are not aware of their contradictory stances on the support of workers for public education. Graff, for example, states "that workers desired educational provision can not be doubted." Graff, *Literacy Myth,* 209. Yet he fails to acknowledge that this differs from the interpretations of Katz.

27. Bowles and Gintis, *Schooling in Capitalist America.*

28. Carnoy and Levin, *Schooling and Work,* 24. Unlike Bowles and Gintis, Carnoy and Levin don't see the capitalists in ascendancy in the struggle for the control of schools until the late nineteenth century. Even in that period, however, Carnoy and Levin appear to exaggerate the role and influence of businessmen in structuring and running the public schools.

29. Soltow and Stevens, *Rise of Literacy.*

30. Lawrence A. Cremin, *American Education: The Colonial Experience,* 1607–1783 (New York: Harper and Row, 1970).

31. Linda K. Kerber, *Women of the Republic: Intellect and Ideology in Revolutionary America* (Chapel Hill: University of North Carolina Press, 1980); Mary Beth Norton, *Liberty's Daughters: The Revolutionary Experience of American Women,* 1750–1800 (Boston: Little, Brown, 1980).

32. Graff, *Literacy Myth.* Carnoy and Levin, *Schooling and Work.*

33. Soltow and Stevens, *Rise of Literacy.*

34. Albert Fishlow, "Levels of Nineteenth-Century American Investment in Education," in *The Reinterpretation of American Economic History,* ed. Robert W. Fogel and Stanley L. Engerman (New York: Harper and Row, 1971), 265–73.

35. David Angus, Jeffrey Mirel, and Maris Vinovskis, "Historical Development of Age-Stratification in Schooling," *Teacher's College Record* 90, no. 2 (winter 1988): 33–58.

36. Mark Blaug, ed., *Economics of Education: Selected Readings,* vol. 1 (Harmondsworth, Eng.: Penguin Books, 1968); C. Arnold Anderson and Mary Jean Bowman, eds., *Education and Economic Development* (Chicago: Aldine, 1965).

37. Gary S. Becker, *Human Capital: A Theoretical and Empirical Analysis with Special Reference to Education,* 3d ed. (Chicago: University of Chicago Press, 1993); Mark Blaug, *The Economics of Education and the Education of an Economist* (New York: New York University Press, 1987); George Psacharopoulos and Maureen Woodhall, *Education for Development: An Analysis of Investment Choice* (New York: Oxford University Press, 1985); David W. Hornbeck and Lester M. Salmon, eds., *Human Capital and America's Future: An Economic Strategy for the '90s* (Baltimore: Johns Hopkins University Press, 1991); Theodore W. Schultz, *Investing in People: The Economics of Population Quality* (Berkeley: University of California Press, 1981); Ray Marshall and Marc Tucker, *Thinking for a Living: Education and Wealth of Nations* (New York: Basic Books, 1992).

38. John Vaizey, *The Economics of Education* (London: Faber and Faber, 1962); E. A. J. Johnson, "The Place of Learning, Science, Vocational Training, and 'Art' in Pre-Smithian Economic Thought," *Journal of Economic History* 24, no. 2 (June 1964): 129–44; Rudolph C. Blitz, "Education in the Writings of Malthus, Senior, McCulloch and John Stuart Mill," in *Readings in the Economics of Education,* ed. Mary Jean Bowman et al. (New York: Unesco, 1968), 40–48.

39. C. Arnold Anderson and Mary Jean Bowman, "Education and Economic Moderniza-

tion in Historical Perspective," in *Schooling and Society: Studies in the History of Education,* ed. Lawrence Stone (Baltimore: Johns Hopkins University Press, 1976), 3–19; Richard A. Easterlin, "A Note on the Evidence of History," in *Education and Economic Development,* ed. C. Arnold Anderson and Mary Jean Bowman (Chicago: Aldine, 1965), 422–29.

40. Graff, *Literacy Myth;* Maris A. Vinovskis, "Horace Mann on the Economic Productivity of Education," *New England Quarterly* 43, no. 4 (Dec. 1970): 550–71; Field, "Educational Expansion."

41. Johnson, "Place of Learning."

42. The best and most balanced treatment of the ideas of the classical English economists on education is Mark Blaug, *Economic History and the History of Economics* (New York: New York University Press, 1986).

43. Adam Smith, *An Inquiry into the Nature and Causes of the Wealth of Nations* (New York: Modern Library, 1937), 739–40.

44. In part this may be due to the fact that all Americans, even conservatives, supported mass education and therefore may have been less reluctant to extol the virtues of schooling for workers. Carl F. Kaestle, " 'Between the Scylla of Brutal Ignorance and the Charybdis of a Literary Education': Elite Attitudes toward Mass Schooling in Early Industrial England and America," in *Schooling and Society: Studies in the History of Education,* ed. Lawrence Stone (Baltimore: Johns Hopkins University Press, 1976), 177–91.

45. Willard Phillips, *A Manual of Political Economy with Particular Reference to the Institutions, Resources, and Condition of the United States* (Boston: Hilliard, Gray, Little, and Wilkins, 1828).

46. Francis Wayland, *The Elements of Political Economy,* 4th ed. (Boston: Gould, Kendall, and Lincoln, 1843), 127. This textbook went through at least twenty-three editions before 1876, sold more than fifty thousand copies, and dominated the field. Cremin, *American Education: The National Experience,* 133.

47. Wayland, *Elements of Political Economy,* 131.

48. Frank Tracy Carlton, *Economic Influences upon Educational Progress in the United States, 1820–1850* (Madison: University of Wisconsin Press, 1908); Kaestle, *Pillars of the Republic.*

49. Perhaps one reason why many early Americans did not focus on the economic productivity of education is because much of the actual training of skilled workers had been provided through the institution of apprenticeship rather than by formal schooling in colonial and early nineteenth-century America. As apprenticeships became more informal and less prevalent in the first quarter of the nineteenth century, alternative sources of training youth were sought. For a useful discussion of the character and demise of apprenticeship in nineteenth-century America, see W. J. Rorabaugh, *The Craft Apprentice: From Franklin to the Machine Age in America* (New York: Oxford University Press, 1986).

50. Seth Luther, *An Address to the Working-Men of New England, on the State of Education, and on the Condition of the Producing Classes in Europe and America* (Boston: Seth Luther, 1832). Attention was also given to the role of education in the writings of supporters of the workers such as Stephen Simpson. Stephen Simpson, *The Working Man's Manual: A*

New Theory of Political Economy, on the Principle of Production the Source of Wealth (Philadelphia: Thomas L. Bonsal, 1831).

51. Graff, *Literacy Myth,* 215. On the later emphasis by both capitalists and workers on vocational education, see Harvey A. Kantor, *Learning to Earn: School, Work, and Vocational Reform in California,* 1880–1930 (Madison: University of Wisconsin Press, 1988).

52. *Fifth Annual Report of the Board of Education Together with the Fifth Annual Report of the Secretary of the Board* (Boston: Dutton and Wentworth, 1842).

53. Merle Curti, *The Social Ideas of American Educators* (Paterson, N.J.: Littlefield and Adams, 1965).

54. Kaestle and Vinovskis, *Education and Social Change in Massachusetts.*

55. *Fifth Annual Report,* 100–101.

56. Ibid., 110–11.

57. Ibid., 93–94.

58. Ibid., 91, 98.

59. For a more detailed discussion of Mann's methodology, see Vinovskis, "Horace Mann."

60. Letter to Horace Mann from thirty-four Bostonians, Jan. 13, 1845, Massachusetts Historical Society.

61. National Teachers' Association, *Journal of Proceedings and Lectures* (Chicago, 1863), 56, as quoted by Curti, *Social Ideas of American Educators,* 113.

62. Field, "Educational Expansion."

63. Douglass C. North, "Capital Formation in the United States during the Early Period of Industrialization: A Reexamination of the Issues," in *The Reinterpretation of American History,* ed. Robert W. Fogel and Stanley L. Engerman (New York: Harper and Row, 1971), 277.

64. Geraldine J. Clifford, " 'Marry, Stitch, Die or Do Worse': Educating Women for Work," in *Work, Youth and Schooling: Historical Perspectives on Vocationalism in American Education,* ed. Harvey Kantor and David B. Tyack (Stanford: Stanford University Press, 1982), 223–68.

65. Susan B. Carter and Mark Prus, "The Labor Market and the American High School Girl, 1870–1928," *Journal of Economic History* 47, no. 1 (Mar. 1982): 163–71.

66. Richard M. Bernard and Maris A. Vinovskis, "The Female School Teacher in Ante-Bellum Massachusetts," *Journal of Social History* 10, no. 3 (spring 1977): 332–45; Richard M. Bernard and Maris A. Vinovskis, "Beyond Catherine Beecher: Female Education in the Antebellum Period," *Signs* 3, no. 4 (summer 1978): 856–69.

67. Graff, *Literacy Myth,* 232.

68. Increased education may have also fostered more long-distance geographic mobility, which helped to redistribute existing economic resources more efficiently. George Borjas, "Self-Selection and the Earnings of Immigrants," *American Economic Review* 77 (Sept. 1987): 531–53; Samuel Bowles, "Migration as Investment: Empirical Tests of the Human Investment Approach to Geographical Mobility," *Review of Economics and Statistics* 52 (Nov. 1970): 356–62; Larry Sjaastad, "The Costs and Returns of Human Migration," *Journal of Political Economy* 70 (1962): 80–93.

69. Vinovskis, "Horace Mann."

70. There is considerable controversy over when and to what degree older workers faced age

discrimination. See, e.g., W. Andrew Achenbaum, *Old Age in the New Land: The American Experience since 1790* (Baltimore: Johns Hopkins University Press, 1978); David Hackett Fischer, *Growing Old in America,* rev. ed. (New York: Oxford University Press, 1978); William Graebner, *A History of Retirement: The Meaning and Function of an American Institution,* 1885–1978 (New Haven: Yale University Press, 1980); Carole Haber, *Beyond Sixty-Five: The Dilemma of Old Age in America's Past* (Cambridge: Cambridge University Press, 1983).

71. John G. Cawelti, *Apostles of the Self-Made Man* (Chicago: University of Chicago Press, 1965); Irwin G. Wyllie, *The Self-Made Man in America: The Myth of Rags to Riches* (New Brunswick: Rutgers University Press, 1954).

72. While the idea of social mobility persisted, the definition of success changed over time with more emphasis on wealth in the mid-nineteenth century. Rex Burns, *Success in America: The Yeoman Dream, and the Industrial Revolution* (Amherst: University of Massachusetts Press, 1976).

73. *Newburyport Herald,* Mar. 2, 1857.

74. Stephan Thernstrom, *The Other Bostonians: Poverty and Progress in the American Metropolis,* 1880–1970 (Cambridge: Harvard University Press, 1973).

75. Stephan Thernstrom, *Poverty and Progress: Social Mobility in a Nineteenth-Century City* (Cambridge: Harvard University Press, 1964). One of the questions has been whether the rates of social mobility for persisters was much higher than for those who had left the community. Until recently, we had no data on this important issue. In a new study, however, Joseph Ferrie analyzed the rates of social mobility for a sample of immigrants in Newburyport, Massachusetts, in 1850. Ferrie found that for immigrant laborers in 1850, those who left actually fared better than those who stayed. For nonlabor immigrants, the situation was reversed. Joseph P. Ferrie, "Up and Out or Down and Out? Immigrant Mobility in the Antebellum United States," *Journal of Interdisciplinary History* 26, no. 1 (summer 1995): 33–55.

76. Stuart Blumin, "Mobility and Change in Ante-Bellum Philadelphia," in *Nineteenth-Century Cities: Essays in the New Urban History,* ed. Stephan Thernstrom and Richard Sennett (New Haven: Yale University Press, 1969), 165–208.

77. Clyde Griffen, "Workers Divided: The Effect of Craft and Ethnic Differences in Poughkeepsie, New York, 1850–1880," in *Nineteenth-Century Cities: Essays in the New Urban History,* ed. Stephan Thernstrom and Richard Sennett (New Haven: Yale University Press, 1969), 49–97.

78. Harmut Kaeble, *Social Mobility in the Nineteenth and Twentieth Centuries: Europe and America in Comparative Perspective* (Leamington Spa, Eng.: Berg Publishers, 1985).

   Based on a review of existing studies ten years ago, Ravitch concluded that "pending further research, it does appear that upward social mobility trends have been established in certain American cities during the nineteenth and early twentieth centuries." Ravitch, *Revisionists Revised,* 88.

79. Ira Mayhew, *Popular Education for the Use of Parents and Teachers and for Young Persons of Both Sexes* (New York: Harper and Brothers, 1850).

80. Cawelti, *Apostles of the Self-Made Man;* Wyllie, *Self-Made Man in America.*

81. Graff, *Literacy Myth,* 114–15.

82. Maris A. Vinovskis, "Quantification and the Analysis of American Ante-Bellum Education," *Journal of Interdisciplinary History* 13, no. 4 (spring 1983): 761–86.

83. Michael B. Katz, Michael J. Doucet, and Mark J. Stern, *The Social Organization of Early Industrial Capitalism* (Cambridge: Harvard University Press, 1982), 275. It is not absolutely clear what variables and data were used in the analysis referred to by Katz and his colleagues because they do not provide any table or cite any table at this point. It is likely that they are referring back to their earlier chapter on social mobility, which includes the information on school attendance for all children in 1861 in a multiple classification analysis.

84. This is particularly the case for very young children because contemporaries were divided on the advisability of sending very young children to school. May and Vinovskis, "Ray of Millennial Light."

85. Thernstrom, *Poverty and Progress,* 22–23.

86. Maris A. Vinovskis, "Patterns of High School Attendance in Newburyport, Massachusetts in 1860" (paper presented at the annual meeting of the American Historical Association, New York City, Dec. 1985); Vinovskis, *Education, Society, and Economic Opportunity.* For another, useful reanalysis of school attendance in Newburyport, see Steven Herscovici, "Ethnic Differences in School Attendance in Antebellum Massachusetts: Evidence from Newburyport, 1850–1860," *Social Science History* 18, no. 4 (winter 1994): 471–96.

87. Emit Duncan Grizzell, *Origin and Development of the High School in New England before 1865* (New York: Macmillan, 1923). By far the best and most recent analysis of the early development of high schools is William J. Reese, *The Origins of the American High School* (New Haven: Yale University Press, 1995).

88. Edward A. Krug, *The Shaping of the American High School, 1880–1920* (Madison: University of Wisconsin Press, 1969), 11. See also Paul E. Peterson, *The Politics of School Reform, 1870–1940* (Chicago: University of Chicago Press, 1985).

89. Vinovskis, "Patterns of High School Attendance."

90. Newburyport was also located in Essex County, Massachusetts. For details on the rates of high school attendance, see Maris A. Vinovskis, "Have We Underestimated the Extent of Antebellum High School Attendance?" *History of Education Quarterly* 28, no. 4 (winter 1988): 551–67; Vinovskis, *Education, Society, and Economic Opportunity,* 142–70.

91. Katz, *Irony of Early School Reform,* 39. For a critique of his estimating procedures, see Vinovskis, "Have We Underestimated?"

92. Vinovskis, "Patterns of High School Attendance." Children of foreign-born parents, however, were particularly unlikely to attend high school.

93. David L. Angus, "A Note on the Occupational Backgrounds of Public High Schools Prior to 1940," *Journal of the Midwest History of Education Society* 9 (1981): 158–83; Reed Ueda, *Avenues to Adulthood: The Origins of the High School and Social Mobility in an American Suburb* (Cambridge: Cambridge University Press, 1987).

94. David F. Labaree, *The Making of an American High School: The Credentials Market and the Central High School of Philadelphia, 1838–1939* (New Haven: Yale University Press, 1988), 37. Similarly, Joel Perlmann found that grades in high school were a better predictor of graduation than social class background. Joel Perlmann, "Who Stayed in

School? Social Structure and Academic Achievement in Determination of Enrollment Patterns, Providence, Rhode Island, 1880–1925," *Journal of American History* 72, no. 3 (Dec. 1985): 588–614.

95. Bowles and Gintis, *Schooling in Capitalist America;* Katz, *Irony of Early School Reform.*

96. Labaree, *Making of an American High School.*

97. Ueda, *Avenues to Adulthood,* 179.

98. Joel Perlmann, *Ethnic Differences: Schooling and Social Structure among the Irish, Italians, Jews, and Blacks in the American City,* 1880–1935 (Cambridge: Cambridge University Press, 1988), 38.

99. While Ravitch suspects that schooling may have fostered social mobility in the past, her review of the few earlier studies found no conclusive evidence either way. Ravitch, *Revisionists Revised,* 90.

100. Richard Jensen, "Education and Life Chances in the Job Market" (paper presented at the meeting of the Social Science History Association, New Orleans, Nov. 1987); Richard Jensen, "The Causes and Cures of Unemployment in the Great Depression," *Journal of Interdisciplinary History* 19, no. 4 (spring 1989): 553–83; Perlmann, *Ethnic Differences.* Joseph Kett suggests that education was becoming a more important factor for getting ahead in the late nineteenth and early twentieth centuries. Joseph F. Kett, *Rites of Passage: Adolescence in America, 1790 to the Present* (New York: Basic Books, 1977).

CHAPTER 7. AN ANALYSIS OF THE CONCEPT AND USES OF SYSTEMIC EDUCATIONAL REFORM

1. For discussions of the patterns and meaning of American education reforms in the past, see Lawrence A. Cremin, *Popular Education and Its Discontents* (New York: Harper and Row, 1990); Henry J. Perkinson, *The Imperfect Panacea: American Faith in Education, 1865–1990,* 3d. ed. (New York: McGraw-Hill, 1991); Diane Ravitch and Maris Vinovskis, eds., *Learning from the Past: What History Teaches Us about School Reform* (Baltimore: Johns Hopkins University Press, 1995); Harold Silver and Pamela Silver, *An Educational War on Poverty: American and British Policy-Making, 1960–1980* (Cambridge: Cambridge University Press, and 1991); and David Tyack and Larry Cuban, *Tinkering toward Utopia: A Century of Public School Reform* (Cambridge: Harvard University Press, 1995).

2. President Bush and the state governors initially developed a list of six national goals. The number of goals was expanded to eight with the enactment of the new legislation, Goals 2000: Educate America Act. As the number of national education goals varies, depending on which time period is being discussed, either six or eight goals will be used in the text as appropriate.

3. While many educators and policymakers focused on the concept of systemic reform, others do not even mention it. For example, in a collection on national educational reforms few authors refer to the concept of systemic reform. John F. Jennings, ed., *National Issues in Education: The Past Is Prologue* (Bloomington, Ind.: Phi Delta Kappa, 1993).

4. There have been few efforts so far to assess the meaning and value of systemic reform. Three particularly useful essays are Susan H. Fuhrman and Diane Massell, "Issues and

Strategies in Systemic Reform," CPRE Research Report Series RR-025 (New Brunswick, N.J.: Consortium for Policy Research in Education, Oct. 1992); Cynthia Y. Levinson and Diane Massell, "Systemic Reform: Literature Review" (unpub. paper, Consortium for Policy Research in Education, Feb. 24, 1992); and Gary Sykes and Peter Plastrik, "Standard Setting As Educational Reform," Trends and Issues Paper no. 8, ERIC Clearinghouse on Teacher Education (Washington, D.C.: American Association of Colleges for Teacher Education, May 1993), 1–67.

5. For an excellent introduction to how ideas become part of the public agenda, see John W. Kingdon, *Agendas, Alternatives, and Public Discourse* (New York: Harper Collins, 1984).

6. National Commission on Excellence in Education, "A Nation at Risk," in *The Great School Debate,* eds. Beatrice Gross and Ronald Gross (New York: Touchstone Books, 1985), 23.

7. Department of Education, *The Nation Responds: Recent Efforts to Improve Education* (Washington, D.C.: Government Printing Office, 1984). Not everyone thinks there has been a significant decline in education in the 1980s and 1990s. See, e.g., the provocative book by David C. Berliner and Bruce J. Biddle, *The Manufactured Crisis: Myths, Fraud, and the Attack on America's Public Schools* (Reading, Mass.: Addison-Wesley, 1995). For a similar, but more balanced exposition of generally the same point of view, see Tyack and Cuban, *Tinkering toward Utopia,* 12–39.

8. For discussions of the recent decentralization and restructuring reform efforts, see Richard F. Elmore, ed., *Restructuring Schools: The Next Generation of Educational Reform* (San Francisco: Jossey-Bass, 1990); Jane Hannaway and Martin Carnoy, eds., *Decentralization and School Improvement* (San Francisco: Jossey-Bass, 1993); and Jane L. David, "School-Based Decision-Making: Kentucky's Test of Decentralization," *Phi Delta Kappan* 75, no. 9 (May 1994): 706–12.

9. For a discussion of these state reforms, see Chester E. Finn, Jr., and Theodor Rebarber, eds., *Education Reform in the '90s* (New York: Macmillan, 1992); Susan H. Fuhrman, Patricia Fry, and Richard F. Elmore, "South Carolina's Flexibility through Deregulation: A Case Study," CPRE Research Report Series TC-007 (New Brunswick, N.J.: Consortium for Policy Research in Education, 1992); Diane Massell and Susan Fuhrman, "Ten Years of State Education Reform, 1983–1993," CPRE Research Report Series RR-028 (New Brunswick, N.J.: Consortium for Policy Research in Education, 1994); and Betty E. Steffy, *The Kentucky Education Reform: Lessons for America* (Lancaster, Pa.: Technomic, 1993).

10. Diane Ravitch, "Developing National Standards in Education" (unpub. paper presented at the American Sociological Association meeting, Pittsburgh, Aug. 22, 1992). The National Council of Teachers of Mathematics (NCTM) published in 1989 a set of curriculum and evaluation standards for teaching mathematics in the elementary and secondary schools.

11. National Goals Panel, *The National Goals Report: Building a Nation of Learners,* 1991 (Washington, D.C.: Government Printing Office, 1991).

12. The National Governors' Association continues to be active in discussing the eight National Education Goals and advocating systemic reforms. See, e.g., National Governors' Association, *Educating America: State Strategies for Achieving the National Education*

Goals (Washington, D.C.: National Governors' Association, 1990); National Governors' Association, *From Rhetoric to Action: State Progress in Restructuring the Education System* (Washington, D.C.: National Governors' Association, 1991); National Governors' Association, *Keys to Changing the System* (Washington, D.C.: National Governors' Association, 1992); and Jane L. David and Paul D. Goren, *Transforming Education: Overcoming Barriers* (Washington, D.C.: National Governors' Association, 1993).

13. Business Roundtable, *The Essential Components of a Successful Education System: Putting Policy into Practice* (Washington, D.C.: Business Roundtable, 1989) [ERIC no. 355628].

14. The word "systemic" has been associated with education developments as early as the early 1970s. For example, it was employed by some analysts who advocated a broader systems approach to educational development. C. Kenneth Tanner, *Designs for Educational Planning: A Systemic Approach* (Lexington, Mass.: D. C. Heath, 1971).

The popular use of "systemic" among educators is indicated by the fact that 454 uses of that word appeared in a search of the ERIC System from 1982 to September 1993. Most of these citations, however, were references to psychological or therapeutic issues relating to education or to other educational topics unrelated to the discussion in this chapter. See, e.g., W. N. Winser, "Fun with Dick and Jane: A Systemic-Functional Approach to Reading" (1991) [ERIC no. ED-355476], or Bradley D. McDowell and Thomas V. Sayger, "Preventive Systemic School Counseling: Revisiting the School-Home-Community Roles of the School Counselor" *Contemporary Education* 64, no. 1 (fall 1992): 25–30 [ERIC no. EJ463308].

Similarly, the word "systemic" appears from time to time in the popular media, usually in regard to topics unrelated to education. See, e.g., Dennis Hevesi, "More Neighborhoods Await the Results of Water Testing," *New York Times,* Aug, 1, 1993, 1:39; Erich Schwarz, "Science and Religion: Still Searching," *Wall Street Journal,* June 16, 1993, A13.

15. The work on systemic reform by O'Day and Smith has been collaborative throughout, and the order of listing the two names in the text will be varied to indicate that collaboration.

16. Marshall Smith has had extensive experience in academe and government. He has an undergraduate background in psychology and an Ed.D. from the Harvard Graduate School of Education with an emphasis on measurement and statistics. During the Carter administration he served as the associate director of the National Institute of Education (1976–77), the assistant commissioner for policy studies, Office of Education (1977–80), and as the executive assistant and chief of staff to the secretary of the Department of Education (1980). He left Washington to become the director of the Wisconsin Center for Education Research (1980–86). In 1986 he became the dean of the Stanford School of Education and then took a leave of absence in 1993 to be the undersecretary for the Department of Education. Throughout his career, he has published extensively on education research and policy issues.

Jennifer O'Day has an undergraduate degree in elementary education and is completing her Ed.D. at the School of Education at Stanford University. Her dissertation is on factors affecting grade retention for students with limited English proficiency. She has taught at San Francisco State University and was the associate director of the Pew Forum for Education Reform at Stanford University. She started working with Smith in 1987, and their essays on systemic reform began to appear the next year. She is currently employed at the University of Wisconsin, Madison.

17. Brenda J. Turnbull, Marshall S. Smith, and Alan L. Ginsburg, "Issues for a New Administration: The Federal Role in Education," *American Journal of Education* 89, no. 4 (Aug. 1981): 396–427.

18. Ibid., 403.

19. Ibid., 408–9.

20. Carl F. Kaestle and Michael S. Smith, "The Federal Role in Elementary and Secondary Education, 1940–1980," *Harvard Educational Review* 52, no. 4 (Nov. 1982): 384–408. Kaestle and Smith discuss the role of the federal government. They acknowledge their preference for more federal involvement in local public schools, but they recognize the political and practical constraints: "Our training, our ideology, and our experience during the 1960s and 1970s incline us to centrally directed solutions in education, especially on issues of fundamental social and constitutional importance. We also believe, on the basis of recent experience, that federal education programs cannot remain peripheral to local public school activities. On the other hand, we also acknowledge, as a lesson of the past ten years, that, though desirable, local control, local initiative, and local variation constrain the number of educational issues the federal government can address and the degree of standardization it can or should impose. Our prescription to federal policymakers, then, is simple: carefully choose educational issues that focus on basic constitutional rights and social justice; use funding and regulation to integrate those goals into the central, day-to-day activities of local schools across the nation; and construct programs that will foster local decision making while transcending local variation." Ibid., 407–8.

21. Michael S. Smith, "Selecting Students and Services for Chapter I," in Denis P. Doyle and Bruce S. Cooper, eds., *Federal Aid to the Disadvantaged: What Future for Chapter* 1 (Philadelphia: Falmer Press, 1988), 119–46.

22. Stewart C. Purkey and Marshall S. Smith, "Effective Schools: A Review," *Elementary School Journal* 83, no. 4 (Mar. 1983): 427–52.

23. Stewart C. Purkey and Marshall S. Smith, "School Reform: The District Policy Implications of the Effective Schools Literature," *Elementary School Journal* 85, no. 3 (Jan. 1985): 353–89.

24. Ibid.

25. For a discussion of the research and development centers as well as an assessment of some of the work of CPRE in particular, see Maris A. Vinovskis, "Analysis of the Quality of Research and Development at the OERI Research and Development Centers and at the OERI Regional Educational Laboratories," (final report, OERI, Department of Education, June 1993).

26. The papers for that conference were published in Elmore, ed., *Restructuring Schools.*

27. Smith wrote a nine-page letter outlining his systemic reform recommendations for the National Science Foundation to improve their mathematics and science education efforts. He stressed the importance of the states, the need to create high quality curriculum frameworks, the coordination of the curriculum framework with the curriculum and student assessments, and the improvement of preservice and in-service teacher

training. Letter of Marshall S. Smith to Bassam Shakhashiri, assistant director of the Science and Engineering Education Division of the National Science Foundation, Aug. 29, 1988 (in the author's possession).

28. Smith and O'Day suggested the need for state curriculum frameworks and for holding local schools accountable for student achievements: "We have argued that a legitimate and effective role for the state would be to provide a broad but explicit curriculum framework to guide teachers' selection of content for instruction. In order for teachers to be able to teach the content embodied in the framework they will need to be systematically exposed to it during pre-service and continuing professional development experiences and to show command of the material before they receive a state license to teach. Insuring that this happens would take considerable leadership on the part of the state. Teachers and other local school officials would be responsible for designing and implementing pedagogical strategies to meet the needs of their students, for making decisions about the content of their instruction within the overall context of the state framework, and for orchestrating the organization and structure of the school. The state would hold the local schools and systems accountable for student achievement within the context of the framework. This strategy would help make sure that schools are held accountable for student progress only if two conditions apply: first, there is an agreed upon body of content which structures the student assessment instruments, and second, the teachers collectively within a school are able to structure the instructional experiences for their particular students in the most effective ways that they know how.

"We did not expect to suggest these policy directions when we started reviewing the research literature on teachers and teaching. The rationale for a state curriculum framework which structures the knowledge needed by the teacher, the content of the schools' curriculum, and student assessment instruments grows out of the research on the importance of content and pedagogical knowledge of teachers. The argument for a common framework is reinforced by the current work on teacher assessment. The work on teaching special populations and teaching strategies provides support for the concept of restructuring and local school control over method and other day to day instructional decisions. We believe that these elements are not incompatible and have suggested an accommodation." Marshall S. Smith and Jennifer O'Day, "Teaching Policy and Research on Teaching" (unpub. paper originally prepared for meeting of the Working Party on the Condition of Teaching, OECD, Paris, France, spring 1988 [Oct. 13, 1988]).

29. Marshall S. Smith and Jennifer O'Day, "Systemic School Reform," in Susan H. Fuhrman and Betty Malem, eds., *The Politics of Curriculum and Testing: The 1990 Yearbook of the Politics of Education Association* (London: Falmer Press, 1991), 234–35.

30. Jennifer A. O'Day and Marshall S. Smith, "Systemic Reform and Educational Opportunity," in Susan H. Fuhrman, ed., *Designing Coherent Education Policy* (San Francisco: Jossey-Bass, 1993), 251.

31. Ibid., 266–67.

32. Ibid., 259.

33. Ibid., 272.

34. There is considerable diversity and confusion in the literature on whether the phrase "opportunity to learn" or "school delivery" standards should be used. Often the terms are

used interchangeably. In an effort to sharpen and clarify current discussions, Andrew Porter has suggested a useful distinction between opportunity to learn standards and school delivery standards: "In distinguishing among the many types of standards, I begin with school delivery standards and opportunity to learn standards. While these two types of standards appear to be used interchangeably, it may be useful to distinguish between them. School delivery standards have no history and so can take on whatever meaning seems useful, while opportunity to learn standards have a history and that history comes [with] a certain meaning. Opportunity to learn describes the enacted curriculum as experienced by the student. In the past, greatest emphasis has been placed on the content of instruction, the particular concepts, skills, and applications that are to be taught. But opportunity to learn has also included the pedagogical quality of instruction and the resources that are available to students and teachers as instruction takes place. Opportunity to learn has not included such organizational features as school leadership, school goals, parent and community support, and district and state support. Neither has opportunity to learn included quality of school life factors such as National Goal 6, that schools should be safe and free from drugs. Thus, school delivery standards are the more inclusive set of standards, including opportunity to learn but also including National Goal 6 as well as organizational features. While all parts of school delivery standards are important, there is value to pulling opportunity to learn out for special attention. The content and pedagogy of instruction are the two best predictors of student achievement, they are the features that describe the curriculum reform of hard content for all students, and they are at the heart of the concept of opportunity to learn." Andrew C. Porter, "Defining and Measuring Opportunity to Learn" (unpub. paper prepared for the National Governors' Association, May 25, 1993), 7–8. Although Smith and O'Day have not employed Porter's distinction, it is useful and would have enhanced their analysis and discussion.

35. O'Day and Smith, "Systemic Reform and Educational Opportunity," 274–75.
36. Ibid., 276. Thus, Smith and O'Day specifically have excluded items such as "a library, or a teachers' room with a separate desk for each teacher, or the human support necessary to allow teachers to have at least one period per day to plan their work together. Though these and other resources may be justifiably viewed as necessary for the instructional program to succeed in many settings, they are not directly part of the systemic curriculum reform and it should be within a school's discretion to allocate certain resources for these and other expenditures it deems more effective in meeting the needs of its students." Ibid., 305n.
37. Ibid., 276.
38. Ibid., 265. They would not welcome providing different frameworks for students in different curriculum tracks. Rather, they would prefer that all students should have the same basic curriculum. Marshall S. Smith, Jennifer A. O'Day, and David K. Cohen, "A National Curriculum in the United States?" *Educational Leadership* 49, no. 1 (Sept. 1991): 74–81.
39. O'Day and Smith, "Systemic Reform and Educational Opportunity," 279–92.
40. Earlier Smith and O'Day had endorsed the concept of a national curriculum and national testing. For example, in an essay with David Cohen, they stated: "In putting

forth these issues and examples, we have tried to suggest that a move towards a national curriculum could benefit education by enabling us to align curriculum, assessment and accountability, and the professional development of teachers. . . . Finally, a national exam could add needed incentives for everyone in the education world, especially students; and the results of the exam would provide all of us with important information necessary to improve continually the education we provide." Marshall S. Smith, Jennifer O'Day, and David K. Cohen, "National Curriculum American Style: Can It Be Done? What Might It Look Like?" *American Educator* 14, no. 4 (winter 1990): 43.

41. Chester E. Finn, Jr., *We Must Take Charge: Our Schools and Our Future* (New York: Free Press, 1991), 247. While Finn accepts certain key components of systemic reform, he rejects others. For example, he opposes the "certification" of state educational content standards or the imposition of opportunity to learn standards by the federal government. Chester E. Finn, Jr., "Unwilling to School," *National Review* 46, no. 1 (Jan. 24, 1994): 16–18. For similar criticisms of systemic reform at the federal level, see Theodor Rebarber, "Proposals for Reauthorizing the Elementary and Secondary Education Act Threaten State and Local Control of Education," *Heritage Foundation Issue Bulletin,* no. 194 (June 14, 1994).

42. "Reasonable people can debate how large that portion [of the total curriculum] should be. My view is that about two-thirds of the high school curriculum, perhaps 80 percent of the middle school program, and virtually all of the content of primary education should be the same for everybody, with the remainder given over to options, preferences, and specialties." Ibid., 254.

43. Ibid., 264–65.

44. For a useful discussion of the politics and recent history of national testing, see Chester E. Finn, Jr., "Who's Afraid of the Big, Bad Test?" (unpub. paper presented at the Brookings conference, "Beyond Goals 2000: The Future of National Standards and Assessments in American Education," Washington, D.C., May 1994).

45. William H. Clune, "The Best Path to Systemic Educational Policy: Standard/ Centralized or Differentiated/Decentralized," *Educational Evaluation and Policy Analysis* 15, no. 3 (fall 1993): 234.

46. Ibid., 250.

47. National Council on Education Standards and Testing, *Raising Standards for American Education: A Report to Congress, the Secretary of Education, the National Education Goals Panel, and the American People* (Washington, D.C.: Government Printing Office, 1992), 3. In a later section on definitions, NCEST clarified what it meant by school delivery standards: "School delivery standards developed by the states collectively from which each state could select the criteria that it finds useful for the purpose of assessing a school's capacity and performance." Ibid., 13.

48. Testimony of Marshall S. Smith, U.S. Congress, House, Subcommittee on Elementary, Secondary, and Vocational Education, *Oversight Hearings on the Report of the National Council on Education Standards and Testing,* 102d Cong., 2d sess., 1992, serial no. 102–105, 50.

49. Ibid., 51.

50. Ibid., 37

51. Testimony of Keith Geiger, Ibid., 120–21.

52. Linda Darling-Hammond, "Opportunity to Learn Standards" (unpub. paper prepared for the National Governors' Association, Nov. 1993).

53. Ibid., 4.

54. Ibid., 4–5.

55. Porter, "Defining and Measuring Opportunity to Learn," 4.

56. Ibid., 9–10.

57. Jane L. David, *Redesigning an Education System: Early Observations from Kentucky* (Washington, D.C.: National Governors' Association, 1993), 3.

58. Robert Barkley, Jr., "Principles and Actions: A Framework for Systemic Change" (paper presented at meeting of the American Educational Research Association, Atlanta, Apr. 1993; rev. Sept. 1993).

59. Ibid., 10.

60. Ibid., 10.

61. Charles M. Reigeluth, "The Need for a Systemic Change Process in Chicago" (unpub. paper, Midwest Regional Educational Laboratory, Mar. 30, 1992).

62. Rex W. Hagans et al., *The State's Role in Effecting Systemic Change: A Northwest Depiction* (Portland, Ore.: Northwest Educational Laboratory, Nov. 1992), 5 [ERIC no. ED354631].

63. Ibid., 9.

64. Ibid., 19–20.

65. Terry A. Astuto et al., *Challenges to Dominant Assumptions Controlling Educational Reform* (final report to the Regional Laboratory for Educational Improvement of the Northeast and Islands, July 1993), 104–5. Much of this material has been published in a shortened and revised essay. David L. Clark and Terry A. Astuto, "Redirecting Reform: Challenges to Popular Assumptions about Teachers and Students," *Phi Delta Kappan* 75, no. 7 (Mar. 1994): 512–20.

66. Astuto et al., *Challenges to Dominant Assumptions,* 57.

67. Ibid., 118, 120, 122–23.

68. There is still considerable suspicion of federal involvement in state and local education issues, even though the adoption of national curriculum standards and assessments would be voluntary. E.g., Lauro Cavazos, the former secretary of education, stated: "I have great reservations about national standards, frankly, and let me explain why. I think that once you establish a standard, although it's voluntary, and we can change it, and people do not have to accept it—I have seen just too many volunteer things started in Washington that subsequently became law. I've seen withholding of funds because we didn't comply in certain areas. And I just want to keep education out of that milieu, that mix of politics, and we're forgetting that we are really trying to educate youngsters. I'm afraid with national standards we're gonna end up lowering the overall quality. We've seen it time and time again on state tests, for example. The youngsters can't pass the test to get out of high school, or perhaps some of the teachers [are] unable to qualify, [and] the standards are pulled down." Transcript of "The Third Annual Conversation with the Secretaries of Education" (Atlanta: Southern Center for International Studies, 1994), 3.

69. Rather than trying to define systemic reform more precisely, some analysts seem content

to see it as a more general, philosophical approach to reforming education. As James Thompson concluded a recent interview: "It is important to keep in mind that systemic reform is not so much a detailed prescription for improving education as a philosophy advocating reflecting, rethinking, and restructuring. Unlike reform efforts that are more limited in scope, systemic reform pervades almost every aspect of schooling. It calls for education to be reconceptualized from the ground up, beginning with the nature of teaching and learning, educational relationships, and school-community relationships." James Thompson, "Systemic Education Reform," *ERIC Digest*, no. 90 (May 1994): 1 [EDO-EA-94–5].

70. As a member of the panel for the continuation grant for the English Standards Project, I had an opportunity to review its progress as of Feb. 1994. Given the amount and quality of work done by the project, it was unlikely that a set of English Standards would be completed within the next couple of years. The Department of Education did not renew the English Standards Project contract.

71. There is still considerable confusion and disagreement among (and within) different disciplines about the meaning and uses of content standards and benchmarks. John Kendall and Robert Marzano have produced a useful document that examines briefly seven important issues: "(1) whether standards are for subject literacy or subject expertise, (2) whether standards should be content or curriculum standards, (3) whether standards should be formed as content or performance standards, (4) whether thinking and reasoning skills can be described independent of content, (5) at what level of generality standards should be tested, (6) how benchmarks could be defined, and (7) how standards organize information." John S. Kendall and Robert J. Marzano, *The Systematic Identification and Articulation of Content Standards and Benchmarks: Update* (Aurora, Colo.: Mid-Continent Regional Educational Laboratory, 1994), 9. See also John S. Kendall and Robert J. Marzano, "The Why, What and How of Standards," in *What's Noteworthy on School Reform*, ed. Sandra Carroll Berger and Jo Sue Whisler (Washington, D.C.: Government Printing Office, 1994), 5–15.

72. Debra Viadero, "Standards in Collision: What Will Happen When All Those Ambitious Plans Reach the Classroom?" *Education Week* (Jan. 19, 1994), 25–27. As Richard Aieta, a member of one national standards panel, put it: "The standards are going to fit if you give me the latitude not to graduate students until they're 28 years old." Ibid., 27.

73. There is concern that the addition of national or state standards will simply complicate matters further. As Gary Stykes and Peter Plastrik have pointed out: "If any single concern underlies this explosion of standard setting it is to provide firm, stable, and shared guidance to the educational system. Yet paradoxically, the sum of so many individual good intentions may be to deepen the disease, not to effect a cure. Policymakers have begun to worry that the pell-mell proliferation of standards may lead not to stronger education for all children, but to continuing discord and fragmentation as various projects collide with one another in supplying contradictory guidance to the education system. As policymakers create all these new standards there is worry that the whole will not hang together." Sykes and Plastrik, "Standard Setting," 1–2. Similarly, Tyack and Cuban have warned that many new reforms are simply layered on top of older

ones so that the final package often contains contradictory and confusing elements. Tyack and Cuban, *Tinkering toward Utopia*, 60–84.

74. Bureau of the Census, *Statistical Abstract of the United States:* 1993, 113th ed. (Washington, D.C.: Government Printing Office, 1993), table 34.

75. Michael Feuer, senior analyst and project director of the Office of Technology Assessment, testified that: "even a modest innovation in testing—revising and updating a conventional multiple-choice test—is costly. It can take from 6 to 8 years to write new items, pilot test, and validate a major revision to a standardized achievement test battery that has been in use for many years." Testimony of Michael Feuer, House Subcommittee, *Oversight Hearings of the Report of the National Council on Education Standards and Testing*, 91.

76. Some urban areas like Chicago are drafting their own standards. Ann Bradley, "Chicago Union, Board Draft Learning Outcomes," *Education Week* (Dec. 8, 1993), 3.

77. Despite the obvious importance of student tests under systemic reform, usually there is little discussion or agreement on the number of state or national tests that students will have to take while they are in the elementary and secondary grades. Some European countries have only one exit examination that measures the achievements of the pupils and helps to determine their future career and educational options. In the United States, many educators and policymakers speak of tests at the end of the fourth, eighth, and twelfth grades. Marshall Smith would reduce the number of tests even further: "I think in the United States we ought to reduce the number of tests, the number of formal tests of the sort we're now talking about, to perhaps two during the entire time the student is in school, K–12. We overtest so much that we make the whole thing absurd. Kids laugh at it, they don't work hard on it, because the tests themselves aren't legitimate." Testimony of Marshall Smith, House Subcommittee, *Oversight Hearings on the Report of the National Council on Education Standards and Testing*, 57. Naturally, the number of national or state tests given has important cost and time implications for implementing systemic reforms.

78. At the same time, there is strong opposition to any single, national examination. For example, David Kearns, the deputy secretary of the Department of Education in the Bush Administration, testified that: "Let me be absolutely clear: the Department of Education does not support a national curriculum. Neither do we support a single national test." Testimony of David Kearns, House Subcommittee, *Oversight Hearings on the Report of the National Council on Education Standards and Testing*, 187.

79. O'Day and Smith suggested that state goals could cover nonacademic items: "Statewide student outcome goals may be an extension and particularization of the national goals developed recently by the governors. They could cover more than academic achievement, including such things as ensuring school readiness, developing students' self-worth and promoting collective responsibility." Smith and O'Day, "Systemic School Reform," 247.

80. George R. Kaplan, "Shotgun Wedding: Notes on Public Education's Encounter with the New Christian Right," *Phi Delta Kappan* 75, no. 9 (May 1994): K6.

81. Lynn Olson, "Who's Afraid of O.B.E.?" *Education Week* (Dec. 15, 1993), 25–27; and

Lonnie Harp, "Ky., Ala. Seen Barometers of State Reforms: Lawmakers are Focus of Feisty Campaigns," *Education Week* (Feb. 9, 1994), 1, 14.

82. There are fragmentary indications that some local districts are facing growing hostility to any efforts to increase reliance on outcomes-based testing. For example, the school board in Littleton, Colorado, voted to return to the traditional graduation requirements instead of using the performance-based system that had been created. Ann Bradley, "Littleton Drops Performance-Based Graduation Requirements," *Education Week* (Feb. 9, 1994), 5.

83. There are some, however, who question the use of any traditional system of rewards and punishments to motivate student achievement. Instead, they would prefer children be taught the Piagetian concept of moral and intellectual autonomy. Constance Kamii, Faye B. Clark, and Ann Dominick, "The Six National Goals: A Road to Disappointment," *Phi Delta Kappan* 75, no. 9 (May 1994): 672–77.

84. There is considerable controversy now over whether the more traditional school inputs have much impact on student achievements. Most earlier reviews of the literature on school inputs did not find much evidence of their effectiveness in fostering student learning. See, e.g., Erik A. Hanushek, "The Impact of Differential Expenditures on School Performance," *Educational Researcher* 18, no. 4 (May 1989): 45–65. A recent reanalysis of this literature challenges this widely accepted notion and argues that school inputs may be effective in helping students. Larry V. Hedges, Richard D. Laine, and Rob Greenwald, "Does Money Matter? A Meta-Analysis of Studies of Differential School Inputs on Student Outcomes," *Educational Researcher* 23, no. 3 (April 1994): 5–14. That reanalysis, however, has been challenged and the controversy is likely to continue. Erik A. Hanushek, "Money Might Matter Somewhere: A Response to Hedges, Laine, and Greenwald," Ibid., 23, no. 4 (May 1994): 5–8; Larry V. Hedges, Richard D. Lane, and Rob Greenwald, "Money Does Matter Somewhere: A Reply to Hanushek," Ibid., 9–10.

85. There is growing skepticism among some analysts about any efforts to develop and follow detailed and comprehensive plans for state and local school reforms. Given the complexity of the schools and the ever-changing environments in which they are located, these scholars call for a more dynamic and unstructured change process. For a useful and thoughtful introduction to this perspective, see Michael Fullan, *Change Forces: Probing the Depths of Educational Reform* (London: Falmer Press, 1993). For comparable discussions on how to manage other organizations and institutions under similar uncertainty, see Richard Pascale, *Managing on the Edge* (New York: Touchstone, 1990); and Ralph D. Stacey, *Managing the Unknowable* (San Francisco: Jossey-Bass, 1992).

86. For a thoughtful and useful survey of some of these earlier reform efforts, see Marshall Sashkin and John Egermeier, *School Change Models and Processes: A Review and Synthesis of Research and Practice* (Washington, D.C.: Government Printing Office, 1993). For a useful discussion of earlier education policy cycles, see Tyack and Cuban, *Tinkering toward Utopia*, 40–59.

87. Preliminary results from surveys of high school principals suggest that many of the changes so far in the secondary schools are proceeding haphazardly and rather slowly. Debra Viadero, "Impact of Reform Said to be Spotty and Not Systemic," *Education Week* (Feb. 9, 1994), 1, 12.

88. Of course, the same mechanisms can and are being used to promote systemic reform today. The question is whether their effectiveness would be the same or greater if the programs were concentrating on some other reform approach such as the Onward to Excellence Program of the Northwest Regional Educational Laboratory.

89. Smith and O'Day recognize that there will be schools that will not respond to this new approach, but they do not give us any indication of the likely extent of noncompliance. "It would be Pollyannaish of us not to acknowledge that many districts will have difficulty in altering their procedures and modes of behavior in the manner we suggest. In some cases the talent is not presently available. In other instances the central administration is simply resistant to significant change. This latter condition is particularly prevalent in many of our larger districts. These are important considerations which threaten any major educational reform. Our belief, however, is that part of the reason for the intractability of central bureaucracies in large districts is that the districts lack the coherent vision and direction that might result from the systemic reforms we suggest in this paper. To an extent, then, the state reforms would increase the chances for important changes to occur at the district level." Smith and O'Day, "Systemic School Reform," 257.

90. Herbert J. Walberg and Richard P. Niemiec, "Is Chicago School Reform Working," *Phi Delta Kappan* 75, no. 9 (May 1994): 715. Walberg and Niemiec looked at the changes in student achievement, student attendance, and graduation and dropout rates for the three years following the Chicago School Reform Act of 1988. They found that "in almost every instance, the scores have declined. . . . the reforms have apparently not succeeded in increasing student attendance. . . . [and] with regard to dropout rates, the situation appears to have worsened." Ibid., 714. For an excellent introduction to and a critique of the recent Chicago school reforms, see Jeffrey Mirel, "School Reform, Chicago Style: Educational Innovation in a Changing Urban Context, 1976–1991," *Urban Education* 28, no. 2 (July 1993): 116–49.

91. On the problems of other recent reforms to achieve their overall goals, see Gary Wehlage, Gregory Smith, and Pauline Lipman, "Restructuring Urban High Schools: The New Futures Experience," *American Educational Research Journal* 29, no. 1 (spring 1992): 51–93.

92. Testimony of Roy Romer, House Subcommittee, *Oversight Hearings on the Report of the National Council on Education Standards and Testing*, 114.

93. For useful introductions to the role of the family in education, see Nancy Feyl Chavkin, ed., *Families and Schools in a Pluralistic Society* (Albany: State University of New York Press, 1993); and William J. Weston, ed., *Education and the American Family: A Research Synthesis* (New York: New York University Press, 1989).

94. Interestingly, in a discussion of national standards by five former secretaries of education, there was considerable emphasis on the vital role of parents in educating children. Transcript, "Third Annual Conversation with the Secretaries of Education."

95. Archie E. Lapointe, "To Learn or Not to Learn: Opportunity vs. Desire," *Education Week* (Dec. 1, 1993), 28; and Harold W. Stevenson and James W. Stigler, *The Learning Gap: Why Our Schools Are Failing and What We Can Learn from Japanese and Chinese Education* (New York: Summit Books, 1992).

96. For an introduction to the role of motivation in classroom performance and school

reform, see Martin V. Covington, *Making the Grade: A Self-Worth Perspective on Motivation and School Reform* (Cambridge: Cambridge University Press, 1992).

97. Thus, Sykes and Plastrik argue that "the systemic reform vision also conceals dilemmas, conflicts, and some heroic assumptions. Perhaps the central dilemma is that the model's potential adverse consequences multiply in direct proportion to its power, defined in terms of the rewards or sanctions attached to compliance with standards. If content and performance standards are instituted as a form of voluntary guidance, many policymakers would predict they will be ignored by schools, teachers, and students. If such standards are attached to powerful stakes such as progress through and graduation from school, admission to higher education and access to employment opportunities and training, the consequences will lay bare and potentially exacerbate our society's continuing, unresolved, and systemic inequities. Furthermore, much evidence indicates that the imposition of external, high-stakes accountability produces negative effects on student motivation and on the character of teaching. Systemic reform advocates argue that the new assessments will not produce the adverse consequences associated with standardized tests of basic skills, but the issue concerns the stakes attached to assessment and their effects on teachers and students, not the form of assessment." Sykes and Plastrik, "Standard Setting," 27–28.

98. National Education Commission on Time and Learning, *Prisoners of Time* (Washington, D.C.: Government Printing Office, 1994), 23.

99. Stevenson and Stigler, *Learning Gap*.

100. National Education Commission on Time and Learning, *Prisoners of Time*, 4.

101. On the importance of summer learning, see Barbara Heyns, *Summer Learning and the Effects of Schooling* (New York: Academic Press, 1978); Barbara Heyns, "Schooling and Cognitive Development: Is There a Season for Learning?" *Child Development* 58, no. 5 (Oct. 1987): 1151–60; Doris R. Entwisle and Karl L. Alexander, "Summer Setback: Race, Poverty, School Composition, and Mathematics Achievement in the First Two Years of School," *American Sociological Review* 57 (Feb. 1992): 72–84; and Gary Walker and Frances Vilella-Velez, *The Summer Training and Education Program (STEP) from Pilot through Replication and Postprogram Impacts* (Philadelphia: Public/Private Ventures, 1992).

102. On the debates over the particular importance of early childhood education, see Ernest L. Boyer, *Ready to Learn: A Mandate for the Nation* (Princeton: Princeton University Press, 1991); Ron Haskins, "Beyond Metaphor: The Efficacy of Early Childhood Education," *American Psychologist* 44, no. 2 (Feb. 1989): 274–82; Lawrence J. Schweinhart, Helen V. Barnes, and David P. Weikart, *Significant Benefits: The High/Scope Perry Preschool Study through Age 27* (Ypsilanti: High/Scope Press, 1993); Maris A. Vinovskis, "Early Childhood Education: Then and Now," *Daedalus* 122, no. 1 (winter 1993): 151–76; and Edward Zigler and Susan Muenchow, *Head Start: The Inside Story of America's Most Successful Educational Experiment* (New York: Basic Books, 1992).

103. On dealing with the needs of pregnant teenagers and young mothers in school, see Joy G. Dryfoos, *Adolescents at Risk: Prevalence and Prevention* (New York: Oxford University Press, 1990); National Research Council, *Losing Generations: Adolescents in High-Risk Settings* (Washington, D.C.: National Academy Press, 1993); Gary Natriello, Edward L.

McDill, and Aaron M. Pallas, *Schooling Disadvantaged Children: Racing against Catastrophe* (New York: Teachers College, 1990); Robert E. Slavin, Nancy L. Karweit, and Nancy A. Madden, *Effective Programs for Students at Risk* (Boston: Allyn and Bacon, 1989); and Maris A. Vinovskis, *An "Epidemic" of Adolescent Pregnancy? Some Historical and Policy Considerations* (New York: Oxford University Press, 1988).

104. In the late 1960s and mid-1970s that office was called the National Institute of Education.

105. Vinovskis, "Analysis of the Quality of Research."

106. There are several research strategies that could be profitably employed to assess the implementation and impact of systemic reform. For example, one might select three states with different approaches to statewide systemic reform. Focusing on schools that historically have been reluctant to undertake any major educational reforms, a stratified sample of those schools in each of the three states could be followed over time in order to ascertain if systemic reforms had an impact. In addition, using a matched sample of comparable schools, two or three different types of seemingly promising reforms could be introduced into those schools (and with an appropriate control group of schools left to themselves in terms of initiating reform activities). Cohorts of children from this subset of schools could be analyzed over a five-year period in order to gauge the impact of state-level and local-level systemic reform on student achievement. For a discussion of this particular research strategy, see the memo by Maris A. Vinovskis, "Further Comments on Proposed FIE Replication and Evaluation of Promising Practices," OERI, May 20, 1994.

CHAPTER 8. A LIFE-COURSE FRAMEWORK FOR ANALYZING EDUCATIONAL RESEARCH PROJECTS

1. This life-course framework was developed while I was a consultant to OERI. I am greatly indebted to a number of individuals who provided thoughtful and useful suggestions. In particular, the staff of OERI were especially stimulating and helpful. Naturally, the views expressed in this chapter are those of the author and do not necessarily reflect those of the Department of Education.

2. For a discussion of the different definitions and uses of the concept of systemic reform, see chap. 6.

3. Evelyn M. Duvall, *Family Development* (Philadelphia: J. B. Lippincott, 1967); Evelyn M. Duvall and Brent C. Miller, *Marriage and Family Development* (New York: Harper and Row, 1985); Reuben Hill, "Methodological Issues in Family Development Research," *Family Process* 3 (1964): 186–206.

4. For critiques of family-cycle models, see Glen H. Elder, Jr., "History and the Family: The Discovery of Complexity," *Journal of Marriage and the Family* 43 (1981): 489–519; Tamara K. Hareven, "Cycles, Courses and Cohorts: Reflections on the Theoretical and Methodological Approaches to the Historical Study of Family Development," *Journal of Social History* 7 (1978): 97–109; Maris A. Vinovskis, "The Historian and the Life Course: Reflections on Recent Approaches to the Study of American Family Life in the Past," in *Life-Span Development and Behavior,* vol. 8, ed. Paul B. Baltes, David L. Featherman, and Richard M. Lerner (Hillsdale, N.J.: Lawrence Erlbaum, 1988), 33–59.

5. Glen H. Elder, Jr., "Family History and the Life Course," in *Transitions: The Family and the Life Course in Historical Perspective,* ed. Tamara K. Hareven (New York: Academic Press, 1978), 20–21.

6. For additional discussions and uses of life-course analysis in other disciplines, see Paul B. Baltes, Hayne W. Reese, and John R. Nesselroade, *Life-Span Developmental Psychology: Introduction to Research Methods* (Monterey, Cal.: Brooks and Cole, 1977); Nancy Datan and Leon H. Ginsberg, eds., *Life-Span Developmental Psychology: Normative Life Crises* (New York: Academic Press, 1975); Glen H. Elder, Jr., *Life Course Dynamics: Trajectories and Transitions,* 1968–1980 (Ithaca: Cornell University Press, 1985); Tamara K. Hareven and Kathleen J. Adams, *Aging and Life Course Transitions: An Interdisciplinary Perspective* (New York: Guilford Press, 1982); Kurt Kreppner and Richard M. Lerner, eds., *Family Systems and Life-Span Development* (Hillsdale, N.J.: Lawrence Erlbaum, 1989).

7. Karl L. Alexander, Doris R. Entwisle, and Susan L. Dauber, *On the Success of Failure: A Reassessment of the Effects of Retention in the Primary Grades* (New York: Cambridge University Press, 1994).

8. Alexander, Entwisle, and Dauber, *On the Success of Failure,* 214.

9. Alan C. Kerckhoff, *Diverging Pathways: Social Structure and Career Deflections* (Cambridge: Cambridge University Press, 1993), 198.

10. The close age-grading of schools in the United States is a fairly recent phenomenon. Although educational reformers had advocated age-grading of schools since the late nineteenth century, they were unable to achieve a close fit between age and grades in most schools until after World War II. For a discussion of the development of age-grading in the United States, see David Angus, Jeffrey Mirel, and Maris Vinovskis, "Historical Development of Age-Stratification in Schooling," *Teacher's College Record* 90, no. 2 (winter 1988): 211–36.

11. One might, of course, also subdivide the lives of individuals according to stages as defined by such scholars as Erik Erikson, Jean Piaget, or Daniel Levinson. Erik H. Erikson, *Childhood and Society,* 2d ed. (New York: W. W. Norton, 1963); Jean Piaget, *The Origins of Intelligence in the Child* (New York: International Universities Press, 1952); Daniel J. Levinson, *The Seasons of a Man's Life* (New York: Alfred A. Knopf, 1978).

   Most recent scholarship, however, questions the reality or utility of such stages. For critical discussions of the uses of stage in cognitive development, see Joachim F. Wohlwill, "Cognitive Development in Childhood," in *Constancy and Change in Human Development,* ed. Orville G. Brim and Jerome Kagan (Cambridge: Harvard University Press, 1980), 359–444; John L. Horn and Gary Donaldson, "Cognitive Development in Adulthood," in Ibid., 445–529; Kurt W. Fischer and Daniel Bullock, "Cognitive Development in School-Age Children: Conclusions and New Directions," in *Development during Middle Childhood: The Years from Six to Twelve,* ed. W. Andrew Collins (Washington, D.C.: National Academy Press, 1984), 70–146.

12. Studies of cognitive development and learning have flourished recently. For a summary of the recent work, see John T. Bruer, *Schools for Thought: A Science of Learning in the Classroom* (Cambridge: MIT Press, 1993).

13. Cynthia A. Berg, "Perspectives for Viewing Intellectual Development Throughout the

Life Course," in *Intellectual Development,* ed. Robert J. Sternberg and Cynthia A. Berg (Cambridge: Cambridge University Press, 1992), 1–15.

14. For a discussion of the importance of summer learning, see Doris R. Entwisle and Karl L. Alexander, "Summer Setback: Race, Poverty, School Composition, and Mathematics Achievement in the First Two Years of School," *American Sociological Review* 57 (Feb. 1992): 72–84; Barbara Heyns, *Summer Learning and the Effects of Schooling* (New York: Academic Press, 1978); Barbara Heyns, "Schooling and Cognitive Development: Is There a Season for Learning?" *Child Development* 58, no. 5 (Oct. 1987): 1151–60; Gary Walker and Frances Vilella-Velez, *Anatomy of a Demonstration: The Summer Training and Education Program (STEP) from Pilot through Replication and Postprogram Impacts* (Philadelphia: Public/Private Ventures, 1992).

15. See, e.g., Doris R. Entwisle, "Schools and the Adolescent," in *At the Threshold: The Developing Adolescent,* ed. S. Shirley Feldman and Glen R. Elliott (Cambridge: Harvard University Press, 1990), 197–224.

16. For a description of the TORUS system, see Pelavin Associates, "Toris, Version 2.0, User Guide" (Washington. D.C.: Pelavin Associates, 1993).

17. Linda Darling-Hammond, Arthur E. Wise, and Stephen P. Klein, *A License to Teach: Building a Profession for 21st-Century Schools* (Boulder, Colo.: Westview Press, 1995), 7.

18. *Federal Register* 60 (Apr. 10, 1995), 18340–42. As a faculty member at the University of Michigan, I was precluded from participating in the discussions on the development of the OERI center priorities. Because I was a consultant to OERI, any involvement I might have had in the center development process could appear to be a conflict of interest if someone at the University of Michigan bid for one of these centers. During the public comment period for the proposed centers, however, I was asked by OERI to comment on the plans since they had been made public.

19. Some of my analysis of the proposed centers draws on my earlier report. See Maris A. Vinovskis, "Analysis of the Quality of Research and Development at the OERI Research and Development Centers and at the OERI Regional Educational Laboratories" (final report, OERI, Department of Educaiton, June 1993).

20. Ibid., 9–94.

21. Ibid., 37–43.

22. Ibid., 45–47.

23. Public Law 103–227, 103d Cong., 2d sess. (Mar. 31, 1994), 108 STAT. 220.

24. Vinovskis, "Analysis of the Quality of Research," 59–60.

25. OERI reviewed the public comments on the proposed R&D centers. Some of the criticisms raised in this section were remedied in the revised Request for Proposals for R&D centers, but many of the problems remain. Because of a possible conflict of interest, I did not participate in the OERI revisions of the center priorities.

CONCLUSION

1. Of course, there are some notable exceptions. See, e.g., Rick Ginsberg and David N. Plank, *Commissions, Reports, Reforms, and Educational Policy* (Westport, Conn: Praeger, 1995).

2. Yet there are some educational historians who have addressed policy questions directly and effectively. See, e.g., Diane Ravitch, *The Troubled Crusade: American Education, 1945–1980* (New York: Basic Books, 1983); Diane Ravitch and Maris A. Vinovskis, eds., *Learning from the Past: What History Teaches Us about School Reform* (Baltimore: Johns Hopkins University Press, 1995); David Tyack and Larry Cuban, *Tinkering toward Utopia: A Century of Public School Reform* (Cambridge: Harvard University Press, 1995); Arthur Zilversmit, *Changing Schools: Progressive Education Theory and Practice, 1930–1960* (Chicago: University of Chicago Press, 1993).

3. On recent developments at public policy schools, see William N. Dunn and Rita Mae Kelly, eds., *Advances in Policy Studies since 1950, Policy Studies Annual Review,* no. 10 (New Brunswick, N.J.: Transaction, 1992).

4. For discussions of how history is used by film makers, see Mark C. Carnes, ed., *Past Imperfect: History According to the Movies* (New York: Henry Holt, 1995); Robert A. Rosenstone, ed., *Revisioning History: Film and the Construction of a New Past* (Princeton: Princeton University Press, 1995). There are also several useful books about movies and American wars, such as Linda Dittmar and Gene Michaud, eds., *From Hanoi to Hollywood: The Vietnam War in American Film* (New Brunswick: Rutgers University Press, 1990); George H. Roeder, Jr., *The Censored War: American Visual Experience during World War Two* (New Haven: Yale University Press, 1993); Lawrence H. Suid, *Guts and Glory: Great American War Movies* (Reading, Mass.: Addison-Wesley, 1978).

5. Similarly, American almanacs, which had a wide circulation in the eighteenth and nineteenth centuries, provided lists of maxims and simple advice for their readers, including materials from Benjamin Franklin. Marion Barber Stowell, *Early American Almanacs: The Colonial Weekday Bible* (New York: Burt Franklin, 1977).

6. For useful critiques of the self-help books and management consultant volumes, see John Micklethwait and Adrian Wooldridge, *The Witch Doctors: Making Sense of the Management Gurus* (New York: Time Books, 1996); Martin E. P. Seligman, *What You Can Change and What You Can't: The Complete Guide to Successful Self-Improvement* (New York: Alfred A. Knopf, 1994).

7. There is considerable disagreement among historians today over the "lessons" of history. Some are skeptical about the usefulness of history altogether while others, including myself, see the value of history for policymakers and the general public. For a range of interpretations, see Salo W. Baron, *The Contemporary Relevance of History: A Study in Approaches and Methods* (New York: Columbia University Press, 1986); J. H. Hexter, *Reappraisals in History* (Evanston: Northwestern University Press, 1962); Michael Howard, *The Lessons of History* (New Haven: Yale University Press, 1991); Harvey J. Kaye, *The Powers of the Present: Reflections on the Crises and the Promise of History* (Minneapolis: University of Minnesota Press, 1991); A. L. Rowse, *The Use of History,* rev. ed. (London: English Universities Press, 1963); Page Smith, *The Historian and History* (New York: Alfred A. Knopf, 1964); Barbara W. Tuchman, *Practicing History: Selected Essays* (New York: Alfred A. Knopf, 1981).

8. George O. Kent, "Clio the Tyrant: Historical Analogies and the Meaning of History," *The Historian* 32, no. 1 (Nov. 1969): 99–106.

9. Arthur M. Schlesinger, Jr., "The Inscrutability of History," in *The Vital Past: Writings on the Uses of History,* ed. Stephen Vaughn (Athens: University of Georgia Press, 1985), 318.

10. For useful discussions of the uses and misuses of historical analogies, see Richard E. Neustadt and Ernest R. May, *Thinking in Time: The Uses of History for Decision-Makers* (New York: Free Press, 1986), 34–57, 75–90; Lester D. Stephens, "Lessons, Analogies, and Prediction," in *The Vital Past: Writings on the Uses of History,* ed. Stephen Vaughan (Athens: University of Georgia Press, 1985), 323–30.

11. Neustadt and May, *Thinking in Time,* 234–35.

12. Ibid., 235–36.

13. Ibid., 237.

14. Ibid., 252.

15. For a discussion of the problems of coordinating and integrating services for children, see Joy G. Dryfoos, *Full-Service Schools: A Revolution in Health and Social Services for Children, Youth, and Families* (San Francisco: Jossey-Bass, 1994); Sharon Lynn Kagan, *Integrating Services for Children and Families: Understanding the Past to Shape the Future* (New Haven: Yale University Press, 1993).

16. For a discussion of the problems of doing interdisciplinary work, see Stephen Jay Kline, *Conceptual Foundations for Multi-Disciplinary Thinking* (Stanford: Stanford University Press, 1995).

17. For a call for more syntheses in history, see Bernard Bailyn, *On the Teaching and Writing of History,* ed. Edward Connery Lathem (Hanover: University Press of New England, 1994).

18. On the extent of knowledge of high school students about American history, see Diane Ravitch and Chester E. Finn, Jr., *What Do Our 17-Year-Olds Know? A Report on the First National Assessment of History and Literature* (New York: Harper and Row, 1987); Alexandra S. Beatty et al., *NAEP 1994 U.S. History Report Card: Findings from the National Assessment of Educational Progress* (Washington, D.C.: Government Printing Office, 1996). It is difficult to translate the lack of knowledge of American history among high school students into the difficulties that adults may encounter because of their limited understanding of our past. For some interesting and useful recent attempts to address such issues, see Michael X. Delli Carpini and Scott Keeter, *What Americans Know about Politics and Why It Matters* (New Haven: Yale University Press, 1996); Norman H. Nie, Jane Junn, and Kenneth Stehlik-Barry, *Education and Democratic Citizenship in America* (Chicago: University of Chicago Press, 1996); Sidney Verba, Kay Lehman Schlozman, and Henry E. Brady, *Voice and Equality: Civic Voluntarism in American Politics* (Cambridge: Harvard University Press, 1995).

19. William Cronon, "The Trouble with Wilderness; or, Getting Back to the Wrong Nature," in *Uncommon Ground: Toward Reinventing Nature,* ed. William Cronon (New York: W. W. Norton, 1995), 69–90. For an interesting discussion of these issues, see William Cronon, "The Trouble with Wilderness; or, Getting Back to the Wrong Nature, *Environmental History* 1, no. 1 (Jan. 1996): 7–28; Samuel P. Hays, "Comment: The Trouble with Bill Cronon's Wilderness," Ibid., 29–32; Michael P. Cohen, "Comment: Resistance to Wilderness," Ibid., 33–42; Thomas R. Dunlap, "Comment: But What

Did You Go Out into the Wilderness to See," Ibid., 43–46; William Cronon, "The Trouble with Wilderness: A Response," Ibid., 47–55.

20. For useful discussions on the nature of presidential appointees and the problems they face, see Hugh Heclo, *A Government of Strangers: Executive Politics in Washington* (Washington, D.C.: Brookings Institution, 1977); G. Calvin MacKenzie, ed., *The In-and-Outers: Presidential Appointees and Transient Government in Washington* (Baltimore: Johns Hopkins University Press, 1987); James P. Pfiffner, *The Strategic Presidency: Hitting the Ground Running*, 2d rev. ed. (Lawrence: University of Kansas Press, 1996).

21. For analyses of the role of career federal civil service employees and their interactions with the presidential employees, see Heclo, *Government of Strangers;* Patricia Wallace Ingraham, *The Foundation of Merit: Public Service in American Democracy* (Baltimore: John Hopkins University Press, 1995); Ronald N. Johnson and Gary D. Libecap, *The Federal Civil Service System and the Problem of Bureaucracy: The Economics and Politics of Institutional Change* (Chicago: University of Chicago Press, 1994); Herbert Kaufman, *The Administrative Behavior of Federal Bureau Chiefs* (Washington, D.C.: Brookings Institution, 1981); MacKenzie, ed., *In-and-Outers*.

22. There are numerous useful books on recent developments in Congress. For a few helpful introductions to changes in Congress, see, e.g., Gary Cox and Mathew McCubbins, *Legislative Leviathan: Party Government in the House* (Berkeley: University of California Press, 1993); Richard Munson, *The Cardinal of Capitol Hill: The Men and Women Who Control Government Spending* (New York: Grove Press, 1993); David Price, *The Congressional Experience* (Boulder, Colo.: Westview Press, 1992); David Rohde and Kenneth A. Shepsle, *Parties and Leaders in the Postreform House* (Chicago: University of Chicago Press, 1991); Barbara Sinclair, *The Transformation of the U.S. Senate* (Baltimore: Johns Hopkins University Press, 1989); Barbara Sinclair, *Legislators, Leaders, and Lawmaking: The U.S. House of Representatives in the Postreform Era* (Baltimore: Johns Hopkins University Press, 1995). For a useful, more in-depth examination of Congress and education issues, see John F. Jennings, ed., *National Issues in Education: Elementary and Secondary Education Act* (Bloomington, Ind.: Phi Delta Kappa, 1995); Andree E. Reeves, *Congressional Committee Chairmen: Three Who Made an Evolution* (Lexington: University of Kentucky Press, 1993); Harry L. Summerfield, *Power and Process: The Formulation and Limits of Federal Educational Policy* (Berkeley: McCutchan Publishing, 1974); Norman C. Thomas, *Education in National Politics* (New York: David MacKay, 1975), 72–109.

23. On the increasing number and growing specialization of congressional staff, see Harrison W. Fox, Jr., and Susan Webb Hammond, *Congressional Staffs: The Invisible Force in American Lawmaking* (New York: Free Press, 1977); Kenneth Kofmehl, *Professional Staffs of Congress* (Lafayette, Ind.: Purdue University Studies, 1962).

24. Occasionally, historians have played a more prominent role. Patricia Graham was the director of National Institute of Education in the late 1970s and Diane Ravitch was the assistant secretary of the Office of Educational Research and Improvement in the early 1990s.

25. For example, the National Library of Education, which has a historian on its staff, has not fully used his interests and skills in that area.

26. Much of this discussion is based on the analyses cited in chap. 1.

27. Interestingly, while the National Library of Education prominently displays about 500 newsletters and periodicals in its reading room, it relegates the *History of Education Quarterly,* the major historical publication in the field, to the back shelves in another room where few nonlibrary staff are likely to encounter it. In my discussions with the OERI staff, it was clear that the *History of Education Quarterly* and other comparable historical journals were rarely consulted. Moreover, recent journals dealing with policy history such as *Journal of Policy History* and *Public Historian* are not even available in the National Library of Education.

28. For useful discussions of the ways in which members of Congress and their staffs obtain information, see David Whiteman, *Communication in Congress: Members, Staff, and the Search for Information* (Lawrence: University Press of Kansas, 1995); William H. Robinson and Clay H. Wellborn, *Knowledge, Power, and the Congress* (Washington, D.C.: Congressional Quarterly, 1991). While such organizations as the American Historical Association do maintain a professional liaison to work with the White House and Congress, the responsibilities of that person appear to be focused on issues more directly affecting historians as scholars and grant recipients than on how to expand the uses and understanding of the past in current policymaking. Other professional academic groups, such as the Society for Research in Child Development (which often have smaller memberships), are more effective in working with the executive and legislative branches to increase the use of scholarly information in the government deliberations.

29. The Congressional Research Service (CRS) sometimes employs historians as part of their staff. For example, Ruth Wasem, a history Ph.D. from the University of Michigan, is employed by CRS to work on a variety of domestic issues including the problem of teenage pregnancies.

30. On the efforts of the White House to develop appropriate briefings for new appointees, see James P. Pfiffner, "Strangers in a Strange Land: Orienting New Presidential Appointees," in *In-and-Outers,* ed. MacKenzie, 141–55.

31. On the activities and demise of the Office of Educational Technology (OTA), see Bruce Bimber, *The Politics of Expertise in Congress: The Rise and Fall of the Office of Technology Assessment* (Albany: State University of New York Press, 1996).

32. This also includes the expenditures of the NIE, the predecessor of OERI.

33. For example, as a consultant to OERI I was asked to do a historical analysis of the development of the concept and recent uses of systemic reform. After my essay was reviewed within the agency, it received considerable internal and external praise and was issued as a working paper within the now defunct Office of Research within OERI. But I was never asked to present a talk or seminar on the topic, although systemic reform was central to the work of OERI and the rest of the Department of Education at that time, nor was my working paper widely distributed or used within the department (though I personally was able to share copies of it with interested policymakers). Subsequently my essay was published in the *American Educational Research Journal* and now appears as chap. 7 in this book.

   It should be pointed out, however, that OERI recently has not been very effective in developing and disseminating policy-oriented work; my experiences, unfortunately, were part of a larger pattern. Nevertheless, it also illustrates the fact that policymakers at OERI and the Department of Education did not feel that a historical discussion of the development of systemic reform was especially needed despite the fact that this new approach was the dominant educational policy paradigm in Washington.

34. Even more recently, when former assistant secretary Diane Ravitch, who directed OERI, and her successor, Sharon Robinson, commissioned me to undertake several policy analyses from a historical perspective, the results of those endeavors were not widely disseminated by OERI to the rest of the department.

35. Some of the staff of the National Library of Education have expressed an interest in developing policy-oriented assistance along the lines of the Congressional Research Service, but they have not had the time nor staff available to pursue this avenue.

36. Emerson Elliott, the able former director of the National Center for Education Statistics (NCES), was concerned that if NCES undertook more in-depth policy analyses, it might engender controversy that could undermine the credibility of NCES as an objective and reliable data collection agency.

37. At the time that Title 1 was created, there was a useful political science investigation of the origins and implementation of that program. Stephen K. Bailey and Edith K. Mosher, *ESEA: The Office of Education Administers a Law* (Syracuse: Syracuse University Press, 1968). Since then, however, very little has been done to write an overall scholarly analysis of the Title 1 program over time. Moreover, as a member of the current Independent Panel to oversee the evaluation of that program, it is clear that there is not much interest among most policymakers in the Department of Education to reassess the current Title 1 effort from a longer and broader historical perspective. For a recent attempt to analyze the effectiveness of the Title 1 program and Head Start from a broader, historical perspective, see Maris A. Vinovskis, "The Development and Effectiveness of Federal Compensatory Education Programs: A Brief Historical Analysis of Title 1 and Head Start" (unpub. paper prepared for the National Commission on Philanthropy and Civic Renewal, Mar. 1997).

38. For an example of the difficulties of assembling recent past information about foreign policy activities toward the Soviet Union because it was scattered throughout the different presidential libraries, see Richard Pipes, *How Washington Makes Soviet Policy: Observations of a Visitor* (Stanford: Hoover Institution Press, 1990), 4.

39. All federal agencies are required, by law, to organize and send their important documents to the National Archives. Unfortunately, few agencies actually do so, and many valuable and important documents disappear.

40. My own experiences in trying to assemble the relevant documents for the studies in this volume testify to the lack of good, systematic record-keeping by the agencies. Most of the Follow Through records, for example, were destroyed in the early 1980s. Many, if not most, of the OERI documents used in my analyses were obtained from individual staff members at that agency rather than from the Department of Education's National Library of Education. Although the staff of the department library have struggled valiantly to collect and preserve the relevant documents, there is little sense of urgency in OERI or the rest of the Department of Education to archive such materials. Fortunately, the new director of the National Library of Education, Blane Dessy, has created a task

force to look into the archival needs of the Department of Education. Moreover, the Department of Education has been a pioneer in the use of developing and disseminating Web pages for contemporary educational documents.

41. On the role of parents in education, see Alan Booth and Judith F. Dunn, eds., *Family-School Links: How Do They Affect Educational Outcomes* (Mahwah, N.J.: Lawrence Erlbaum, 1996); David W. Grissmer et al., *Student Achievement and the Changing American Family* (Santa Monica, Calif.: RAND, 1994); William J. Weston, ed., *Education and the American Family: A Research Synthesis* (New York: New York University Press, 1989).

42. On the importance of summer learning, see Doris R. Entwisle and Karl L. Alexander, "Summer Setback: Race, Poverty, School Composition, and Mathematics Achievement in the First Two Years of School," *American Sociological Review* 57 (Feb. 1992): 72–84; Barbara Heyns, *Summer Learning and the Effects of Schooling* (New York: Academic Press, 1978); Gary Walker and Frances Vilella-Velez, *Anatomy of a Demonstration: The Summer Training and Education Program (STEP) from Pilot through Replication and Postprogram Impacts* (Philadelphia: Public/Private Ventures, 1992). For a useful, historical discussion of summer learning, see Kenneth Gold, "'Mitigating Mental and Moral Stagnation': The Role of Summer Education in American Schools, 1840–1990" (Ph.D. diss., University of Michigan, 1997).

43. For a thoughtful discussion of this problem from the perspective of the U.S. Congress, see Jennifer Mittelstadt, "Educating 'Our Girls' and 'Welfare Mothers': Discussions of Education Policy for Pregnant and Parenting Adolescents in Federal Hearings, 1975–1995," *Journal of Family History* 22, no. 3 (July 1997): 326–53. On federal programs for pregnant teenagers, see Dionee J. Jones and Stanley F. Battle, eds., *Teenage Pregnancy: Developing Strategies for Change in the Twenty-First Century* (New Brunswick, N.J.: Transaction, 1990); Kristin Luker, *Dubious Conception: The Politics of Teenage Pregnancy* (Cambridge: Harvard University Press, 1996); Theodora Ooms, ed., *Teenage Pregnancy in a Family Context: Implications for Policy* (Philadelphia: Temple University Press, 1981); Maris A. Vinovskis, *An "Epidemic" of Adolescent Pregnancy? Some Historical and Policy Considerations* (New York: Oxford University Press, 1988).

44. For discussions of the evolution of nineteenth- and early-twentieth-century high schools, see Jurgen Herbst, *The Once and Future School: Three Hundred and Fifty Years of American Secondary Education* (London, Routledge, 1996); Michael B. Katz, *The Irony of Early School Reform: Educational Innovation in Mid-Nineteenth-Century Massachusetts* (Cambridge: Harvard University Press, 1968); David F. Labaree, *The Making of an American High School: The Credential Market and the Central High School in Philadelphia, 1839–1939* (New Haven: Yale University Press, 1988); Joel Perlmann, *Ethnic Differences: Schooling and Social Structure among the Irish, Italians, Jews, and Blacks in the American City, 1880–1935* (Cambridge: Cambridge University Press, 1988); William J. Reese, *The Origins of the American High School* (New Haven: Yale University Press, 1995); Reed Ueda, *Avenues to Adulthood: The Origins of the High School and Social Mobility in an American Suburb* (Cambridge: Cambridge University Press, 1987); Maris A. Vinovskis, *Education, Society, and Economic Opportunity: A Historical Perspective on Persistent Issues* (New Haven: Yale University Press, 1995); Maris A. Vinovskis, *The Origins of Public High*

Schools: A Reexamination of the Beverly High School Controversy (Madison: University of Wisconsin Press, 1985).

45. Gross enrollment ratio based on school enrollment of all ages in grades 9 to 12 divided by the fourteen- to seventeen-year-old population. National Center for Education Statistics, *Digest of Education Statistics,* 1995 (Washington, D.C.: Government Printing Office, 1995), 68.

46. Sherman Dorn, *Creating the Dropout: An Institutional and Social History of School Failure* (Westport, Conn.: Praeger, 1996); Joseph F. Kett, "School Leaving: Dead End or Detour?" in *Learning from the Past: What History Teaches Us about School Reform,* ed. Diane Ravitch and Maris A. Vinovskis (Baltimore: Johns Hopkins University Press, 1995), 265–94.

47. Herbert M. Kliebard, *The Struggle for the American Curriculum, 1893–1958* (London: Routledge and Kegan Paul, 1986); Herbert M. Kliebard, *Forging the American Curriculum: Essays in Curriculum History and Theory* (London: Routledge, 1992); George Willis et al., eds., *The American Curriculum: A Documentary History* (Westport, Conn.: Praeger, 1994).

48. David Angus and Jeffrey Mirel, "Rhetoric and Reality: The High School Curriculum," in *Learning from the Past: What History Teaches Us about School Reform,* ed. Diane Ravitch and Maris A. Vinovskis (Baltimore: Johns Hopkins University Press, 1995), 295–328.

49. Michael W. Sedlak, "Attitudes, Choices, and Behavior: School Delivery of Health and Social Services," in *Learning from the Past: What History Teaches Us about School Reform,* ed. Diane Ravitch and Maris A. Vinovskis (Baltimore: Johns Hopkins University Press, 1995), 57–94.

50. The average length of the public school year did rise from 144.3 days in 1899–1900 to 172.7 days in 1929–30, but then only increased to 178.0 days in 1959–60 and 179.8 days in 1990–91. Moreover, while we do not have good historical data on the length of the school day, that may have actually decreased during these years. National Center for Education Statistics, *Digest of Education Statistics,* 1995, 50. On the changes in the school year and school day and the importance of time considerations, see Cheryl M. Kane, *Prisoners of Time Research: What We Know and What We Need to Know* (Washington, D.C.: Government Printing Office, 1994); National Education Commission on Time and Learning, *Prisoners of Time: Schools and Programs Making Time Work for Students and Teachers* (Washington, D.C.: Government Printing Office, 1994).

51. For a useful discussion of the problems of urban schools in Michigan and why they have deteriorated over time, see Jeffrey Mirel, *The Rise and Fall of an Urban School System: Detroit, 1907–81* (Ann Arbor: University of Michigan Press, 1993).

52. On the problems of the children of the Baltimore adolescent mothers, see Jeanne Brooks-Gunn and P. Lindsay Chase-Lansdale, "Adolescent Childbearing: Effects on Children," in *Encyclopedia of Adolescence,* ed. Richard M. Lerner, Anne C. Petersen, and Jeanne Brooks-Gunn (New York: Garland, 1991), 103–10; Frank F. Furstenburg, Jr., Jeanne Brooks-Gunn, and P. Lindsay Chase-Lansdale, "Teenaged Pregnancy and Childbearing," *American Psychologist* 44, no. 2 (1989): 313–20.

53. On the problems of inferring the current potential effectiveness of programs on the basis

of much earlier model efforts using longitudinal data, see Deanna S. Gomby et al., "Long-Term Outcomes of Early Childhood Programs: Analysis and Recommendations," *Future of Children* 5, no. 3 (winter 1995): 6–21.

54. Henry J. Perkinson, *The Imperfect Panacea: American Faith in Education, 1865–1990,* 3d ed. (New York: McGraw-Hill, 1991).

55. Carl F. Kaestle, *Pillars of the Republic: Common Schools and American Society,* 1780–1860 (New York: Hill and Wang, 1983); Edith Nye MacMullen, *In the Cause of True Education: Henry Barnard and Nineteenth-Century School Reform* (New Haven: Yale University Press, 1991); Jonathan Messerli, *Horace Mann: A Biography* (New York: Alfred A. Knopf, 1972).

56. Barbara Beatty, *Preschool Education in America: The Culture of Young Children from the Colonial Era to the Present* (New Haven: Yale University Press, 1995); Victoria Getis and Maris A. Vinovskis, "History of Child Care in the United States before 1950," in *Child Care in Context: Cross-Cultural Perspectives,* ed. Michael E. Lamb et al. (Hillsdale, N.J.: Lawrence Erlbaum, 1992), 185–206; Michael Steven Shapiro, *Child's Garden: The Kindergarten Movement from Froebel to Dewey* (University Park: Pennsylvania State University Press, 1983).

57. On the enactment of the Elementary and Secondary Education Act of 1965, see Stephen K. Bailey and Edith K. Mosher, *ESEA: The Office of Education Administers a Law* (Syracuse: Syracuse University Press, 1968); Julie Roy Jeffrey, *Education for Children of the Poor: A Study of the Origins and Implementation of the Elementary and Secondary Education Act of* 1965 (Columbus: Ohio State University Press, 1978).

58. On the American ethos of individualism, see James Leiby, *A History of Social Welfare and Social Work in the United States* (New York: Columbia University Press, 1978); Barry Alan Shain, *The Myth of American Individualism: The Protestant Origins of American Political Thought* (Princeton: Princeton University Press, 1994).

59. On the role of education in dealing with inequalities in American society, see Raymond Boudon, *Education, Opportunity, and Social Mobility: Changing Prospects in Western Society* (New York: John Wiley, 1973); James S. Coleman, *Equality and Achievement in Education* (Boulder, Colo.: Westview Press, 1990); Christopher Jencks et al., *Inequality: A Reassessment of the Effect of Family and Schooling in America* (New York: Harper and Row, 1972); Christopher Jencks et al., *Who Gets Ahead? The Determinants of Economic Success in America* (New York: Basic Books, 1979); Frederick Mosteller and Daniel P. Moynihan, eds., *On Equality of Educational Opportunity* (New York: Vintage, 1972); Caroline Hodges Persell, *Education and Inequality: The Roots and Results of Stratification in America's Schools* (New York: Free Press, 1977).

60. On the complex issues of black education, see Reginald M. Clark, *Family Life and School Achievement: Why Poor Black Children Succeed or Fail* (Chicago: University of Chicago Press, 1983); David L. Kirp, *Just Schools: The Idea of Racial Equality in American Education* (Berkeley: University of California Press, 1982); Ellen Condliffe Lagemann and Lamar P. Miller, eds., *Brown v. Board of Education: The Challenge for Today's Schools* (New York: Columbia University Press, 1996); Charles V. Willie, Antoine M. Garibaldi, and Wornie L. Reed, eds., *The Education of African-Americans* (New York: Auburn House, 1991).

61. Patricia Albjerg Graham, "Assimilation, Adjustment, and Access: An Antiquarian View of American Education," in *Learning from the Past: What History Teaches Us about School Reform,* ed. Diane Ravitch and Maris A. Vinovskis (Baltimore: Johns Hopkins University Press, 1995), 3–24

62. Tyack and Cuban, *Tinkering toward Uptopia.*

63. On comparisons of U.S. education to other countries, see National Center for Education Statistics, *Education in States and Nations: Indicators Comparing U.S. States with Other Industrialized Countries in* 1991, 2d ed. (Washington, D.C.: Government Printing Office, 1996).

64. On Head Start, see chap. 3.

65. On Even Start, see chap. 5.

66. On Follow Through, see chap. 4.

67. Diane Ravitch, "Adventures in Wonderland: A Scholar in Washington," *American Scholar* 64, no. 4 (autumn 1995): 497–516.

68. Zilversmit, *Changing Schools,* 121.

69. On school choice, see John E. Chubb and Terry M. Moe, *Politics, Markets, and America's Schools* (Washington, D.C.: Brookings Institution, 1990); Terry M. Moe, ed., *Private Vouchers* (Stanford: Hoover Institution Press, 1995); Paul E. Peterson, "The New Politics of Choice," in *Learning from the Past: What History Teaches Us about School Reform* , ed. Diane Ravitch and Maris A. Vinovskis (Baltimore: Johns Hopkins University Press, 1995): 217–40; Edith Rasell and Richard Rothstein, eds., *School Choice: Examining the Evidence* (Washington, D.C.: Economic Policy Institute, 1993); Claire Smrekar, *The Impact of School Choice and Community in the Interest of Families and Schools* (Albany: State University of New York Press, 1996).

On the development of curriculum standards, see Diane Ravitch, ed., *Debating the Future of American Education: Do We Need National Standards and Assessments?* (Washington, D.C.: Brookings Institution, 1995); Diane Ravitch, *National Standards in American Education: A Citizen's Guide* (Washington, D.C.: Brookings Institution, 1995); Robert Rothman, *Measuring Up: Standards, Assessment, and School Reform* (San Francisco: Jossey-Bass, 1995).

On changes in school finances and governance, see Susan H. Fuhrman, ed., *Designing Coherent Education Policy: Improving the System* (San Francisco: Jossey-Bass, 1993); Michael W. Kirst, "Who's in Charge? Federal, State, and Local Control," in *Learning from the Past: What History Teaches Us about School Reform* (Baltimore: Johns Hopkins University Press, 1995), 25–56; Allan R. Odden, ed., *Rethinking School Finance: An Agenda for the 1990s* (San Francisco: Jossey-Bass, 1992); Allan R. Odden and Lawrence O. Pincus, *School Finance: A Policy Perspective* (New York: McGraw-Hill, 1992).

On the debate over multiculturalism in schools, see Gary B. Nash, "American History Reconsidered: Asking New Questions about the Past," in *Learning from the Past: What History Teaches Us about School Reform,* ed. Diane Ravitch and Maris A. Vinovskis (Baltimore: Johns Hopkins University Press, 1995), 135–63; Arthur M. Schlesinger, Jr., *The Disuniting of America: Reflections on a Multicultural Society* (Knoxville, Tenn.: Wittle Direct Books, 1991); Reed Ueda, "Ethnic Diversity and National Identity in Public School Texts," in *Learning from the Past: What History Teaches Us about School Reform,* ed. Diane Ravitch and Maris A. Vinovskis (Baltimore: Johns Hopkins University Press, 1995), 113–34.

70. On the earlier assessments of the regional educational laboratories, see Maris A. Vinovskis, "Analysis of the Quality of Research and Development at the OERI Research and Development Centers and at the OERI Regional Educational Laboratories" (final report, OERI, Department of Education, June 1993).

71. On some of the earlier assessments of the Title 1 program, see Launor F. Carter, "The Sustaining Effects Study of Compensatory and Elementary Education," *Educational Researcher* 13, no. 7 (Aug./Sept. 1984), 4–13; Milbrey Wallin McLaughlin, *Evaluation and Reform: The Elementary and Secondary Education Act of 1965, Title I* (Cambridge, Mass.: Ballinger, 1975); Michael J. Puma et al., *Prospects: The Congressionally Mandated Study of Education Growth and Opportunity, Interim Report* (Bethesda, Md.: Abt Associates, 1993); Michael J. Wargo et al., *ESEA Title I: A Reanalysis and Synthesis of Evaluation Data from Fiscal Year 1965 through 1970,* final report (Palo Alto, Calif.: American Institutes for Research, 1972).

72. On activities of the NIE's policy board, see Maris A. Vinovskis, "Changing Views of the Federal Role in Educational Statistics and Research" (unpub. paper prepared for OERI, Washington, D.C., Sept. 1995).

Index